Movie Classics

Other titles in
Chambers Compact Reference

Catastrophes and Disasters
Crimes and Criminals
50 Years of Rock Music
Great Inventions Through History
Great Modern Inventions
Great Scientific Discoveries
Masters of Jazz
Musical Masterpieces
Mythology
The Occult
Religious Leaders
Sacred Writings of World Religions
Saints
Space Exploration

To be published in 1993

Great Cities of the World
Movie Stars
Operas
World Folklore

Movie Classics

Editor
Allan Hunter

Chambers

EDINBURGH   NEW YORK   TORONTO

Published 1992 by W & R Chambers Ltd
43–45 Annandale Street, Edinburgh EH7 4AZ
95 Madison Avenue, New York N.Y. 10016

Library of Congress Cataloging-in-Publication Data applied for

ISBN 0 550 17008 1

Cover design   Blue Peach Design Consultants Ltd
Typeset by Hewer Text Composition Services, Edinburgh
Printed in England by Clays Ltd, St Ives plc

Acknowledgements

Contributors   Allan Hunter, Kenny Mathieson

Chambers Compact Reference Series Editor   Min Lee

Allan Hunter would like to thank Gay Cox, Gill Crawford, Shirley Gilmour, Rosemary Goring, Jim Hickey, Trevor Johnston, Kenny Mathieson, Richard Mowe

Illustration Credits

Contents

Introduction

The essential qualities of a Movie Classic can sometimes prove elusive. The contenders for the accolade covered within these pages certainly include a selection of the most popular films ever made, the most critically lauded and the most commercially successful of all time – but the book is not primarily concerned, Guinness-like, with records of the biggest or the best, however compelling the information.

A Movie Classic can perhaps only be measured on an unscientific scale of public affection and esteem. Films like *Battleship Potemkin* and *Citizen Kane* are clearly Movie Classics because they have profoundly influenced the shape of the moviemaking landscape and their impact on the art form has stood the test of time. The sheer popularity of a *Gone With the Wind* or *The Sound of Music*, the symbolic significance of a *Rome, Open City* or *Breathless* in heralding new trends in cinema techniques or the awards showered upon a *Ben-Hur* or *Dances With Wolves* more than earn them a place in the roll-call of greats.

Sometimes it is only posterity that can bestow classic status upon a specific title. When Frank Capra's *It's a Wonderful Life* was released just after World War II, it wound up over $500 000 in the red and failed to receive a single Oscar. Capra was felt to have lost his popular touch and the career of star James Stewart was seen to falter after a five-year absence at war. However, subsequent generations have taken the film to their hearts, admiring the humanity of Capra's vision and the richness of Stewart's performance; the film is now a rep house, video and television perennial and as much a part of the Yuletide season as presents and Santa Claus.

French filmmaker Jean Vigo died tragically young in Paris in 1934 believing that his final film *L'Atalante* had been a failure after brutal interference from its distributor. However, the years have allowed restorations to be made and his original intentions to be vindicated, resulting in acclaim for one of the most romantic of French features.

From *L'Atalante* to *Touch of Evil*, *It's a Wonderful Life* to *Night of the Hunter*, the book is full of titles that were disowned, maligned or merely misunderstood at the time of their initial release but now stand unquestioned in the pantheon of greats.

The selection of titles, which runs chronologically from *The Great Train Robbery* in 1903 to *Silence of the Lambs* in 1991, therefore represents the gamut of what constitutes a film classic whether it is the sheer entertainment value of a *Singin' In The Rain* and *Casablanca* that can be seen time and time again, the controversy and passions aroused by a *Peeping Tom* or *Fatal Attraction* or the unchallenged artistry of a Buster Keaton comedy, a Fred Astaire musical routine or an Ingmar Bergman drama.

The films chosen for inclusion within the book have been heavily influenced by the research undertaken for the earlier *Chambers Film and Television Handbook*. Material originally compiled for that volume by the current editor, Kenny Mathieson and Trevor Johnston has been completely revised, corrected where necessary, and expanded to fit the form of this new book. Numerous new entries have also been researched and written by myself and Kenny Mathieson.

Each film is now represented by an entry that provides a short plot synopsis, selected technical credits, a cast list and a commentary which aims to give background detail on the production of a film or pinpoint its significance within cinema history, or the career of a particularly innovative filmmaker. Where relevance and space permits the entry also conveys a sense of the film's box-office performance and whether it received Oscar awards.

Throughout the book films are listed in alphabetical order with the foreign-language films listed under the name by which they are best known in the UK. Thus Kurosawa's epic will be found under *The Seven Samurai* and not *Shichinin No Samurai* whilst Federico Fellini's study of decadent Roman mores will be found under *La Dolce Vita* rather than *The Sweet Life*.

The aim of this book is is to provide an easy reference for those seeking a sense of the landmarks of world cinema and an instant aide-memoire for all those who have looked back in langour on the memory of a film that moved, informed, delighted or entertained them.

The inimitable James Stewart once recounted an anecdote that seems to sum up the value of Movie Classics and our affection for them. He was in a remote location at work on a western when a fan approached him and complimented him on a simple scene from a film he had seen some 15 years previously. The man rather tentatively commented that he hoped Stewart hadn't objected to the intrusion and doubted that the comment had meant anything much to him. Stewart recalled, 'When he told me that it was the most moving . . . I tell you, it was better than getting a fistful of fine notices. Did it mean anything? Why, it means everything to me. When they get round to writing my epitaph, I'll settle for, I'll be happy with, "He sure gave us a lot of pleasure over the years." I wouldn't mind that at all – to die knowing . . . knowing you've given people just a little piece of . . . a small piece of time they'll never forget.'

This book then is a celebration of the films containing those little pieces of time that are part of the collective consciousness and will never be forgotten as long as cinema survives; King Kong straddling the Empire State, Dorothy venturing over the rainbow, Death offering a game of chess, the quest for an elusive black bird, a man joyously splashing in the rain, a hand reaching for a butterfly. In short, a whole host of Movie Classics.

The Adventures of Robin Hood

Michael Curtiz and William Keighley, USA, 1938

Sherwood Forest swashbuckler

Errol Flynn is the definitive Robin of Locksley in an adventure of unsurpassed élan.

The story

When King Richard is held for ransom, Prince John appoints himself regent. Only Robin of Locksley opposes him and turns outlaw to raise the ransom. One raid brings him the company of Maid Marian who soons falls under his spell. Prince John and his ally, Guy of Gisbourne, manage to lure Robin into the trap of an archery contest. However, Marian warns his men of what has befallen him and they snatch their leader from the jaws of certain death. When Richard returns he joins with Robin and his men in infiltrating John's coronation. A furious fight ensues in which Robin skewers the evil Gisbourne, King Richard banishes John, grants amnesty to the merry men, restores Robin his lands and gives him the hand of Marian in marriage.

Comment

Robin Hood has been roaming through a celluloid Sherwood Forest since 1908 with his most celebrated interpreters including Douglas Fairbanks Senior in *Robin Hood* (1922), Sean Connery in *Robin and Marian* (1976) and, most recently, Kevin Costner in *Robin Hood: Prince of Thieves* (1991). Whatever the individual merits of each version, there are few who would dispute Errol Flynn's claim to the honour of being the screen's most dashing, romantic, athletic and mischievous Robin:

Originally planned as a change of pace for Warners' star James Cagney in 1935, this production was shelved when Cagney left the studio in dispute over his contract. By the time the notion was revived, Flynn had established himself as the sound era's leading swashbuckler and romantic hero in films like *Captain Blood* (1935) and *The Charge of the Light Brigade* (1936). Thus with Flynn in the lead, filming commenced under William Keighley with Bidwell Park in California standing in for Sherwood Forest. He had completed most of the exterior work when Jack L Warner decided to replace him with Michael Curtiz who took charge of all the interior scenes and a modest amount of additional exterior shooting. The end product however is a seamless piece of storytelling in which every element contributes to the whole and stands as testament to the all-round craftsmanship possible under the old studio system.

The Adventures of Robin Hood's excellence lies not just in Errol Flynn's athleticism, Basil Rathbone's dastardly villainy or De Havilland's demure heroine, but also in the rousing musical soundtrack by Erich Wolfgang Korngold, the sumptuous use of colour and the set design by Carl Jules Weyl. Winner of Oscars for Weyl, Korngold and editor Ralph Lawson, the film set standards for adventure yarns that have never been surpassed.

A Warner Brothers Production
Producers Hal B Wallis and Henry Blanke
Screenplay Norman Reilly Raine and Seton I Miller
Photography Tony Gaudio, Sol Polito and W Howard Greene
Editor Ralph Lawson
Art Director Carl Jules Weyl
Music Erich Wolfgang Korngold
Running time 102 mins *colour*

Cast
Errol Flynn (Robin Hood)
Olivia De Havilland (Maid Marian)
Basil Rathbone (Sir Guy of Gisbourne)
Claude Rains (Prince John)
Patric Knowles (Will Scarlet)
Eugene Pallette (Friar Tuck)

The African Queen

John Huston, USA, 1951

Wartime adventure

Hostility melts into romance on the treacherous rivers of war-torn Africa.

The story

Central Africa, World War I. A German attack results in the death of a missionary. His prim sister Rose is given sanctuary aboard *The African Queen*, a river launch captained by the gin-sodden Charlie Allnutt who reluctantly agrees to her plan for a daring raid on a German gunboat. Surviving a hazardous journey over rapids engenders a mutual admiration that blossoms into love. Eventually they arrive at the lake where the *Louisa* is moored. Allnut equips his vessel with torpedoes but they are captured before action can be taken. Sentenced to be hanged, they are wed as the *Louisa* drifts into contact with the derelict *African Queen* and explodes, throwing them free of further danger.

Comment

Hard to imagine now with anyone but the potent star pairing of Humphrey Bogart and Katharine Hepburn, *The African Queen* had once been envisaged both for Bette Davis and David Niven. When John Huston came to the project, he insisted on filming some 1100 miles up the Congo; the gamble paid off for the very real difficulties of the surroundings are lucidly preserved on screen and help to overshadow the narrative's many moments of improbability. The film's sentimentality (as opposed to the cynical world-view expressed in the director's earlier *Treasure of the Sierra Madre* (1947) for example) ensures that it is always fondly recalled. Humphrey Bogart was to receive the year's Best Actor Academy Award for his portrait of the dissolute Canadian boat captain in the face of stiff competition from Marlon Brando's Stanley Kowalski in *A Streetcar Named Desire* (1951) (see p208) as well as Montgomery Clift in *A Place in the Sun*, Arthur Kennedy in *Bright Victory* and Fredric March in *Death of A Salesman*. Encountering some difficulty with the prissiness of her character, Hepburn found the key to the humour in the role when Huston instructed her to play Rose with the lady-like exactitude of Eleanor Roosevelt.

Huston would return to the theme of two ill-matched souls brought together by adversity in films like *Heaven Knows Mr Allison* (1957) which teamed Deborah Kerr's nun with Robert Mitchum's marine, whilst Hepburn was to appear in a variation on the theme, partnered by a drink-guzzling John Wayne in *Rooster Cogburn* (1975). Uncredited co-writer Peter Viertel's 1953 novel *White Hunter, Black Heart*, which chronicles Huston's obsessional excesses, was creditably filmed in 1990 by actor/director Clint Eastwoood.

A Horizon-Romulus Production
Producer S P Eagle (Sam Spiegel)
Screenplay James Agee and John Huston, based on the novel by C S Forrester
Photography Jack Cardiff
Editor Ralph Kemplen
Art Director Wilfred Shingleton
Music Alan Gray
Running time 105 mins Technicolor
Cast
Humphrey Bogart (Charlie Allnut)
Katharine Hepburn (Rose Sayer)
Robert Morley (Rev Samuel Sayer)
Peter Bull (Captain of the *Louisa*)
Theodore Bikel (First Officer)
Walter Gotell (Second Officer)

L'Age d'Or

Luis Buñuel, France, 1930

Surrealist fantasy

Buñuel and Salvador Dali collaborate on a most influential surrealist film.

The story

The film begins with a short documentary about scorpions. When some bishops take over an island, they separate a young couple in the throes of passion and have the man placed under arrest. The couple meet again at a party given by the woman's mother at which nothing is allowed to disrupt the social calm, even the appearance of a cart and a kitchen fire that sends a maid scurrying into their midst. The couple's next attempt to make love is curtailed when the man is called to the telephone and the girl is left to suck on the toe of a statue. In a medieval castle, a group of disciples of the Marquis De Sade emerge, including the Christlike Duc De Blangis who re-enters with a young girl. A bloodcurdling scream is subsequently heard.

Comment

The iconoclastic Spaniard Luis Buñuel's collaboration with his equally eccentric countryman Salvador Dali marks a key moment in the development of the European film as art. Following their groundbreaking work together on the celebrated short *Un Chien Andalou* (1928), noted for its opening shot of an eye brazenly sliced open by a straight razor, Buñuel more firmly allied himself to the surrealist movement and was fortunate to find a wealthy sponsor in the Vicomte De Noailles (also a supporter of Man Ray and Jean Cocteau), who handed the director a million francs and a free hand with it. *L'Age d'Or* was filmed over the course of a month at the Billancourt Studios in Paris

and later on location at Dali's Spanish home. The result, considered a blasphemous assault on conventional morality and the pernicious influence of the church, caused a riot on its first appearance at the Studio 28 where members of the right-wing League of Patriots and the Anti-Jewish League combined to club fellow audience members and virtually destroy the building. Withdrawn from Paris after a week, the film remained unshown in France until 1979.

Following its own dislocated dream logic and making dissonant use of sound and music, the piece focuses on two lovers forever kept apart by the constraints of the church and the hypocrisy of a bourgeois morality that had defiled the purity of love and sowed the seeds of its own destruction. The themes, methods and and typical surrealist juxtapositions in the film were to become constants throughout Bunuel's long and distinguished career: his particular brand of ecclesiastical satire was later even more apparent in the blasphemous *Viridiana* (1961), while his obsession with *amour fou* surfaced most bizarrely in *Belle de Jour* (1967).

A Vicomte De Noailles Production
Producer Luis Buñuel
Screenplay Luis Buñuel and Salvador Dali
Photography Albert Dubergen
Art Director Pierre Schilzneck
Music Mozart, Beethoven, Mendelssohn, Debussy and Wagner
Running time 60 mins b/w

Cast
Gaston Modot (The Man)
Lya Lys (The Woman)
Max Ernst
Pierre Prevert
Jose Antigas
Caridad de Laberdesque

Aguirre, Wrath of God

Werner Herzog, Germany, 1972

Epic adventure

This epic account of the destructive effects of the rage for power raises moral issues on how far the filmmaker should go.

The story

Peru, 1560. A mighty expedition of Conquistadors sets out in search of the legendary Inca city of gold, El Dorado. On reaching the Amazon, their leader, Pizarro, sends out a small party of forty on rafts to seek out the city, under the command of Don Pedro de Ursua and his wife Inez. The rafts soon come under attack from natural disaster and hostile Indians, while internal tensions turn to open strife as the deluded second-in-command, Aguirre, the self-proclaimed Wrath of God, takes over the expedition. Driven on by his maniac quest as his men die all around him, Aguirre is left declaring his defiance to an unrelenting jungle.

Comment

Werner Herzog's epic study of delusion and the power of myth was made on a tiny budget in horrifically difficult conditions on the Amazon. The film hinges around Klaus Kinski's depiction of the increasingly demented Aguirre, and is an immensely powerful study of the warping effects of a monomaniac drive for power, the real motivation behind his lunatic quest.

The film begins in a spectacularly realist mode, as the expedition negotiates its route down a steep mountain path to the river which blocks their way. As the rafts make the long journey, though, Herzog evolves an increasingly fantastic visual narrative to correspond to the growing disorder and absurdity of events.

The world which he creates moves further and further from empirical reality, into a darkly dreamy otherworld of the imagination which invites, but does not insist upon, a metaphorical reading. The final shot of Aguirre as the last man alive on a raft overrun by monkeys, still babbling of a conquering triumph, is an unforgettable image.

Herzog's *Fitzcarraldo* (1982) is set in a much later historical period, but centres on a similarly grandiose and lunatic scheme to build an opera house in the jungle. It required the dangerous transport of a steamship over a mountain, recorded in Les Blank's compelling documentary *Burden of Dreams* (1982). Both films raised serious questions about how far it is permissible to go in making a film. Herzog admitted that the shooting was extremely hazardous (not to say exploitative) for cast and crew, but his own driving need to realize his visions took precedence – an attitude which brought him much criticism, but also the Best Director Award at Cannes in 1982.

A Werner Herzog Filmproduktion
Producer Werner Herzog
Screenplay Werner Herzog, from the journal of Gaspar De Carvajal
Photography Thomas Mauch
Editor Beate Mainka-Jellinghaus
Special Effects Juvenal Herrera and Miguel Vazquez
Music Popol Vuh
Running time 93 mins *colour*

Cast
Klaus Kinski (Don Lope de Aguirre)
Helena Rojo (Inez de Atienza)
Ruy Guerra (Pedro de Ursua)
Del Negro (Gaspar de Carvajal)
Peter Berling (Don Fernando de Guzman)
Cecilia Rivera (Flores de Aguirre)
Dany Ades (Perucho)
Armando Polanah (Armando)
Edward Roland (Okello)

Alexander Nevsky

Sergei Eisenstein, USSR, 1938

Historical epic

Eisenstein brings a dramatic sweep and operatic mood to the depiction of Russian history.

The story

Having defeated the Swedish invaders on the Neva, Prince Alexander Nevsky has assumed a quiet existence among the simple peasantry where he maintains the belief that the German Teutonic Knights are the biggest threat to Russia's peace and security. Novgorod becomes the last stronghold to withstand the might of the German advance and Nevsky accedes to a request that he lead a last stand only on the condition that the strategy is one of attack rather than defence. He assembles a vast force and at Lake Peipus in 1242 fights a decisive pitched battle in which the combination of peasants, nobles and Prince Nevsky's leadership drives the German army to a watery grave in the lake.

Comment

While Sergei Eisenstein's pioneering 1920s' works, such as *Battleship Potemkin* (1925) (see p29) and *October* (1928) formulated the innovative editing technique of montage and focused on the Soviet masses as collective hero, the films that were to follow in subsequent decades, *Alexander Nevsky* and the *Ivan the Terrible* (1942–6) diptych, seem much more traditional both in formal terms and in their narrative focus upon one heroic individual. Eisenstein had visited America in 1929 and worked on an abortive attempt to film *An American Tragedy* for Paramount. Other projects of the day include the unfinished *Que Viva Mexico* and the suppressed *Bezhin Meadow* and thus ten years had past before he began work on *Nevsky*, the first flowering of this later style. However, the film should not be viewed as a retreat from the cerebral cinematic explorations of the earlier period but as an advance in developing his method to meet the political and technological demands of the time.

Dramatizing Prince Nevsky's drive to expel the brutal Teutonic Knights from 13th-century Holy Russia, the film draws on established literary and artistic means of representation and, given the extent to which the impressive pageant of action is fused with Prokofiev's stirring score, Eisenstein himself called the structure 'symphonic'. To contemporary eyes raised largely on classical American cinema, it thus remains one of his most accessible works, with the breathtaking 'Battle of the Ice' sequence more than a match for many a Hollywood epic set-piece, and itself paid tribute to by Ken Russell in *Billion Dollar Brain* (1967). Unsurprisingly, the film was withdrawn during the German-Soviet pact of 1938 and released afresh when the Germans invaded the following year.

A Mosfilm Production
Screenplay Sergei Eisenstein and Peter Pavlenko
Photography Edward Tisse
Music Sergei Prokofiev
Running time 112 mins b/w

Cast

Nikolai Cherkassov (Prince Alexander Yaroslavich Nevsky)
Nikolai P Okhlopov (Vassily Buslai)
Alexander L Abrikosov (Gavrilo Olexich)
Dmitri N Orlov (Ignat, Master Armourer)
V K Novikov (Pavsha, Governor of Pskov)
N N Arski (Domash, Nobleman of Novgorod)

All About Eve

Joseph L Mankiewicz, USA, 1950

Backstage melodrama

A vitriolic thespian tussle inspires one of Hollywood's most incisive and cultured entertainments.

The story

An apparent star-struck innocent, the scheming Eve Harrington ingratiates herself with star actress Margo Channing, charms her coterie of friends and colleagues, and secures the position of Margo's undestudy. Margo's belligerent response to this leads the gullible Karen Richards to detain her in the country and allow Eve her big chance. Eventually Eve's treachery is revealed, but Margo retains the love of director Bill Simpson and can no longer be harmed. Karen however finds her marriage to playwright Lloyd Richards endangered, before critic Addison de Witt intervenes to ruthlessly make his claim to Eve's affections. Established as a star, Eve becomes the target of another ambitious aspiring actress.

Comment

A venomous story of backbiting showbusiness folk, with dialogue etched in acid and cynicism expressed in the most piquant and quotable of manners, *All About Eve* remains one of Hollywood's wittiest and sharply scripted entertainments with memorable performances from all the cast, especially an electrifying Bette Davis as grande dame Margo Channing and George Sanders as sardonic drama critic Addison de Witt.

A true incident in the life of actress Elisabeth Bergner, which was transformed into the short story *The Wisdom of Eve* by writer Mary Orr, the item was first published in *Cosmopolitan* in 1946 and had also seen service as a 1949 radio drama before Joseph L Mankiewicz urged Twentieth Century-Fox

to purchase the screen rights. Long attracted to the notion of conveying the life of a great actress and the personal sacrifices necessary for professional success, he felt that the story provided the perfect starting-point for just such a film. Early casting suggestions included Jeanne Crain as Eve with either Barbara Stanwyck or Claudette Colbert as Margo; Colbert had signed to play the role before a ruptured disc forced her withdrawal from the project. Gertrude Lawrence was the second choice before Mankiewicz approached Bette Davis and gave her the role that would revitalize a career in need of fresh impetus after her break in 1949 from an increasingly unhappy long-term association with Warner Brothers. A triumph for all concerned, the film was nominated for 14 Academy Awards and was named the year's Best Picture, with Oscars also awarded to Mankiewicz (as writer and director) and to George Sanders, as well as for the Sound Recording and Costume Design. Often revived, it also served as the basis of the Broadway musical *Applause* (1970) which earned a Tony for Lauren Bacall.

A Twentieth Century-Fox Production
Producer Darryl F Zanuck
Screenplay Joseph L Mankiewicz, based on the story *The Wisdom of Eve* by Mary Orr
Photography Milton Krasner
Editor Barbara McLean
Art Directors Lyle Wheeler and George W Davis
Music Alfred Newman
Running time 138 mins b/w

Cast
Bette Davis (Margo Channing)
Anne Baxter (Eve Harrington)
George Sanders (Addison De Witt)
Celeste Holm (Karen Richards)
Gary Merrill (Bill Simpson)
Hugh Marlow (Lloyd Richards)
Marilyn Monroe (Miss Casswell)

All Quiet on The Western Front

Lewis Milestone, USA, 1930

Pacifist drama

A grim depiction of the realities of war makes a definitive statement for pacifism.

The story

World War I. Inspired by a sense of patriotism and the rhetoric of their school-teachers, a group of boys join the Army and are sent to the front. Veteran soldiers scoff at their naivety and the first experiences of gunfire prove sobering. Slowly, they are hardened by battle and the death of friends. The sensitive Paul Baumer finds that his attitudes quickly change when he is forced to kill, and a brief return home leaves him feeling alienated from those he had once loved. He is relieved to return to the few comrades who remain. Later, as he reaches out from his trench to catch a butterfly, he is shot dead by a French sniper. His is but one of thousands of young lives lost on the battlefields.

Comment

The image of a hand stretching out to touch a butterfly remains one of the most famous moments in all cinema, and Lewis Milestone's film even today is regarded as a definitive anti-war statement. Following the pattern set by the 1925 silent block-buster *The Big Parade* and echoed as recently as 1989 in Oliver Stone's *Born on the Fourth of July*, this faithful adaptation of Erich Maria Remarque's famous novel follows the fortunes of volunteer recruits as they have their patriotic illusions of glory shattered by the grim horrors of battle. Although Lew Ayres (a conscientious objector during World War II who served as a medic and chaplain's aide) takes top billing, the focus

on the group makes it more of an ensemble movie, with the real triumph perhaps being director Milestone's bravura staging of the action sequences. Taking over a huge California ranch, he was the first to use a giant crane with which to sweep the camera across the bullet-riddled, muddy landscapes, whilst castors from Howard Hughes Machine Tool Shop allowed him to make swift tracking shots along the trenches. The startling results have only rarely been bettered by the likes of Stanley Kubrick's *Paths of Glory* (1957) (see p160). It is also worth noting George Cukor's input in rehearsing the actors' performances, which pleased the studio enough to set him off on a lauded, though very different, Hollywood canon that includes *The Philadelphia Story* (1940) (see p166) and *A Star Is Born* (1954) (see p206).

Nominated for four Academy Awards, *All Quiet on The Western Front* was named Best Film, with Milestone honoured as Best Director. 1979 brought a television remake but *The Road Back* (1937), a sequel directed by James Whale, is all but forgotten.

A Universal Production
Producer Carl Laemmle Jnr
Screenplay Del Andrews, Maxwell Anderson and George Abbott, based on the novel *Im Westen Nichts Neues* by Erich Maria Remarque
Photography Arthur Edeson
Editor Edgar Adams
Music David Broekman
Running time 138 mins b/w

Cast
Lew Ayres (Paul Baumer)
Louis Wolheim (Katczinsky)
John Wray (Himmelstoss)
George 'Slim' Summerville (Tjaden)
Raymond Griffith (Gerard Duval)
Russell Gleason (Muller)

All The President's Men

Alan J Pakula, USA, 1976

Political thriller

A documentary-style thriller converts front page news into purposeful entertainment.

The story

While reporter Bob Woodward learns that one of the five men apprehended at the Democratic Party headquarters in Washington is a former CIA operative, his colleague Carl Bernstein links the men to Charles Colson, Special Counsel to the President. Advised by informant 'Deep Throat' they uncover a 'dirty tricks' fund operated by the Committee to Re-Elect the President (CRP) administered by former Attorney General John Mitchell. They overcome the scepticism of colleagues and silence of key witnesses until a former CRP Treasurer implicates White House Chief of Staff Bob Haldeman and the matter is confirmed by 'Deep Throat'. They continue to work on the story that will topple the President as Nixon is sworn in for a second term.

Comment

A comparative rarity in American cinema for its engagement with the political realities of the day, *All the President's Men* (1976) is a skilful fusion of the liberal concerns and star clout of Robert Redford with director Alan J Pakula's fascination with obsessive individuals and the minutiae of the workings of large power-structures, in this case the media and the Government. Redford's interest in the Watergate break-in was first stimulated during his promotional tour for *The Candidate* (1972). Encouraged by Redford's support, *Washington Post* reporters Woodward and Bernstein turned their experiences into a book that had sold a reported 2 750 000 copies by the end of 1975. Warner Brothers purchased the rights for Redford's Wildwood Enterprises for $450 000 and the film project grew from the initial plan of a low-budget production with unknown actors into a major motion picture in which Redford felt obliged to co-star with Dustin Hoffman in order to protect the by now considerable investment.

Using a documentary-like approach to the welter of information and characters, Pakula also manages to elicit the maximum amount of suspense from the thriller elements in a grand puzzle unravelled by the detective work of two combative Davids who are facing the Goliath of labyrinthine Government corruption. He makes characteristic use of light and deep-focus photography to render the Washington Post offices as bright and open as possible and contrasts this with the dark shadows of the city and scurrying silhoettes of the participants in a dangerous network of deceit and revelation. The film grossed $30 million, received eight Academy Award nominations and won Oscars for Best Sound, Art Direction, Screenplay and Best Supporting Actor Jason Robards as *Post* Editor Ben Bradlee.

A Wildwood Enterprises Production
Producer Walter Coblenz
Screenplay William Goldman, based on the book by Carl Bernstein and Bob Woodward
Photography Gordon Willis
Editor Robert L Wolfe
Art Director George Jenkins
Music David Shire
Running time 138 mins *colour*

Cast
Dustin Hoffmann (Carl Bernstein)
Robert Redford (Bob Woodward)
Jack Warden (Harry Rosenfeld)
Martin Balsam (Howard Simons)
Hal Holbrook (Deep Throat)
Jason Robards (Ben Bradlee)

An American in Paris

Vincente Minnelli, USA, 1951

Sophisticated musical

Recreating Paris on the backlot, Kelly and his collaborators take the musical to new artistic heights.

The story

GI Jerry Mulligan has remained in Paris after the war to become a painter. He enjoys the romance of struggling in a Montmartre pension, the neighbourhood children, the lugubrious wit of his friend Adam Cook and the encouragement of Henri Baurel who is about to marry a beautiful young dancer. Soon he is discovered by rich widow Milo Roberts who introduces his work to her affluent friends. Celebrating in a nightclub, he meets and falls in love with Lise Bouvier who resists a romance because she is the one engaged to Baurel. When Roberts demands more of him than artistic promise he spurns her future help. However, Baurel realises it is hopeless to stand in the way of true love and Jerry is joyously reunited with Lise.

Comment

An American in Paris is an important milestone in the development of the musical as one of the first of the genre to win serious respect from the critical establishment and the American Academy. Sprung from producer Arthur Freed's influential musical unit at M-G-M, which was responsible for a string of classics including *Singin' in the Rain* (1952) (see p198) and *The Band Wagon* (1953) (see p23), the film's origin in an orchestral piece by George Gershwin and its climactic 17-minute modern ballet sequence, designed in the visual style of French artist Raoul Dufy and drawing on the work of Lautrec, Manet and others, announced unprecedented aspirations to higher artistic credibility. While

these very same qualities have latterly seen the film criticized for its over-ripe pretension, the high-falutin' trappings are actually quite germane to the typical Vincente Minnelli approach of telling the story through a combination of song, dance, dialogue and décor, and the degree of sophistication in all aspects of the production remains a testament to the studio's high standards of creative excellence. Most significantly perhaps, the focus on actor-choreographer Gene Kelly's exuberant and contemporary routines greatly expanded the filmic dance vocabulary and challenged the received notion that a popular audience would not accept ballet forms in mainstream entertainment. (With a box-office gross of $4.5 million, the film was the third most popular attraction of 1951 in America.) While the film received six of the eight Academy Awards for which it was nominated, including Best Picture, Kelly's efforts were also singled out with a special award for his 'versatility as an actor, singer, director and dancer, and specifically for his brilliant achievements in the art of choreography on film'.

An M-G-M Production
Producer Arthur Freed
Screenplay Alan Jay Lerner
Photography Alfred Gilks and John Alton
Editor Adrienne Fazan
Art Directors Cedric Gibbons and Preston Ames
Music George and Ira Gershwin
Running time 113 mins *colour*

Cast

Gene Kelly (Jerry Mulligan)
Leslie Caron (Lise Bouvier)
Oscar Levant (Adam Cook)
Georges Guetary (Henri Baurel)
Nina Foch (Milo Roberts)
Eugene Borden (George Mattieu)

Silence is golden
Movie history before *The Jazz Singer*

The initial efforts of the Lumière Brothers, Georges Méliès or Thomas Edison in placing images on film caught the public's attention as a form of novelty that held up a mirror to the world around them and captured a sneeze, a kiss or a train arriving at a station. However, as cinema progressed beyond the status of just another amusement arcade diversion, certain basic narrative techniques began to develop in short dramatic films like *The Great Train Robbery* (1903) (see p100) in which the title act and subsequent chase involved the use of editing between points of view to create tension and also a close-up for dramatic punctuation. Although time has rendered such innovations elementary, at the turn of the century their impact was revolutionary.

Perhaps the man who is most readily identified as the figure who transformed filmmaking into an art form is D W Griffith. An innovator in film technique, he is recognized as the first American to make expressive use of dramatic devices like close-ups, flashbacks and cross-cutting and the scale of his storytelling can be seen in such seminal works as *The Birth Of A Nation* (1915) (see p36) and *Intolerance* (1916) (see p110). Griffith worked on some of Mary Pickford's early films and also made extensive use of the waif-like skills of Lillian Gish in *Broken Blossoms* (1919) and *Way Down East* (1920) and it was due to the popularity of figures like Pickford, Gish, Chaplin and Fairbanks that the star system developed. In 1919, Griffith, Pickford, Fairbanks and Chaplin formed United Artists to gain greater creative control over their work and the results included such adventure classics as *Robin Hood* (1922) and *The Thief of Bagdad* (1924) (see p218) as well as *The Gold Rush* (1925) (see p94). Although Fairbanks was unrivalled as the screen's most dashing swashbuckler, Chaplin's domin-ance of the comedy field was always challenged; contemporary audiences have tended to find more humour in the daredevil antics of Harold Lloyd in *Safety Last* (1923) (see p186) or the blank-faced grace of Buster Keaton in *The General* (1926) (see p88).

As American cinema very quickly came to be the slave of commercial concerns and popular taste, further artistic innovations and experimentation tended to come from other parts of the globe. German Expressionism, which attempted to give visual expression to inner turmoil and feelings, made a highly original use of light and shadow, distorted camera angles and sets in such influential productions as *The Cabinet of Dr Caligari* (1919) (see p50), *Nosferatu* (1922) (see p151) and *Metropolis* (1926) (see p142) and would soon have a lasting effect on the gangster and horror genres in America. The Surrealist movement of the 1920s eventually turned to film-making with such eye-catching results as *Un Chien Andalou* (1928) and *L'Age D'Or* (1930) (see p5). To this day their liberating sense of iconoclasm and use of symbolism are seen in diluted form in cinemas worldwide. Meanwhile, in Russia, cinema was used to serve explicitly propagandist purposes and Sergei Eisentein's theory of montage, in which a visually dramatic or emotional moment can be created through editing, is best illustrated by the famed Odessa Steps sequence in *Battleship Potemkin* (1925) (see p29).

From Erich Von Stroheim's chronicles of sexual mores, to Cecil B De Mille's Biblical epics and including such poetic achievements as *Sunrise* (1927) (see p211), *The Wind* (1928) (see p237) and *The Crowd* (1928) (see p60), the silent cinema was achieving some of its finest masterpieces at exactly the time technology was about to render it obsolete.

The Birth of a Nation *(1915) Directed by D W Griffith (Lillian Gish)*

The Jazz Singer *(1927) Directed by Alan Crosland (May McAvoy, Al Jolson)*

Blackmail *(1929) Directed by Alfred Hitchcock*
(Alfred Hitchcock (left), John Longden (seated centre))

Becky Sharp *(1935) Directed by Rouben Mamoulian (Miriam Hopkins)*

Andrei Rublev

Andrei Tarkovsky, USSR, 1966

Historical parable

Icon painter Rublev inspires a powerful parable of artistic expression, faith and integrity.

The story

15th-century Russia. During his peregrinations, icon painter Andrei Rublev is entertained by a buffoon whose irreverence is harshly punished. He assists Theophanes in painting a new church, argues the case against a strict adherence to the Old Testament, watches as peasant revellers are slain and his own companions are slaughtered, and witnesses a vision of the dead Theophanes who urges him not to abandon himself to despair but to continue his art. Inspired, he kills a Tartar to protect a deaf-mute girl who is subsequently carried off and watches as Boriska completes the painstaking task of creating a new bell. Tears of joy stream down his face as the work is completed and there is a montage of his religious paintings.

Comment

Although completed as far back as 1965, Andrei Tarkovsky's epic panorama of medieval life waited until the 1969 Cannes Film Festival before it was first seen in the West. Subsequently screened in Britain shorn of some forty minutes, it faced a further three-year delay before distribution in the USSR. Apparently objecting to the film's violent realism and a mood that was felt to be too sombre for the 50th-anniversary celebrations of the October Revolution, the Soviet authorities who shelved the film for so long were, paradoxically, also responsible for providing the first in a series of lavish budgets that Tarkovsky would receive for works of uncompromisingly distinctive artistry, including the ruminative science fiction pieces *Solaris* (1972) and *Stalker* (1979) and the highly personal recollections of *Mirror* (1974).

Perhaps appropriately, Andrei Rublev dramatizes the time-honoured dilemma of the artist's relationship with society and the opposing pulls of dispassionate observation or passionate, involved interaction. The eponymous hero, a monk and icon painter who lived during the 15th century, bears witness to a world of constant misery and brutality as the Tartar hordes plunder all before them, and begins to ponder the worth of his existence until he watches a peasant waif's extraordinarily confident supervision of the casting of a prestigious church bell. The young lad's instinctive drive towards the completion of his project is proof to the doubting protagonist that the God-given gift of creativity flourishes even in times of the profoundest social turmoil, and as Tarkovsky bursts into colour to linger over Rublev's exquisite icons, the parallel with the position of the pre-perestroika Soviet artist is taken as read.

A Mosfilm Production
Screenplay Andrei Mikhalkov-Konchalovsky and Andrei Tarkovsky
Photography Vadim Yusov
Art Director Yevgeni Tcherniaiev
Music Vyacheslav Ovchinnikov
Running time 185 mins *colour* and *b/w*

Cast
Anatoly Solonitsyn (Andrei Rublev)
Ivan Lapikov (Kirill)
Nikolai Grinko (Daniel the Black)
Nikolai Sergeyev (Theophanes the Greek)
Irma Raush (Deaf-and-dumb Girl)
Nikolai Burlyayev (Boriska)

Annie Hall

Woody Allen, USA, 1977

Soul-searching comedy

An autobiographical romance captures the essence of Woody Allen.

The story

Introduced at a tennis club, comedian Alvy Singer and aspiring singer Annie Hall embark on a romance and set up house together. Recording tycoon Tony Lacey's interest in Annie arouses Alvy's jealousy and a quarrel leads to separation. Alvy plunges into an affair with journalist Pam but eventually the couple are reunited. Lured to Hollywood, he is accompanied by Annie. They attend one of Lacey's parties and on the homeward flight to New York they make a decision to part, with Annie returning to Lacey in California. Alvy makes a futile attempt at reconciliation and then writes a play resolving his feelings about their relationship. When they meet by accident in New York an affection and friendship is still evident between them.

Comment

With *Annie Hall*, Woody Allen leaves behind the dominant parodic (*Love and Death*, 1975) or revue-style modes (*Bananas*, 1971) in which the former gag-writer and nightclub comedian's work had been pitched to achieve the first unified work in the self-conscious, East Coast Jewish upper-middlebrow manner now his trademark. Although the earlier films had established the Allen sceen persona of the aspirant romantic as existential schmuck, here he manages a more emotionally satisfying narrative core by contextualizing his star turn in a directly confessional love story that draws on his own highly public Seventies liaison with co-star Diane Keaton. Filmed under characteristic secrecy with the working title of 'Anhedonia' (the inability to enjoy oneself), the film was described by Allen as being about 'real problems besetting some fairly neurotic characters trying to exist in male-female relationships in America in 1977. So it turns out to be more serious than anything I've ever tried before'.

Without totally eschewing the comic tricks of yore – one scene uses subtitles to hilariously reveal the characters' true feelings, another gag utilizes an appearance by media guru Marshal MacLuhan for its effect – the film parades Allen's personal neuroses (the transience of love and happiness) with a blend of aphoristic wit and would-be seriousness. As such, it's the pivotal entry in Allen's filmography, establishing a template for his later, more accomplished variations on a similar theme and setting him on a path towards recognition as one of America's most respected film talents, a fact acknowledged by the American Academy who rewarded the film with five nominations and four Oscars including Best Film, Best Director and Best Screenplay.

A Jack Rollins-Charles H Joffe Production for United Artists
Producer Charles H Joffe
Screenplay Woody Allen and Marshall Brickman
Photography Gordon Willis
Editors Ralph Rosenblum and Wendy Greene Bricmont
Art Director Mel Bourne
Music Various
Running time 93 mins *colour*

Cast

Woody Allen (Alvy Singer)
Diane Keaton (Annie Hall)
Tony Roberts (Rob)
Carol Kane (Allison)
Paul Simon (Tony Lacey)
Shelley Duvall (Pam)

The Apartment

Billy Wilder, USA, 1960

Bittersweet romantic comedy

A bittersweet satire on contemporary morality allows Billy Wilder to grow 'a rose in a garbage pail'.

The story

Insurance clerk C C Baxter finds his corporate rise assisted by providing his superiors with access to his apartment as a locale for their extra-marital affairs. A surprise promotion is engineered by company director J D Sheldrake in return for his use of the apartment. Baxter is now emboldened to pursue his love of elevator operator Fran Kubelik but is dismayed to discover that she is Sheldrake's mistress. When Sheldrake chooses Christmas Eve to inform her that marriage will never be an option, she takes an overdose and is discovered by Baxter who tenderly nurses her back to health. Declaring his apartment off-limits, the conscience-stricken Baxter quits his job and is rewarded with Fran's love.

Comment

Warmly impressed by their first collaboration on *Some Like It Hot* (1959) (see p203), writer-director Billy Wilder vowed to Jack Lemmon that he would create a role designed specifically to display the range of his talents. The result was *The Apartment* (1960), a bittersweet critique of the moral laxitude abroad in the go-getting corporate jungle of contemporary America that would be echoed a generation later in Oliver Stone's *Wall Street* (1987).

Respected for his equal ability with hard-nosed drama or frequently risqué comedy, Wilder combines both in *The Apartment* and uses the approachability of three central performers primarily associated with light comedy to draw the audience into a dramatically bleak vision of social relations. Lemmon's innate likeability has rarely been more skilfully employed and is deftly complemented by MacLaine's shop-soiled vulnerability and MacMurray's seldom exploited affinity with the all-American heel. A veteran of Wilder's *Double Indemnity* (1944) (see p71), MacMurray was a last-minute replacement for Paul Douglas who died during the film's pre-production period.

Marked by a moving sense of compassion throughout, Wilder escapes the harsh bitterness of which he was sometimes capable (*Kiss Me Stupid*, 1964) to achieve perhaps the most emotionally resonant film of his career and certainly one of the most popular. Listed among the top ten box-office hits of 1960, it was nominated for ten Academy Awards and won Wilder the hat trick of Best Picture, Best Director and Best Screenplay (with I A L Diamond). The triumvirate of Billy Wilder, Lemmon and MacLaine were subsequently reunited on *Irma La Douce* (1963).

A United Artists Picture
Producer Billy Wilder
Screenplay Billy Wilder and I A L Diamond
Photography Joseph LaShelle
Editor Daniel Mandell
Art Director Alexander Trauner
Music Adolph Deutsch
Running time 125 mins b/w Panavision

Cast
Jack Lemmon (Calvin Clinton 'Bud' Baxter)
Shirley MacLaine (Fran Kubelik)
Fred MacMurray (J D Sheldrake)
Jack Kruschen (Dr Dreyfus)
Ray Walston (Mr Dobisch)
Edie Adams (Miss Olsen)

Apocalypse Now

Francis Coppola, USA, 1979

Vietnam odyssey

A surrealistic Vietnam journey identifies the evil that lurks within all mankind.

The story

Vietnam. Battle-weary Captain Willard is ordered to execute Colonel Kurtz, an American officer who has established a dictatorship deep in the jungle. The journey upriver begins with a helicopter assault led by gung-ho Colonel Kilgore and grows increasingly surreal as he leaves supposed civilization behind. Willard enters Kurtz's kingdom and Kurtz explains his philosophy that a victor must utilize man's primordial instinct to kill without compassion or moral dilemma and invites him to terminate his life. Willard attacks him with a machete, an act mirrored in the ritualistic slaughter of a water-buffalo. Kurtz dies uttering 'the horror, the horror', and Willard sails away, haunted by guilt and the insanity of all slaying.

Comment

'My film is not about Vietnam. It is Vietnam.' Such was the characteristically flamboyant statement of Francis Coppola at the first unveiling of *Apocalypse Now*. The critical success of *The Godfather* (1972) (see p89), *The Godfather, Part II* (1974) and *The Conversation* (1974) (see p59) had firmly established Coppola as one of the most exciting and visionary directors of his generation and now he embarked on his long-planned magnum opus, a major artistic statement on America's military involvement in South East Asia.

The troubled shooting of the film on location in the Philippines, revealed in the documentary *Hearts of Darkness* (1991), ironically echoed the real events. Sets were destroyed by tropical storms, star Harvey Keitel was replaced by Martin Sheen who suffered a near-fatal heart attack, shooting stretched from a planned 17 weeks to 238 days and the budget steadily escalated from $12 to $31 million.

Coppola's approach to his country's recent history proved a highly allusive one. Taking the story outline and thematic thrust of Joseph Conrad's *Heart of Darkness* and overlaying the 'fisher king' myth of death and regeneration adopted by T S Eliot's *The Waste Land*, the film provides an operatic examination of the deep-rooted evil in the human soul rather than a specific focus on the ideological contours of the Vietnam conflict. Vietnam War correspondent Michael (*Dispatches*) Herr's wise narration, The Doors' contemporary rock music, and the impressively-marshalled military hardware effectively date the proceedings, but the film's real achievement lies in moments of hallucinatory carnage where the sensual delirium, horror and absurd beauty of wartime are disturbingly conveyed.

An Omni-Zoetrope Production
Producer Francis Coppola
Screenplay John Milius and Francis Coppola, based on *Heart of Darkness* by Joseph Conrad
Photography Vittorio Storaro
Editors Walter Murch, Gerald B Greenberg and Lisa Fruchtman
Production Designer Dean Tavoularis
Music Carmine Coppola, Francis Coppola, Wagner, The Doors etc
Running time 141 mins (70 mm) (35mm version with end title sequence: 153 mins)
colour Technicolor

Cast

Marlon Brando (Colonel Walter E Kurtz)
Robert Duvall (Lt-Col Bill Kilgore)
Martin Sheen (Captain Benjamin L Willard)
Frederic Forrest ('Chef' Hicks)
Larry Fishburne ('Clean')
Dennis Hopper (Photo-journalist)
Harrison Ford (Colonel Lucas)

Ashes and Diamonds
(Popiol I Diament)
Andrzej Wajda, Poland, 1958

Wartime resistance drama

Wajda's masterly film opened up political and historical debate previously silenced in post-war Poland.

The story

Poland, on the last day of World War II. Maciek is the youngest member of a Nationalist resistance movement in a small Polish town. He is ordered to kill the new Communist district secretary, Szczuka, a wartime comrade. A violent assassination at the beginning of the film establishes that Maciek has no qualms about killing, but he is torn between devotion to duty and the absurdity of the situation. As he waits in the hotel, he meets a woman, Krystyna, and spends the night with her, further fuelling his doubts. They part after reading an inscription in a churchyard, and Maciek goes to his inevitable tragic confrontation with Szczuka. He shoots his rival, but is in turn shot by a drunken officer from a banquet in which the new Poland is emerging, and dies, symbolically, on a giant scrap-heap.

Comment

Andrzej Wajda was the first Polish filmmaker to make a major impression beyond the boundaries of his own country. He belonged to a generation which had grown up in the shadow of the fascist occupation of his country, and began to make films in the equally dark shadow of the post-war Communist régime.

His work has taken a steady look at the political and historical realities which gave birth to the new Poland, and *Ashes and Diamonds*, adapted from a famous novel by Jerzy Andrzejewski, is arguably the finest example of it. The film completed an informal trio begun with *A Generation (Pokolenie*, 1955) and *Sewer (Kanal*, 1957 (*They Loved Life*)).

The conflict which divides Maciek and Szczuka contains resonances which go well beyond the specific human dimension of the film, but one of its great strengths is that the politics remain subservient to the working out of that human drama.

The gritty realism of the film is constantly augmented by Wajda's distinctly symbolic vision, and simple objects take on layers of significance in relation to the emerging Poland. The filmmaker catches his nation on the very cusp of war and peace, and the haunted uncertainties and fragile attachments of the characters speak with great eloquence and artistry of that history.

A Film Polski Production
Producer Stanisław Adler
Screenplay Andrzej Wajda and Jerzy Andrzejewski
Photography Jerzy Wójcik
Editor Halina Nawrocka˙
Art Director Roman Mann
Music Polish Radio Rhythm Quintet
Running time 105 mins b/w

Cast
Zbigniew Cybulski (Maciek Chelmicki)
Ewa Kryzjewska (Krystyna)
Wacław Zastrżezyński (Szczuka)
Adam Pawlikowski (Andrzej)
Jan Ciecierski (The Porter)
Bogumił Kobiela (Drewnowski)
Stanislaw Milski (Pieniazjek)

L'Atalante

Jean Vigo, France, 1934

Timeless romantic drama

A simple tale of two lovers becomes a universal hymn to romance.

The story

Jean, the captain of the barge *L'Atalante*, marries country girl Juliette and brings her aboard the vessel. She attempts to cope with the monotony and masculinity of this claustrophobic environment but grows lonely when Jean attends to his duties, and yearns for the excitement of Paris. She is befriended by the garrulous old mate Père Jules, but this merely arouses Jean's jealous nature. When she slips ashore, an incensed Jean casts off without her. United by their distant longing for each other, the couple are tormented by the separation. At Le Havre, Père Jules sets off in search of Juliette and is blessed by good luck in discovering her. She is joyously reunited with the lovelorn Jean and they happily resume the voyage.

Comment

The 1990 restoration and reissue of Jean Vigo's *L'Atalante*, pieced together from prints in British, French and Belgian archives to conform to the director's original intentions, cemented Vigo's critical status as one of the most accomplished of film artists. While his earlier short work, the scathing 'documentary' *A Propos De Nice* (1929) and the schoolboy anarchy of *Zéro De Conduite* (1932) confirmed a trenchant and idiosyncratic talent at work, when hired by major French studio Gaumont to work on a potentially hack-neyed waterway romance, Vigo's response was to respect only the outline of the material, make the best of difficult shooting conditions, and turn in the uniquely quirky hymn to romance that is *L'Atalante*.

From the simplest of scenarios, Vigo creates a rich cavalcade of ever-changing moods, switching from broad comedy to moments of tension and from surreal visions to a celebration of desire. Perhaps the most extraordinary sequence has the fervent lovers momentarily estranged, and as Vigo deftly cuts between separate beds, from restless body to restless body, he does evoke a memorably poetic and palpable sense of erotic need. Faced with the uncategorizable end result however, Gaumont barred the director from the editing room while they recut the film, replaced some of Maurice Jaubert's dreamy score with a currently popular song and released the film under the title *Le Chaland Qui Passe*. Vigo died in Paris of rheumatic septicaemia at the age of 34 a mere two weeks later.

Bernardo Bertolucci pays his tribute to the film in *Last Tango in Paris* (1972) (see p125) when the Jean-Pierre Leaud character is shooting a scene on a barge and throws a lifebelt overboard. As it hits the water, the word *L'Atalante* is seen printed on the perimeter.

A Gaumont production
Producer J-L Nounez
Screenplay Jean Vigo and Albert Riera, based on a story by Jean Guinee
Photography Boris Kaufman and Louis Berger
Editor Louis Chavance
Art Director Francis Jourdain
Music Maurice Jaubert
Running time 85 mins b/w

Cast
Michel Simon (Père Jules)
Dita Parlo (Juliette)
Jean Daste (Jean)
Gilles Margaritis (Pedlar)
Louis Lefebvre (Boy)
Maurice Gilles (Head Clerk)

Au Revoir Les Enfants

Louis Malle, France/West Germany, 1987

Autobiographical wartime remembrance

This unsentimental but moving story is based on a true wartime incident in the life of the young Malle in Occupied France.

The story

Occupied France, 1944. 12-year-old Julien Quentin and his brother François are reluctantly packed off to a Catholic boarding school near Fontainbleu by their anxious mother. Julien is asked by Father Jean to befriend a mysterious newcomer, Jean Bonnet. In the course of their growing friendship, Julien discovers that Jean is a Jewish boy, one of three hidden in the school by the Fathers. When the black-market operation run by Joseph the kitchen boy is discovered, he reports Father Jean to the Gestapo in retaliation for his dismissal. The Nazis remove the Father and the three boys, and close the school. Bonnet later dies at Auschwitz.

Comment

Au Revoir Les Enfants marked Louis Malle's return to France, in both literal and figurative terms, after a series of films set in America. The simple but highly evocative story is based on Malle's own childhood experience in wartime France, one which he has said 'may well have determined my vocation as a filmmaker'.

The relationship between the two boys is completely credible, if perhaps slightly idealized. Quentin is a high-spirited, rather mischievous, but well-liked boy, while the newcomer is an outsider from the beginning. They are brought together by their mutual love for books, and Bonnet's accomplishments in playing jazz on piano, and forge a strong friendship.

Malle allows their relationship to develop in a leisurely and deliberately understated fashion, concentrating on the daily rituals of school life rather than the momentous events beyond the walls. Only the occasional intrusion, as in the scene when the two boys are lost during a treasure hunt and are picked up and returned to the school by German soldiers, provides intimations of what is to come.

The betrayal, when it arrives, comes from their friend Joseph, an orphaned kitchen boy who runs a black-market operation in the school, involving some of the boys. Joseph's piqued and perhaps unthinking act of revenge seals the fate of Bonnet, the other Jewish boys, and Father Jean.

The film was released in France during the trial of Klaus Barbie for war crimes in Lyons, and took on additional relevance in the wake of the infamous remark by Jean Le Pen, the leader of the French National Front, that the holocaust was just a detail in the history of World War II.

A Nouvelles Editions de Films/MK2 Productions/Marian Karmitz (Paris)/Stella Film/NEF (Munich) Production

Producer Louis Malle
Screenplay Louis Malle
Photography Renato Berta
Editor Emmanuelle Castro
Art Director Willy Holt
Music Schubert and Saint-Saëns
Running time 104 mins *colour*

Cast
Gaspard Manesse (Julien Quentin)
Raphael Fejtö (Jean Bonnet)
Francine Racette (Mme Quentin)
Stanislas Carré de Malberg (François Quentin)
Phillipe Morier-Genoud (Father Jean)
François Berléand (Father Michel)
François Negret (Joseph)
Peter Fitz (Muller)

L'Avventura

Michelangelo Antonioni, Italy, 1960

Contemporary alienation

Alienation is explored through visual framing and character in a groundbreaking study of non-communication.

The story

Reunited after a month apart, Anna and her fiancé, architect Sandro, make love, but Anna seems unhappy with their situation as they drive off with Claudia to join friends for a boating holiday off the Sicilian coast. Anna attempts to communicate her feelings to Sandro and is later found to be missing from the boat. Despite extensive exploration, her body is not found. As they continue to search, Claudia and Sandro are attracted to each other and later book into a sumptuous hotel. That evening, Claudia catches him making love to a prostitute he had met earlier. Sandro follows Claudia as she rushes from the hotel but it is Claudia who wistfully comforts his tearful figure as night ends and day begins.

Comment

Greeted with a slow handclap and catcalls at its first Cannes screening in May 1960 and subsequently judged to be a 'nightmarish masterpiece of tedium' by *Time* magazine, Michelangelo Antonioni's characteristically langorous evocation of contemporary alienation elicited both admiration and dismay from the critics and would go on to bemuse and irritate many an international audience on its surprisingly successful box-office release.

Although obviously presaged by the director's earlier work (*Le Amiche*, 1955 and *Il Grido*, 1957), a combination of distinctive thematic and stylistic elements were to establish *L'Avventura* as a contentious, must-see picture on the then burgeoning art-house circuit. Disregarding the usual narrative expectations (whether Anna committed suicide, lived or died is never explained for instance, and ultimately is of little importance), Antonioni also disdains audience identification with the plight of the central couple through achingly slow pacing, limited use of dialogue, distanced camera-work and by the pair's halting attempts at communication and joyless, if not pointless, sexuality.

Such overwhelming social malaise is of course a common current in much 20th-century European art, but Antonioni's work is significant for the way in which the alienation of individuals from each other is conveyed not through the shaping of the narrative but by a certain formal astringency and the visual motif of the characters' alienation from their surroundings. It was an art he was to develop against a memorable variety of backdrops from the Rome stock exchange (*L'Eclisse*, 1962) to swinging London (*Blow-Up*, 1966), from hippy California (*Zabriskie Point*, 1969) to arid North Africa (*The Passenger*, 1975).

A Cino Del Duca Produzioni Cinématografiche Europée/Societé Cinématographique Lyre Film.
Producer Amato Pennasiliio
Screenplay Michelangelo Antonioni, Elio Bartolini and Tonino Guerra, based on a story by Antonioni
Photography Aldo Scavarda
Editor Eraldo Da Roma
Art Director Piero Poletto
Music Giovanni Fusco
Running time 145 mins b/w

Cast
Gabriele Ferzetti (Sandro)
Monica Vitti (Claudia)
Lea Massari (Anna)
Dominique Blanchar (Giulia)
Renzo Ricci (Anna's Father)
James Addams (Corrado)

The Band Wagon

Vincente Minnelli, USA, 1953

Showbusiness musical

The Broadway comeback of a Hollywood hoofer is a musical highlight of the Fifties.

The story

Concerned about his fading popularity, ageing Hollywood star Tony Hunter is persuaded to try a Broadway show. Despite misgivings and the indifference that greets his arrival in New York, he agrees. His loyal friends Lester and Lily Marton conceive a musical show for his talents and he plunges into the fray despite a leading lady, ballerina Gaby Berard, whom he considers inappropriate, and a director, the flamboyant Jeffrey Cordova, who seems intent on sabotaging their efforts with his extreme vision of the material. The opening night is a predictable disaster. Stealing victory from the jaws of despair, they all collaborate on a lighter, less pretentious falderol, Tony falls in love with Gaby and the show is a hit.

Comment

Along with *Singin' In the Rain* (1952) (see p198), *The Band Wagon* stands as a supreme example of the standards reached by the Arthur Freed unit at M-G-M in the 1950s. Written by Betty Comden and Adolph Green, who were also responsible for the screenplay of *Singin' In the Rain*, the film adopts a behind-the-showbusiness-scenes formula familiar from the earlier production and satirizes both the Broadway theatre of the period and (affectionately) the figure of Fred Astaire himself as he worries over his age, the height of his co-star and the perfectionism that has been his hallmark.

Constructed around the catalogue of songs by Howard Dietz and Arthur Schwartz, the soundtrack includes such numbers as 'A Shine on Your Shoes', 'Triplets', 'That's Entertainment' and 'Dancing in the Dark' which Gene Kelly once cited as his favourite number from all the dancing duets in Astaire's canon. Also included is the by now inevitable balletic sequence, 'Girl Hunt Ballet' (written by Alan Jay Lerner), a spoof of the Mike Hammer-Mickey Spillane school of tough-guy heroics popular at the time.

A witty and sophisticated screen entertainment, Vincente Minnelli's direction makes characteristically effective use of colour throughout and also subtly deploys the musical numbers to express the psychological and emotional development of the Astaire character; songs such as 'By Myself' give way to the likes of 'I Guess I'll Have to Change My Plans' as he abandons his despondent sense of isolation to embark on a new path of romance and a shared future.

Nominated for Academy Awards for Scoring Of A Musical Picture, Costume Design and the Original Screenplay, the film went unrewarded but assured of its unassailable position in the history of the screen musical.

An M-G-M Production
Producer Arthur Freed
Screenplay Betty Comden and Adolph Green
Photography Harry Jackson (George Folsey)
Editor Albert Akst
Art Directors Cedric Gibbons and Preston Ames
Music Howard Dietz and Arthur Schwartz
Running time 112 mins colour

Cast
Fred Astaire (Tony Hunter)
Cyd Charisse (Gaby)
Oscar Levant (Lester Marton)
Nanette Fabray (Lily Marton)
Jack Buchanan (Jeffrey Cordova)
Ava Gardner (Guest Star)

'You ain't heard nothing yet'
Movie history from *The Jazz Singer* to World War II

Al Jolson's first words in *The Jazz Singer* (1927) (see p115) signalled both the beginning and the end of an era. The film's vast popularity ensured that the talking picture was not a passing fad but the shape of things to come, whilst the advent of sound meant that the one universal language of artistic communication had now been rendered a Tower of Babel. The technological restraint of the new advances produced a short period of crude and immobile productions that compared unfavourably with the expressive fluidity of the silent film at its peak.

Across the Atlantic, Alfred Hitchcock made the first British talkie in *Blackmail* (1929) (see p38) and gave a glimpse of the artistic possibilities in the use of sound with a sequence in which the soundtrack mutes every word except 'knife', the latter becoming a devastating verbal reminder of the leading lady's fatal misdemeanour.

The 1930s now reveal the Hollywood studio system functioning at its peak, and while there have been justifiable criticisms of the tyranny imposed by such movie moguls as Louis B Mayer and Harry Cohn and the near servile conditions in which stars were bound to a studio by seven-year contracts, the era did produce some of the most sublime and enduring classics of American film. Each studio had a distinctive style and roster of contract artists so that it became possible to recognize a film's place of origin often from just a reading of the supporting cast list. Warner Brothers became famous for its gangster cycle, Busby Berkeley musicals, Bette Davis melodramas and the adventures of Errol Flynn. Paramount had a sophisticated sheen in the work of Ernst Lubitsch, Marlene Dietrich and Gary Cooper, as well as much-needed commercial viability in the *double entendres* of Mae West. M-G-M, considered the Rolls

Royce of studios, boasted 'more stars than there are in heaven' and had a list of talents that ranged from Clark Gable to Judy Garland and Greta Garbo. R-K-O was the home of Astaire and Rogers, Katharine Hepburn and *King Kong* (1933) (see p123), along with *Dracula* (1930) and *Frankenstein* (1931), Universal established itself as the chief innovator in the fantasy and macabre genres, whilst Harry Cohn's poverty-row enterprise at Columbia entered the big league mainly thanks to the work of Frank Capra on films like *It Happened One Night* (1934) (see p112) and *Mr Deeds Goes to Town* (1936).

The pre-War era also witnessed one of the richest periods in French cinema as René Clair delighted audiences with the sparkling whimsy of such films as *Le Million* (1931), Jean Renoir's warm humanism was given its most eloquent expression in *La Grande Illusion* (1937) (see p97) and *La Règle Du Jeu* (1939) (see p181), and the collaboration of writer Jacques Prévert, director Marcel Carné and actor Jean Gabin in films like *Le Jour Se Lève* (1939) (see p120) resulted in vivid encapsulations of the national mood as the war clouds gathered.

In Hollywood the war was met with a flood of suitably morale-boosting adventures, comedies and musicals, notably the patriotic *Yankee Doodle Dandy* (1942) (see p239). However, it also saw Orson Welles enter the medium with *Citizen Kane* (1941) (see p55), still the prime contender for the title of the greatest film ever made, and *The Magnificent Ambersons* (1942) (see p136), and in Britain wartime restrictions provided the impetus for Michael Powell and Emeric Pressburger to make such ravishing work as *The Life and Death of Colonel Blimp* (1943) (see p132), for Olivier's *Henry V* (1944) (see p103) and David Lean's *Brief Encounter* (1945) (see p45).

All Quiet on The Western Front *(1930) Directed by Lewis Milestone (Lew Ayres)*

Paths of Glory *(1957) Directed by Stanley Kubrick*
(Adolphe Menjou, Kirk Douglas, George MacReady)

The Blue Angel *(1930) Directed by Josef Von Sternberg (Marlene Dietrich)*

Queen Christina *(1933) Directed by Rouben Mamoulian (Greta Garbo)*

Batman

Tim Burton, USA, 1989

Comic-strip adventure

The dark side of the comicbook hero is emphasized in an archetypal Eighties blockbuster.

The story

Gotham City. Millionaire recluse Bruce Wayne doubles as mysterious crime-fighter Batman. When crime boss Carl Grissom arranges the murder of Jack Napier, Batman's intervention tips him into a vat of chemicals instead. He survives, deformed and deranged, to become The Joker and exact his revenge on Grissom. Meanwhile, reporter Vicki Vale falls for Wayne unaware of his split personality. However, when she is kidnapped by the Joker it is Batman who swings to her rescue. Discovering that Wayne's parents were killed by the young Jack Napier she begins to unravel the mystery. Taking Vicki hostage, The Joker challenges Batman to a duel. Confronting each other atop a cathedral belfry, The Joker is bested and falls to his death.

Comment

Perhaps the supreme example of contemporary Hollywood's approach to filmmaking as a commercial enterprise, *Batman* was hyped, merchandized and budgeted to the hilt to ensure maximum media exposure and saturation audience awareness of the 'product' being sold. Its reported budget of $50 million was one of the highest ever, and Jack Nicholson is reputed to have earned up to $60 million from his profit participation in a venture that easily lent itself to the selling of a soundtrack album, a distinctive T-shirt, dolls, books, posters etc. Given the weight of expectations, the film, in parts, even managed to live up to its advance publicity.

Under the direction of Tim Burton, the film interestingly chooses to stress the darker, schizophrenic qualities of the Batman/Bruce Wayne vigilante figure and finds a visual equivalent of his troubled personality in the brooding, imposing vision of Gotham City provided in the awesome sets of Oscar-winner Anton Furst. Ultimately, however, it is Jack Nicholson's Joker who both steals and unbalances the film as the actor contributes one of his most flamboyant and operatic turns, cannily aware that in a production so heavily dominated by technology and set design a performance had to be on a grand scale to make any kind of impact.

One of the highest-grossing films of all time, *Batman*'s success sent Hollywood in search of some similarly heroic box-office propositions: *Dick Tracy* (1990) may have proved less to the public taste but *Robin Hood* (1991), complete with men of Sherwood dolls and chart-topping Bryan Adams single, appears to vindicate the possibilities of the formula. *Batman Returns* is currently in production, although future generations may wonder what all the fuss was about.

A Guber-Peters Company Production in association with Polygram Pictures
Producers Jon Peters and Peter Guber
Screenplay Sam Hamm and Warren Skaaren, based on a story by Hamm using characters created by Bob Kane
Photography Roger Pratt
Editor Ray Lovejoy
Production Designer Anton Furst
Music Danny Elfman; songs by Prince
Running time 126 mins colour

Cast

Jack Nicholson (The Joker/Jack Napier)
Michael Keaton (Bruce Wayne/Batman)
Kim Basinger (Vicki Vale)
Robert Wuhl (Alexander Knox)
Pat Hingle (Commissioner Gordon)
Billy Dee Williams (Harvey Dent)

The Battle of Algiers
(La Battaglia Di Algeri)

Gillo Pontecorvo, Italy/Algeria, 1965

Political drama

A balanced and urgent account of a struggle for independence sets new standards in cinéma-vérité-style drama.

The story

October 1957. Trapped in his home, Algerian Liberation Army (FLN) leader Ali La Pointe reflects on his three-year involvement with the struggle for independence from the French. In 1954, when the town centre becomes the focal point of resistance, a campaign of bombing is waged by both sides. Early in 1957 French paratroopers arrive under the command of Colonel Mathieu who instigates a brutal wave of torture and repression. The FLN stage a general strike but Mathieu escalates the killings until only La Pointe remains. A comrade is tortured into revealing his hiding place and in the October he is blown up for his refusal to surrender. Opposition to the French however never dies and in 1962 Algeria gains its independence.

Comment

Gillo Pontecorvo's film is a meticulously detailed recreation of the historical events surrounding the successful rebellion against the French colonial régime in Algeria. Shooting on the actual locations with a cast mainly drawn from local non-professionals, his grainy monochrome images resonate with the authenticity of the newsreel. Yet a statement in the opening titles reminds us that no actuality footage was used – thus the film is not only a committed political testament but a commentary on the techniques of the documentary itself.

As former partisan fighter and a Youth Secretary of the Italian Communist Party,

Pontecorvo's sympathies are never in doubt, but while the studiously harrowing scenes of torture at the hands of the French military construct a compelling case against such human rights violations, the film admirably refuses to draw its characterization in easy ideological shorthand. The colonial Colonel is prepared to admit to the inevitability of the historical process, for example, and a sequence leading up to a rebel bomb attack pulls no punches on the civilian cost to be paid for violent political struggle. By eschewing the caricatures of villainy and heroism and admitting the fictiveness of his filmmaking strategies, Pontecorvo acknowledges the flexibility of political and aesthetic values, thus strengthening rather than weakening his impact.

Nominated as the Best Foreign Film of 1966, the complex Academy rules then pertaining to the eligibility of foreign work for the main awards meant that Pontecorvo found himself an unsuccessful nominee for his script and direction in 1968. His subsequent career has produced only a very modest body of work, notably *Quiemada!* (1969) starring Marlon Brando.

A Casbah Films-Igor Films Production
Producers Antonio Musu and Yacef Saadi
Screenplay Franco Solinas, based on a story by Solinas and Gillo Pontecorvo
Photography Marcello Gatti
Editors Mario Serandrei and Mario Morra
Art Director Sergio Canevari
Music Ennio Morricone and Gillo Pontecorvo
Running time 135 mins b/w

Cast

Jean Martin (Colonel Mathieu)
Yacef Saadi (Saari Kader)
Brahim Haggiag (Ali La Pointe)
Tommaso Neri (Captain Dubois)
Fawzia El Kader (Haahmal)
Michele Kerbash (Fathia)

Battleship Potemkin
(Bronenosets Potemkin)
Sergei Eisenstein, USSR, 1925

Russian landmark

A sailors' revolt establishes the international reputation of Soviet cinema.

The story

Conditions aboard the battleship *Potemkin* have driven the crew to the brink of revolt. When certain sailors refuse to eat rancid meat, they are ordered to be executed but Vakulinchuk intervenes and convinces the guards not to carry out the order and insurgence breaks out. The sailors gain control and sail to Odessa where they erect a shrine to Vakulinchuk who has been slain. His heroic sacrifice inspires the citizens of Odessa to join the sailors in opposing the Czar. Troops arrive and many civilians are slaughtered. The *Potemkin*'s crew use their guns to destroy the military headquarters. Fearing reprisals, they steam in trepidation towards the remainder of the fleet; however their comrades decide to join their cause.

Comment

The worldwide success of Sergei Eisenstein's *Battleship Potemkin* immediately focused international attention on the new Soviet cinema, fulfilling, to some extent, the Bolshevik authorities' hopes that their state-funded programme of filmmaking for explicitly propagandist purposes would not only consolidate the Revolution at home but promote the notion of class-consciousness abroad.

Commissioned to mark the 20th anniversary of the 1905 Revolution, Eisenstein chose to concentrate in particular on the naval mutiny and subsequent Tsarist massacre of civilians in the seaport of Odessa. The film embodies the idea of the collective hero that he had absorbed from his days creating a new revolutionary art in the theatre under Meyerhold, using the idea of typage to cast real sailors and actual citizens for greater authenticity of performance. Most significantly however, *Potemkin* was a textbook demonstration of Eisenstein's theoretical and practical approach to montage. From Marx's dialectical materialism, Pavlovian work on stimuli and response, Freudian psychology and the post-Revolution Soviet wave of Constructivist art, Eisenstein had worked out a highly mathematical concept of montage according to which a film's meaning was created from the series of synthetic collisions between image and subsequent image. Although few of today's films adopt Eisenstein's doctrinaire approach to the technique, his basic thesis added immeasurably to the widening of film grammar; *Battleship Potemkin*'s typically precise sequence of slaughter on the Odessa steps became one of the cinema's best-known moments, frequently imitated and paid homage to most recently in Brian De Palma's *The Untouchables* (1987).

A Goskino Production
Producer Jacob Bliokh
Screenplay Sergei Eisenstein and Nina Agadzhanova-Shutko
Photography Edward Tisse and V Popov
Editor Sergei Eisenstein
Art Director Vasili Rakhals
Music Edmund Meisel
Running time 75 mins b/w

Cast

Alexander Antonov (Vakulinchuk)
Vladimir Barsky (Commander Golikov)
Grigori Alexandrov (Senior Officer Giliarovski)
Mikhail Gomorov (Sailor Matiushenko)
Levchenko (Boatswain)
Repnikova (Woman on the Steps)

Becky Sharp

Rouben Mamoulian, USA, 1935

Colourful period piece

The lush beauty of full Technicolor is revealed for the first time.

The story

Orphan Becky Sharp is determined to obtain all the privileges and status of a lady. First she sets her sights on the buffoonish Joseph Sedley, brother of her dearest friend Amelia. Then while a governess in the Crawley household she charms the son Rawdon and they are wed. Soon Rawdon is ordered to Brussels where Becky meets the Marquis of Steyne who becomes her conduit to the highest reaches of London society. However, as debts mount Rawdon is forced to defend his honour. Becky offers herself to Steyne in return for money but Rawdon interrupts their tryst and declares their marriage over. Reduced to singing in a tavern, Becky rises again by duping money from Rawdon's brother and resuming her friendship with Joseph.

Comment

Just as *The Jazz Singer* (1927) (see p115) has come to be regarded as the key film in the sound revolution, *Becky Sharp* has a similar position of historical significance as the first film to utilize the three-strip Technicolor process that signalled the advent of effective full-colour films. Throughout the 1920s the Technicolor company had been offering a system which cemented together simultaneously filtered (through red and green) 'recordings' to produce an effect far superior to earlier efforts at tinting or stencilling colour onto film. The major breakthrough however came in 1928 when a new printing method was developed to produce a single final print that combined the twin filter strips without having to glue them together. This method would also permit printing from three different filtered images (through cyan, magenta and yellow) so creating the first truly modern colour process. Walt Disney became the first to try out the new technology with *Flowers and Trees* (1932) in the Silly Symphonies series of cartoons, and the live-action short *La Cucaracha* (1934). Originally begun by Lowell Sherman, who died during the shooting, *Becky Sharp* was the first three-strip Technicolor feature. Sherman's replacement, Rouben Mamoulian, tried to alter the colour to reflect the emotional tonality of the story and the results were seen in their full glory when the UCLA Film Archive recently completed a painstaking three-year restoration of the film from the few prints still extant in archives around the world. Lush in the reds of military uniforms and the blues and yellows of crinoline dresses and capes, the film may not entirely stand the test of time in terms of its dramatic qualities and overwrought performances, but its luxurious and pioneering use of colour has earned it a place in history.

A Pioneer Pictures Production
Producer Kenneth MacGowran
Screenplay Francis Edward Faragoh, based on a play by Langdon Mitchell and Vanity Fair by William Makepeace Thackeray
Photography Ray Rennehan
Editor Archie Marshek
Art Director Robert Edmond Jones
Music Roy Webb
Running time 83 mins colour

Cast

Miriam Hopkins (Becky Sharp)
Frances Dee (Amelia Sedley)
Cedric Hardwicke (Marquis of Steyne)
Billie Burke (Lady Bareacres)
Alison Skipworth (Miss Crawley)
Nigel Bruce (Joseph Sedley)

Ben-Hur

William Wyler, USA, 1959

Biblical epic

A saga of revenge and faith brings intimacy to the pyrotechnics of the epic genre.

The story

Jerusalem. When Judah Ben-Hur refuses to turn informer for his boyhood friend Roman Tribune Messala the latter responds by condemning him to galley slavery and having his mother and sister imprisoned. Years pass, but when Ben-Hur saves the life of the Consul Quintus he is rewarded by being adopted as his son. He returns to Jerusalem and his beloved Esther and is later able to revenge himself on Messala in a spectacular chariot race. The dying Messala informs Ben-Hur that his family reside in the Valley of the Lepers. Seeking the help of Jesus, he witnesses the crucifixion and recognizes the carpenter's son who had once shown him mercy. He is later reunited with a mother and sister now both miraculously cured.

Comment

The 1950s' advent of television as a truly popular entertainment medium initiated the decline of the Hollywood film industry's lucrative primacy. The studios' response was technological innovation designed to emphasize the movie screen's sheer dimensional scale over the flickering cathode-ray image on the box at home. Fox's lavish Biblical spectacular *The Robe* (1953) was the first feature film shot in their new widescreen format of Cinemascope, its success demonstrating that the expansive frame needed expansive action to fill it and thus provoking a slew of similar vast superproductions like *War and Peace* (1956), *Around the World in 80 Days* (1956) and *The Ten Commandments* (1956).

Impressed by the profit and loss accounts on these ventures, M-G-M decided to risk the future of the company on a $15 million remake of General Lew Wallace's platitudinous novel. An earlier adaptation starring Ramon Navarro had cost an unprecedented $4 million in 1925. This version would be entrusted to the professionalism of William Wyler, who had worked in a lowly fashion on the silent one, with Cesare Danova initially announced as the star before Charlton Heston was persuaded to offer a further essay in heroic fortitude. Filmed in Italy over a period of ten months, *Ben-Hur* came to be regarded as the artistic peak of the genre with Wyler's direction emphasizing the intimate human drama amidst the epic conflicts and the staggering second-unit work of Andrew Marton and Yakima Canutt offering some of the screen's liveliest action sequences, particularly the famed chariot race. With an American box-office gross of around $40 million it achieved its purpose of saving M-G-M, and its tally of 11 Academy Awards remains a record for an individual film.

An M-G-M Production
Producer Sam Zimbalist
Screenplay Karl Tunberg (with uncredited contributions from Christopher Fry, Maxwell Anderson, S N Behrman and Gore Vidal) from *A Tale of Christ* by General Lew Wallace
Photography Robert Surtees
Editors Ralph E Winters and John D Dunning
Art Directors William A Horning and Edward Carfagno
Music Miklos Rosza
Running time 217 mins colour Technicolor

Cast
Charlton Heston (Judah Ben-Hur)
Stephen Boyd (Messala)
Haya Harareet (Esther)
Jack Hawkins (Quintus Arrius)
Hugh Griffith (Sheikh Iiderim)
Martha Scott (Miriam)

The Best Years of Our Lives

William Wyler, USA, 1946

The post-war home front

The problems of servicemen readjusting to civilian life are captured with skill and sensitivity.

The story

Returning servicemen Al Stephenson, Fred Derry and Homer Parrish share the worry of how they will adjust to civilian life. Awkward reunions ensue; Al begins to drink heavily whilst Fred finds that his glamorous wife Marie has become a stranger to him and that Al's daughter Peggy offers a much more sympathetic shoulder. Homer, who has lost both arms in a torpedo blaze, finds that his worries have been groundless as fiancée Wilma insists that nothing has changed her love for him. By the time of their wedding Al has happily readjusted to the comfort of his old ways and wife Millie whilst Fred has left his wife and seems free to pursue Peggy.

Comment

One of the Hollywood establishment's most admired filmmakers, William Wyler exercized his skills on a broad range of generic material and earned the nickname '90 Take Wyler' for his legendary on-set perfectionism. Whilst the seeming absence of any recurring thematic consistency places him outside the auteurist consensus lionizing a John Ford or an Orson Welles, Wyler could be relied on to handle prestige projects with unerring competence. Having just returned from the field – where his undemonstrative sensibility made him a fine war documentarist (*The Memphis Belle*, 1944) – he proved an apt choice for *The Best Years of Our Lives*, the most significant fictional account of America's post World War II homecoming.

Inspired by an article in *Time* magazine,

Sam Goldwyn had hired McKinlay Kantor to write a 50-page treatment for the film. Kantor spent the advance and rewarded Goldwyn with a 268-page novel written in free verse. Tenacious in the extreme, Goldwyn also paid him to adapt that novel into a screenplay before writer Robert E Sherwood and Wyler were assigned to the project. Collaborating with his regular cameraman Gregg Toland to frame the landscape of small town middle-class middle America in immaculately composed detail, Wyler proceeded to sympathetically record the pains of readjustment to civilian society. Avoiding overt sentimentality, its responsible and accurate treatment of issues affecting most of the population made it a wide commercial success and perhaps the finest representation of Wyler's consummate, if impersonal, craftsmanship.

Nominated for eight Academy Awards, it won six including Best Picture, and non-professional Harold Russell was given a further special award for bringing 'hope and courage to his fellow veterans'.

A Samuel Goldwyn Production
Producer Samuel Goldwyn
Screenplay Robert E Sherwood, based on the verse novel *Glory for Me* by MacKinlay Kantor
Photography Gregg Toland
Editor Daniel Mandell
Art Directors Perry Ferguson, George Jenkins and Julia Heron
Music Hugo Friedhofer
Running time 182 mins b/w

Cast
Myrna Loy (Millie Stephenson)
Fredric March (Al Stephenson)
Dana Andrews (Fred Derry)
Teresa Wright (Peggy Stephenson)
Virgina Mayo (Marie Derry)
Harold Russell (Homer Parrish)

Bicycle Thieves
(Ladri Di Biciclette)

Vittorio De Sica, Italy, 1948

Neorealist classic

An everyday occurrence signifies a cry of despair from the Roman underclass.

The story

Rome. Antonio Ricci is offered a job as billposter on the understanding that he supplies his own bike. During his first day on the job the bike is stolen. The event is an everyday occurrence for the police who suggest he search for the thief himself. He sets off accompanied by his ten-year-old son Bruno. They first catch sight of the man at the flea markets and Ricci later follows him into a brothel where he denies the accusation. An unsympathetic crowd gathers and the man has an epileptic fit; nothing is resolved. A despairing Ricci then steals a bike but is immediately caught. The owner does not press charges but Bruno has witnessed this humiliation and offers a comforting hand as they trek wearily onwards.

Comment

Former Italian screen idol turned director Vittorio De Sica's *Bicycle Thieves* (*Ladri Di Biciclette*) remains one of the best-known films from the Italian neorealist school which flourished in the 1940s as a response to the glossily anodyne state-sponsored 'white telephone' movies of the previous Fascist period. As developed by its major theorists, including screenwriter Cesare Zavattini and director Roberto Rossellini, neorealism embodied a moral (and hence an aesthetic) position aiming to confront audiences with 'reality', encouraging the viewer to question the 'real' world instead of merely soaking up the lavishly-prepared images of the screen entertainment industry. As De Sica himself remarked, 'Why should we filmmakers go in search of extraordinary adventures when we are confronted in our daily lives with facts that cause genuine anguish?'

Encountering immense difficulty in finding finance for the film, De Sica had scoured the world and even rejected an offer from David O Selznick who had added the proviso that Cary Grant play the billposter. Eventually three Italian businessmen backed his plan and De Sica was able to use a cast of non-professionals and film in the capital's most downbeat corners to create an accurate picture of struggling ordinary folk. Yet despite such trappings and their accompanying neorealist claims to truthful objectivity, the film garners its emotional impact from the deliberate sentimental styling of the narrative. Antonio, of course, finds himself surrounded by bicycles just after his own machine is stolen; lo! bells ring on the soundtrack; it's all part of the contrivance that is film storytelling. The trick is – and De Sica manages it with moving panache – that you don't notice the contrivance.

A Produzione De Sica Production
Producer Vittorio De Sica
Screenplay Vittorio De Sica, Oreste Bianco, Suso Cecchi D'Amico, Adolfo Franci, Gherado Gherardi and Gerardo Guerrieri, adapted by Cesare Zavattini from the novel by Luigi Bartolini
Photography Carlo Montuori
Editor Eraldo Da Roma
Art Director Antonio Traverso
Music Alessandro Cicognini
Running time 90 mins b/w

Cast
Lamberto Maggiorani (Antonio Ricci)
Enzo Staiola (Bruno Ricci)
Lianella Carell (Maria Ricci)
Vittorio Antonucci (The Thief)
Elena Altieri
Gino Saltamerenda

The Big Sleep

Howard Hawks, USA, 1946

Private-eye mystery

Humphrey Bogart essays the definitive Philip Marlowe in a baffling thriller.

The story

Philip Marlowe is hired by General Sternwood to rid him of a blackmailer who possesses nude photographs of his daughter Carmen. The man is murdered but Marlowe is now intrigued by the deceased's landlord, gambler Eddie Mars, and by Carmen's sultry sister Vivian. He ultimately tracks the missing Mrs Mars to a garage and, piecing the case together, confronts Mars, claiming that he has deliberately faked his wife's disappearance to lay suspicion on Sean Regan who had been killed by Carmen. Vivian has been paying blackmail money to protect her sister. Eddie willingly admits this, safe in the knowledge that his men have their rendezvous surrounded. Marlowe forces him into the open where he is killed by a hail of bullets.

Comment

At one point during the filming of *The Big Sleep*, the frustrated filmmakers contacted Raymond Chandler to seek clarification of a particular plot point. Chandler later recalled, 'Bogart and Hawks sent me a wire asking whether one of the characters was murdered or committed suicide and, dammit, I didn't know either.' One of the most labyrinthine plots in thriller history, the film succeeds because the unravelling of the mystery is made secondary to the crackling dialogue and interplay between the characters, especially the insolent banter exchanged like tennis balls between Bogart and Bacall. The couple had been introduced to each other during the making of Hawks'

To Have and Have Not (1944) and were now man and wife.

There have been many actors who have attempted to fill the shoes of Chandler's private detective Philip Marlowe, notable among them Dick Powell in *Murder, My Sweet* (1945) (UK: *Farewell My Lovely*) and Robert Montgomery in *The Lady in the Lake* (1946) but Bogart's remains arguably the definitive interpretation. His screen persona and the character as written meld into the world-weary, reluctant Sir Galahad that he had perfected in such films as *The Maltese Falcon* (1941) (see p137) and *Casablanca* (1942). Based on Chandler's first novel, *The Big Sleep* (a laconic euphemism for death) was watered down for the screen to comply with a then dominant code of censorship that restricted the ability to deal with pornography and drug-addiction on screen. An inept remake set in London, and made in 1978 when anything was possible on screen, was but a distant relation of the original with Robert Mitchum bringing little of the flair to Marlowe that had made his approach to the character so pleasurable in *Farewell My Lovely* (1975).

A Warner Brothers-First National Production
Producer Howard Hawks
Screenplay William Faulkner, Leigh Brackett and Jules Furthman, based on the novel by Raymond Chandler
Photography Sid Hickox
Editor Christian Nyby
Art Director Carl Jules Weyl
Music Max Steiner
Running time 114 mins b/w

Cast
Humphrey Bogart (Philip Marlowe)
Lauren Bacall (Vivian Rutledge)
John Ridgley (Eddie Mars)
Martha Vickers (Carmen Sternwood)
Dorothy Malone (Bookshop Proprietress)
Peggy Knudsen (Mrs Eddie Mars)

'A cast of thousands'
The epic

Bigger isn't necessarily better but, with the scale of resources at its command, Hollywood has been able to place some of the most spectacular scenes of historical reconstruction on screen. Italian productions like *Cabiria* (1914) were what inspired D W Griffith to work on such an expansive scale in his Southern epic *The Birth of A Nation* (1915) (see p36) and in *Intolerance* (1916) (see p112), the Babylonian sets are amongst the largest in film history. However, the silent era also witnessed such large-scale Douglas Fairbanks ventures as *Robin Hood* (1922) and *The Thief of Bagdad* (1924) (see p218), as well as the vast futuristic city in the science-fiction epic *Metropolis* (1926) (see p142) and the earliest work of Cecil B De Mille.

The son of an Episcopalian minister, De Mille worked in many genres but his reputation rests on the showmanship, flair and vulgarity he brought to action-packed spectaculars, often culled from the Bible, that adopted a high moral tone as they wallowed in whichever of the seven deadly sins he chose to condemn. His most famous productions include *The Ten Commandments* (in 1923 and 1956), *King of Kings* (1927) and *Samson and Delilah* (1949). Perhaps because of De Mille's dominance the epic is most commonly seen as having some form of Biblical connection; it reached its peak in the 1950s when Hollywood chose to tackle the threat from television by providing the kind of expansive and expensive entertainment with which the small screen could not hope to compete. Thus the wide-screen process of cinematography known as Cinemascope was first used on a feature film in Twentieth Century-Fox's *The Robe* (1953) starring Richard Burton. Public response to the film was such that it easily emerged as the year's most successful production, with a gross estimated to be at least twice that of its nearest rival, and soon screens were filled with the likes of *Demetrius and the Gladiators* (1954), *The Ten Commandments* (1956) and *Ben-Hur* (1959) (see p31), as well as such non-Biblical but equally impressive presentations as *War and Peace* (1956) and *Around the World in 80 Days* (1956).

Box-office evidence confirmed the theory that productions on this scale were the solution to luring audiences away from the home front and soon every possible genre was blown-up to epic scale from the war film (*The Longest Day*, 1962) to the western (*How the West Was Won*, 1962) and the comedy (*Those Magnificent Men in Their Flying Machines*, 1965) etc. Eventually, prohibitive costs and the influence of *Easy Rider* (1969) (see p75) in encouraging a generation of filmmakers interested in low-budget productions and contemporary subject matters signalled the virtual demise of that particular style of filmmaking. It is estimated that to make *Ben-Hur* at today's prices would cost well in excess of $100 million.

Notable foreign-language directors to have worked in the epic genre include Sergei Eisenstein, who deserves mention for the Battle of the Ice sequence in *Alexander Nevsky* (1938) (see p7), Sergei Bondarchuk, who created a grandiloquent eight-hour version of Tolstoy's *War and Peace* (1966–7), Sergio Leone who covered a rich canvas in *Once Upon A Time in the West* (1968) and Werner Herzog, whose operatic intensity has inflamed the journeys at the heart of *Aguirre, Wrath of God* (1972) (see p6) and *Fitzcarraldo* (1982).

The contemporary English-language epic is a rare creature but Richard Attenborough keeps the De Mille tradition alive in films like *A Bridge Too Far* (1977) and *Gandhi* (1982) whilst the success of Kevin Costner's *Dances With Wolves* (1990) (see p62) may yet start a revival of the genre.

The Birth of a Nation

D W Griffith, USA, 1915

Innovative silent epic

Innovative artistry and explicit racism combine in a problematic milestone in cinema history.

The story

1860. The Stonemans visit the Southern Camerons for the last time before Civil War renders them enemies. Many die but Ben Cameron is spared and nursed by Elsie Stoneman when he is captured. In peacetime, Phil Stoneman and his Negro protégé Silas Lynch are sent to enforce emancipation in the South. White supremacist Ben Cameron forms the Ku-Klux Klan and executes the Negro Gus for provoking the suicide of his sister Flora. Open warfare results in which Stoneman and the Camerons find themselves on the same side. When Lynch holds Elsie captive, the Klan rides to her rescue also liberating the cabin where Margaret Cameron has been under siege. An uneasy peace reigns as Elsie and Ben and Margaret and Phil are married.

Comment

David Wark Griffith's *The Birth Of A Nation* is one of the most problematic milestones in all of cinema history: artistically, it remains a prime achievement in the development of film narrative; ideologically, it is one of the most explicitly racist films ever made. In his myriad shorts from 1908 onwards Griffith had virtually invented the grammar of film: from the close-up and long-shot to the idea of cutting between points of interest to create tension, from the first use of titles to the creation of the flashback, Griffith did it first.

Inspired by the international success of Giovanni Pastrone's Italian epic *Cabiria* (1914), he sought to create an American work on a similar scale, choosing as his source the Rev Thomas F Dixon's melodrama *The Clansman*. Himself a Southerner raised in the values of the Old South, Griffith ultimately exhorts both Confederates and Unionists to unite against their common enemy, the unruly and sexually avaricious Negro, through the organization of the Ku-Klux Klan ('the saviour of white civilization' runs one intertitle). Playing on the most blatant racial stereotypes (the coloured characters are played by whites in black faces) and hysterical fears of miscegenation, the merest synopsis today is enough to horrify, but with its expansive battle scenes and detailed plotting *The Birth Of A Nation* attracted unprecedented audiences, earning a reputed $5 million return on its $91 000 budget and causing no less a figure than President Woodrow Wilson to comment, 'It's like writing history with lightning'. However, while Griffith's admirers still regard him as a giant among American filmmakers, others are less willing to confer lasting greatness on an artist whose work suffers such grave flaws of conception.

An Epoch Production
Producer D W Griffith
Screenplay D W Griffith and Frank E Woods based on the novel and play *The Clansman* and the novel *The Leopard's Spots* by Thomas Dixon Jnr
Photography G W Bitzer
Editor James Smith
Music Joseph Carl Breil and D W Griffith
Running time 180 mins approx (Subsequently 165 mins) b/w

Cast
Lillian Gish (Elsie Stoneman)
Mae Marsh (Flora Cameron, the Little Sister)
Henry B Walthall (Ben Cameron, the Little Colonel)
Miriam Cooper (Margaret Cameron)
Mary Alden (Lydia Brown, Stoneman's Mulato Housekeeper)
Ralph Lewis (The Honourable Austin Stoneman)

Black Narcissus

Michael Powell and Emeric Pressburger, UK, 1947

Sensual melodrama

This visually stunning battle between religion and eroticism has achieved the classic status denied on its release.

The story

A party of nuns set up a religious community in a remote and spectacular mountain-top monastery in India. Their building has previously been the house where the ruling general kept his harem, and the nuns are troubled by intimations of eroticism from the very first, in the paintings on the walls, and in the presence of both the handsome young son of the General with his pervasive Black Narcissus perfume, who insists they educate him, and the English factor Mr Dean, a powerful sexual presence. Both Sister Clodagh and Sister Ruth are attracted to him, but the latter is driven to madness, and attempts to kill Sister Clodagh in a climactic, literally cliff-hanging confrontation. The chastened sisters abandon the wild place and return to civilization.

Comment

Black Narcissus was part of a sequence of films made by the team of Powell and Pressburger in the late 1940s and early 1950s which have come to be seen as classics, although they were not well-understood or received at the time. Powell is generally credited with the extraordinary visual appeal of the films, while Pressburger is thought of more as a screen-writer, but their contributions overlapped in all areas of their filmmaking.

Black Narcissus is centrally concerned with the divisive and ultimately tragic effects of the tensions created when ascetic religion runs headlong into eroticism. The dramatic location and sexual presences of the two men have different but palpable effects on all five nuns, and only the most straightforward and uncomprehending sisters, Honey and Briony, manage to adjust to the dangerous atmosphere of this wild mountain retreat.

Sister Phillipa, the eldest, realizes that she cannot maintain her faith in such a place, and requests that she be sent back, but events overtake the community. The clash is reflected in the reactions of the Mother Superior, Sister Clodagh, and the errant Sister Ruth, to Mr Dean: Clodagh, a beautiful girl, keeps herself at a distance, but her feelings cause her to question her vocation; Ruth, on the other hand, succumbs to the powerful emotions generated by her irreconcilable dichotomy, and ultimately dies in the act of attempting to kill Sister Clodagh.

Perhaps the most remarkable aspect of *Black Narcissus* is that the wild Himalayan location was in fact Pinewood Studios and a garden in Horsham, Sussex. Powell felt that location filming would dissipate the delicate, hothouse balance of the story; in the studio he was able to exercise his trademark penchant for remarkable colour effects with greater control.

An Archers Production
Producers Michael Powell and Emeric Pressburger
Screenplay Powell and Pressburger, based on the novel by Rumer Godden
Photography Jack Cardiff
Editor Reginald Mills
Art Director Alfred Junge
Music Brian Easdale
Running time 100 mins *colour*

Cast

Deborah Kerr (Sister Clodagh)
Sabu (The Young General)
David Farrar (Mr Dean)
Flora Robson (Sister Philippa)
Esmond Knight (The Old General)
Jean Simmons (Kanchi)

Blackmail

Alfred Hitchcock, UK, 1929

Pioneering 'talkie' thriller

Britain's first talkie establishes the themes and style of the master of suspense.

The story

During dinner with her fiancé, Scotland Yard detective Frank Webber, Alice White finds herself flattered by the attentions of an artist whom she later accompanies to his studio. As she prepares to pose for him, he advances on her. She kills him with a bread knife and flees, leaving her gloves behind, one of which is discovered by Webber, who has been assigned to the case, and the other by Tracy who uses it to blackmail Webber. A guilt-ridden Alice finds her attempts to confess to the police continually thwarted. Meanwhile, Webber calls Tracy's bluff and a chase through London climaxes at the British Museum where Tracy plunges to his death from the roof of the Reading Room. Webber returns the gloves to White as they are reunited.

Comment

Officially regarded as the first sound film to be shot in Britain, *Blackmail* is doubly notable as a progenitor of much of Alfred Hitchcock's later thematic and stylistic manner. Assigned to shoot the film silent, with the innovation of sound featuring only in the final reel, Hitchcock managed however to 'dub' synchronized dialogue on to the earlier passages and release *Blackmail* as a talkie. One of his biggest technical challenges came in masking the heavy accent of his Czechoslovakian leading lady Anny Ondra who mimed her lines while actress Joan Barry spoke them just off-camera. Synchronizing the two efforts led to numerous retakes of individual scenes. As in most early sound efforts, some of the dialogue stretches are dreadfully slow, but with one striking sequence Hitchcock demonstrates the artistic potential of the new medium: having fended off the rape attack Ondra breakfasts with the family the next morning but the soundtrack mutes the entire conversation excepting the word 'knife', each repetition a piercing reminder of her crime.

The central figure of the guilty woman was to recur in Hitchcock's work (eg *Notorious*, 1946; *Psycho*, 1960 (see p169); *Marnie*, 1964), as was the notion of the ordinary protagonist plunged into chaos (*The Thirty-Nine Steps*, 1935; *North By Northwest*, 1959, among many others), but what might be most important about *Blackmail* is that it sets the precedent of subjugating the actual meaning of the plot to the string of darkly comic suspense games that may be extracted from it along the way. Hitch cameo-spotters might also like to keep an eye open for a scene on the underground where a certain familiar figure finds his attempts to read disrupted by a bothersome boy.

An Elstree Production
Producer John Maxwell
Screenplay Alfred Hitchcock, Benn W Levy and Charles Bennett based on Bennett's play
Photography Jack Cox
Editor Emile De Ruelle
Art Directors Wilfred C Arnold and Norman Arnold
Music Hubert Bath and Henry Stafford
Running time 86 mins (silent version: 75 mins)
b/w

Cast
Anny Ondra (Alice White)
John Longden (Frank Webber)
Donald Calthrop (Tracy)
Cyril Ritchard (The Artist)
Sara Allgood (Mrs White)
Charles Paton (Mr White)

The Blue Angel
(Der Blaue Engel)
Josef Von Sternberg, Germany, 1930

The cruelty of infatuation

The mystique of the Dietrich legend begins as Lola-Lola ensnares a devoted audience.

The story

Professor Immanuel Rath, a pillar of the community, ventures to The Blue Angel nightclub, planning to harangue his hedonistic students but finds himself captivated by sultry entertainer Lola-Lola. Giddy with delight, he quaffs champagne and stays the night. The next morning at school he is the laughing-stock and when news of his extra-curricular activities reaches the principal he is dismissed. Despondent, he returns to Lola-Lola who convinces him that they should be wed. Soon he is reduced to little more than her lackey. When the show returns to his home town he is ritually humiliated in front of the crowd and discovers Lola-Lola in the arms of another. All self-respect gone, he returns in abject misery to the school and dies.

Comment

Originally conceived as a starring vehicle for Emil Jannings, *The Blue Angel* is now revered as the first film to reveal the glamorous allure of screen legend Marlene Dietrich. One of the most respected stars of the silent era, Jannings had won the first Oscar for his performances in Josef Von Sternberg's *The Last Command* (1928) and *The Way Of All Flesh* (1928), but found that with the advent of talkies, his highly theatrical style and guttural German accent signalled an end to his American aspirations. Returning to Germany, he planned a reunion with Von Sternberg on a script about Rasputin and it was this director who suggested instead that they film Heinrich Mann's 1904 novel *Professor Unrat*. Briggite Helm, best known

from *Metropolis* (1926) (see p142), was selected as the nightclub temptress before Mann suggested Berlin entertainer Trude Hesterberg. It was only when these other possibilites were exhausted that Dietrich was signed, thus initiating one of the greatest of all director-actress partnerships.

The film's basic outline of the weak and masochistic male trapped by an indifferent and enigmatic temptress held an undoubted autobiographical charge for Von Sternberg and he was to use it time and time again in his 1930s' series of perversely stylish Dietrich showcases for Paramount (*Morocco*, 1930; *Blonde Venus*, 1932; *The Scarlet Empress*, 1934; *The Devil Is A Woman*, 1935 etc). Always highly aware of her screen image, Dietrich, already a screen veteran of some 17 unremarkable movies, conspired in Von Sternberg's complete absorption in filmic style. She was a sculpted presence to be lit and dressed as his often fetishistic impulses demanded – the result a pessimistic and highly personal vision of an existence ruled remorselessly by the unfathomable demands of pleasure.

Producer Erich Pommer
Screenplay Robert Liebmann, Karl Vollmoller and Carl Zuckmayer, based on the novel *Professor Unrat* by Heinrich Mann
Photography Gunther Rittau and Hans Schneeberger
Editor Sam Winston
Art Directors Ottot Hunte and Emil Hasler
Music Friedrich Hollander
Running time 103 mins b/w

Cast

Emil Jannings (Professor Immanuel Rath)
Marlene Dietrich (Lola Frohlich)
Kurt Gerron (Kiepert, A Magician)
Rosa Valette (Guste, His Wife)
Hans Albers (Mazeppa)
Eduard Von Winterstein (Principal of the School)

Blue Velvet

David Lynch, USA, 1986

Murderous melodrama

The placid surface of a small town conceals a maelstrom of murder, mendacity and evil.

The story

When Jeffrey Beaumont discovers a human ear, Sandy Williams reveals that it may be connected with her father's investigations into singer Dorothy Vallens. Drawn into Vallens's desire for a sadomasochistic relationship, he witnesses her humiliation by the deranged Frank Booth and concludes that Booth is holding her husband and daughter hostage. Frank teases him over the thin line between his venality and Jeffrey's purity and he discovers that Williams's partner is implicated in the mayhem. When Dorothy appears naked in the street, he comforts her and returns to her apartment where her husband and Williams's partner have been killed. Frank appears but Jeffrey kills him and life in Lumberton returns to something approaching normality.

Comment

Once described as 'Jimmy Stewart from Mars', director David Lynch has proved himself one of the most distinctive talents in contemporary American cinema, disturbing audiences with the images and ambience of his feature *Eraserhead* (1976). His move into the mainstream had produced the mixed results of his Academy Award nomination as Best Director for the moving Victorian true-life drama *The Elephant Man* (1980), and the commercial and artistic failure of his bloated attempt to bring Frank Herbert's science-fiction novel *Dune* (1984) to the screen. Putting aside other projects, he then set about creating *Blue Velvet*, a flamboyant surrealistic thriller that expressed his fondness for peering under the apparently idyllic rose-picketed surface of small-town American life to expose the seething mass of sexual, emotional and criminal perversion that exists there. The film is a Dantesque vision of what might really be taking place in the lives of apple-pie Andy Hardy innocents, and Lynch would subsequently refine this preoccupation into a fine and bizarre art in the cult television series *Twin Peaks*.

Redolent of Hitchcock's *Vertigo* (1958) (see p230) or Michael Powell's *Peeping Tom* (1959) (see p161) in the seductive lustre that Lynch brings to the depiction of the forbidden sadomasochistic relationship between Beaumont and Dorothy, its commentary on voyeurism and the similarities implied between the supposedly wholesome Beaumont and the vicious psychopath Booth (played with almost feral intensity by Dennis Hopper), *Blue Velvet* is also one of the richest and most provocative visual and aural experiences to emerge from American cinema in the 1980s and earned Lynch a second Best Director Academy Award nomination.

A De Laurentiis Entertainment Group Production
Screenplay David Lynch
Photography Frederick Elmes
Editor Duwayne Dunham
Art Director Patricia Norris
Music Angelo Badalamenti
Running time 120 mins colour

Cast
Kyle MacLachlan (Jeffrey Beaumont)
Isabella Rossellini (Dorothy Vallens)
Dennis Hopper (Frank Booth)
Laura Dern (Sandy Williams)
Hope Lange (Mrs Williams)
Dean Stockwell (Ben)

Bonnie and Clyde

Arthur Penn, US, 1967

Criminal character-study

Sixties America is defined by a bloody evocation of its outlaw past.

The story

Bored by small-town life, waitress Bonnie Parker is easily beguiled by the boastful manner of robber Clyde Barrow and responds to his promise of an exciting future. Joined by garage mechanic C W Moss, Clyde's brother Buck and his wife Blanche, they form the Barrow gang and rob banks. Their newspaper notoriety and folk-hero status appeal to the fame-hungry Bonnie but the law gradually catches up and at one ambush Buck is killed and Blanche is blinded. Moss finds them sanctuary with his father and Bonnie has a poem published but their sense of impending death is potent. Moss's father betrays them in return for his son's safety and in a rural clearing Bonnie and Clyde are caught like rag dolls in police crossfire.

Comment

One of the key films of its decade, *Bonnie and Clyde* was developed by writers David Newman and Robert Benton as a means of defining the state of America in the 1960s by evoking the spirit of America in the 1930s through two characters who perfectly embodied the attractiveness of an amoral, fame-conscious, anti-establishment counter-culture. Heavily influenced by the French 'New Wave', they had approached both François Truffaut and Jean-Luc Godard with this most American of subject matters before the project came to the attention of Warren Beatty who chose to produce as well as star in the film. His current paramour Leslie Caron was obviously ill-suited to play a Depression-era Southern girl in search of excitement and among those considered for the role of Bonnie before Dunaway were Natalie Wood, Carol Lynley, Tuesday Weld and Sue Lyon.

Brilliantly directed by Arthur Penn, the film captures breakthrough performances from performers like Dunaway and Hackman, and features a brilliantly-used banjo score and insistent screen violence of unprecedented intensity. However, while Dunaway's beret may have launched new fashion trends, the deep resonance of the piece and source of its appeal to young contemporary audiences lay in its evocation of the conflict between personal impulse and society's constricting, often corrupt, network of control. After weathering a storm of negative publicity over its energetic juxta-positions of violence and humour, explicit rhyming of sexual satisfaction and lawless-ness, and its alleged glorification of banditry, the film grossed $30 million in its first year of release and received ten Academy Award nominations, including Best Picture, winning Oscars for Estelle Parsons as Best Supporting Actress and for the cinematography.

A Tatira-Hiller-Warner Brothers Production
Producer Warren Beatty
Screenplay David Newman and Robert Benton, with uncredited contributions by Robert Towne
Photography Burnett Guffey
Editor Dede Allen
Art Directors Dean Tavoularis
Music Charles Strouse
Running time 111 mins *colour*

Cast

Warren Beatty (Clyde Barrow)
Faye Dunaway (Bonnie Parker)
Michael J Pollard (C W Moss)
Gene Hackman (Buck Barrow)
Estelle Parsons (Blanche)
Denver Pyle (Frank Hamer)
Gene Wilder (Eugene Grizzard)

Le Boucher

Claude Chabrol, France/Italy, 1969

Rural murder mystery

A village schoolteacher shelters a psychotic killer in an unconventional psychological thriller.

The story

The film open at a wedding in the village of Le Trémolat in Périgord, where the camera picks out a couple from the happy throng. Mlle Hélène is the local schoolteacher, Popaul the butcher. She gives him a cigarette-lighter as a gift, but she ensures that their relationship is one of friendship, rather than as lovers, as Popaul wishes. While taking her pupils to visit the nearby caves in which Cro-Magnon man lived, Hélène discovers the body of a young girl, and finds a cigarette-lighter beside it, which she conceals. Following a climactic confrontation in her deserted school, Popaul kills himself, leaving Hélène to her guilt.

Comment

Chabrol emerged as a leading light of the French New Wave in the late 1950s, and arguably embodies the much-disputed notion of the filmmaker as auteur more fully than any other director. Indeed, there are those who believe that he has taken Jean Renoir's dictum that every great filmmaker makes the same film over and over to excessive lengths.

In *Le Boucher*, an understated tragic love story told as an unconventional thriller, the clash between the sophisticated but aloof schoolteacher Hélène and the butcher Popaul, a gentle and considerate character with a brutal, atavistic underside, seems remorselessly pre-ordained.

Characters bearing these names recur throughout Chabrol's films, as does the theme of a fated triangular relationship, in this case filled in by Mlle Hélène's relationship with her pupils, rather than another lover. When she discovers that Popaul is probably a murderer, she chooses to hide what she knows, thereby condemning herself to an agony of guilt and indecision.

Her real guilt, though, is that she has been unable or unwilling to respond to Popaul's obvious need for her, or to offer him any help when he stalks her in the darkened school, not as the killer, but as a kind of victim. Popaul kills himself rather than her, but leaves an unresolved residue of guilt and complicity which she must carry with her.

Chabrol has said that he likes simple plots with complicated characters. The action proceeds slowly and by subtle indirection, building a complex picture of the relationship through the small accumulation of carefully observed detail, as in the doubling of the opening wedding with the very different atmosphere of the subsequent funeral. It is the most accomplished statement of his perennial theme.

A La Boetie/Euro International Production
Producer André Génovès
Screenplay Claude Chabrol
Photography Jean Rabier
Editor Jacques Gaillard
Art Director Guy Littaye
Music Pierre Jansen
Running time 94 mins *colour*

Cast
Stéphane Audran (Hélène Marcoux)
Jean Yanne (Popaul Thomas)
Antonio Passalia (Angelo)
Mario Beccaria (Léon Hamel)
Pasquale Ferone (Father Charpy)
Roger Rudel (Police Inspector)
William Guérault (Charles)

Breathless
(A Bout De Souffle)
Jean-Luc Godard, France, 1959

New wave drama

Love on the run leaves an insolent calling-card from the French 'New Wave'.

The story

In the Riviera, Michel Poiccard steals a car and heads for Paris intent on collecting money owed to him and meeting his beloved Patricia, an American student and aspiring journalist. Pursued by two motorcycle cops, he kills one of them. Unable to retrieve his money, he steals and exhorts Patricia to join him in a life of adventure. When he returns from a date, she finds Michel in her bed and his ardour seems unaffected by the disclosure that she may be pregnant. Meanwhile, the police draw ever closer. After a night together, she telephones the police with his whereabouts and returns to justify the necessity of her actions and the need for independence. Shocked, he rushes into the street and is gunned down.

Comment

Jean-Luc Godard's *Breathless* (*A Bout De Souffle*) was an explosive salvo alerting the rest of the film community that the French nouvelle vague, or New Wave, had well and truly arrived. As one of the young critics (including later directors François Truffaut, Claude Chabrol and Eric Rohmer), who from the mid-1950s had been expounding the *politique des auteurs* (Americanized by Andrew Sarris as the 'auteur theory') in the influential pages of the film magazine *Cahiers du Cinema*, Godard and his peers gave vent to a radical polemic that insisted on the director as the author of his or her film and rejected the discipline of admired French art cinema to acclaim the profundity of hard-boiled American directors like Sam Fuller and Nicholas Ray. An upturn in modestly-budgeted French independent production was to allow Godard to give celluloid expression to these ideas. Co-written by Truffaut and with Chabrol as technical adviser, *Breathless* makes no aspiration to social realism or the adaptation of literary values. The film's then shocking formal play of jump cuts, scenes extended beyond any narrative function, and unashamed 'quotations' from other movies emphasizes cinema-as-cinema, revealing the mechanism of signification so long hidden by the polish of classical narrative styles.

Modernist film par excellence it might be, but 30 years on its B-movie plotting, its nods to Humphrey Bogart, and the laconically iconic presence of Jean-Paul Belmondo and Jean Seberg, seem to align *Breathless* more closely to the doomed romanticism of the Hollywood love-on-the-run sub-genre – which is precisely how American director Jim McBride remade it in 1983 with Richard Gere and Valerie Kaprisky.

A SNC/Les Films Georges De Beauregard/ Imperia Production
Producer Pierre Rissient
Screenplay Jean-Luc Godard based on an idea by François Truffaut
Photography Raoul Coutard
Editor Cecile Decugis
Art Director none
Music Martial Solal
Running time 90 mins b/w

Cast
Jean Seberg (Patricia Franchini)
Jean-Paul Belmondo (Michel Poiccard/ 'Laszlo Kovacs')
Daniel Boulanger (Inspector Vital)
Henri-Jacques Huet (Antonio Berrutti)
Liliane Robin (Minouche)
Roger Hanin (Carl Zubart)

Bride of Frankenstein

James Whale, USA, 1935

Macabre fantasy

A masterful mixture of mirth and the macabre brings fresh ideas to an enduring genre.

The story

Miraculously surviving the inferno in the old mill, the Monster is once again on the rampage. His creator Henry Frankenstein recovers from his injuries whilst resisting the disgraced Dr Pretorius's offer of a partnership. Briefly incarcerated by the authorities, the Monster finds shelter with a blind hermit who teaches him to speak. He is later befriended by Pretorius who secures Frankenstein's cooperation in the creation of a mate by abducting his wife. However, the new creature recoils in horror from her intended partner. Angered by her rejection, the tearful Monster allows Henry and Elizabeth their freedom before pulling a lever that brings the castle crumbling around himself and the other miscreants.

Comment

Conceived under the working titles of 'Frankenstein Lives Again!' and the less inspired 'The Return of Frankenstein', this sequel to James Whale's 1931 shocker readily surpasses its predecessor. Indulging fully in the macabre, Whale embraces the extreme in almost every aspect of the production from the gigantic sets to the splendidly eccentric characterizations. However, the reason for the film's classic status lies in its superb use of humour, not necessarily in the obvious 'comedy' supplied by Una O'Connor's hysterical maid but in the striking figures of Elsa Lanchester's hissing mate, a role once evisaged for either Louise Brooks or Brigitte

Helm, and Ernest Thesiger's droll academic, Dr Pretorius.

Planned for Claude Rains, who had 'appeared' in Whale's version of *The Invisible Man*, Pretorius is a man at home in the solitary dank of a mausoleum who has created a group of tiny people called homunculi and who invites Frankenstein to join him in toasting 'a new world of gods and monsters' with a glass of gin – 'my only weakness'.

Blending terror with dark wit and the undiminished pathos of Boris Karloff's characterization, *Bride of Frankenstein* avoided the more common inferiority found in such sequels of the period as *Son of Kong* (1934), and set new standards for the fantasy genre.

Karloff would play his most famous creation only once more in *Son of Frankenstein* (1939) but did return to the series as meddlesome scientist Dr Niemann in *House of Frankenstein* (1944) and featured as the last of the dynasty in the unfortunate *Frankenstein – 1970* (1958). Mel Brooks provided an accurate and affectionate pastiche of the Whale film in *Young Frankenstein* (1974) with Peter Boyle as the Monster.

A Universal Production
Producer Carl Laemmle Jnr
Screenplay William Hurlbut and John L Balderston
Photography John Mescall
Editor Ted Kent
Art Direction Charles D Hall
Music Franz Waxman
Running time 76 mins b/w

Cast
Boris Karloff (The Monster)
Colin Clive (Henry Frankenstein)
Valerie Hobson (Elizabeth Frankenstein)
Elsa Lanchester (Mary Shelley/The Bride)
O P Heggie (The Hermit)
Una O'Connor (Minnie)
Ernest Thesiger (Dr Septimus Pretorius)

Brief Encounter

David Lean, UK, 1945

Melancholy romance

A simple exploration of suppressed suburban passion strikes a universal chord.

The story

Milford Junction railway station. In the buffet, suburban housewife Laura Jesson is abandoned by Dr Alec Harvey. At home, she reflects on the events that led to this abrupt farewell. A speck of grit in her eye had brought the first encounter with this kind stranger. They met again by accident and arranged first a visit to the cinema and then other outings to the park, the country and a restaurant where Laura was embarrassed to meet some old friends. A visit to a stranger's flat had also ended in shame. Inevitably, Alec had declared his love and informed her of the only honourable option: his departure for foreign climes. Distraught, she had contemplated suicide but returned instead to the cosy familiarity of her grateful husband.

Comment

Written and produced by celebrated playwright/actor/celebrity Nöel Coward, David Lean's *Brief Encounter* forever preserves on screen a particularly English, especially middle-class, love story. Presented mainly in flashback, the placing of the action in the context of Celia Johnson's melancholic reverie licenses the film's Rachmaninoff-accompanied tone of romantic delirium, a heightening of the senses that makes even the most ordinary visit to the park or a restaurant chime with heartfelt intensity. Furthermore, the couple's visit to the cinema where they watch a trailer for a forthcoming epic, *The Flames of Passion*, should alert us to the element of filmic fantasy working its magic here too, for although the so-called realism of *Brief Encounter* is often remarked upon, the artful treatment of the settings (dimly-lit interiors and gloomy streets contrast with invigorating interludes in natural surroundings) shows Lean finding a pictorial expression for the theme of emotional containment. His responsiveness throughout to the pair's mingled feelings of elation and fatalism seems much less calculating and rather more moving than the monumental vacuousness of later superproductions *Doctor Zhivago* (1965) and *Ryan's Daughter* (1970).

Chosen as one of the best films at the first Cannes Film Festival in 1946, *Brief Encounter* also achieved the comparatively rare British feat of securing American Academy Award nominations for Best Director and Best Actress. A 1974 television remake with Richard Burton and Sophia Loren making an unlikely suburban couple proved little short of disastrous but the material was more profitably explored by Richard Kwietniowski's *Flames of Passion* (1990), a gay reflection on the central romance.

An Independent Producers/Cineguild Film
Producer Noel Coward
Screenplay David Lean, Ronald Neame and Anthony Havelock-Allan, based on Noël Coward's play *Still Life*
Photography Robert Krasker and B Francke
Editors Jack Harris and Harry Miller
Art Directors L P Williams and G E Calthorp
Music Rachmaninoff's Second Piano Concerto
Running time 85 mins b/w

Cast
Celia Johnson (Laura Jesson)
Trevor Howard (Dr Alec Harvey)
Cyril Raymond (Fred Jesson)
Stanley Holloway (Albert Godby, station guard)
Joyce Carey (Myrtle Bagot)
Margaret Barton (Beryl Waters)

The kings of comedy

Whilst the silent era produced the Keystone Kops, 'Fatty' Arbuckle and Harry Langdon, comedy was dominated by Charlie Chaplin, whose downtrodden, acrobatic little tramp was first seen in 1913 and achieved some of his most poignant moments in *The Gold Rush* (1925) (see p94) and *City Lights* (1931) (see p56). For many years Buster Keaton's reputation remained secondary to Charlie Chaplin's but his eschewal of sentimentality, greater flair for the mechanics of filmmaking and characterization of an unsmiling, game figure challenged but not defeated by the intricacies of the world have endeared him much more to posterity and have seen work like *The Navigator* (1924) and *The General* (1926) (see p88) hailed as masterpieces. Harold Lloyd, the master of daredevil comedy for his high-rise antics in *Safety Last* (1923) (see p186) also remained an undervalued talent for many years.

The partnership of Laurel and Hardy was formed in the silent era but achieved their greatest successes with the advent of sound, winning an Oscar for the short film *The Music Box* (1932) and adding musical routines to their bowler-hatted tomfoolery in *Bonnie Scotland* (1935) and *Way Out West* (1937) (see p232). Double-acts like Abbott and Costello never captured the public's affection in quite the same manner although the 'Road To . . .' comedies of Bing Crosby, Bob Hope and Dorothy Lamour revealed a warm, bantering relationship while the anarchy and surrealism of The Marx Brothers at their peak in *Duck Soup* (1933) and *A Night at the Opera* (1935) (see p145) would prove highly influential. The 1930s also witnessed the advent of screwball comedies like *It Happened One Night* (1934) (see p112) and *Bringing Up Baby* (1938) (see p49) in which the likes of Katharine Hepburn or Cary Grant were seen to cavort through a series of illogical escapades that combined a verbal sophistication with an obvious sense of physical humour, an unusual edge of class-conscious satire and liberated, strong-willed heroines. Echoes of the genre's most mirthful moments can be heard in the glorious knockabout character romps of Preston Sturges and, alongside Grant and Hepburn, the most skilled practitioners of romantic comedy have included Hepburn and Spencer Tracy, Doris Day and Rock Hudson, Walter Matthau and Jack Lemmon, Judy Holliday, Tony Curtis and an endless list of leading lights.

Homegrown talents have always surfaced in Britain but international renown came with the post-war Ealing comedies, including *Kind Hearts and Coronets* (1949) (see p122), the long-running *Carry On* series and the communal and individual endeavours of The Monty Python team, particularly *Time Bandits* (1980) and *A Fish Called Wanda* (1988). Following in the footsteps of Ernst Lubitsch, Billy Wilder proved himself a master of the bittersweet farce in *Some Like It Hot* (1959) (see p203) and *The Apartment* (1960) (see p17) whilst other talents of enduring note include brash satirist Mel Brooks and Woody Allen whose probing autobiographical New York confessions from *Annie Hall* (1977) (see p16) onwards have been a cornerstone of contemporary American comedy. Allen's sophistication is now something of a rarity from a country whose comedy appears ranging from the sophomoric antics of the *Porkys* crowd to the crass star vehicles of *Saturday Night* alumni like Bill Murray and Eddie Murphy, although the work of Steve Martin and Robin Williams combines warmth with inventiveness. However, the worldwide success of *Police Academy* 1–6, made with awesome regularity between 1984 and 1989, suggests that audience tastes may not have changed that much since the days of the Keystone Kops.

The General *(1926) Directed by Clyde Bruckman and Buster Keaton (Buster Keaton)*

Safety Last *(1923) Directed by Sam Taylor (Harold Lloyd)*

A Night at the Opera *(1935) Directed by Sam Wood*
(Groucho Marx, Margaret Dumont, Chico Marx, Harpo Marx)

Way Out West *(1937) Directed by James W Horne (Stan Laurel, Oliver Hardy)*

Bringing up Baby

Howard Hawks, USA, 1938

Crazy comedy

The screwball comedy reaches its peak with the meeting of a palaeontologist, an heiress and a leopard called Baby.

The story

On the eve of his wedding, palaeontologist David Huxley is a contented man, his recreation of a brontosaurus almost complete, but an embarrasing encounter with dizzy heiress Susan Vance turns his life upside-down. Discovering that her dog may have taken a bone vital to his work, he follows her to a Connecticut farm and is embroiled in various humiliating adventures with pet Brazilian leopard Baby and crazed big game hunter Horace Applegate, which finally land him in jail. However, Susan's overwhelming personality proves irresistible. His work is funded by her aunt and now Susan is to be his bride although her discovery of the missing bone and destruction of his dinosaur do not promise a peaceful future.

Comment

With a frenetic plotline that almost defies logical description, *Bringing Up Baby* has come to be regarded as the finest example of the screwball comedy genre that emerged in pre-War Hollywood. A particularly zany antidote to the gloom of the real world, the films involved attractive characters cavorting through a series of illogical escapades and combined a verbal sophistication with an obvious sense of physical humour (pratfalls, slapstick etc) and an infectiously anarchic spirit. Noted for their liberated, strong-willed heroines who easily outwitted the nominal male hero and an unusual edge of satire and class-consciousness, the genre more or less began in 1934 with *It Happened One Night* (see p112) and *Twentieth Century* and reached its zenith around the time of *Bringing Up Baby*.

Directed by Howard Hawks with a vigour and pace that he would intensify even further in *His Girl Friday* (1940), the film marks one of the four highly productive screen partnerships between Hepburn and Cary Grant, the latter in a role that had apparently been turned down by Ray Milland, Ronald Colman and Robert Montgomery. Losing his clothes and his dignity, exploding with frustration behind horned-rimmed glasses, he is the perfect foil to Hepburn's sleek and spoiled heiress. Despite warm reviews, the film was not a box-office success; it lost $365 000, contributed to Hepburn being labelled 'box-office poison' by exhibitors and led to the end of her association with R-K-O and to her return to the theatre. Hawks too paid for the failure by losing the opportunity to direct *Gunga Din* for the studio and the film received no Academy Award nominations. Now it is regarded as one of the highpoints of screen comedy from its decade and served as the role model for Peter Bogdanovich's homage in *What's Up Doc?* (1972).

An R-K-O Production
Producer Howard Hawks
Screenplay Dudley Nichols and Hagar Wilde, based on a story by Wilde with uncredited contributions from Robert McGowan and Gertrude Purcell
Photography Russell Metty
Editor George Hively
Art Directors Van Nest Polglase and Perry Ferguson
Music Roy Webb
Running time 102 mins b/w

Cast
Katharine Hepburn (Susan Vance)
Cary Grant (David Huxley)
Charles Ruggles (Major Horace Applegate)
May Robson (Aunt Elizabeth)
Walter Catlett (Constable Slocum)
Barry Fitzgerald (Gogarty)

The Cabinet of Dr Caligari
(Das Kabinett Des Dr Caligari)

Robert Wiene, Germany, 1919

Expressionist fantasy

A madman's wildest imaginings are vividly conveyed in a cinematic flourishing of German Expressionism.

The story

Seated comfortably, Francis recounts his involvement with Dr Caligari. When his friend Alan had been killed following a visit to a fair where Caligari and his somnambulist Cesare were a prime attraction, Francis had suspected Caligari. His girlfriend Jane was subsequently carried off by Cesare who died during the ensuing chase. Francis managed to uncover accounts of a murderous 18th-century Caligari and confronted the doctor with his accusations. Francis was carried away in a straitjacket. The story completed, he returns to an asylum where he is an inmate with Jane and Cesare. The Doctor believes that progress is being made in his case and that Francis can be cured of the madness that has led to these fictions.

Comment

Generally recognized as the first major film in the German Expressionist manner, *The Cabinet of Dr Caligari* was to inspire the likes of F W Murnau's *Nosferatu* (1922) (see p151) and, arguably, G W Pabst's *Die Buchse Der Pandora (Pandora's Box)* (1929), and subsequently influence the stylistic development of the horror genre in Hollywood. On its British release in 1922 the film was billed as 'Europe's greatest contribution to motion picture art'. Certainly, the 'art' was there for everyone to see, for with its disturbing storyline and decors, all misshapen angles and false perspectives, painted shadows and weirdly overemphatic performances, the film made great play of its association with the artists of the Expressionist movement, their distorted anti-naturalist figures indicative of a fragmenting social fabric.

Any creative work is of course a product of the ideological moment, and commentators have fruitfully defined the way in which Caligari is indicative of the mood of post World War I Germany. Whilst the original screenplay clearly seems an anti-authoritarian statement, the final version (as amended by the producer) in which the horrifying central narrative is revealed as a madman's delusions and the Caligari figure his benevolent psychiatrist, has been read as an expression of the German psyche's fear that individual freedom encourages chaos and must hence be contained by the harshest of leadership.

Given the raw power the film derived from its incarnation of Expressionist principles and the particular historical circumstances in which it was made, a remake would have seemed an unlikely and unprofitable venture. It proved just that in a 1962 colour American version directed by Roger Kay.

A Decla-Bioscop Production
Producer Erich Pommer
Screenplay Carl Mayer and Hans Janowitz, based on a story by Janowitz
Photography Willy Hameister
Art Directors Hermann Warm, Walter Rohrig and Walter Reimann
Running time 78 mins approx b/w

Cast
Werner Krauss (Dr Caligari)
Conrad Veidt (Cesare)
Friedrich Feher (Francis)
Lili Dagover (Jane)
Hans Heinz von Twardowski (Alan)
Rudolf Lettinger (Dr Olsen)

Casablanca

Michael Curtiz, USA, 1942

Wartime romance

A doomed romance, a world rent by war, an act of impossible nobility. You must remember this . . .

The story

Casablanca has become a sanctuary for those refugees seeking exit-visas to Lisbon and thence America. One of the city's favourite haunts is Rick's Café Americain run by the cynical Richard Blaine. His unexpected possession of two stolen letters of transit makes him much sought-after by the authorities and by newly arrived underground leader Victor Laszlo and his wife Ilsa, Rick's former lover who had deserted him in Paris on receiving news that her husband had survived the concentration camp. Ilsa rekindles his romantic feelings but, recognizing the importance of Laszlo's work, he devises a plan that puts Ilsa and Laszlo on the plane to Lisbon and leaves him and police chief Renault to face an uncertain but patriotic future.

Comment

The ever-increasing popularity of this 50-year-old Best Picture Academy Award winner provides continuing evidence of the power of cinematic nostalgia. No better, no worse than any number of similar fare from the period, *Casablanca* has since become a phenomenon, perhaps the best loved and most frequently screened of all old Hollywood movies.

Based on a play that had never been staged, offered to three other directors before Michael Curtiz took the assignment, and at one time planned as a vehicle for either Dennis Morgan and Michele Morgan or Ronald Reagan and Ann Sheridan, the film's origins hardly inspire, yet for today's audiences it exemplifies the kind of snappily-crafted studio entertainment synonymous with the golden age of Hollywood and now a thing of the past. We revel in the cherishable array of supporting actors (particularly Claude Rains's Academy Award nominated performance as the suavely sinister police chief), in the tart dialogue exchanges and quotable lines ('Here's looking at you kid', 'Play it Sam' etc) and the film's memorable song 'As Time Goes By'. The presence of Humphrey Bogart in a role that established the world-weary antihero of his future screen persona makes us forget the implausibilities of the plotting and the dullness of fugitive couple Bergman and Henreid. Certainly it satisfies the current appetite for retro-chic, but the film's enduring appeal may lie in the way its attitudes have somehow remained contemporary – the notion of doomed romance in a world on the brink of chaos still affects us – thus enabling a functional product to transcend its original source and pass into the realm of folklore.

Woody Allen paid homage to the film and a general desire to emulate Bogart's attitudes in his play and film *Play It Again, Sam* (1972).

A Warner Brothers-First National Production
Producer Hal B Wallis
Screenplay Julius J and Philip G Epstein and Howard Koch, based on the play *Everybody Comes to Rick's* by Murray Burnett and Joan Alison
Photography Arthur Edeson
Editor Owen Marks
Art Director Carl Jules Weyl
Music Max Steiner
Running time 102 mins b/w

Cast

Humphrey Bogart (Rick Blaine)
Ingrid Bergman (Ilsa)
Paul Henreid (Victor Laszlo)
Claude Rains (Captain Louis Renault)
Conrad Veidt (Major Strasser)
Sydney Greenstreet (Senor Farrari)
Peter Lorre (Ugarte)

Chariots of Fire

Hugh Hudson, UK, 1981

Inspirational drama

A celebration of faith and honour cheers the beleaguered British film industry.

The story

Cambridge, 1919. Spurred by a personal strggle against anti-semitism, ambitious runner Harold Abrahams is the first man for seven centuries to cover the perimeter of Caius College courtyard in 46 seconds. Meanwhile in Scotland, missionary's son Eric Liddell is gaining his running nickname of 'The Flying Scotsman'. The two men meet at a French-Scottish track event in Edinburgh which Liddell wins. In 1924, both are chosen to represent Britain in the Paris Olympic Games. Refusing to run on the Sabbath, Liddell is forced to withdraw from the 100 metres event and Abrahams wins ahead of the American Scholz. Liddell now runs in the 400 metres and, carried by his faith, wins in record time.

Comment

Bewildered by audience reactions to his production of *Midnight Express* (1978) and disappointed with his American tale *Foxes* (1980), producer David Puttnam returned to Britain determined to make a film that was intrinsically British and celebrated the human values in which he believed. 'I wanted to make a film like *A Man for All Seasons* about someone who didn't behave in an expedient manner.' The result was what he would later term 'an absolutely Cinderella picture' that became the highest-grossing foreign film ever seen in America to that date.

Chariots served to indicate that British producers need not opt for the risky and often unsatisfying compromise of mid-Atlantic product, but could indeed win success with indigenous subject-matter, providing the budget was modest and the treatment effective. Skilfully performed, with its anachronistic but hauntingly hummable theme music and attractive visual polish, courtesy of top adman turned debutant director Hugh Hudson, the film offered inspiration and hope to a cinema-going population that had often found themselves bereft of both.

Nominated for seven Academy Awards and winner of four, including Best Picture and Best Original Score, the film's success also prompted Best Original Screenplay winner Colin Welland to give his famous warning to the members of the American Academy – 'The British Are Coming'. Even if this fervently expressed threat was not fulfilled in the succeeding years, *Chariots of Fire* secured its place in British screen history for (at least momentarily) restoring the faith in the home industry after a decade which had witnessed an apparently inexorable decline in production statistics and creative standards.

An Enigma Production
Producer David Puttnam
Screenplay Colin Welland
Photography David Watkin
Editor Terry Rawlings
Art Directors Anna Ridley and Jonathan Amberston
Music Vangelis
Running time 123 mins colour

Cast

Ben Cross (Harold Abrahams)
Ian Charleson (Eric Liddell)
Nigel Havers (Andrew Lindsey)
Nick Farrell (Aubrey Montague)
Daniel Gerroll (Henry Stallard)
Ian Holm (Sam Mussabini)

Chinatown

Roman Polanski, USA, 1974

Film noir recreation

Murder, incest and the pursuit of power are the perfect ingredients for a thirties private eye mystery.

The story

Los Angeles, 1937. Private eye J J Gittes is hired by Ida Sessions, posing as Evelyn Mulwray, to follow her husband. The photos he takes of Mulwray with a young girl, Katherine, appear in a scandal rag. When Mulwray's body is discovered, his real wife threatens to sue Gittes for defamation of character. Gittes's investigations uncover Sessions's body, pinpoint Mulwray as crucial to the construction of a water dam and lead him to landowner Noah Cross. Despite threats of violence he discovers that Cross is behind the murders and that Evelyn is his daughter and Katherine both her daughter and sister as the result of her rape by Cross. He tries to help the women escape to Mexico but they are trapped in Chinatown where Evelyn is killed.

Comment

A stunningly textured vision of individual naivety and the forms of wider evil and corruption attendant on the birth of a nation like America, *Chinatown* meticulously recreates the ambience of 1930s Los Angeles, paying homage to the detective genre of Hammett and Chandler, but infuses that world with a very contemporary sensibility that refuses to add a patina of triumphant goodness to a catalogue of conscienceless acts in which the bad guys win. Writer and former cop Robert Towne developed his script for Paramount vice-president Robert Evans with the character of cynical but chivalrous private eye J J Gittes

tailor-made for Jack Nicholson and the complex femme fatale/enigmatic victim of Evelyn Mulwray envisaged for Evans's then wife Ali McGraw. In the 18 months the script took to write, McGraw had departed to become Mrs Steve McQueen and Faye Dunaway was drafted as a replacement, with Roman Polanski hired as a director. Bringing a foreign cinéaste's view of Los Angeles to the screen, Polanski also insisted on a bleaker ending to the film than that originally planned by Towne in which the young girl Katherine is at least allowed to escape from the web of Cross. In Polanski's film there would be no dawn of false hope.

Featuring excellent performances from Nicholson and especially Dunaway, the film engrosses as both thriller and character-study. It received 11 Oscar nominations, winning a solitary award for Towne's screenplay. The long-delayed and much-troubled sequel *Two Jakes* (1990), directed by Nicholson, failed to repeat the impact of the original and would seem to place in doubt the viability of a concluding part to Towne's proposed trilogy which would be set in 1959 and feature private eye Gittes being sued by his own wife.

A Paramount Production
Producer Robert Evans
Screenplay Robert Towne
Photography John A Alonzo
Editor Sam O'Steen
Art Director W Stewart Campbell
Music Jerry Goldsmith
Running time 131 mins colour

Cast

Jack Nicholson (J J Gittes)
Faye Dunaway (Evelyn Mulwray)
John Huston (Noah Cross)
Perry Lopez (Escobar)
John Hillerman (Yelburton)
Darrell Zwerling (Hollis Mulwray)

Cinema Paradiso
(Nuovo Cinema Paradiso)

Giuseppe Tornatore, Italy/France, 1989

Sentimental cinematic nostalgia

A valentine to the halcyon days of cinema-going finds an international welcome.

The story

The death of his mentor Alfredo reminds filmmaker Salvatore Di Vitta of his misspent childhood in the village cinema Paradiso where he acquired his love of all things filmic from projectionist Alfredo. When Alfredo loses his sight in a fire, Salvatore becomes his eyes and eventually the projectionist as well. During his adolescence, he makes a documentary, falls in love with a girl, completes his National Service and follows Alfredo's advice to leave home and become a filmmaker. His return is tinged with sadness as the Paradiso is under demolition and his family have become strangers; however Alfredo's legacy of a reel of all the kissing scenes that were censored from the films of his youth vindicates his devotion to film.

Comment

Although similar to fellow Italian Ettore Scola's *Splendor* (1988) which also deals in nostalgia for the cinema's past, it was Giuseppe Tornatore's sentimental evocation of the pre-television days when cinema played an important role in the fabric of community life that struck an international chord and saw the film showered with awards including a special Jury Prize at the Cannes Film Festival and the Oscar for Best Foreign Film.

Unlike a film like *The Last Picture Show* (1971) (see p124) in which the closure of the local cinema serves as a lament for the passing of an era, *Cinema Paradiso* is more intent on celebrating than mourning the past and is able to reach out to audiences all over the world. This is because in the specific details of the incidents that occurred in the cinema Paradiso in a small Sicilian village, Tornatore is able to reflect the cinema-going experiences that were then common to all audiences in the heyday prior to the later assembly-line characterless efficiency of the multiplex and modern multi-screen endeavours. His depiction of the eccentric patrons, unruly children, masturbating adolescents and snoring geriatrics is the story of all those who have participated in the communal experience of a Saturday night at the movies.

Despite the irresistible warmth of the director's approach, and the obvious skill in the performances of veteran Noiret and endearing moppet Cascio, the film needed the endorsement of foreign acclaim and the loss of 30 minutes before finding an audience in Italy. Its success launched Tornatore as a skilled manipulator of the heartstrings and, at the time of writing, there has been increasing speculation of an impending American remake that would feature Bruce Willis and Macaulay Culkin in the central roles.

A Cristaldifilm/Films Ariane Production
Producer Franco Cristaldi
Screenplay Giuseppe Tornatore
Photography Blasco Giurato
Editor Mario Morra
Art Director Andrea Crisanti
Music Ennio Morricone
Running time 123 mins (originally 155 mins)
colour

Cast
Philippe Noiret (Alfredo)
Jacques Perrin (Salvatore Di Vitta)
Salvatore Cascio (Salvatore as a child)
Mario Leonardi (Salvatore as an adolescent)
Agnese Nano (Elena)
Pupella Maggio (Maria)

Citizen Kane

Orson Welles, USA, 1941

Cinema milestone

A legendary tycoon's final word sparks a dazzling investigation of the American Dream.

The story

Charles Foster Kane dies uttering the word 'Rosebud'. A journalist attempts to discover the significance of this by quizzing his former friends and employees. Kane inherited his wealth as a youngster and was placed in the care of banker Walter Thatcher. Later, he takes charge of the *New York Inquirer* and becomes a newspaper tycoon. He is married but falls in love with Susan Alexander. Exposure of their affair proves the downfall of his political aspirations when he stands for Governor. Divorced, he marries Susan but his manipulation and the hollowness of their life lead her to abandon him. He dies alone. As the journalist leaves the Xanadu estate, there is a glimpse of a childhood sled bearing the name Rosebud.

Comment

François Truffaut's oft-quoted statement that 'Everything that matters in cinema since 1940 has been influenced by *Citizen Kane*' meets with little disagreement from the critical consensus. A former child prodigy whose acclaimed work with his own Mercury Theatre Company on stage and radio seemed to genuinely merit the word 'genius', the 24-year-old Welles was put under contract to R-K-O in 1939. In two years there, his work on such unrealized projects as a version of *Heart of Darkness* and the thriller *The Smiler With the Knife* allowed him to absorb a wealth of information on film technique and led to the observation that the studio's resources were 'the biggest toy train set any boy ever had'.

Although based on real-life mogul William Randolph Hearst (whose minions worked to ensure the film's suppression), and known as 'American' and 'John Citizen, USA' before shooting began, the film's widely-admired structure deploying overlapping narratives from various witnesses was influenced by *The Power and The Glory*, a 1933 film that recounts the life of a callous industrialist through flashback. Examining the complex relationship between individual power, personal choice and the context of society that Welles found fascinating in Shakespeare and was to return to in his own work, *Citizen Kane* was also a milestone in the developing art and style of the cinema. Eschewing the conventional *mise-en-scène* of edited long-shot/medium-shot/close-up in favour of deep-focus composition within the frame, Welles reveals meaning through the way in which the characters are positioned in their surroundings (the dying Kane, for instance, lost in the expansive void of his mansion). As writer/producer/director/star, Welles's protean achievements remain undimmed by the passage of half a century.

A Mercury Production for R-K-O
Producer Orson Welles
Screenplay Herman J Mankiewicz and Orson Welles
Photography Gregg Toland
Editors Robert Wise and Mark Robson
Art Directors Van Nest Polglase, Darrell Silvera and Hilyard Brown
Music Bernard Herrmann
Running time 119 mins b/w

Cast
Orson Welles (Charles Foster Kane)
Joseph Cotten (Jedediah Leland)
Dorothy Comingore (Susan Alexander)
Everett Sloane (Mr Bernstein)
Ray Collins (James W Gettys)
George Colouris (Walter Parks Thatcher)
Agnes Moorehead (Kane's Mother)

City Lights

Charles Chaplin, USA, 1931

Heartrending comedy

A sacrifice made for love gives the little tramp his most poignant moments.

The story

Sleeping rough, the impecunious little tramp finds his heart stolen by the beauty of a blind flower seller. Befriended by a drunken millionaire, who fails to recognize him when he is sober, he convinces the girl that he is a handsome, wealthy man-about-town. A series of misadventures that land him in jail also provide the money to finance an eye operation for the girl. Returning after his prison sentence, he is overjoyed that her sight has been restored. Gazing through her florist shop window, he attracts her attention and she steps out to offer him a flower and a coin. Face to face, she recognizes her benefactor for the figure he is and is both crushed and uplifted by the generosity of his spirit.

Comment

In 1928 Charles Chaplin temporarily halted production on his latest feature. The realization that the cinema's recently-found ability to talk was no passing fad left him pondering the status of his newest self-financed silent movie. The completed *City Lights* was eventually to open in January 1931, with an added musical score by Chaplin and occasional sound effects but, to all intents and purposes, it was a silent film released in the fifth year of the sound era. It was a risky venture but Chaplin's name alone guaranteed an astonishing level of public interest in the finished work; Winston Churchill and George Bernard Shaw attended the film's première, as did Eisenstein who was moved to tears. The initial welcome from a public already nostalgic for the glories of the wordless past augured well, and by the end of the year the film featured in the top five money-makers with a gross of $1 million. Six decades later it stands as one of Chaplin's most universally loved films.

Never an influential formalist in the manner of say D W Griffith or F W Murnau, Chaplin's almost total concentration here on the pantomime expertise and appeal of his emblematic little tramp confirmed that the core of his art lay in the performance before the camera and so transcended the day's technical innovation behind it. A simple narrative offers plenty of scope for the transition from broad comedy to tear-strewn tragedy, with the sophistication of expression that Chaplin brought to his role very probably at its peak. In his 1949 essay 'Comedy's Greatest Era', critic and screen-writer James Agee was moved to write of the tramp and the girl's moving climactic reunion: 'It is enough to shrivel the heart to see, and it is the greatest piece of acting and the highest moment in movies.'

A Charles Chaplin Production
Producer Charles Chaplin
Screenplay Charles Chaplin
Photography Roland Totheroh
Editor Charles Chaplin
Art Director Charles D Hall
Music Charles Chaplin
Running time 86 mins b/w

Cast
Charles Chaplin (The Tramp)
Virginia Cherrill (The Blind Girl)
Harry Myers (The Millionaire)
Hank Mann (The Boxer)
Allan Garcia (The Butler)
Florence Lee (Grandmother)

'Th . . . that's all folks'
The animator's art

In many eyes, Walt Disney and animation are synonymous and from *Snow White and the Seven Dwarfs* (1937) (see p202) to *Beauty and The Beast* (1991) the studio has produced hours of some of the best-loved feature-length animation using a largely unvarying formula of endearing anthropomorphic characters, skilfully etched villains and cheery songs. The detail, craftsmanship and use of multi-plane camera techniques to add a richness and depth of vision in early films like *Pinocchio* (1940) and *Bambi* (1943) can still stir the senses, and some of the more affectionately recalled Disney classics include *The Lady and The Tramp* (1956), *One Hundred and One Dalmatians* (1961) and *The Jungle Book* (1967).

However, there is more to the genre than the classical animation typical of Disney. Early pioneers in the field include Winsor McKay whose *Gertie the Dinosaur* appeared in 1909, the French cartoonist Emile Cohl and New Zealander Len Lye. Disney arrived in Hollywood in the early 1920s and worked on a number of series before the creation of his most famous character Mickey Mouse (originally to be called Mortimer). The subsequent gallery of characters that appeared in the Silly Symphonies series contributed to Disney winning more Oscars than any other individual in film history.

Among the few serious rivals to Disney's kingdom was Max Fleischer who gave life to *Popeye* and *Betty Boop* and also entered feature-length animation with *Gulliver's Travels* (1939). However most of the major studios ran animation departments making regular series of short cartoons featuring such figures as Bugs Bunny and Tom and Jerry. Innovative figures in this area include Tex Avery and Chuck Jones whose anarchic and irreverent approach balanced the sweet nature of Disney's work. Disney continued to experiment in

films like *Fantasia* (1940) (see p83), but it was the M-G-M Studios who mixed live action and animation with Jerry the mouse seen to dance with Gene Kelly in *Anchors Aweigh* (1944).

Less conventional aspects of animation can be seen in the career of Norman McLaren who worked in a diversity of forms including hand-drawn films and paper-cut films; his *Love on the Wing* (1939), for instance, was drawn directly with pen and ink frame-by-frame on to raw film stock. Ray Harryhausen's Dynamation process used stop-motion photography to breathe life into outlandish creatures for such films as *The Seventh Voyage of Sinbad* (1958) and *Jason and the Argonauts* (1963) whilst Ralph Bakshi brought animation into the world of X-rated adventures with his amorous moggy *Fritz The Cat* (1972). The more surrealistic side of animation can be seen in the films of Ladislaw Starewicz and Jan Svankmajer who has used puppets, trick photography, animation and live action to depict his mordantly comic obsessions. His feature-length work includes *Alice* (1988), an individualistic interpretation of *Alice in Wonderland*.

In the commercial field, Disney mixed animation and live action in *Mary Poppins* (1964) and achieved spectacular results when he was collaborating with Steven Spielberg's company and animator Richard Williams on *Who Framed Roger Rabbit* (1988). The success of that film plus a return to traditional techniques in *The Little Mermaid* (1989) heralded the ongoing renaissance in animation that has seen Dublin-based Don Bluth studios making *An American Tail* (1986), *The Land Before Time* (1988) and others, Richard Williams finally complete *The Thief and The Cobbler* (1991) and British animator Nick Ward win an Oscar for *Creature Comforts* (1990), one illustration of the very healthy animation scene currently existing in this country.

Close Encounters of the Third Kind

Steven Spielberg, USA, 1977

Awe-struck science fiction

State-of-the-art effects stress the benevolence of aliens who come in peace.

The story

Investigating a power shortage, lineman Roy Neary witnesses an alien spacecraft. He later meets Jillian Guiler and her son Barry who have also experienced similar encounters. Neary neglects his work and family to make sense of this whilst the Guilers are visited by the aliens who abduct Barry. Meanwhile, scientist Claude Lacombe and his team have devised a musical language that will allow them to communicate with the aliens. Neary, Guiler and many others make their way to the Devil's Tower in Wyoming. An enormous craft appears and responds to the messages of peace, opening its cargo door to release many earthlings, including Barry. Neary joins the team who have volunteered to accompany the aliens into space.

in which a young courting couple encountered a UFO. Finally in a position to have his dream financed after the success of *Jaws*, he first allowed noted scenarist Paul Schrader to work on a version of the script before embarking on his own. He had originally envisaged the older Jack Nicholson in the role of Neary but subsequently cast his *Jaws* star Richard Dreyfuss who had come to represent something of a cinematic alter ego for the director. Originally budgeted at a highly conservative $7 million the cost of special-effects sent that figure spiralling upwards to some $21 million; however the film earned more than $77 million on its first release in America and received eight Academy Award nominations, winning only one Oscar for Cinematography. In 1980, Spielberg released a new version of the film, *Close Encounters of the Third Kind – The Special Edition* in which he had edited certain sections and added scenes in which the Dreyfuss character is seen entering the alien spacecraft to be met by a stunning array of lights and machines.

Comment

Once entitled 'Watch the Skies', Spielberg's first film since *Jaws* (1975) (see p114) used state-of-the-art special-effects (courtesy of Douglas Trumbull), colourful mixtures of blinding light and uplifting music to illustrate the quasi-religious simplicity of his childlike vision of loving extra-terrestrials who visit planet earth. Unlike classic science-fiction films of the 1950s that reflected the paranoia of the Cold War era in their depiction of bellicose aliens intent on destruction, Spielberg convincingly asserts that it is equally possible for their intentions to be peaceful and harmless, an assertion embellished in the subsequent *E.T.* (1982) (see p74).

Drawn to the notion of UFOs since childhood, Spielberg had written a short story as early as 1970 entitled 'Experiences'

A Columbia Production
Producers Julia and Michael Phillips
Screenplay Steven Spielberg
Photography Vilmos Zsigmond and John A Alonzo, William A Fraker, Laszlo Kovacs, Douglas Slocombe, Dave Stewart, Robert Hall, Don Jarel, Dennis Muren and Richard Yuricich
Editor Michael Kahn
Art Director Dan Lomino
Music John Williams
Running time 135 mins *colour*

Cast
Richard Dreyfuss (Roy Neary)
François Truffaut (Claude Lacombe)
Teri Garr (Ronnie Neary)
Melinda Dillon (Jillian Guiler)
Cary Guffey (Barry Guiler)
Bob Balaban (Interpreter Laughlin)

The Conversation

Francis Coppola, USA, 1974

Character study

Acting greatness and technical virtuosity combine in a disturbing examination of personal responsibility.

The story

The recording of a conversation between a young couple penetrates the once rigid objectivity of surveillance expert Harry Caul. Contracted to deliver the tape to a company director, his curiosity grows when he glimpses the couple in the office building and he assumes some danger in the words 'He'd kill us if he got the chance'. Even though his task is completed, he goes to a hotel room neighbouring the one cited in the tape where he hears a violent struggle and witnesses a bloody figure through the frosted glass of a terrace window. At the company offices, the couple are facing press queries about the sudden death of her father – the director. Caul is warned not to get involved and he retreats to his gutted apartment.

Comment

Overshadowed by the sweep and scale of Coppola's achievements as the creator of *The Godfather* (1972) (see p89), *The Conversation* is one of his most rewarding films, tautly combining the paranoia and suspense of a Hitchcock-style thriller with a painfully detailed character study of a man destroyed by his guilt-ridden conscience and a need to assume responsibility for his actions.

Loosely based on sound expert Hal Lipset and inspired by the Antonioni film *Blow-Up* (1966), the film's script was first developed by Coppola in the late 1960s as a modern-day horror film that would explore the notion of privacy. Made possible by the success of *The Godfather* (1972), it gained added currency with its appearance at the same time as the full extent of the Watergate scandal was haemorrhaging out across America. However, the Watergate element is almost incidental to a film that allows Coppola to underline the validity of his concerns about personal responsibility, individual guilt, redemption and contemporary alienation, and is exemplary in its use of sound and narrative structure. It also allows Hackman (in a role once briefly envisaged for Marlon Brando) to give one of the most haunting performances in American cinema of the 1970s as an angst-torn loner. The sheer ordinariness and face-in-the-crowd quality of Hackman's screen persona have rarely been more effectively deployed than in the depiction of a cautious, self-protective individual tortuously unravelling at the edges as he runs the gamut from clinical detachment to passionate turmoil in the course of two hours. Winner of the Palme D'Or at the Cannes Film Festival, *The Conversation* was not a box-office success and was unsuccessful in converting any of its three Oscar nominations into awards.

A Coppola Company–Directors Company Production
Producers Francis Ford Coppola and Fred Roos
Screenplay Francis Ford Coppola.
Photography Bill Butler
Editor Richard Chew
Art Director Dean Tavoularis
Music David Shire
Running time 113 mins *colour*

Cast
Gene Hackman (Harry Caul)
John Cazale (Stan)
Allen Garfield (Bernie Moran)
Frederic Forrest (Mark)
Cindy Williams (Ann)
Harrison Ford (Martin Stett)

The Crowd

King Vidor, USA, 1928

A face in the crowd

King Vidor finds universal truths in the daily grind of the common man.

The story

John Sims is born on 4 July 1900. Orphaned as a young man, he determines to make his way in the world and journeys to New York and employment as an office clerk. At Coney Island, he meets Mary and they fall in love. Married life is not easy but the birth of two children brings happiness and when John wins $500 things seem to be on the up. However, when their daughter is struck and killed by a lorry John is distraught; he drifts from job to job and grows apart from Mary. At his lowest ebb, he attempts suicide but the sight of his little boy gives him the strength to keep trying and he is reunited with Mary. Together the family forget their troubles by sharing in the laughter of the crowd at a variety show.

Comment

One of the silent-film directors determined to explore film as a medium for social comment and artistic expression as well as mass entertainment, King Vidor had an abiding interest in the dramatic presentation of the fabric of everyday American lives that reached its apotheosis in this simple but insightful account of a face in the crowd and the ebb and flow of its owner's daily grind. Though a universal and timeless story that benefited from Vidor's refusal to sentimentalize or romanticize his subject, much of the film's enduring strength results from the documentary-like search for realism that Vidor pursued by focusing on the details of daily domestic routines, casting an unknown in the lead role and experimenting with on-location shooting, something of a rarity at the time. While much of the film was made in the M-G-M studios at Culver City in California, Vidor and his crew also filmed in Detroit and New York with his use of the imposing city skyscrapers, bustling crowds and the heavy traffic then a novelty emphasizing the insignificance of the individual in the modern age.

The film was honoured at the first Academy Awards with nominations for Best Director and Artistic Quality of Production but confirmed the M-G-M hierarchy's view that the general public did not want to see a bittersweet reflection of their own lives on cinema screens. Leading man James Murray, plucked from obscurity, found it impossible to capitalize on the acclaim for his work in this film and subsequently drifted into alcoholism, his pride preventing him from accepting a smaller role in Vidor's 1934 production *Our Daily Bread*. He then disappeared until his body was dredged from the Hudson River in 1936 and it was determined that he had taken his own life.

An M-G-M Production
Producer King Vidor
Screenplay King Vidor, John V A Weaver and Harry Behn, based on a story by Vidor
Photography Henry Sharp
Editor Hugh Wynn
Art Directors Cedric Gibbons and Arnold Gillespie
Running time 95 mins b/w

Cast

James Murray (John)
Eleanor Boardman (Mary)
Bert Roach (Bert)
Estelle Clark (Jane)
Daniel G Tomlinson (Jim)
Dell Henderson (Dick)

Cyrano De Bergerac

Jean-Paul Rappeneau, France, 1990

Period piece

Bold adventure and heartrending pathos combine in a peerless adaptation of a theatrical classic.

The story

Paris, 1640. Sensitive about his substantial proboscis, swordsman and poet Cyrano De Bergerac is reluctant to profess his love for Madeleine Robinot, known as Roxane. Unaware of his feelings, she tells him of her love for Christian De Neuvillette and when the oafish lad is at a loss how to woo her, Cyrano writes exquisitely romantic letters on his behalf. Soon the couple are wed. When Christian and Cyrano are ordered into battle against the Spanish, Cyrano maintains the correspondence in his comrade's name. Roxane arrives at the front in time for her beloved Christian to die in her arms. Roxane retreats to a convent but years later the dying Cyrano staggers to her side and reveals that it was his words that had won her heart.

Comment

One of the most successful foreign-language films of all time, *Cyrano* has also become one of the most fêted, recouping its budget of 100 million francs and winning universal acclaim for a towering central performance from Gérard Depardieu that received the rare accolade of a Best Actor Oscar nomination. The success of the film, quite conventional in style, can be attributed not only to the quality of the performances and the care and attention given to the period setting, but also in the adroit manner in which director and co-scenarist Jean-Paul Rappeneau creates a work that is gloriously alive for contemporary audiences without violating the spirit or intent of Rostand's original.

Rappeneau had first seen Cyrano as a boy at the Comédie Française during the war. A triumphant 1984 revival at the Theatre Mogador led to the notion of a new film version which Rappeneau was asked to make. Plans fell through but he returned to the project a number of years later, watching a spectrum of screen *Cyrano*s from two silent versions to José Ferrer's Oscar-winning 1950 performance, and even exploring the plans that Orson Welles had to tackle the subject when the rights were held by Alexander Korda. With Jean-Claude Carrière he developed a script that removed obscure references from the original text and managed to give equal weight to the elements of poet, humorist, warrior and tragedian that are encompassed in Cyrano, all the while couching the dialogue in alexandrine verse which had received an accomplished interpretation in the English translation by Anthony Burgess. Depardieu was the only choice for Cyrano because, as Rappeneau claimed, 'I knew him capable of expressing both aspects of the character simultaneously: his brilliance and his suffering.'

A Hachette Première et Cie/Camera One/ UGC/DD Productions/Films A2 Production
Producer Michel Seydoux
Screenplay Jean-Paul Rappeneau and Jean-Claude Carrière, based on the play by Edmond Rostand
Photography Pierre L'Homme
Editor Noelle Boisson
Art Directors Jacques Rouxel and Tamas Banovich
Music Jean-Claude Petit
Running time 138 mins colour

Cast
Gerard Depardieu (Cyrano De Bergerac)
Jacques Weber (Comte De Guiche)
Anne Brochet (Roxane)
Vincent Perez (Christian De Neuvillette)
Roland Bertin (Ragueneau)
Philippe Morier-Genoud (Le Bret)

Dances With Wolves

Kevin Costner, USA, 1990

Frontier epic

The western returns from Boot Hill with an epic saga of self-discovery and genocide.

The story

1863. Decorated for bravery, Lieutenant John J Dunbar subsequently requests a posting to the remote Fort Sedgwick. A wolf is his sole companion at the abandoned farmhouse where he makes his home under the vigilance of the native Sioux Indians. Later, he is befriended by the tribe, hunting buffalo with them, confronting a Pawnee war party and falling in love with Stands With a Fist (a white woman, captured as a child). Returning to Fort Sedgwick, he is apprehended by the cavalry and treated as a traitor. However, a Sioux ambush effects his release. Dunbar and Stands With a Fist then take their leave of the tribe to prevent bloody retribution.

Comment

Cited as evidence of the western's enduring popularity and the malleability of the genre in supporting the dramatic demands of successive generations, *Dances With Wolves* proved to be an unexpected international box-office sensation and the recipient of seven Oscars, including Best Picture. An epic saga of personal fulfilment, a paean to the simpler values of a vanished age, a rousing adventure yarn and a statement on America's guilty legacy of racism and genocide, the film is the kind of reckless gamble that Hollywood is no longer supposed to take.

Running for three hours and making extensive use of Lakota Sioux dialect, it marked an impressive début behind the camera for Costner who confounded those critics who had dubbed the film 'Kevin's Gate' during its production. A devotee of the genre who has cited *How The West Was Won* (1963) as his favourite film, Costner had previously acted in the western *Silverado* (1985) and won a Best Director Oscar for his work here. Showing an eye for landscape, he confidently judges the pacing of the story and invests the drama with a gentle and engaging humanism that treats the audience with intelligence.

Standing alongside *Broken Arrow* (1950) and *Cheyenne Autumn* (1964) as a rare celluloid voice on behalf of the native American, the film also seemed to strike a very contemporary chord in its advocacy of the community, family, environmentally-sound action and an almost utopian mode of existence. It was also at the vanguard of a number of productions dealing with the problems of native Indians in American culture from both historical and contemporary perspectives, among them *War Party* (1990) and *Thunderheart* (1991).

A Tig production in association with Majestic
Producers Kevin Costner and Jim Wilson
Screenplay Michael Blake, based on his own novel
Photography Dean Semler
Editors William Hoy, Stephen Potter and Chip Masamitsu
Production Designer Jeffrey Beecroft
Music John Barry
Running time 180 mins *colour*

Cast
Kevin Costner (Lieutenant John J Dunbar)
Mary McDonnell (Stands With A Fist)
Graham Greene (Kicking Bird)
Rodney A. Grant (Wind In His Hair)
Floyd Red Crow Westerman (Ten Bears)
Tantoo Cardinal (Black Shawl)

Day for Night
(La Nuit Americaine)

François Truffaut, France, 1973

A celebration of filmmaking

The tribulations of a crew shooting an ill-fated movie create a classic film about filmmaking.

The story

A film crew are shooting a movie called *Meet Pamela*, in which a young Frenchman brings his British bride home to meet his parents, with tragi-comic consequences. Ferrand, the director, has to cope with the problems of his crew behind the scenes: Julie, the wife, is recovering from a nervous breakdown; Alphonse, the lead actor, falls in love with a flirtatious script girl who runs away with a stuntman; Severine, the mother in *Meet Pamela*, despairs over her daughter's illness. Julie attempts to sooth the heart-broken Alphonse, but he promptly falls in love with her, and telephones her husband to demand that he divorce her. Julie locks herself away and swears she will never come out, but her understanding husband arrives to restore calm. Alexander, the father in *Meet Pamela*, is killed in a car accident. A double is used to finish the film, and they go their separate ways.

Comment

'Day for Night' refers to a technique of daytime shooting with a special filter which makes the scene appear to be happening at night, a device used in early westerns where budgets were lean, which is why the French call it 'la nuit Americaine'.

Truffaut's use of it for a title not only signals that this film is very much a film about filmmaking, but is also an ironic reminder that film not only creates an illusion, but the process of that creation can often be very different from what ends up on screen.

The dreadful film they are actually supposed to be shooting provides the occasion for the real subject of *Day For Night*, which is the behind-the-scenes tribulations which the director, played with superb assurance by Truffaut himself, must manipulate and juggle in order to finish his film.

These events encompass personal tragedy, broken hearts, marital misunderstandings and ultimately even the death of one of the lead actors in a car accident. Remarkably, they are all based on actual events which occurred in the making of earlier Truffaut films (including the death of François Dorleac in a car accident during the making of *The Soft Skin*), and the director pulls no punches in exposing the fragile egos and petulant tantrums of the film world.

That alone would not give the film its immensely satisfying flavour, however. Truffaut succeeds in transcending the in-jokes and recondite references of the film-maker's trade by presenting us with a pageant of absurd but believable characters facing equally real dilemmas, and does so with genuine style, wit and panache.

A Les Films Du Carrosse/PECF/PIC Production
Producer Marcel Berbet
Screenplay François Truffaut, Jean-Louis Richard and Suzanne Schiffman
Photography Pierre-William Glenn
Editors Yann Dedet and Martine Barraque
Art Director Damien Lanfranchi
Music Georges Delerue
Running time 120 mins colour

Cast
François Truffaut (Ferrand)
Jacqueline Bisset (Julie)
Jean-Pierre Léaud (Alphonse)
Valentina Cortese (Severine)
Jean-Pierre Aumont (Alexandre)
Dani (Lilianna)
David Markham (Julie's Husband)
Jean Champion (Bertrand)
Natalie Baye (Assistant)

Days of Heaven

Terrence Malick, USA, 1978

Rural relationships

*Malick's mythic love story defies the
conventions of American cinema.*

The story

Bill, a migrant labourer, his young sister
Linda and girlfriend Abby flee the city for
the heartlands of America in the early 1900s,
after he has killed a foreman in anger. In
Texas, they are hired by a reclusive, invalid
farmer to work his harvest. The farmer falls
in love with Abby, and when Bill discovers
the farmer's illness, he pretends that Abby is
his sister in order to encourage a marriage
which will see them inherit the property on
the farmer's death. They live harmoniously
together for a short time, until Abby begins
to fall in love with the farmer. Bill leaves,
only to return later to claim Abby. The
farmer realizes he has been betrayed, and the
duel between the two men destroys the
fragile peace which has been created, as a
plague of locusts descends upon the farm.

Comment

Malick has directed only two films, but both
Badlands (1973) and *Days of Heaven* reveal an
idiosyncratic and highly original aesthetic
approach to cinema. *Days of Heaven* achieves
the timeless tragedy of myth in a way that
few – and perhaps no – other American films
have, and does so in a film of quite
remarkable visual depth and beauty.

Malick is perhaps a little guilty of effecting
a god-like lack of regard for the humans at
the centre of his story, an impression
exacerbated by his insistence on a stoically

underplayed, and at times almost mask-like,
restraint from his actors.

Instead of allowing vent to the passions at
the heart of the central *ménage à trois*, Malick
concentrates on larger forces, notably the
eternal workings of mother nature, and the
relentlessly unavoidable fate which first
creates a kind of artificial kingdom of peace
in the farmhouse, and then rends it apart as
the two males do battle for the love of Abby.

If the visual dimension of the film
foregrounds the sweeping Texas plains to
the diminishment of the characters, so too
does the soundtrack emphasize the heightened rustle of the wind in the wheat, or the
final horrific buzz of the locusts, over the
snatches of often nearly inaudible dialogue,
all of which serves to sharpen the mythic
dimension of the film. It is not what the
characters say that is important, but the
context – natural and mythic – in which they
are ensnared.

An OP Production
Producers Bert and Harold Schneider
Screenplay Terrence Malick
Photography Nestor Almendros and Haskell
Wexler
Editor Billy Weber
Art Director Jack Fisk
Music Ennio Morricone and Leo Kottke
Running time 95 mins *colour*

Cast

Richard Gere (Bill)
Brooke Adams (Abby)
Sam Shepard (The Farm Owner)
Linda Mantz (Linda)
Robert Wilke (The Foreman)

Dirty Harry

Don Siegel, USA, 1971

Rogue cop

The scourge of the establishment or a mindless thug? Clint Eastwood states the case for the defence.

The story

San Francisco. The mysterious 'Scorpio' holds the city to ransom by threatening to kill one person per day. When a girl is buried alive, the mayor decides to pay. Inspector Harry Callahan is viciously assaulted delivering the money but manages to knife his fleeing assailant. Identifying the blackmailer through the treatment of his wounds, Callahan apprehends him in typically brutal fashion. However, the girl is dead and 'Scorpio' is released because of inadmissible evidence. When he subsequently hijacks a school bus Callahan intervenes and gives chase, ensuring there will be no restrictive legal technicalities by administering a fatal blast from his 44 Magnum handgun. He then throws his police badge into the river.

Comment

Dirty Harry passed through several stars before it became a Clint Eastwood project. Steve McQueen, Paul Newman and John Wayne had all been approached about playing the title character before Frank Sinatra accepted the part. A hand injury and impending 'retirement' forced him to relinquish the role and brought Eastwood on to the picture.

Eastwood had seen Harry as articulating the frustrations of his fellow citizens who wanted justice to be seen to be done and not impeded by legal machinations or subverted by recourse to socio-psychological justifications. Yet to many critics, the only difference between Harry and the psychopathic killer in the film is that Harry wears a badge.

The film opens on a memorial plaque stating 'In Tribute to the Police Officers of San Francisco who gave their lives in the line of duty'. On one level it then develops into a compulsive contemporary thriller whose commercial success would inspire the cycle of vigilante films typified by *Death Wish* (1974). It could be argued that the film is a bitterly anti-liberal tract that condones police violence and embraces a fascist mentality; yet Harry is typical of the Siegel loner, operating within his own moral code and growing anachronistic within a world that confuses him. Harry's climactic disposal of his police badge is evidence that his particular brand of individualistic endeavour has no place within the proper restraints of today's law-enforcement agencies. It's hardly a call-to-arms for would-be vigilantes.

The thematic richness of the film enhances its status as a popular thriller and Eastwood was to return to the character with generally less provocative if consistently lucrative results in *Magnum Force* (1973), *The Enforcer* (1976), *Sudden Impact* (1983) and *The Dead Pool* (1988).

A Malpaso Production for Warner Brothers
Producer Don Siegel
Screenplay Harry Julian Fink, Rita M Fink and Dean Reisner, based on a story by the Finks
Photography Bruce Surtees
Editor Carl Pingitore
Art Director Dale Hennessy
Music Lalo Schifrin
Running time 101 mins *colour*

Cast
Clint Eastwood (Harry Callahan)
Harry Guardino (Lt Bressler)
Reni Santoni (Chico)
John Vernon (The Mayor)
Andy Robinson (Killer)
John Larch (Chief)

Distant Voices, Still Lives

Terence Davies, UK, 1988

Family ties

The painful wounds of individual memory are distilled into a luminous work of art.

The story

Distant Voices: 1950s Liverpool. Eileen's wedding evokes a flood of family memories concerning the stern patriarch that was their late father. A brutal man capable of both violence and sentimentality, he is recalled refusing to let sister Maisie go to a dance and insisting that she scrub the cellar floor, hitting their mother, slapping Eileen in the air-raid shelter and then insisting she sing for everyone, and in a rare moment of serenity as he grooms a horse. *Still Lives:* Eileen's marital harmony is shortlived. Maisie's pregnancy gives cause for celebration with a night at the pub which ends in tears. Her mother continues a life of hardship. Brother Tony marries Rose. After Maisie's baby's christening she walks off arm-in-arm with her mother and husband.

Comment

Terence Davies's autobiographical diptych *Distant Voices, Still Lives,* with its admiring reception at the 1988 Cannes Film Festival, the prelude to a virtual apotheosis upon the film's later domestic release, justifiably remains the most lauded British film of the late 1980s. As in his earlier *Trilogy* (1974–83), wherein a terminally-ill cancer patient contemplates the tension between Catholicism and homosexuality which has marked his entire experience, a concentrated cinematic technique elevates the fearless revelation of deeply personal scars towards the dignity of a true work of art.

Seamlessly fusing two short films – *Distant Voices* was shot in Autumn 1985, *Still Lives* two years later – he chronicles the turbulent fortunes of his own working-class Liverpool family through the 1940s and 1950s, the first half concentrating on the domineering violence of his autocratic father, the second documenting the marital discord of the household's next generation. Isolating key moments into a mosaic of short scenes (weddings, funerals, christenings, wartime) Davies's elliptical approach cumulatively coheres into a moving picture of alienated male authority tyrannically suppressing feminine domesticity. Yet despite the film's insistence on the courageous silent suffering of the women, Davies avoids utter bleakness by stressing the period's close-knit sense of community and celebrating the cathartic potency of popular culture – the pub singalongs, movie musicals and songs on the radio teem with words of hope and romance. The distance between lyric and image, art and reality, ironically opposes our capacity for love and its sparing manifestation in family life's ongoing daily grind.

A British Film Institute Production
Producer Jennifer Howarth
Screenplay Terence Davies
Photography William Diver and Patrick Duval
Editor William Diver
Art Directors Miki Van Zwanenberg, and Jocelyn James
Running time 84 mins *colour*

Cast
Freda Dowie (Mother)
Peter Postlethwaite (Father)
Angela Walsh (Eileen)
Dean Wiliams (Tony)
Lorraine Ashbourne (Maisie)
Sally Davies (Eileen as a Child)

Neorealism

Arising in opposition to the perceived artificiality of the 'white telephone' middle-class dramas prevalent under the Fascists, and partially inspired by the 'poetic realism' in eve-of-war French productions like *Le Jour Se Lève* (1939) (see p120), neorealism was a style of filmmaking adopted by Italian directors in the immediate post-war period. It involved a documentary-like approach to fictionalized, socially-aware stories of ordinary people and everyday events and attempts as realistic a presentation of these events as possible through the use of authentic locations and, where possible, non-professional actors. Luchino Visconti's *Ossessione* (1942) (a version of James M Cain's *The Postman Always Rings Twice*) with its unflattering provincial backdrop was seen to be a precursor of the short-lived movement but Roberto Rossellini's *Rome – Open City (Roma – Città Aperta)* (1945) (see p183), conveying the experiences of life during the last days of the German occupation, is the first of the genuine neorealist films. Other notable works include Rossellini's episodic *Paisa* (1946), and the films produced by the collaboration between screenwriter Cesare Zavattini and director Vittorio De Sica.

Sympathetically dealing with the plight of the downtrodden working-classes, the poverty-stricken and those denied human compassion or justice under the bourgeois mores and laws of the country, De Sica once declared that their intention had been to show 'the indifference of society towards suffering. They are a word in favour of the poor and unhappy.' The films from their union include *Shoeshine (Sciuscia)* (1946) which traces the aspirations that lead two shoeshine boys to reform school, *Bicycle Thieves (Ladri Di Biciclette)* (1948) (see p33), the allegorical whimsy of *Miracle in Milan (Miracolo A Milano)* (1950) in which an orphan grows to become a leader to the homeless poor in Milan and, their final film, *Umberto D* (1952) which focused on the heartrending circumstances of an impoverished pensioner who contemplates suicide.

As Rossellini embarked upon his professional and personal association with Ingrid Bergman, and De Sica moved into more polished and conventional mainstream comedies and melodramas, the brief flourish of neorealism ended, its demise unmourned by the Italian government which had done its utmost to discourage such an overtly damning and unpatriotic view of their country. However, its impact was to prove far-reaching. In America, *Shoeshine* received a special Oscar because 'the high quality of this motion picture, brought to eloquent life in a country scarred by war, is proof to the world that the creative spirit can triumph over adversity' and thus established what would become the annual Best Foreign Film category. The movement's influence can also be seen on the documentary-like thrillers produced by Hollywood in the post-war years, including *The House on 42nd Street* (1946) and *Call Northside 777* (1947), and the later Free Cinema movement in Britain whose members aimed to make 'committed' films capturing ordinary lives and everyday events. Directors from the movement eventually moved into feature-length narrative cinema in the era of 'kitchen sink' drama and among their best known work is *Saturday Night and Sunday Morning* (1960) (see p188) and *This Sporting Life* (1963). The influence of the neorealists on contemporary Italian cinema is visible in the films of the Tavianis Brothers and in Ermanno Olmi's *The Tree of Wooden Clogs (L' Albero Degli Zoccoli)* (1978) (see p224) and provided the basis of Maurizio Nichetti's affectionate parody in the recent comedy *The Icicle Thief (Ladri Di Saponette)* (1989).

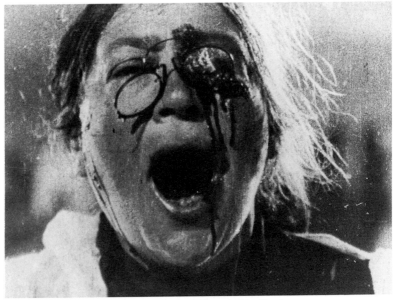

Battleship Potemkin *(1925) Directed by Sergei Eisenstein (Repnikova)*

Metropolis *(1926) Directed by Fritz Lang*

Le Jour Se Lève (1939) *Directed by Marcel Carné (Jules Berry, Jean Gabin)*

M (1931) *Directed by Fritz Lang (Peter Lorre)*

La Dolce Vita
(The Sweet Life)

Federico Fellini, Italy/France, 1960

Decadence revisited

Memorable images and dazzling set pieces combine in an epic fresco on the decadence of modern Rome.

The story

Rome. Gossip columnist and aspiring serious writer Marcello Rubini serves as a witness to decadent high-society life as he drifts through a series of parties, incidents and encounters with a string of women including his girlfriend Maddalena and his fiancée Emma. He covers the arrival of starlet Sylvia Rank and awaits a promised miracle where a lame man is killed in the crush. He determines to take his writing more seriously but his sense of bafflement and self-disgust are exacerbated by a visit from his father and the news that a friend has killed himself and his children. During a night of debauchery, he is revealed as only a publicity agent and watches as the guests assemble on the beach to witness a large fish being hauled ashore.

Comment

A widespread *succès de scandale* for a supposed sexual candour mild by today's standards, *La Dolce Vita* fully established Federico Fellini as an internationally acclaimed auteur, the movie's cachet such that its title and the name given to one of its characters – the sleazy press photographer Paparazzo – have since passed into the language. A sort of rake's progress following Mastroianni's hack through the vigorously decadent urban landscape of contemporary Rome, the film charts a week of caricatured activity: from the protagonist's infidelities to the arrival of a statue of Christ by helicopter, from a vision of the Madonna that causes a riot to a bout of orgiastic revelry at the climax.

It has often been said of the film that Fellini pretends to expose the moral collapse and spiritual malaise of an entire society while all the time gleefully enjoying the extremities of its lifestyle, but the Italian is hardly an ideas man in the first place. The religious imagery and the suicide of the film's token intellectual character matter much less than the showmanlike display of the director's varied peccadillos and the tangible emotional effects evoked by his bizarre tableaux. Rather than shoot on Rome's famous Via Veneto, Fellini built his own version in the city's Cinecitta studios and the use of black-and-white photography as well as wide-screen add a sense of scale and flamboyance that dominate the social and personal statements being made. It's arguable that no other major filmmaker has so little to say but such a striking way of saying it – a position addressed by Fellini himself in his subsequent masterly extravaganza $8\frac{1}{2}$ (1963) (see p76).

A Riama Films/Pathé Consortium Cinema Production
Producers Giuseppe Amato and Angelo Rizzoli
Screenplay Federico Fellini, Ennio Flaiano, Tullio Pinelli and Brunello Rondi
Photography Otello Martelli
Editor Leo Cattozo
Art Director Piero Gherardi
Music Nino Rota
Running time 174 mins b/w

Cast

Marcello Mastroianni (Marcello Rubini)
Yvonne Furneaux (Emma)
Anouk Aimee (Maddalena)
Anita Ekberg (Sylvia Rank)
Alain Cuny (Steiner)
Annibale Ninchi (Marcello's Father)

Double Indemnity

Billy Wilder, USA, 1944

Femme fatale

An archetypal femme fatale lures a corruptible man into the perfect murder.

The story

Wounded insurance salesman Walter Neff enters his company office and begins dictating a confession. After calling on the seductive Phyllis Dietrichson, his lust had lured him into fraudulently writing a double-indemnity accidental death policy on her husband and then conniving with her in murdering him. Claims investigator Keyes however had suspected foul play and ultimately saw Phyllis and her lover Nino Zachette as the guilty parties. An increasingly disgusted Neff decided to silence the poisonous Phyllis (also guilty of murdering Dietrichson's first wife). However, before he kills her, she shoots him. The last of his testimony is overheard by Keyes who phones the police before comforting his dying friend.

Comment

Adapted from James M Cain's story by fellow crime fiction doyen Raymond Chandler and acerbic director Billy Wilder, it is hardly surprising that *Double Indemnity* so effectively epitomizes the narrative concerns of the film noir. Although their working relationship was by all accounts a strained one, Chandler and Wilder did succeed in bringing from page to screen the familiar fatalistic package of stinging dialogue, cold-blooded slaying and sexual duplicity that marks out the genre. The confident male protagonist who soon becomes the confused victim of the predatory female is a recurrent notion in film noir plotting (eg *The Killers*, 1946; *Out of the Past*, 1947; *Body Heat*, 1981 etc) which frequently investigates the disruption of patriarchal structures by the sexual manipulation of the dangerous but desirable woman.

In the case of *Double Indemnity*, Wilder had offered the role of corrupt insurance man to Alan Ladd and George Raft, among others, before striking on the idea of casting Fred MacMurray against his amiable all-American image. The actor took some persuading to depart from a successful type but later recalled the role as one of his finest. Stanwyck and Wilder were to receive two of the film's seven Oscar nominations but Wilder claimed that some of his best work never made it to the screen. In the original ending to the film, MacMurray is convicted for murder and Robinson witnesses his death at a gas chamber in San Quentin. Thought to be too shocking for wartime audiences, the 20 minutes were dropped although Wilder claims they were among the best he directed. The footage is said to still exist in the vaults of Paramount Studios. Television remakes of the story in 1954 and 1973 have done nothing to dint the dark and corrosive power of the original.

A Paramount Production
Producer Joseph Sistrom
Screenplay Raymond Chandler and Billy Wilder, based on a short story in the book Three Of A Kind by James M Cain
Photography John F Seitz
Editor Doane Harrison
Art Directors Hasn Dreier and Hal Pereira
Music Miklos Rozsa
Running time 106 mins b/w

Cast

Fred MacMurray (Walter Neff)
Barbara Stanwyck (Phyllis Dietrichson)
Edward G Robinson (Barton Keyes)
Porter Hall (Mr Jackson)
Jean Heather (Lola Dietrichson)
Tom Powers (Mr Dietrichson)

Dracula

Terence Fisher, UK, 1958

Gothic horror

Hammer adds Gothic style and sexuality to the telling of the Dracula legend.

The story

Working as a librarian to the mysterious Count Dracula, Jonathan Harker is bitten in the neck by a vampire woman. Before succumbing to her will, he drives a stake through her heart but is subsequently killed by the Count, who journeys to London seeking revenge on Harker's beautiful fiancée Lucy Holmwood. Investigating Harker's disappearance, expert vampirologist Van Helsing finds a reference to the Count and is soon on the case as Dracula takes Lucy under his power and attempts to control her brother's wife Mina. Van Helsing eventually tracks the vampire to his lair. Keeping the Count at bay with a hastily improvised candlestick cross, he tears open curtains to reveal the lethal sunlight which reduces the Count to a pile of dust.

Comment

Having already enjoyed some measure of success with their colour version of *The Curse of Frankenstein* (1956) in which Peter Cushing had played the meddling Baron and Christopher Lee the miscreant result of his misguided experiments, the British company Hammer moved, quite logically, to a new version of Bram Stoker's *Dracula* with Lee an aristocratic Count and Cushing as his sworn adversary, the fearless Van Helsing.

In Lee's autobiography *Tall, Dark and Gruesome*, he recalls that the film was produced on a budget of £90 000 from which he received the princely sum of £750. However, a lack of financial resource was compensated for by an inventiveness in other areas and the film established the style and approach that was to characterize Hammer's great early successes within the horror and fantasy genres. Choosing to be more faithful to the Stoker novel than either the Expressionist *Nosferatu* (1922) (see p151) or the celebrated Bela Lugosi *Dracula* (1931), the film makes the Count a suave and handsome figure, thus placing an emphasis on the previously implicit sexual allure of the vampire figure. Director Terence Fisher adopts a distinctively Gothic style that consists of richly sensual colours, dripping blood, and a sense of purpose that is underlined by the fast pace of the editing and the unrelenting pitch of the jangling musical accompaniment.

Hugely successful at home and abroad, the film is said to have achieved the highest cost/profit ratio of any British film ever made and launched Lee, Cushing and Fisher on productive careers as maestros of the macabre. However, despite a slew of lucrative sequels from *Brides of Dracula* (1960) to the *Satanic Rites of Dracula* (1973), nothing could quite match the impact and chill of this original, particularly the rather spectacular way in which Lee's Count meets his demise.

A Hammer Production
Producer Anthony Hinds
Screenplay Jimmy Sangster, based on the novel by Bram Stoker
Photography Jack Asher
Editors Bill Lenny and James Needs
Art Director Bernard Robinson
Music James Bernard
Running time 82 mins *colour*

Cast
Peter Cushing (Van Helsing)
Christopher Lee (Count Dracula)
Melissa Stribling (Mina Holmwood)
Michael Gough (Arthur Holmwood)
Carol Marsh (Lucy Holmwood)
John Van Eyssen (Jonathan Harker)

The Draughtsman's Contract

Peter Greenaway, UK, 1982

Labyrinthine mystery

This playful fusion of experimental formalism with a country house murder mystery scored an unexpected commercial success.

The story

Wiltshire, England, 1694. Neville, an artist, is hired by an aristocratic lady, Mrs Herbert, to make a series of twelve drawings of their house and estate as a surprise present to her unfaithful husband in his absence. As a condition of accepting the commission, Neville insists that Mrs Herbert indulges in a sexual act with him for each of the drawings, to which she agrees. Neville also dallies with the Herberts' married daughter, Mrs Talmann, who wants an heir her husband cannot provide, and incurs the displeasure of her husband, who resents the artist's obvious influence over the household. After Neville completes the drawings and departs, Mr Herbert is discovered dead in the moat. The family blame Neville, and when he returns to make a final drawing, he is blinded and killed. The real murderer, it then emerges, is Mr Talmann.

Comment

This film marked Peter Greenaway's passage from making highly experimental films to a more commercial form of cinema. He has described the film as being an elaborate charade or conceit of the kind common in Restoration drama, and he takes great delight in the formal as well as thematic interplay between plot, imagery, and Michael Nyman's music.

The film was an unexpected success at the box-office, at least on the art-house circuit, and established the director as the leading representative of the avant-garde tendency in British filmmaking, at least in the public estimation, where his work is better known than that of, for example, Derek Jarman or Ken McMullen.

It is a more conventional piece of filmmaking than his later more fragmented and visceral films, and devotes much time and care to an examination of the house and grounds. Like his earlier, abstract film *Vertical Features Remake* (1979), it pursues a visual concern with vertical forms in a landscape, shot at different times and in different light, and makes a rich (if at times uneven) concoction from its fusion of familiar genres (the period drama, the murder mystery) with overtly formal considerations unusual in British cinema, where the dominant tradition has been literary and realist.

Greenaway's film, though, takes strength from his use of that tradition, albeit in a parodic fashion, and can be enjoyed on multiple levels, enabling the viewer to tease out significances from behind the playful sex and murder mystery on the film's attractive surface. It remains the most conventional and accessible of Greenaway's feature films.

A BFI Production
Producer David Payne
Screenplay Peter Greenaway
Photography Curtis Clark
Editor John Wilson
Art Director Bob Ringwood
Music Michael Nyman
Running time 108 mins colour

Cast
Anthony Higgins (Mr Neville)
Janet Suzman (Mrs Herbert)
Anne Louise Lambert (Mrs Talmann)
Hugh Fraser (Mr Talmann)
Neil Cunningham (Mr Noyles)
Dave Hill (Mr Herbert)
David Gant (Mr Seymour)

E. T. – The Extra-Terrestrial

Steven Spielberg, USA, 1982

Alien encounters

The sentimental saga of a boy and his extra-terrestrial captures the hearts of the world.

The story

Accidentally abandoned by its spacecraft, an extra-terrestrial takes refuge in the grounds of a suburban home where it is discovered by ten-year-old Elliott. Elliott gives the being sanctuary, introduces it to his sister Gertie and older brother Michael and searches for the relevant equipment that will allow it to communicate with its spacecraft and 'phone home'. As E. T. weakens in the alien environment, Elliott also falls ill. Eventually, the authorities track the boy and the being to his home. Under their care, Elliott recovers but E. T. dies. However, it revives upon receipt of a message from 'home'. Elliott ensures its release and transports the being to the woods, where the spacecraft returns and E. T. departs.

Comment

Steven Spielberg's *E. T.* seems to transcend categorization as a mere movie, but stands instead as a fully-fledged cultural phenomenon. It is estimated that worldwide more than 240 million people have seen the film, earning it in excess of $700 million in box-office revenues, while the associated merchandizing jamboree turned into one of the first multi-media movie 'events' now ubiquitously assailing the consumer with numbing regularity.

The highly lucrative source of all this public and critical adoration is the sentimental tale of a lonely suburban youngster and his one true friend that is redolent of the boy-and-his-dog school of weepie and was described by the American trade magazine *Variety* as 'the best Disney movie that Disney never made'.

The protagonist's deep and abiding companionship with his sexless, ageless, extra-terrestrial offers a vision of profound and reciprocated affection in a world where the institutions of home (much play is made of the absent father) and organized religion no longer offer such much-needed succour. The film's overwhelming emotional appeal lies in the opportunity it affords the audience to participate in this genuinely childlike love, an experience heightened by the drama of the creature's 'death' and resurrection. The alien Other of paranoid 1950s science fiction has thus become man's best friend and the Christ figure rolled into one, the feel-good Spielbergian theology of space as heaven sending us out of the cinema reassured by its notion of the great nuclear family in the sky.

The one institution that was to remain unmoved by the film was the American Academy, where *E. T.*'s nine nominations resulted in only three victories in the lesser categories.

An Amblin production for Universal
Producers Steven Spielberg and Kathleen Kennedy
Screenplay Melissa Mathison
Photography Allen Daviau
Editor Carol Littleton
Production Designer James D Bissell
Music John Williams
Running time 115 mins *colour*

Cast
Dee Wallace (Mary)
Henry Thomas (Elliott)
Peter Coyote ('Keys')
Robert MacNaughton (Michael)
Drew Barrymore (Gertie)
K C Martel (Greg)

Easy Rider

Dennis Hopper, USA, 1969

State of the nation

A cross-country journey reflects the dispiriting state of the nation in 1960s America.

The story

Replete with funds from a drugs deal, bikers Wyatt and Billy set off for the New Orleans Mardi Gras. Sleeping rough and travelling light, they pause briefly at a hippy commune. In one town, their unwelcome presence leads to arrest and imprisonment alongside alcoholic lawyer George Hanson. Attracted by their free spirits, he arranges their release and joins the journey. When they are subsequently attacked by the sheriff, Hanson is clubbed to death. Travelling onwards, they pick up two girls from a brothel, reach the disappointing Mardi Gras and experience a bad trip. Deciding to stay on the road to Florida, they are taunted by a redneck truck driver who accidentally shoots Billy in the stomach and returns to kill Wyatt as well.

Comment

Although *Easy Rider* was not the first film to examine the mood and aspirations of late 1960s' America's burgeoning youth counter-culture, it was perhaps the first to do so from within. Inspired by an article that Hopper had read about two bikers found dead on the side of a rural road, it was made on a tiny budget by a crew shooting fast and travelling as light as the film's protagonists and proved a triumph for independent production at a time when the studios were in decline. The $20 million box-office gross accumulated by the film in America alone highlighted just how out of touch the majors were from the day's predominantly young moviegoing audiences.

The odyssey of the bikers-cum-outlaws penetrates the heart of Middle America, where the degree to which their whole ethos of drugs, rock and anti-establishment attitudes is disaffected from the mainstream becomes radically apparent; such is the paranoia of this deeply conservative society, its bigots can only respond with bullets. However, if Hopper and Fonda's lyrical cruise represents the only true freedom left, the film's various visions of social alternatives prove unanimously limited. Sincere, portentous, rather over-directed, *Easy Rider* has dated badly but remains both eulogy and elegy for a crucial moment in cultural history and gateway to the new Hollywood of the 1970s and the film that finally launched Jack Nicholson after a decade of work in mostly exploitation subjects. Rip Torn had originally been cast as the liberal lawyer whose personal sense of the American Dream's failure embodied the disillusionment of a generation. Leaving the cast over 'creative difficulties', he was to have been replaced by Bruce Dern before Nicholson stepped into the role and received a Best Supporting Actor Oscar nomination, one of two earned by the film.

A Pando Company/Raybert Production
Producer Peter Fonda
Screenplay Peter Fonda, Dennis Hopper and Terry Southern
Photography Laszlo Kovacs
Editor Donn Cambren
Art Director Jerry Kay
Music various
Running time 94 mins *colour*

Cast

Peter Fonda (Wyatt)
Dennis Hopper (Billy)
Antonio Mendoza (Jesus)
Phil Spector (Connection)
Mac Mashourian (Bodyguard)
Jack Nicholson (George Hanson)

8½
(Otto E Mezzo)

Federico Fellini, Italy, 1963

Fellini compendium

This masterly exploration of the creative process is also an ambivalent but vital celebration of life itself.

The story

Guido, a successful director, is struggling to make his new film. He has built lavish sets, but cannot get under way. He is besieged by his colleagues and the complexities of his private life, which are augmented by the arrival of both his wife and his mistress on set. His insubstantial plot, about a man who meets and is rejected by his ideal woman, constantly changes in the light of his childhood memories, sexual fantasies, and present experiences, including meeting his own 'ideal' Claudia, but he gets no further on. He hides from the press and his producers, seeking shelter first with a band of clowns, and then the cast of the film. The unresolved conclusion leaves him facing widely differing options, including suicide, renouncing filmmaking, or making his peace with the world.

Comment

Like all Fellini's films, $8\frac{1}{2}$ is both ambiguous and uneven. He is not a maker of exquisite, rounded masterpieces; his cinema has an epic, mythical quality, a sprawling, self-indulgent canvas which often seems to be a kind of vast freak-show, a circus exploring the decline and fall of both Italian civilization and Italian cinema.

At the same time, his caustic vision is usually balanced by affirmation; beneath the cynicism, Fellini really does love his freak-show. He also loves ambivalence, and

nowhere more so than in this film. The viewer is left to disentangle meanings and significances from his highly allusive, metaphorical transformations of experience.

The central character in $8\frac{1}{2}$, the film director Guido, has made precisely the same number of films as Fellini (which is the significance of the enigmatic title), and invites an obvious connection. While it is never safe to assume the obvious with Fellini, there are few contemporary artists who have worked themselves so directly into their creations, while simultaneously disengaging from a realist, directly autobiographical aesthetic in the process.

Some viewers find the film irritatingly piecemeal and unresolved; others delight in its ambiguities, and its engagement with the difficulties not only of producing art, but of reconciliation with life itself. It is a masterly interweaving of thematic and temporal strands rarely achieved in a medium obsessed with linear narrative, and a fascinating stripping bare of the creative process.

A Cineriz Production
Producer Angelo Rizzoli
Screenplay Fellini, Ennio Flaiano, Tullio Pinelli and Brunello Rondi
Photography Gianni Di Venanzo
Editor Leo Catozzo
Art Director Piero Gherardi
Music Nino Rota
Running time 138 mins b/w

Cast
Marcello Mastroianni (Guido Anselmi)
Claudia Cardinale (Claudia)
Anouk Aimée (Luisa Anselmi)
Sandra Milo (Carla)
Rossella Falk (Rossella)
Barbara Steele (Gloria Morin)
Guido Alberti (Pace, the Producer)

Les Enfants Du Paradis
(Children of Paradise)

Marcel Carné, France, 1944

The ironies of love

The Paris theatre world of the 19th century is the setting for a masterpiece of French cinema.

The story

Infatuated with Garance, Baptiste Debreau takes her to the Grand Relais where she falls in love with his friend Lemaitre. Implicated in a robbery, the innocent Garance is saved by the intervention of the Count Edward De Monteray. Years later, she is his mistress, Baptiste has married the devoted Natalie and Lemaitre drowns his disappointment in wine. The Count suspects her of still loving Lemaitre but subsequently discovers her in the arms of Debureau and challenges him to a duel. The lovers spend a final night together unaware that underworld denizen Lacenaire has fatally stabbed the Count. Natalie begs Garance to leave them in peace, and she is last seen disappearing from view pursued by Baptiste in his stage Pierrot costume.

Comment

It's not too fatuous to suggest Marcel Carné's *Les Enfants Du Paradis* as a French equivalent to *Gone With the Wind* – the culmination of pre-war studio production expertise at its most lavish, most perfectly finished, most appealing to the emotions. The troubled gestation of Selznick's sweeping vision has its match too in the absurd folly of Pathé mounting France's most expensive ever project at a time when the country was languishing under Nazi occupation. The romantic pessimism of Carné's celebrated collaborations with poet and screenwriter Jacques Prévert, *Les Quai Des Brumes* (*Port of Shadows*) (1938) and *Le Jour Se Lève* (*Daybreak*) (1939) (see p120),

saw them banned under the Germans – forcing the pair towards the less successful medieval allegory of *Les Visiteurs Du Soir* (*The Devil's Envoys*) (1942). The 18th-century setting of *Les Enfants Du Paradis* would enable it to escape the Nazi censor, even though the film was intended as a paean to the enduring vitality of the French spirit.

As the Nazis had forbidden any film to be longer than 90 minutes the duo shot their swirling fresco as two: *The Boulevard of Crime* and *The Man in White*, over a lengthy period between August 1943 and March 1944. Carné stalled progress in the hope, eventually fulfilled, that the movie's première would take place after the liberation. Its sumptuous trappings making the historical tableaux tangibly immediate, Carné's masterpiece charts the ebb and flow of an *ingénue* actress's contesting affections for three very different men, bringing the most delicate of emotions into crystalline focus. As the determinedly independent Garance, Arletty's central performance places her alongside Vivien Leigh's Scarlett O'Hara in the pantheon of the screen's great romantic heroines.

An SN Pathé-Cinema Production
Producer Fred Orain
Screenplay Jacques Prévert
Photography Roger Hubert and Marc Fossard
Editors Henri Rust and Madeleine Bonin
Art Director Alexandre Trauner
Music Joseph Kosma and Maurice Thiriet
Running time 195 mins (subsequently 188 mins) b/w

Cast

Arletty (Garance)
Jean-Louis Barrault (Baptiste Debureau)
Pierre Brasseur (Frederick Lemaitre)
Marcel Herrand (Lacenaire)
Pierre Renoir (Jericho)
Maria Casares (Natalie)

The Exorcist

William Friedkin, USA, 1973

The devil inside her

Demonic possession brings commercial respectability to the horror genre.

The story

The sudden inexplicable changes in 12-year-old Regan baffle her mother and members of the medical profession who suggest she consult the Church. As Regan grows increasingly violent and uncontrollable, her mother approaches Father Karras, a young priest whose faith is at a low ebb. He concludes that she has been possessed by the devil and enlists the services of Father Merrin, a specialist in exorcism. One evening they engage in a titanic struggle for the girl's soul. The effort is too much for Merrin who suffers a heart attack. Karras continues the ceremony and brings the demon forth. When it enters his body, he hurls himself from a window and dies having sacrificed himself to save Regan.

Comment

A major current in 1970s' cinema was the commercial recognition of the previously marginalized horror and science-fiction genres, with both *Jaws* (1975) (see p114) and *Star Wars* (1977) (see p207) in their day the most successful films ever released. Similarly phenomenal in its ability to draw in a broad spectrum of the mainstream audience (with an $82 million box-office gross), Friedkin's *The Exorcist*, a $10 million diabolical thriller with a highly respectable cast, drew on the talk-show currency of the 'Is God dead?' debate to wrap its graphically exploitative study of demonic possession in an aura of thematic credibility. Thrill-seekers could therefore ostensibly ponder society's crisis of faith at the same time as they revelled in Friedkin's gloating spectacle of profanity, levitation, pea-soup vomit, swivelling heads and – the *pièce de resistance* – masturbation with a crucifix.

However, the notion of the monster within emphasized the degree of anxiety created by the nuclear family in crisis; the same ruptured domesticity had surfaced earlier in *Rosemary's Baby* (1968) (see p185) and *Night of the Living Dead* (1968) (see p150) while Richard Donner's *The Omen* (1976) and Larry Cohen's *It's Alive* (1973), both with sequels, concentrated firmly on the demonic offspring factor. Necessarily, the exorcist's stricken daughter is 'cured' by a surge of faith courtesy of the Catholic church, though the box-office imperative meant the treatment was not successful enough to prevent a couple of wayward sequels in John Boorman's *Exorcist II: The Heretic* (1977) and *Exorcist III: Legion* (1990) directed by William Peter Blatty, the source novelist and writer/producer of the original instalment who had won one of the film's two Oscars from a tally of ten nominations including Best Picture and Best Director.

A Hoya Production for Warner Brothers
Producer William Peter Blatty
Screenplay William Peter Blatty, based on his own novel
Photography Owen Roizman and Billy Williams
Editors Norman Gay, Jordan Leondopoulos, Evan Lottman and Bud Smith
Art Director Bill Malley
Music Jack Nitzche
Running time 121 mins colour

Cast
Ellen Burstyn (Mrs MacNeill)
Max Von Sydow (Father Merrin)
Jason Miller (Father Karras)
Lee J Cobb (Lt Kinderman)
Jack MacGowran (Burke)
Linda Blair (Regan)
Mercedes McCambridge (Voice of the Demon)

Fanny and Alexander
(Fanny Och Alexander)

Ingmar Bergman, Sweden, 1982

The rigours of childhood

Bergman's farewell is a magical remembrance of things past.

The story

Christmas 1907. In a small Swedish town, Alexander Ekdahl and his sister Fanny revel in the joys of the family festivities. Shortly thereafter, their father Oscar collapses with a fatal heart attack. Their mother Emilie hastily weds Bishop Vergerus and they become virtual prisoners under his religious tyranny with Alexander subject to stern discipline. However, the children are eventually rescued by Isak Jacobi and hide in his antique shop. Soon they are joined by their mother who has drugged Vergerus to effect her escape. Later, the cleric is burned alive in an accidental blaze. Restored to her family, the birth of Emilie's daughter brings further celebrations and grandmother Helena contemplates a return to the stage.

Comment

Self-consciously intended as a farewell to the cinema, Ingmar Bergman's serio-comic tableau *Fanny and Alexander* is an intriguing and enjoyable index to a memorable career. To some degree autobiographical, Bergman's film foregrounds the magic lantern apparatus as a metaphor for the cinema itself, while the theatrical setting and references to Shakespeare and Strindberg deliberately underscore the director's characteristic examination of psychological/metaphysical tensions within the dreamplay of filmic representation, most notably in *Persona* (1966) (see p165); the lingering spiritual doubts (see *Winter Light* (*Nattvards-gasterna*), 1961) reveal how the obsessions of the man are created in the Dickensian travails of the young boy. Perhaps the most unexpected element among the recognizable threads from his life and references to his work is the ultimate mood of the film which proves to be uncharacteristically exuberant and life-affirming as if Bergman, once regarded as the 'apostle of doom', had resolved the conflicts with all his personal demons and found faith in celebrating the sheer joy involved in being alive and happy.

The receipt of six Academy Award nominations was a major achievement in itself for a foreign-language entry up against the promotional budgets and hype of the Hollywood studios. However, it also won four Oscars for Best Foreign Language Film, Costume Design, Art Direction–Set Decoration and the luminous Cinematography of Bergman's regular collaborator Sven Nykvist, previously an Oscar-winner for Bergman's *Cries and Whispers* (*Viskingar Och Rop*, 1972). If, as seems increasingly likely, Bergman remains true to his word and never directs for the cinema again, *Fanny and Alexander* is an entirely apt and entrancing swansong.

A Cinematograph Production for the Swedish Film Institute/Swedish Television SVT 1/Gaumont/Personafilm/Tobis Filmkunst
Producer Ingmar Bergman
Screenplay Ingmar Bergman
Photography Sven Nykvist
Editor Sylvia Ingemarsson
Art Director Anna Asp
Music Daniel Bell
Running time 189 mins (TV version: 300 mins) colour

Cast
Pernilla Allwin (Fanny Ekdahl)
Bertil Guve (Alexander Ekdahl)
Gunn Wallgren (Helena Ekdahl)
Allan Edwall (Oscar Ekdahl)
Ewa Froling (Emilie Ekdahl)
Borje Ahlstedt (Carl Ekdahl)

Gotta sing, gotta dance
The American musical

Given the acclaim for the part-musical *The Jazz Singer* (1927) (see p115) as the first talking picture, it is hardly surprising that almost every Hollywood studio in the early sound era rushed into production with an all-singing, all-dancing, all-talking extravaganza like *Hollywood Revue* of 1929 or *Broadway Melody* (1929) which won the second-ever Best Picture Oscar. The fad proved shortlived but musical escapism flourished throughout the Depression-era as Broadway director Busby Berkeley brought his kaleidoscopic routines involving multitudes of chorus girls to the screen in films like *42nd Street* (1933) and *Gold Diggers of 1933* (see p90). 1933 also saw the release of *Flying Down to Rio*, in which the supporting terpsichorean work of Fred Astaire and Ginger Rogers caught the public's eye and resulted in one of the art form's most sublime partnerships. Backed by the choreography of Hermes Pan, stunning art direction, the work of composers like Irving Berlin, Ira Gershwin and Cole Porter, Astaire and Rogers revolutionized the musical with their effortless perfectionism and ability to tell stories through dance. Their greatest achievements included *Top Hat* (1935) (see p222) and *Swing Time* (1936), but the 1930s produced a wide diversity of musical talents from the operettas of Jeanette MacDonald and Nelson Eddy, to Alice Faye and Bing Crosby, child sensations like Shirley Temple and Deanna Durbin and, towards the end of the decade, such all-round juvenile performers as Mickey Rooney and Judy Garland, the latter finding her theme song of 'Over the Rainbow' in *The Wizard of Oz* (1939) (see p238). Doris Day achieved popularity at Warner Brothers and Betty Grable and Carmen Miranda were an indispensable part of the colourful Twentieth Century-Fox roster of talents, but any history of the musical is dominated by the production

unit at M-G-M headed by Arthur Freed and celebrated in the compilation *That's Entertainment* (1974). Using the most gorgeous palette of colours and allowing creative figures to test the technical and aesthetic boundaries of the musical, the Freed unit created *Meet Me in St Louis* (1944) and *The Pirate* (1947), and brought Fred Astaire out of retirement for a run of successes from *Easter Parade* (1948) to *The Belle of New York* (1952) and *The Band Wagon* (1953) (see p23). It allowed Gene Kelly and director Stanley Donen to take the musical on to the streets of New York in *On The Town* (1949) (see p153) and recreate the coming of sound in Hollywood for the backdrop of the joyous *Singin' In the Rain* (1952) (see p198), whilst Kelly and Vincente Minnelli created one of the most admired sequences of screen ballet in *An American in Paris* (1951) (see p11).

Unaccountably, the original screen musical began to lose favour in the late 1950s. With the exceptions of increasingly asinine star vehicles for the likes of Elvis Presley, lavish productions of proven Broadway hits became the norm such as *The King and I* (1956) and Oscar-winners *West Side Story* (1961) and *The Sound of Music* (1965) (see p204). Bob Fosse's innovative choreography and approach provided some high points in *Sweet Charity* (1968) and *Cabaret* (1972); the Liza Minnelli of that film and *New York, New York* (1977) or the Barbra Streisand of *Funny Girl* (1968) and *Yentl* (1983) are among the few contemporary stars to shine in the musical genre. The Bette Midler of *The Rose* (1979) and *For the Boys* (1991), John Travolta in *Saturday Night Fever* (1977) and *Grease* (1978), a lavish-budget *Annie* (1982) or a disappointing *Stepping Out* (1991) still offer filmgoers echoes of what used to be, whilst endless re-runs on television and video testify to the enduring glories of the musical's past.

The Wizard of Oz (1939) Directed by Victor Fleming
(Jack Haley, Ray Bolger, Judy Garland, Bert Lahr)

Yankee Doodle Dandy (1942) Directed by Michael Curtiz
(Jeanne Cagney, James Cagney, Joan Leslie, Walter Huston, Rosemary De Camp)

Singin' In The Rain *(1952) Directed by Stanley Donen (Cyd Charisse, Gene Kelly)*

Top Hat *(1935) Directed by Mark Sandrich (Ginger Rogers, Fred Astaire)*

Fantasia

Samuel Armstrong, James Algar, Bill Roberts, Paul Satterfield,
Hamilton Luske, Jim Handley, Ford Beebe, T Hee, Norman Ferguson,
Wilfred Jackson, USA, 1940

Animated musical fantasy

*Classical music and Disney
animation combine in a unique
fusion of distinctive art forms.*

The story

Leopold Stokowski and the Philadelphia
Symphony Orchestra take their places
whilst a narrator separates music into that
which tells a story, that which paints a
picture and 'absolute music' which exists for
its own sake. The latter is illustrated with
Bach's *Toccata and Fugue*, which is followed
by a terpsichorean interpretation of
Tchaikovsky's *Nutcracker Suite*. Then Mickey
Mouse appears as Dukas's Sorcerer's
Apprentice and the cycle of the planet's
birth and regeneration complements
Stravinsky's *Rite of Spring*. Nymphs and
centaurs perform Beethoven's 'Pastoral'
Symphony whilst a ballet serves *The Dance
of the Hours* by Ponichielli. Finally, the Black
God of Mussorgsky's *Night on the Bare
Mountain* gives way to the serenity of *Ave
Maria*.

Comment

In the course of the 1930s the Walt Disney
operation had grown from a small
production company to a substantial studio
complex capable of mounting the first
cartoon feature *Snow White and the Seven
Dwarfs* (1937) (see p202). The same year,
however, Disney was also looking for a new
vehicle to re-establish the pre-eminence of his
favourite Mickey Mouse – latterly eclipsed
by the burgeoning popularity of one Donald
Duck Esq – and approached noted
conductor Leopold Stokowski with the
notion of featuring America's foremost
rodent in an animated setting of Paul
Dukas's orchestrated fairy tale *The Sorcerer's
Apprentice*. As work progressed into 1938,
Disney began to conceive of a complete
concert feature visualising classical favourites
in this way and so *Fantasia* was born. While
vulgarization of the music is not entirely
avoided, the film's moves away from
anthropomorphic pictorialism towards a
free abstraction (as in the J S Bach *Toccata
and Fugue*) proved stylistically influential,
though some sections work better than
others – the frolicsome bestiary of
Ponchielli's *Dance of the Hours*, for instance,
is rather more winning than the greeting
card religiosity of Schubert's *Ave Maria*. Still,
Disney's commitment to broadening the
scope of the medium is self-evident, and the
prohibitively expensive 'Fantasound' multi-
speaker system developed an early precursor
of stereo recording, even if the full impact
has only been fully realized by the expansive
digital Dolby of the film's restored 50th-
anniversary reissue.

A Walt Disney Production
Producer Walt Disney
Screenplay Lee Blair, Elmer Plummer, Sylvia
Moberly-Holland, Norman Wright, Albert
Heath, Bianca Majolie, Graham Heid, Phil
Dike, Perce Pearce, Carl Fallberg, William
Martin, Leo Thiele, Robert Sterner, John
Fraser McLeish, Otto Englander, Webb
Smith, Erdman Penner, Joseph Sabo, Bill Peet,
George Sallings, Campbell Grant, Arthur
Heinemann
Art Directors Robert Cormack, Al Zinnen,
Curtiss D Perkins, Arthur Byram, Bruce
Bushman, Tom Codrick, Charles Philippi,
Zack Schwartz, MacLaren Stewart, Dick
Kelsey, Hugh Hennessy, Kenneth Anderson, J
Gordon Legg, Herbert Ryman, Yale Gracey,
Lance Nolley, Kendall O'Connor, Harold
Doughty, Ernest Nordli, John Hubley, Kay
Nielsen, Terrell Stapp, Charles Payzant, Thor
Putnam
Running time 124 mins *colour*

Fatal Attraction

Adrian Lyne, USA, 1987

Revenge thriller

Casual infidelity provokes a nightmare of psychotic retribution.

The story

Happily married Dan Gallagher's impulsive sexual liaison with Alex Forrest becomes something that he is not allowed to walk away from or easily dismiss. His repeated attempts to end their involvement are met by Alex's suicide bid and the news that she is pregnant. Increasingly desperate, she pours acid over his car and cooks his daughter's pet rabbit. He reports her to the police and confesses his infidelity to his wife Beth. When Alex takes his daughter for the afternoon and a distraught Beth crashes their car, he nearly murders Alex in rage. Later, she enters the family home intent on killing Beth. In the ensuing struggle, Dan appears to have drowned her when she rises again and Beth shoots her dead.

Comment

A kind of *Brief Encounter* meets *Friday, The 13th*, *Fatal Attraction* grossed $156 million and struck a chord far in excess of its derivative plot and approach. The year's major cinematic talking-point, it also came to be interpreted as a metaphor for the AIDS era, a brutal plea for monogamy, a reactionary genuflection to the morality of America's New Right or a misogynistic attack on the sexually liberated, single career-woman.

The project began as a 30-minute short film by James Dearden entitled 'Diversion'. Dearden subsequently expanded it into a feature-length screenplay that was entrusted to fellow Britisher Adrian Lyne, then best known for $9\frac{1}{2}$ *Weeks* (1986). Whilst highly effective in manipulating viewers' emotions, orchestrating shock moments and helping to elevate the film to the talking-point it became, Lyne's direction is also the reason that the film is included in this book more as a social phenomenon than as an example of great moviemaking. With the excellent performances of Close, Douglas and Archer, this is a film more about style than substance, which implies culture through arias from *Madame Butterfly*, defines taste as luxury and glitz, telegraphs exactly what it intends to do without subtlety or suspense and plunders shamelessly from other films, most notably a climax borrowed from *Les Diaboliques* (1955). The motivation behind Close's character crumbles as she is increasingly depicted as a psycho-killer who must be destroyed. Lyne later recalled the original ending before the studio insisted it be changed: 'Michael Douglas went to jail because his fingerprints were on the knife that Glenn Close used to commit suicide. I thought, "This is great. She got him from beyond the grave." ' After test screenings in America a different ending was filmed with the original seen only in Japan.

A Paramount Production
Producers Stanley R Jaffe and Sherry Lansing
Screenplay James Dearden
Photography Howard Atherton
Editors Michael Kahn and Peter E Berger
Art Director Jack Blackman
Music Maurice Jarre
Running time 120 mins colour

Cast
Michael Douglas (Dan Gallagher)
Glenn Close (Alex Forrest)
Anne Archer (Beth Gallagher)
Ellen Hamilton Latzen (Ellen Gallagher)
Stuart Pankin (Jimmy)
Ellen Foley (Hildy)

A Fistful of Dollars
(Per un Pugno di Dollari)

Sergio Leone, Italy/West Germany/France, 1964

Spaghetti western

The Man With No Name rides into town and initiates the 'spaghetti' western.

The story

When a stranger rides into town and kills four of the Baxters, he is hired by their sworn enemies, the Rojos. He proceeds to intensify their feud. Having witnessed Ramon Rojo slaughter scores of Mexican soldiers to acquire a shipment of gold, he poses two of the corpses in a cemetery. He then deceives the Rojos into thinking the Baxters have secured witnesses to their misdeeds. The ensuing confrontation leaves many dead. He also frees the beautiful Marisol from Ramon's clutches and is brutally beaten for his efforts. Ramon now burns the Baxters' home and tortures Silvanito who has been the stranger's ally. However, the stranger re-emerges to gun down the entire Rojo gang. He rides out, determined to return the gold.

Comment

By the early 1960s, the western genre was no longer the filmic wellspring of pioneer values it had once seemed: the sturdy myths of old had already been questioned by the psychologically probing 1950s' films of directors like Anthony Mann, while television's ubiquitous horse operas nightly played out the same situation to the point of redundancy. Then, along came Italian director Sergio Leone whose fresh approach comprised pushing the genre into an operatic sense of overstatement.

Securing a budget of $200 000, he began searching for a leading actor, preferably somebody known to the public, but ideally someone inexpensive. Steve Reeves was ruled out, James Coburn's salary demand was regarded as prohibitive and Richard Harrison was gainfully employed elsewhere, but he did make one suggestion: try *Rawhide* star Clint Eastwood. Inspired by the script, Eastwood journeyed to Spain at a modest fee of $15 000 to film a project then entitled 'The Magnificent Stranger'.

An unofficial remake of Akira Kurosawa's *Yojimbo* (1961), the film adopted a baroque approach that became synonymous with what was tagged the 'spaghetti western'. Paring dialogue to a minimum and refusing to give him a name lent a mystique to the central character, and the film was further distinguished by a style that detailed violence in brutal, lingering close-ups and orchestrated endlessly drawn-out ritualistic confrontations to the memorably shrieking accompaniment of Ennio Morricone's music. The result made Eastwood a star, revolutionized the western and led to a slew of generally inferior imitations.

A Jolly Film-Constantin Film-Ocean Film Production
Producers Harry Colombo and George Papi
Screenplay Sergio Leone and Ducci Tessari, based on a story by Tony Palombi
Photography Massimo Dallamano
Editor Robert Cinquini
Art Director Carlo Simi
Music Ennio Morricone
Running time 95 mins (originally 100 mins) *colour*

Cast

Clint Eastwood (The Man With No Name)
Marianne Koch (Marisol)
John Welles (Gian Maria Volonte) (Ramon Rojo)
Wolfgang Lukschy (John Baxter)
Sieghardt Rupp (Esteban Rojo)
Antonio Prieto (Benito Rojo)

Five Easy Pieces

Bob Rafelson, USA, 1970

Class drama

Confused and alienated by America's class divisions, Jack Nicholson becomes a symbol of a generation.

The story

Rejecting his musical talents and comfortable family background, Bobby Dupea works as an oil rigger. When his girlfriend Rayette announces her pregnancy, he quits work and visits his sister Partita who informs him of their father's ailing condition and suggests that he pay a visit. Rayette accompanies Bobby to Washington. His father has lost the power of speech and communication is even more difficult than ever but he attempts to explain the choices he has made in life. Strongly attracted to his brother's fiancée Catherine, Bobby vainly tries to persuade her to leave with him. On the road again with Rayette, he abandons her at a gas station to hop a ride on a truck bound for Alaska and another fresh start.

Comment

More than a decade after his film debut, Jack Nicholson finally achieved recognition and acclaim with his Oscar-nominated performance in *Easy Rider* (1969) (see p75). The charisma and perception he brought to the subsequent, and not dissimilar, character of Bobby in *Five Easy Pieces* confirmed his new star status and crystallized his image as a symbol of the confusion and alienation experienced by the counterculture generation of Americans.

Adrien Joyce, a pseudonym for Carol Eastman, claims to have based the central character on her late brother and partly on Nicholson himself and there is a tangible feeling of conviction in her study of a man adrift from the values of his family and class but unable to find an alternative or a sense of belonging elsewhere. Rare in the annals of contemporary American cinema for its thoughtful and perceptive approach to issues of class consciousness, the problems between the generations and the struggle to find an identity and something worth committing to, one could almost view it as a more mature reflection on the issues faced by James Dean's *Rebel Without A Cause* a generation earlier.

Ably supported by Karen Black, Nicholson's particular brand of lethal charm and iconoclasm are well placed and underpinned with a sense of tragedy and vulnerability, whilst his relish of comic situations is rarely more apparent than in the celebrated restaurant scene where the escalating frustrations in his attempt to place a simple order for wheat toast are somehow symbolic of all that angers and thwarts him in life. Although ultimately unrewarded by the American Academy, the film was nominated for four Oscars – Best Picture, Screenplay, Actor and Supporting Actress for Karen Black.

A BBS Production
Producers Bob Rafelson and Richard Wechsler.
Screenplay Adrien Joyce (Carol Eastman), based on a story by her and Rafelson
Photography Laszlo Kovacs
Editors Gerald Shepard and Christopher Holmes
Art Director Toby Rafelson
Running time 96 mins *colour*

Cast
Jack Nicholson (Robert Eroica Dupea)
Karen Black (Rayette Dipesto)
Lois Smith (Partita Dupea)
Susan Anspach (Catherine Van Ost)
Billy 'Green' Bush (Elton)
Fannie Flagg (Stoney)

From Here to Eternity

Fred Zinnemann, USA, 1953

Army life

The sprawling life of an army barracks sets new standards in adult drama.

The story

1941. Schofield Barracks, Honolulu. New arrival Prewitt's blinding of a past opponent fires his refusal to fight on behalf of the company and leads to his ostracization by all but the wiry, hot-headed Maggio. As Prewitt falls in love with prostitute Lorene, steadfast Sergeant Warden embarks on a passionate liaison with Karen Holmes, bored wife of the commander. When Maggio dies from his brutal treatment by stockade sergeant Judson, Prewitt avenges him and hides out with Lorene. When the Japanese launch a surprise attack on Pearl Harbour, Prewitt is accidentally killed trying to return to his men whilst Warden re-applies himself to the thing he knows best – soldiering. Karen and Lorene return to America on the same ship.

Comment

Famed above all for the surf-enveloped seashore writhe involving Deborah Kerr and Burt Lancaster, *From Here to Eternity* was one of the films in the 1950s-that began to challenge the prevailing censorship codes and demand that Hollywood adopt a more mature approach in its depiction of sex. Released in the very same year as Otto Preminger's *The Moon Is Blue* which shocked by bandying about such hitherto forbidden words as 'virgin', it has also stood the test of time as one of the more intelligent all-star adaptations of a popular novel and as the film that firmly established the dramatic abilities of Frank Sinatra.

The film may have been an entirely different prospect if Columbia studio boss Harry Cohn's choices and not the wishes of director Fred Zinnemann had dictated the cast list. Cohn had been keen to use either of contract players Aldo Ray or John Derek for the part of Prewitt, Zinnemann insisted on Clift. Eli Wallach was the first choice for Maggio with Sinatra begging and borrowing favours and accepting a miserly $8 000 before he was entrusted with the role, whilst it was really only a disagreement over the wardrobe which saw the replacement of Joan Crawford with Deborah Kerr, despite Cohn's expostulation over agent Bert Allenberg's entreaties on her behalf: 'Can you imagine, that sonofabitch suggested that English virgin from Metro?'. The role completely shattered Kerr's prim English-rose image.

Nominated for 13 Oscars, *From Here to Eternity* won eight, the most for a single picture since *Gone With the Wind* (1939) (see p95) and was the second top moneymaker in America for 1953, just behind *The Robe*, with an impressive haul of $12 500 000. A television remake in 1979 starred Natalie Wood and William Devane and led to a shortlived series.

A Columbia Production
Producer Buddy Adler
Screenplay Daniel Taradash (Dalton Trumbo) based on the novel by James Jones
Photography Burnett Guffey
Editor William Lyon
Art Director Gary Odell
Music George Duning
Running time 118 mins b/w

Cast

Burt Lancaster (Sgt Milton Warden)
Montgomery Clift (Private Robert E Lee Prewitt)
Frank Sinatra (Angelo Maggio)
Deborah Kerr (Karen Holmes)
Donna Reed (Lorene)
Ernest Borgnine (Sgt 'Fatso' Judson)

The General

Clyde Bruckman and Buster Keaton, USA, 1926

Silent comedy

Comedy, action, adventure and romance are effortlessly united in the stony-faced artistry of Buster Keaton.

The story

When the Civil War breaks out engineer Johnnie Gray attempts to enlist in the Confederate Army but is rejected because of the importance placed on his occupation. Dubbing him a coward, his girl Annabelle ends their engagement. A year later, Annabelle is on board his beloved engine 'The General' when Union soldiers hijack the train. Johnnie gives chase and, deep in enemy territory, he rescues Annabelle, takes control of 'The General' and now the chase is reversed. Once over the Rock River Bridge, Johnnie sets fire to it and sends a Union supply train hurtling to a watery demise. Later, his bravery is accidentally responsible for a Southern victory and he is rewarded with a commission and the devotion of Annabelle.

Comment

The General remains the best known of the masterly silent comedy features directed by and starring stony-faced clown Buster Keaton, an artist whose ill-deserved but unavoidable decline during the sound era has since been substantially countered by a great resurgence in critical admiration. While the one-time vaudevillian fortunately lived long enough to appreciate this belated recognition, *The General* provides ample evidence of his uniquely lugubrious comic persona, spellbinding physical agility and clinical filmmaking control.

Loosely based on actual events during the American Civil War (which Disney would film with more sobriety in 1956), Keaton's film strove to create an absolutely genuine evocation of the costumes, weaponry, technology and scenery of the period, even shooting in Oregon because it possessed the narrow-gauge track required to run the ancient steam locomotives that he insisted on using. Keaton's typically inconsequential railway engineer remain drolly implacable throughout a cavalcade of memorable sight gags, among them the risky spectacle of the hero seated on his engine's moving driving bar and the famous cannon-shot from train to train. All are presented in long-shot to reveal the authentically daring stuntwork and Keaton's habitually precise camera placement is often crucial to the comic impact; it compares favourably with Chaplin's functional *mise-en-scène* which is concerned solely with recording the little tramp's pantomimic paces. The direction or the seamless integration of the various action set pieces into the narrative is scarcely noticed however, for the keynote of Buster Keaton's art and his deliciously unharried performance is the way their meticulous élan comes across as effortless.

A Buster Keaton Productions Incorporated Film
Producer Joseph M Schenck
Screenplay Al Boasberg and Charles Smith, based on a story by Keaton and Bruckman from *The Great Locomotive Chase* by William Pittinger
Photography J Devereaux Jennings and Bert Haines
Editors Sherman Kell and Harry Barnes
Art Director Fred Gabourie
Running time 74 mins b/w

Cast
Buster Keaton (Johnnie Gray)
Marion Mack (Annabelle Lee)
Glen Cavender (Capt Anderson)
Jim Farley (Gen Thatcher)
Frederick Vroom (Southern General)
Charles Smith (Annabelle's Father)

The Godfather

Francis Coppola, USA, 1972

Dynastic drama

The power and influence of a blood-soaked dynasty illustrate the artistry of Francis Coppola.

The story

A lavish family wedding underlines the power and influence of Mafia Godfather Don Vito Corleone, whose subsequent disapproval of rival mobster Sollozzo's move into narcotics leads to his being gunned down in the street; only the intervention of his son Michael thwarts a further attempt on his life. Michael avenges this affront by killing Sollozzo and his police protector McCluskey before retreating to Sicily where he is married. Warfare erupts in which Sonny Corelone is killed and Michael is widowed. He returns to America and assumes the leadership of the family as Vito dies. Marrying Kay Adams, he ruthlessly arranges the slaying of his enemies and consolidates his position as the new Godfather.

Comment

The Godfather proved that a blockbuster movie need not be bereft of artistic achievement or social significance and it is Francis Coppola's greatest strength that he was able to combine the traditional Hollywood values of star names, production values and narrative clarity with a genuine auteur's handling of muted colour, densely-textured composition and the nuances of performance.

Mario Puzo's novel had been purchased by Paramount for $35 000. After the failure of the Mafia saga *The Brotherhood* (1968), it was felt that public interest in this criminal fraternity would be modest and so the budget was set at a lowly $2 million. Arthur Penn and Peter Yates are known to have been offered the project before Coppola who was regarded as a skilled writer and, perhaps, a more affordable name. His tenacity moulded the project as he held out for Marlon Brando in the face of studio opposition (Frank Sinatra, Laurence Olivier, Orson Welles and Edward G Robinson had all been mentioned for the role), stuck to his suggestion of Pacino when Warren Beatty declined the role of Michael, managed to increase the budget and saw much more in the project than a bloody gangster chronicle. The results were sensational – revitalizing Brando's reputation, breaking box-office records with a gross of over $80 million and winning three Oscars from a tally of ten nominations. It also established the notion of the Corleones as the apotheosis of the American Dream, a dynastic encapsulation of the country's emotional, moral and economic history orchestrated in large operatic tones. Coppola carried those notions forward in the even more richly textured *The Godfather, Part II* (1974), also a Best Picture Oscar winner, and the *King Lear*-like *The Godfather III* (1990).

A Paramount Production
Producer Albert S Ruddy
Screenplay Mario Puzo and Francis Coppola, based on Puzo's novel with uncredited contributions from Robert Towne
Photography Gordon Willis
Editors William Reynolds, Peter Zinner, Marc Laub and Murray Solomon
Art Director Warren Clymer
Music Nino Rota
Running time 175 mins *colour*

Cast
Marlon Brando (Don Vito Corleone)
Al Pacino (Michael Corleone)
James Caan (Sonny Corleone)
Richard Castellano (Clemenza)
Robert Duvall (Tom Hagen)
Sterling Hayden (McCluskey)

Gold Diggers of 1933

Mervyn LeRoy, USA, 1933

Putting on a show

Musical archetypes are established in a kaleidoscopic Depression-era extravaganza.

The story

Unemployed chorus girls Carol, Trixie and Polly are relieved to learn that producer Barney Hopkins has a new show, but joy is shortlived when his lack of money is revealed. However, their apparently impecunious songwriter/neighbour Brad Roberts offers to lend $15 000 and the show goes on with Brad added to the cast and falling for Polly. He is really the son of high society stock and his brother Lawrence appears to end his undignified dabbling in show-business. Mistaking Carol for Polly he attempts to buy her off but winds up in love with her and ends the family's opposition to Brad and Polly's marriage. All ends well and it appears that Trixie also has a beau in the shape of the Bradfords' lawyer Peabody.

Comment

Hollywood's response to the widespread Depression of the early 1930s took various forms including such 'social conscience' movies as *I Was A Fugitive From A Chain Gang* (1932), but the industry, for the most part, concentrated on escapist product to distract the audience from harsh everyday realities, initiating a successful era for screen comedy, the horror genre and the resurgent film musical. The *annus mirabilis* of 1933 saw Warner Brothers's ace choreographer Busby Berkeley, entirely revitalize the genre with a trio of classic 'puttin' on a show' extravaganzas: *42nd Street, Footlight Parade* and *Gold Diggers of 1933*, adapted from the 1929 stage play.

Sharing much of the same cast, notably love-interest duo Dick Powell and Ruby Keeler, and pretty much the same plot (threatened Broadway show goes ahead with the plucky chorus girl drafted into starring role), the films' rudimentary wish-fulfilment narratives would barely be worthy of note were it not for the startling artifice of Berkeley's production numbers. These well-drilled cavalcades of objectified sexuality – flesh at times turns to mere abstraction as the aerial camera peers down on Berkeley's characteristic kaleidoscopic patterning – proved hugely influential in the development of the medium by deviating from the set notion of filmed theatrical hoofing. To some extent, *Gold Diggers*'s most famous numbers, the ironic 'We're in the Money' and the elegiac 'My Forgotten Man' sequences, are the most intriguing of all, because here at least the brilliant dance director's filmic world teasingly, obliquely offers comment on life outside the movie house. Subsequent sequels include *Gold Diggers of 1935* and *Gold Diggers of 1937* (1936).

A Warner Brothers Production
Producer Robert Lord
Screenplay Erwin Gelsey, James Seymour, David Boehm and Ben Markson, based on the play *Gold Diggers of Broadway* by Avery Hopwood
Photography Sol Polito
Editor George Amy
Art Director Anton Grot
Music Harry Warren and Al Dubin
Running time 96 mins b/w

Cast
Warren William (J Lawrence Bradford)
Joan Blondell (Carol King)
Aline MacMahon (Trixie Lorraine)
Ruby Keeler (Polly Parker)
Dick Powell (Brad Roberts/Robert Treat Bradford)
Guy Kibbee (Faneuil H Peabody)

Once upon a time in the West

One of the few truly American art forms, the western was a significant part of Hollywood history for 70 years and those most closely associated with the genre have been among the stars making the most consistent number of appearances in the top-ten chart of box-office attractions. *The Great Train Robbery* (1903) (see p100) was one of the first productions to use film as narrative, and throughout the silent era westerns were a popular entertainment medium for pure storytelling, with Tom Mix and William S Hart proving upright heroes of unimpeachable virtue. The epic qualities of the west were more fully realized with efforts like *The Covered Wagon* (1923) and *The Iron Horse* (1924) and, as technical advances allowed on-location filming and the recording of sound, the western responded with such films as *In Old Arizona* (1929), *The Big Trail* (1930), starring a youthful John Wayne, and *Cimarron* (1931) which achieved the rare feat of winning the Oscar for Best Picture. However, the 1930s also witnessed the genre becoming a preserve of low-budget, assembly-line second-features and singing cowboys. However, 1939 saw the trend reversed with the release of *Jesse James*, the comic *Destry Rides Again*, teaming James Stewart and Marlene Dietrich, and *Stagecoach* (see p205) which belatedly bestowed lasting stardom upon John Wayne and once again underlined John Ford's mastery of the genre. Ford was to prove himself the poet of the western, offering affectionate homage to the men who won the west in films like *My Darling Clementine* (1946), *Fort Apache* (1948) and *She Wore A Yellow Ribbon* (1949). The post-war era saw the western graced with more psychological depth and flawed heroes, a trend most apparent in the fruitful star-director partnerships forged by Randolph Scott and Budd Boetticher and James Stewart and Anthony Mann. Stewart was also seen in *Broken Arrow* (1950) which was notable for its sympathetic perspective on the treatment of the Red Indian. A genre for all seasons, the western could now serve a multiplicity of intentions with Gary Cooper's lone law enforcer in *High Noon* (1952) (see p107) symbolic of those isolated by the anti-communist witch-hunts, and even John Wayne portraying the moral ambiguity of a ruthless pioneer in *The Searchers* (1956) (see p189) before reverting to the more traditionally dependable icon seen in *Rio Bravo* (1959) (see p182).

Developments in the early 1960s strove for a note of elegy rather than action in films like *Ride the High Country* (UK: *Guns in the Afternoon*) (1961) and Ford's *The Man Who Shot Liberty Valance* (1962) whilst the plethora of television westerns suggested that the genre was no longer commercially viable on the big screen. However, Italian filmmaker Sergio Leone imaginatively revitalized it with *A Fistful of Dollars (Per Un Pugno Di Dollari)* (1964) (see p85) which made Clint Eastwood a star and established the 'spaghetti' western taking standard elements of the American western to operatic extremes with its graphic savagery. Leone reached his apotheosis with *Once Upon A Time in the West (C'era Una Volta Il West)* (1968) and his use of violence bled back into the American western in such productions as *The Wild Bunch* (1969) (see p235), *Soldier Blue* (1970) and Clint Eastwood's own *The High Plains Drifter* (1973). John Wayne's poignant swansong in *The Shootist* (1976) (see p195) and Eastwood's *The Outlaw Josey Wales* (1976) really did seem to signal the demise of the western and, with the odd exception of *Silverado* (1985) or *Young Guns* (1988), the western has been little seen in recent years although the immense success of *Dances With Wolves* (1990) (see p62) suggests that it can never entirely be consigned to Boot Hill.

Stagecoach *(1939) Directed by John Ford (George Bancroft, John Wayne, Louise Platt)*

The Shootist *(1976) Directed by Don Siegel (John Wayne)*

Sullivan's Travels *(1941) Directed by Preston Sturges (Joel McRae, Veronica Lake)*

Sunset Boulevard *(1950) Directed by Billy Wilder*
(Erich Von Stroheim, Gloria Swanson)

The Gold Rush

Charles Chaplin, USA, 1925

The frozen north

Hunger and larceny in the frozen wastes inspire peerless comic invention.

The story

Taking shelter in a remote cabin whilst the villainous Black Larson goes in search of food, the little tramp and Big Jim McKay grow desperate with hunger. A dinner of boiled boots fails to satisfy but the accidental shooting of a bear resolves their plight. McKay leaves only to find that Larson has discovered his gold strike. In a fight, McKay is rendered amnesiac by a blow to the head and Larson is buried under an avalanche. In a boom town, the tramp falls for showgirl Georgia whom he invites to his New Year festivities. His memory restored, McKay arrives back and recruits the tramp to help him find his gold mine. They become rich beyond their wildest dreams and on the voyage home the tramp is reunited with Georgia.

Comment

Chaplin's critical reputation began to decline sometime around the late 1950s, a process spurred on by the failure of his final features *A King in New York* (1957) and *A Countess from Hong Kong* (1967), and the belated rediscovery of Buster Keaton, whose work appears rather more interesting as cinema (eg *The General* (see p88)) and whose understated personality has much more contemporary appeal than Chaplin's ripe sentimentality. Nonetheless, Chaplin's achievement should not be undervalued: he is after all the one figure who first embodied the cinema's worldwide power of communication and *The Gold Rush* represents a joyful highpoint in his art before the sound revolution, marital problems and political controversy rendered his subsequent output rather more contentious.

Typically, the film contrasts the innate goodness of the outcast little tramp with the rampant unscrupulousness of his fellow prospectors, while all concerned struggle for survival in Alaska's frozen wastes; his roommate's half-starved delirium might very well transform our hero into a human chicken to be pursued around the room, but Chaplin's protagonist still retains his benevolence of spirit and an enviable resourcefulness. Thus, the famous scene in which he fends off the thought of cannibalism by tucking into his boots (the hobnails becoming bones to be sucked dry, the laces succulent strands of spaghetti) creates from the most humdrum of props one of the screen's most enduring comic moments. Vastly popular on its release, the film was one of the highest-grossing of all silent films with a take estimated at close to $2.5 million and was reissued in 1942 with a musical soundtrack and somewhat flat-footed narration spoken by Chaplin himself.

A Charles Chaplin Production
Producer Charles Chaplin
Screenplay Charles Chaplin
Photography Roland Totheroh
Editor Charles Chaplin
Art Direction Charles D Hall
1942 Re-Issue Music and Narration Charles Chaplin
Running time 82 mins b/w

Cast
Charles Chaplin (Lone Prospector)
Georgia Hale (Georgia)
Mack Swain (Big Jim McKay)
Tom Murray (Black Larson)
Betty Morrissey, Kay Desleys and Joan Lowell (Georgia's Friends)

Gone With The Wind

Victor Fleming, USA, 1939

Civil-War romance

This romance played out against the sweep of the Civil War is probably the most popular film of all time.

The story

1861. At the Twelve Oaks ball Scarlett O'Hara encounters the dashing Rhett Butler and discovers that Ashley Wilkes is to marry Melanie Hamilton. Scarlett weds Melanie's brother who dies of measles. Rhett continues to feature in her life and comes to the rescue as Atlanta becomes a raging inferno. Scarlett vows to see the family estate at Tara rise again and still harbours an unrequited love for Ashley. When her second husband is killed she finally marries Rhett and gives birth to a daughter. However, when the infant dies their marriage crumbles. When Melanie dies Scarlett realizes the depths of Ashley's love for his late wife and attempts a reconciliation with Rhett. He leaves but she resolves to win him back.

Comment

If D W Griffith's *Birth of a Nation* (see p36) encapsulates the panoply of American film technique up to 1915, then another Civil War epic, producer David O Selznick's truly phenomenal screen presentation of Margaret Mitchell's *Gone With the Wind*, takes us up to 1939. Having secured the rights before publication to a source novel whose popularity was to rank second only to the Bible, the ambitious Selznick single-mindedly set out to turn the melodramatic story of Southern belle Scarlett O'Hara's wartime romance with dangerously dashing rogue Rhett Butler into the biggest movie event America had yet experienced. Over the next three years, every move Selznick made was calculated to whip up a flurry of excited publicity: he wrested Clark Gable, the biggest male star of the day, from M-G-M; he conducted a high-profile search to find the ideal Scarlett (Katharine Hepburn and Paulette Goddard are among the many to have been considered), before casting almost unknown English actress Vivien Leigh; he battled the Production Code over the final inclusion of a mild expletive; and in honour of a final product that was the longest and most expensive film ($4.25 million) ever made, he held three days of celebrations before the Atlanta world première in December 1939. A slew of writers may have worked on the script and a trio of directors – Victor Fleming, George Cukor and Sam Wood – may have been involved, but the flamboyant sweep, charismatic star performances and tearful emotional appeal of this intimate spectacular have continued to win over audiences and preserve its status as the most famous of Hollywood pictures. Nominated for a record 13 Academy Awards, the film won eight Oscars, and audiences now wait to see what the vast resources of contemporary Hollywood can bring to the sequel *Scarlett* (1991).

A Selznick International production
Producer David O Selznick
Screenplay Sidney Howard, based on the novel by Margaret Mitchell
Photography Ernest Haller
Editors Hal C Kern and James E Newcom
Art Director Lyle Wheeler
Music Max Steiner
Running time 222 mins *colour*

Cast

Clark Gable (Rhett Butler)
Vivien Leigh (Scarlett O'Hara)
Leslie Howard (Ashley Wilkes)
Olivia De Havilland (Melanie Wilkes)
Laura Hope Crewes (Aunt 'Pittypat' Hamilton)
Hattie McDaniel (Mammy)

The Graduate

Mike Nichols, USA, 1967

The young generation

Fresh out of college, a worried Benjamin enrols in the school of life.

The story

Naive recent Honours graduate Benjamin Braddock returns home to Los Angeles and uncertainty about both his future and the affluent circles in which his parents move. At a homecoming party, friend of the family Mrs Robinson asks him to drive her home and attempts to seduce him. They embark on an affair but Benjamin finds himself drawn to her daughter Elaine, also a college graduate. Mrs Robinson tries to end their romance by informing Elaine that Benjamin raped her. When subsequently presented with Benjamin's version of events Elaine chooses to believe him but is already committed to marrying wealthy student Carl Smith. Benjamin arrives at the church as the ceremony ends and runs off with the newly-wed bride.

Comment

Having made a triumphant entry into the film world with his excoriating version of *Who's Afraid of Virginia Woolf?* (1966), director Mike Nichols then set his sights on making a film that would satirize various aspects of the Los Angeles lifestyle and also dramatize the doubts and worries of the current generation of American youth who felt unable to relate to the values of their parents. The result was *The Graduate*.

Casting possibilities on the film had provided a number of interesting options before the final choices were made. Robert Redford, for instance, was offered the title role which he rejected on the perfectly reasonable ground that no one would believe he would encounter difficulties in meeting girls. Doris Day was sought for the role of Mrs Robinson, and at one point Gene Hackman was cast as Mr Robinson before a dissastisfied Mike Nichols felt compelled to replace him.

The final film made a star of the then relatively unknown 30-year-old Broadway performer Dustin Hoffman, who touched a nerve as the middle-class innocent whose affair with a predatory married woman leaves him questioning the cosy bourgeois values it's assumed he will comfortably and unquestioningly adopt. Nichols consistently shoots from this character's point of view, often distorting the image to formally italicize the protagonist's gnawing alienation. Stylistic panache aside, the eminently agreeable pop soundtrack and a sympathetic eye for the real social traumas of young adulthood were more than enough to make this one of the most popular films of the 1960s with an American box-office gross of around $50 million. Nominated in seven Academy Award categories, the film won Mike Nichols a Best Director Oscar.

An Avco Embassy Production
Producer Lawrence Turman
Screenplay Calder Willingham and Buck Henry, based on the novel by Charles Webb
Photography Robert Surtees
Editor Sam O'Steen
Art Director Richard Sylbert
Music Dave Grusin (songs: Paul Simon)
Running time 105 mins *colour*

Cast
Anne Bancroft (Mrs Robinson)
Dustin Hoffman (Benjamin Braddock)
Katharine Ross (Elaine Robinson)
Murray Hamilton (Mr Robinson)
William Daniels (Mr Braddock)
Elizabeth Wilson (Mrs Braddock)

La Grande Illusion

Jean Renoir, France, 1937

Anti-war statement

Renoir's masterpiece illustrates the passing of an era and the power of wartime camaraderie.

The story

World War I. Shot down during a mission, pilots Marechal and De Boeldieu are offered every hospitality by German ace Von Rauffenstein before being escorted to a barracks at Hallbach where they are befriended by French captain Rosenthal. Their escape tunnel is almost completed when they are transferred to Wintersborn which is run by the now retired Von Rauffenstein, who is as courteous as his circumstances will permit. Later, De Boeldieu creates a distraction whilst the two others escape, and is reluctantly shot by the gentlemanly Von Rauffenstein. During their 200-mile journey they are given food and shelter by a young German widow whom Marechal promises to return for after the war. Finally free, they cross into Switzerland.

Comment

La Grande Illusion is the most popular work by French director Jean Renoir, whose richly varied oeuvre spanning some 45 years has seen certain commentators acclaim him as the finest filmmaker of all. Renoir's agility across a broad spectrum of thematic approaches has often tended to befuddle the strictest of auteurist critics whose championing of the mischievous satiric escapade *La Règle du Jeu* (1939) (see p181) has perhaps threatened to overshadow the achievement of *La Grande Illusion*. Although the latter is more usually read as a more conventional exercise in anti-war humanism, both pieces offer wise reflection on the flexibility of previously rigid social structures.

Based on a true story from World War I, the film illustrates how the camaraderie between officers and soldiers on both French and German sides transcends the barriers of class, creed, rank and even nationality. Thus, when Pierre Fresnay's upper-class French officer allows his opposite number and fellow aristocrat Erich Von Stroheim to shoot him, his fatal self-sacrifice is as much an admission of the passing of the old order and the dawn of a new society as it is an act of patriotic heroism. However, in the brave new world outside, two escaped men are still looked on as working-class ruffian and hated Jew, the great illusion referred to in the title ironically drawing out the contrast between the ideals of brotherhood experienced in confinement and the stubborn prejudices of 'free' society. Made only after Renoir had struggled for three years to secure funding, the film was the year's most successful production in its native France and received a prize for the Best Artistic Ensemble at the Venice Film Festival.

A Cinedis Production
Screenplay Jean Renoir and Charles Spaak
Photography Christian Matras
Editor Marguerite Renoir
Music Joseph Kosma
Running time 117 mins b/w

Cast

Jean Gabin (Marechal)
Pierre Fresnay (Capt De Boeldieu)
Erich Von Stroheim (Von Rauffenstein)
Marcel Dalio (Rosenthal)
Dita Parlo (Peasant Woman)
Carette (An Actor)

The Grapes of Wrath

John Ford, USA, 1940

The dignity of man

The voice of the people gains eloquent expression in a definitive adaptation of Steinbeck.

The story

Having served time for killing a man in self-defence, Tom Joad returns to his father's cotton farm in Oklahoma to discover that the family have been evicted from their land. Tom joins them on the arduous journey to California. Work and hospitality are scarce along the way, hardship a common companion. At one camp the preacher Casy is murdered when he attempts to organize a strike against the appalling conditions. Tom revenges his death but then becomes a fugitive, finding temporary refuge at one well-run government transit camp where he vows to his mother that he will continue the fight for the rights of the working class. She responds with a doughty determination to hold the family together whatever the future may hold.

Comment

Perhaps the most remarkable thing about *The Grapes of Wrath* is that John Steinbeck's emotive novel of Depression-era America should have reached the screen intact in the Hollywood of 1940. Published in March of 1939, the book was an instant bestseller and the screen rights were purchased by Twentieth Century-Fox for $70 000 with the proviso that they would respect the 'social intent' of the literary property. A controversial novel that had been banned and burned in various locations across America, it was felt that a major screen adaptation would merely legitimize its socialist concerns.

Strongly resisting such reactionary views, studio head Darryl F Zanuck assigned former newspaper reporter Nunnally Johnson to write the script and hired John Ford to direct. In the 1960s, Ford told Peter Bogdanovich, 'the story was similar to the famine in Ireland, when they threw people off the land and left them wandering on the roads to starve. That may have had something to do with it – part of my Irish tradition – but I liked the idea of this family going out to try and find their way in the world.'

Ma Joad's final profession of faith in 'the people' certainly runs true to the life-giving communal spirit that is frequently the keystone of Ford's work. The plight of the Okies here is not so far from that of the townsfolk in *My Darling Clementine* (1946), the cavalry division in the *Fort Apache* (1948)-led trilogy, or even the native Americans in *Cheyenne Autumn* (1964) – the Fordian imperative throughout is the quest by the group to secure a peaceful home they call their own.

Nominated for seven Academy Awards, including Best Actor for Fonda's magnificent performance, the film received Oscars for Ford and Jane Darwell.

A Twentieth Century-Fox Production
Producer Darryl F Zanuck
Screenplay Nunnally Johnson, based on the novel by John Steinbeck
Photography Gregg Toland
Editor Robert Simpson
Art Directors Richard Day, Mark Lee Kirk and Thomas Little
Music Alfred Newman
Running time 125 mins *b/w*

Cast
Henry Fonda (Tom Joad)
Jane Darwell (Ma Joad)
John Carradine (Casy)
Charley Grapewin (Grampa Joad)
Dorris Bowdon (Rosaharn)
Russell Simpson (Pa Joad)

Great Expectations

David Lean, UK, 1946

Dickens adaptation

David Lean's mastery of cinematic narrative and composition illuminate Dickens's classic text.

The story

Grabbed by escaped convict Magwitch in a graveyard, the terrified young Pip brings him food and a file for his chains. An orphan, he is sent to play with Estella, the ward of eccentric Miss Haversham, and grows infatuated with her. As a young man an anonymous benefactor provides him with the means to live like a gentleman and he moves to London, sharing lodgings with Herbert Pocket. Increasingly haughty, he is shocked to discover that his benefactor has been the still outlawed Magwitch, but does help him in a vain attempt at flight. Magwitch dies and Pip discovers that Estella is his daughter. On his return home, he learns of Miss Haversham's death in a fire and saves Estella from a similarly reclusive life and incipient madness.

Comment

Perhaps even more so than in such epic productions as *The Bridge on the River Kwai* (1957) and *Lawrence of Arabia* (1962) (see p127), David Lean's gifts as a master cinematic storyteller are illustrated in his post-war adaptations of Dickens's *Great Expectations* and *Oliver Twist* which followed in 1948. His ability to create pace and tension through masterful editing, control of period, location and atmosphere evoked through a use of light and shadow, and effective deployment of incisive character actors in a wide range of sometimes unexpected roles, are well shown in the opening sequence of this film which combines all these elements in a gripping encounter between Pip and Magwitch (a grizzled and forbidding Finlay Currie) when the convict suddenly appears from behind a tombstone amidst the eerie calm of the marshland graveyard.

Previously filmed during the silent era and again by Universal in a nearly forgotten 1934 version, Lean's *Great Expectations* was partly inspired by an earlier stage adaptation of the novel by Alec Guinness whom he cast as Herbert Pocket, his official film début and the first of six collaborations between director and actor. Filmed in the marshlands of East Kent, along the Thames Estuary, the film is beautifully enhanced by the black-and-white photography of Guy Green and the performances of a staggering who's who of British talent. Acclaimed in some quarters as 'probably the best British film yet made', it travelled to America in 1947 and received five Academy Awards nominations, including Best Picture and Best Director, and won Awards for Best Cinematography and Best Art Direction. Jean Simmons, cast as Estella in Lean's film, would play Miss Haversham in the most recent 1989 television mini-series based on the novel.

A Rank/Cineguild Production
Producer Ronald Neame
Screenplay David Lean, Ronald Neame, Anthony Havelock-Allan, Cecil McGivern and Kay Walsh, based on the novel by Charles Dickens
Photography Guy Green
Editor Jack Harris
Art Directors John Bryan and Wilfrid Shingleton
Music Walter Goehr
Running time 118 mins b/w

Cast
John Mills (Pip Pirrip)
Valerie Hobson (Estella/Her Mother)
Bernard Miles (Joe Gargery)
Francis L Sullivan (Jaggers)
Martita Hunt (Miss Havisham)
Finlay Currie (Abel Magwitch)

The Great Train Robbery

Edwin S Porter, USA 1903

Primitive western

An action-packed western establishes the narrative potential of movies.

The story

Two marauders assault a telegraph clerk and tie him up as a train pulls into a station. Joined by four other desperados, they attack the refuelling train and burst in on the guard as he tries to secure the strong-box, which they steal. The train's passengers are lined up along the track and asked to deposit their valuables with the robbers. One man is shot in the back whilst trying to escape. The robbers unhitch the engine from the train, travel onwards and run towards their waiting mounts. Meanwhile, the clerk's daughter rescues him and raises the alarm. A posse is quickly formed and the robbers are hunted down. Trapped whilst sharing out their spoils, the men are killed in the shootout with the posse.

Comment

At the turn of the century the newfangled nickelodeon was just one of a number of forms of popular entertainment alongside stage melodrama, circuses, vaudeville and magic lantern shows; the challenge to the new medium was to develop as an art form whilst at the same time communicating with the audience in a way they could understand. As one of America's first story films, Edwin S Porter's *The Great Train Robbery* was a significant point in the process.

Billed as 'The sensational and startling "hold up" of the "gold express" by famous western outlaws', the significance of the film was that its 20 shots connected to tell the story of an exciting chase, and as such its complexity and impact dwarfed the mere curiosity value of the single-scene subjects so common in the era when the movies were not much more than a fairground attraction. Although each piece of action was presented unedited as a kind of visual tableau, Porter was among the first to generate excitement by cutting between two points of view. After a climactic gunbattle, Porter then pulls off his most extraordinary visual coup when the film's first close-up has an unruly varmint pointing his rifle straight into the camera; for an audience who had never actually seen a close-up of any kind before it was a moment as thrilling as the first sight of the Lumière brothers' train pulling into the station that had signalled the birth of cinema in 1895.

Porter remained a prolific if less innovative director over the next decade before retiring from filmmaking in 1916. Leading actor 'Bronco Billy' Anderson appeared in some four hundred short westerns before retiring from the screen in 1920, returning only for a one-off cameo appearance in *The Bounty Killer* (1965).

Produced by the Thomas Edison Company
Cast includes G M 'Bronco Billy' Anderson, George Barnes, A C Abadie and Marie Murray
Running time 11 mins approx b/w

Greed

Erich Von Stroheim, USA, 1924

Epic of obsession

Von Stroheim's most expansive work is a masterful examination of human avarice.

The story

McTeague, a young miner, becomes an apprentice to a travelling dentist before settling in San Francisco where he meets veterinarian Marcus Schouler and becomes enamoured of his cousin and fiancée Trina. Marcus gallantly steps aside for his friend but grows resentful when Trina wins $5000 in a lottery. After McTeague and Trina are married money becomes the central obsession of their lives. Marcus ruins McTeague by exposing him for practising without a licence and then leaves town. He takes refuge in alcohol and turns violent towards Trina, later abandoning her and then returning to murder her for her money. Marcus pursues him to Death Valley where they die handcuffed together under the scorching desert sun.

Comment

Not one of the films made by the extravagant Austrian expatriate Erich Von Stroheim exists today in the form he originally intended. The greater part of his 1920s' output offered a sardonic vision of European decadence, with *Foolish Wives* (1921) the first evidence that his relentless eye for authenticity would create results too expansive or outrageous for the producers of the day. Adapted from Frank Norris's chronicle of San Franciscan low-life *McTeague*, the subject matter of *Greed* made it an exception in Von Stroheim's oeuvre, but the film's treatment at the hands of production company Metro-Goldwyn still exemplifies the ongoing conflict of creative cinematic artist and intransigent moneymen.

Von Stroheim achieved a visual equivalent of Norris's Zolaesque naturalism by shooting everything on location, but this heavily detailed realist style pushed the running time of the finished result to lengths unprecedented even by Von Stroheim's ever-generous standards. From his first nine-hour assembly he reduced the footage to seven and then four hours, but the studio still baulked at the notion of screening the film over two consecutive nights. Metro then carried out their own drastic cuts, replacing Von Stroheim's original titles and preserving only the skeleton of his original conception in a final release print under three hours in length. For all that, the version of *Greed* remaining today is still a film of tremendous visceral power, its final desperate scenes of murder and betrayal under the pitiless Death Valley skies a searing indictment of human avarice. Because the studio burned all the cut material to extract the silver nitrate in the stock, the full amplitude of Von Stroheim's work cannot be assessed.

A Metro-Goldwyn Company Production
Producer Irving Thalberg
Screenplay Erich Von Stroheim and June Mathis, based on the novel *McTeague* by Frank Norris
Photography Ben Reynolds and William Daniels
Editors Erich Von Stroheim, Frank Hull and Marguerite Faust
Art Directors Richard Day and Erich Von Stroheim
Music Leo A Kempinsky
Running time originally 160 mins approx b/w

Cast
Tempe Piggot (Mother McTeague)
Gibson Gowland (McTeague)
Gunther Von Ritzau (Dr 'Painless' Potter)
Jimmy Wang (Chinese Cook)
Jean Hersholt (Marcus Schouler)
Zasu Pitts (Trina)

Heaven's Gate

Michael Cimino, USA, 1980

Perfectionist western

American disdain cannot obscure the beauty and spectacle of Cimino's grandiloquent 'socialist western'.

The story

Over 20 years after their graduation from Harvard, lawman James Averill encounters Billy Irvine who informs him that cattleman's leader Frank Canton is planning a massed attack on the immigrant community in Johnson County. Averill warns John Bridges and vainly seeks protection from the local army commander. He begs his mistress, prostitute Ella Watson, to leave town but she chooses the company of his rival, hired gun Nathan Champion. When Canton's men arrive, they kill Champion. The immigrants ride out to meet the gunmen and a battle ensues in which it is Canton who is forced to seek help from the army. In Rhode Island in 1903, Averill reflects on the subsequent deaths of Ella and John Bridges and his own killing of Canton.

Comment

Fresh from the Oscar-winning success of *The Deer Hunter* (1978), director Michael Cimino received the go-ahead from United Artists for a new movie based on the little-known Johnson County War. From historical events surrounding the massacre by Wyoming's wealthy Stock Growers' Association of the immigrant community then farming the land, Cimino was to weave together *Heaven's Gate*, a huge yet financially disastrous epic that remains one of the most controversial offerings to come out of latter-day Hollywood.

With a thirst for authenticity that extended to the transportation of a period locomotive halfway across the continent, Cimino's schedule soon fell by the wayside and his budget expanded from an initial (rather unlikely) $7.5 million to a highly-publicized final tally of around $36 million. In the hope that the final product would be a huge blockbuster United Artists continued to support his efforts, but were surely unprepared for the degree of unwarranted critical vitriol that the revisionist four-hour spectacular would attract on its initial engagement. After a swift withdrawal and the reissue of a somewhat mangled shorter cut, American public response continued to be disdainful of Cimino's apparent profligacy, but a highly favourable reappraisal of the film by European commentators apportioned at least part of the disastrous US reception to *Heaven's Gate*'s unpalatable ideological stance. While one French newspaper called it 'the first socialist western', American audiences (and critics) seemed unwilling to accept the film's passionate and strikingly beautiful account of Yankee entrepreneurism's human toll. The final failure of the film precipitated the end of United Artists as a viable production company and led to the sale of the studio. Steven Bach's book *Final Cut* chronicles the travails of making the film.

A Partisan Production
Producer Joann Carelli
Screenplay Michael Cimino
Photography Vilmos Zsigmond
Editors Tom Rolf, William Reynolds, Lisa Fruchtman and Gerald Greenberg
Art Directors Tambi Larsen, Spencer Deverill and Maurice Fowler
Music David Mansfield
Running time 210 mins *colour*

Cast
Kris Kristofferson (James Averill)
Christopher Walken (Nathan D Champion)
John Hurt (William C Irvine)
Sam Waterston (Frank Canton)
Brad Dourif (Mr Eggleston)
Isabelle Huppert (Ella Watson)
Joseph Cotten (Reverend Doctor)

Henry V

Laurence Olivier, UK, 1944

Morale-boosting Shakespeare

Patriotism and cinematic artistry combine in a milestone of literary adaptation.

The story

A performance at London's Globe Theatre expands into a vast panorama of colour, drama, landscape and conflict as the story of Henry V is recounted. In 1415, Henry leaves England to fight the time-honoured enemy of the French. With an army of 30 000 he lays siege to northern France for 60 days and secures many victories with little loss to his own numbers. At Agincourt on 25 October however, his much-depleted force must withstand a French army of 60 000, but with effective deployment of his archers and a rallying cry to English patriotism he achieves a notable victory. A peace treaty is signed at Rouen, Henry woos the French Princess Katherine and the two royal families are united as the drama returns to the Globe Theatre.

Comment

By the 1940s the screen had already seen its fair share of Shakespearean adaptations, including the all-star *A Midsummer Night's Dream* (1935) and an *As You Like It* (1936) featuring Laurence Olivier. However, as the first film to offer an idiomatic rendering of the Bard's enduring verse and to use the resources of the cinema to capture the scope of Shakespeare's historical conception, Olivier's *Henry V* marked an instant milestone. Securing leave from his Fleet Air Arm duties, he embarked on a hawkish film interpretation of *Henry V* that would contribute to the ongoing propaganda effort. William Wyler and Carol Reed were among those he approached before assuming the director's reins himself. Still under contract to David O Selznick, Vivien Leigh was refused permission to play Queen Katherine and, similarly beholden to M-G-M, Robert Donat felt it unwise to accept the role of the Chorus. However, Olivier was able to collect a splendid cast and filmed on the estate of Lord Powerscourt at Enniskerry in Ireland with extras drawn from the local Home Guard. Betraying none of the expediences under which it was filmed, the production used a cut text to place the emphasis on the famous English victory at Agincourt and illustrates Olivier's filmmaking boldness as he sweeps the camera across the fields in the film's stirring battle scenes and intriguingly situates the action within the framework of an actual Elizabethan performance in the original Globe Theatre. Actor/director Kenneth Branagh's muddily impressive 1989 *Henry V* tones down the wartime jingoism of its earlier counterpart to offer a more sobering account of the price of conflict, but in the famous 'Saint Crispin's Day' oration the leonine fire of the Olivier performance still retains a charge that carries all before it.

A Rank/Two Cities Production
Producers Laurence Olivier and Filippo Del Giudice
Screenplay Alan Dent and Laurence Olivier, based on the play by William Shakespeare
Photography Robert Krasker
Editor Reginald Beck
Art Director Paul Sheriff
Music William Walton
Running time 137 mins *colour*

Cast
Laurence Olivier (King Henry V)
Robert Newton (Ancient Pistol)
Leslie Banks (Chorus)
Renee Asherson (Princess Katherine)
Esmond Knight (Fluellen)
Leo Genn (Constable of France)

Down the mean streets
Film noir

A French term meaning 'dark film'; the antecedents of this cinema style can be discerned in a variety of sources including the German Expressionist films of the inter-war years (examples include *The Cabinet of Dr Caligari* (1919) (see p50), *Nosferatu* (1922) (see p151), *Metropolis* (1926) (see p142) and *M* (1931) (see p134)), the vein of poetic realism in the menacing, foggy, pre-war French dramas combining the talents of actor Jean Gabin, screen-writer Jacques Prévert and director Marcel Carné, as exemplified by *Quai Des Brumes* (1938) and *Le Jour Se Lève* (1939) (see p120) and in the hardboiled detective fiction of writers Dashiell Hammett and Raymond Chandler, both of whom were also to work intermittently as screen-writers.

Derived from the term *roman noir* ('dark novel') which described English gothic fiction of the 19th century, *film noir* has come to describe the style in a disparate series of Hollywood films from the 1940s and early 1950s that reflected the gloomy, post-war mood of the nation in their explorations of corruption and betrayal with characters that stoically faced an inescapable, doom-laden fate seen to reflect the worry and confusion of those now living in the nuclear age.

Set in the rain-drenched, shadow-enshrouded mean streets of an urban jungle, the films used expressive contrasts of light and shade, distorted perspectives and new levels of screen violence to achieve their atmospheric results. The earliest signs of the emergent style can probably be seen in John Huston's adaptation of Hammett's *The Maltese Falcon* (1941) (see p137) whilst the establishment of the *femme fatale*, often crucial to the unravelling of the plot or the reckless indiscretions of the once dependable hero, can be witnessed in the characters played by Gene Tierney in

Laura (1944) (see p126) and especially by Barbara Stanwyck in *Double Indemnity* (1944) (see p71). The most archetypal examples of the genre include Fritz Lang's *The Woman in The Window* (1944), Edgar J Ulmer's *Detour* (1945), Howard Hawks's *The Big Sleep* (1946) (see p34), Robert Siodmak's *The Killers* (1946), Jacques Tourneur's *Out of the Past* (UK: *Build My Gallows High*) (1947) and Jules Dassin's *Night and the City* (1950), which tend to make use of an intricate flashback structure to convey their narrative and often have plots predicated on the irresistible allure of a beautiful woman.

With time the brutality and pessimism darkened even further, the mood grew ever more nihilistic, and the films focused on the twisted psychology and neuroses of such characters as the mother-fixated gangster Cody Jarrett (played by James Cagney) in Raoul Walsh's *White Heat* (1949) (see p234), the psychotic screen-writer Dixon Steele (Humphrey Bogart) in Nicholas Ray's *In A Lonely Place* (1950) and the thug-like sadist of Mickey Spillane's private eye Mike Hammer in Robert Aldrich's *Kiss Me Deadly* (1955) (almost the last example of its kind).

A combination of factors from the onset of the cosy patriarchy of the Eisenhower era to the cinema's experimentation with wide-screen and colour processes signalled an end to the development of this style of filmmaking, but there have been recent attempts to evoke the form and ambience of the films, most notably *Chinatown* (1974) (see p53), the steamy *Body Heat* (1981) and *Blood Simple* (1984), and it survives in the current fascination with the work of pulp novelist Jim Thompson that has, thus far, produced *The Kill-Off* (1989), *The Grifters* (1990) and *After Dark My Sweet* (1990).

White Heat *(1949) Directed by Raoul Walsh (James Cagney, Edmond O'Brien)*

The Big Sleep *(1946) Directed by Howard Hawks (Lauren Bacall, Humphrey Bogart)*

Rebel Without A Cause *(1955) Directed by Nicholas Ray (James Dean, Corey Allen)*

Some Like It Hot *(1959) Directed by Billy Wilder (Marilyn Monroe, Tony Curtis)*

High Noon

Fred Zinnemann, USA, 1952

Cold War western

Facing fear as the clock strikes twelve, a courageous man stands alone.

The story

Hadleyville, June 1865. The celebrations for retiring marshal Will Kane's marriage to Amy are interrupted by the news that outlaw Frank Miller has been pardoned and will be arriving on the noon train to seek vengeance on Kane. His sense of integrity commands him to stay despite Amy's assertion that she will leave with or without him but he subsequently discovers that no-one will fight alongside him. Frightened and alone, he prepares to face the gang of four as the train pulls into town. In a prolonged shoot-out he kills three of the men and Amy, who has been persuaded to remain by Kane's former mistress Helen, kills the other assailant. Kane disgustedly throws his marshal's badge into the dust and the newly-weds ride off together.

Comment

Loosely suggested by the John Cunningham short story 'The Tin Star' which had appeared in a 1947 edition of *Collier's* magazine, *High Noon* was developed over a number of years by screenwriter Carl Foreman and producer Stanley Kramer, with the lead role once announced for Kirk Douglas. Foreman had developed an interest in writing a western and in using the device of telling events in real time that had proved effective in the prize-fighting drama *The Set-Up* (1949). As he continued to develop the story, the Hollywood community came increasingly under the scrutiny of the anti-Communist House of Un-American

Activities Committee. Foreman himself would later be called an uncooperative witness and subsequently blacklisted from the industry and saw the events happening to him and the story of a town gripped by fear as paralleled in the western he wrote.

Director Fred Zinnemann was attracted to the material for the expression it gave to a common theme of his work: the individual who follows the dictates of conscience rather than a more self-serving agenda. He would return to this time and time again in films like *A Man For All Seasons* (1966) and *Julia* (1977).

A key film in the psychological maturing of the western genre during the 1950s, *High Noon* owed much of its eventual success not to the underlying political subtext but to the astringency of the direction, the use of the song 'Do Not Forsake Me Oh My Darlin'' and the presence of leathery genre icon Cooper as a courageous man riven with real fears. Hired for $60 000 and a percentage of the profits instead of his normal $275 000 fee, Cooper was rewarded with his second Best Actor Academy Award and a film that returned well over $3 million on an investment of approximately $750 000.

A Stanley Kramer production
Screenplay Carl Foreman, based on the story 'The Tin Star' by John W Cunningham
Photography Flod Crosby
Editor Elmo Williams
Art Director Rudolph Sternad
Music Dmitri Tiomkin
Running time 84 mins b/w

Cast

Gary Cooper (Will Kane)
Thomas Mitchell (Jonas Henderson)
Lloyd Bridges (Harvey Pell)
Katy Jurado (Helen Ramirez)
Grace Kelly (Amy Kane)
Otto Kruger (Percy Mettrick)

The Hunchback of Notre Dame

William Dieterle, USA, 1939

Beauty and the beast

Charles Laughton captures the spiritual beauty within the physical deformity of the Hunchback.

The story

Gypsy girl Esmeralda comes to Paris to intercede with the King on behalf of her people as the hunchbacked Notre Dame bellringer Quasimodo is crowned King of the Fools. An attractive dancer, she catches the eye of the Archdeacon Claude who dispatches Quasimodo to kidnap her. She is rescued by Proebus, the captain of the guard who is subsequently stabbed by the Archdeacon who tortures Esmeralda into confessing to his crime. She is sentenced to hang but saved by the intervention of the devoted Quasimodo, who offers her the Cathedral's sanctuary. Using all of his ingenuity and agility to protect her from the King's men and the crowd, he is killed, but Esmeralda lives and is reunited with her lover, the gypsy poet Gringoire.

Comment

Although filmed on many occasions, from *Esmeralda* (1906) to Anthony Hopkins's television version in 1982, Victor Hugo's novel received its most inventive and best recalled screen treatment in this lavish 1939 R-K-O production. In a concerted effort to build a more prestigious image for the studio, R-K-O had gone talent-hunting, signing, for instance, Orson Welles, and offering Charles Laughton a five-picture contract that brought him back to Hollywood for the first time since *Mutiny on the Bounty* (1935).

Filmed on a budget of $1 826 000, *The Hunchback* used $250 000 of that on a reproduction of the 15th-century square around Notre Dame Cathedral; it achieves a powerful sense of the squalor and grotesquerie of the medieval period through its imposing set design, tumultuous crowd scenes and tone of realism with which it undercuts the poignancy of the Beauty and the Beast love-story played out between the Hunchback and Esmeralda, a role that marked Maureen O'Hara's American début.

Barely recognizable under the five hours of make-up applied to create the pitiful deformity of the Hunchback's body, Charles Laughton gives a performance of heartbreaking gentleness and great physical dexterity as he scampers around the Notre Dame bell tower, pours boiling oil on the crowd as they attack, and swings Tarzan-like to Esmeralda's rescue. Forever troubled by his own lack of physical beauty, Laughton can only have invested the character with his personal torment; this, and the exhausting conditions under which the film were made, as well as his own emotions about the outbreak of war in Europe, contribute immensely to one of the finest pieces of acting ever captured on film. Astonishingly, he was not even nominated for a Best Actor Oscar in a year in which Mickey Rooney's performance in *Babes in Arms* was!

An R-K-O Production
Producer Pandro S Berman
Screenplay Sonya Levien and Bruno Frank, based on the novel by Victor Hugo
Photography Joseph August
Editors William Hamilton and Robert Wise
Art Director Van Nest Polglase
Music Alfred Newman
Running time 115 mins b/w

Cast
Charles Laughton (The Hunchback)
Sir Cedric Hardwicke (Frollo)
Thomas Mitchell (Clopin)
Maureen O'Hara (Esmeralda)
Edmond O'Brien (Gringoire)
Alan Marshal (Proebus)

In the Realm of the Senses
(Ai No Corrida)

Nagisa Oshima, France/Japan, 1976

Graphic sexual drama

This heightened study of an obsessive sexual relationship caused outrage over its explicit treatment of the subject.

The story

A servant girl and former prostitute, Sada, becomes obsessed with her employer Kichizo after seeing him make love to his wife. The obsession quickly becomes mutual, Kichizo makes her his mistress, and they run away together. While travelling around and living in hotels and geisha-houses, the pair indulge in constant sexual activity, interrupted only occasionally by more practical necessities. The couple play erotic games with knives and razors, prefiguring the eventual outcome of their obsessive relationship. Kichizo is physically unable to stand up to their passion, and ultimately consents to being strangled by Sada, in the hope of attaining a supreme sexual fulfilment. Sada severs her dead lover's penis, and is arrested several days afterwards as she wanders in a daze.

Comment

Oshima was prosecuted for obscenity in Japan over this film, and although found not guilty, did not succeed in overturning the strict obscenity laws of that country. The film, which is also known as *Empire of the Senses*, is a relentlessly explicit study of sexual obsession.

The story is based on an actual case, when a woman named Sada Abe strangled and castrated her lover with his consent, and was later arrested with his penis still in her possession. Most of the film consists of sexual acts between the central pair Kichizo and Sada, occasionally with other participants. The level of obsession in their coupling is such that not only do they largely ignore the other demands of life around them, but also bring anyone who comes into contact with them into their sexual activity.

Oshima chooses simply to present this, with little comment, analysis or justification. Sada moves from complacent servant to dominant partner, a role-reversal which goes against the grain of Japanese (and even Western) social expectations. His clinical, rather distanced observation of their act refuses the titillatory intention of pornography, but it was not only the Japanese censors who saw the distinction as a fine one.

It remains the benchmark for on-screen treatment of the sexual act, but it is ironic that the single most powerful and eloquent expression of Kichizo's absorption in Sada comes in one of the few scenes which is not of a sexual nature, when, temporarily parted from her, he walks down a street completely oblivious of a column of soldiers and a cheering crowd.

An Oshima Productions/Argos Films/Shibata Organization Production
Producer Anatole Dauman
Screenplay Nagisa Oshima
Photography Hideo Ito
Editor Keiichi Uraoka
Art Director Jusho Toda
Music Minoru Miki
Running Time 105 mins *colour*

Cast

Tatsuya Fuji (Kichizo)
Eiko Matsuda (Sada)
Aoi Nakajima (Toku)
Meika Seri (Maid Matsuko)
Taiji Tonoyama (Old Beggar)
Hiroko Fuji (Maid Tsune)

Intolerance

D W Griffith, USA, 1916

Multi-story epic

Railing against injustice through the ages, Griffith expands the horizons of silent cinema.

The story

Inspired by lines from Walt Whitman's *Leaves of Grass*, 'Out of the cradle endlessly rocking' and 'Endlessly rocks the cradle Uniter of Here and Hereafter', the film opens and closes with the image of a woman rocking a cradle that provides the link be-tween four increasingly interrelated stories illustrating man's inhumanity to man and the enduring emotion of intolerance: a modern couple's fight for justice as an innocent Irish Catholic boy is sentenced to the gallows, the Passion Play and Christ's crucifixion, 539BC when King Belshazzar is betrayed and Babylon falls to the invading Persian forces, and France in 1572 when Catholicism is responsible for the St Bartholomew's Day massacre of the Huguenots.

Comment

In the autumn of 1914 *The Birth of A Nation* (1915) (see p36) was being edited and D W Griffith began work on his next film, *The Mother and The Law*, a contemporary saga of social deprivation set against the backdrop of labour agitation, which he had more or less completed by the time his epochal Civil War story opened to widespread adulation. Spurred on by the favourable response to *Birth of A Nation*'s epic scope and keen to respond to the censorious charges of racism levelled against that work by eloquently asserting his right to free speech, he now proposed to expand his recently shot material into a new film that would be his most ambitious project to date. 'The purpose of the production,' he explained, 'is to trace a universal theme through various episodes of the race's history,' adding, 'not only beauty but thought is our goal, for the silent drama is peculiarly the birthplace of ideas.'

With an emphasis on editing as a ruling aesthetic principle that was to prove a central influence on the Soviet school of the 1920s, *Intolerance* pictured the mother of ages rocking the cradle of history as the linking footage between selected moments in time, each of which in some way manifested a struggle against oppression. Despite notable set-pieces (the Babylonian sets are amongst the largest ever constructed), *Intolerance* was not a financial success on its initial release and continues to divide critical opinion: for some, its formal compexity and thematic richness make the film an American masterpiece; others share the feelings of confused audiences of the time that Griffith's obtrusive cross-cutting does not adequately convey the film's meaning. Unfortunately, no prints of Griffith's original version have survived.

A D W Griffith Production
Producer D W Griffith
Screenplay D W Griffith
Photography G W Bitzer and Karl Brown
Editors James and Rose Smith
Art Director Frank 'Huck' Wortman
Running time 220 mins approx b/w

Cast
Lillian Gish (The Woman Who Rocks The Cradle)
Mae Marsh (The Dear One)
Miriam Cooper (The Friendless One)
Erich Von Stroheim (Pharisee)
Bessie Love (The Bride of Cana)
Constance Talmadge (The Mountain Girl)

Invasion of the Bodysnatchers

Don Siegel, USA, 1956

Science-fiction paranoia

A low-budget genre movie with no stars has proved to be an enduring examination of paranoia and dehumanization.

The story

Los Angeles. A dishevelled man tries desperately to convince the authorities that the earth has been invaded by pods which are able to take over the minds and bodies of human beings. The film tells his tale in flashback. He is a doctor in the small community of Santa Mira. A number of local people begin to act in an 'unreal' fashion. Fears are crystallized when he and Becky find a half-formed version of a friend in a strange pod. Their discoveries of the pods quickly escalate, and they realize Santa Mira's inhabitants are being taken over in their sleep. They attempt a desperate escape, but finally even Becky is taken over. Back in the present, his story is not believed until someone reports an accident involving a lorry filled with strange pods.

Comment

The opening and closing sequences which establish that Bennell's story is ultimately believed by the authorities were not approved by Siegel, who had no such wish to allow his viewers off the hook. Like screenwriter Daniel Mainwaring, he wanted to depict a society which was literally and irrevocably being swallowed up by pods.

Made in the wake of the McCarthy witch hunts and amid rampant Cold War paranoia, it is a grippingly convincing thriller. It does not rely on violence or gore to make its point, unlike the far less successful 1978 remake by Philip Kaufman, in which Siegel played a cameo role. Instead, it presents an insidiously chilling vision of a society slowly being transformed by an apparently indestructible threat, against which the rebellious human is all but powerless. Bennell's refusal to succumb to the blandishments of conformity grows increasingly desperate as all around him fall, and the viewer can only share his helplessness.

The moment when he kisses Becky, the young widow with whom he has formed a relationship, and realizes that she, too, has gone over to the pods, is hugely poignant. It precipitates the real climax of the film, a memorable sequence in which Bennell, now completely isolated, flees from his love and the rest of the pod-people, and finds himself in a nightmarish stream of cars, none of which will stop to hear his dreadful warning.

Kevin McCarthy judges his performance beautifully, and resists the temptation to over-react, an essential ingredient in the success of a film which in essence offers everyday normality as the source of sublime horror. It is not really surprising that producer Walter Wanger got cold feet and insisted upon the conciliatory preface and coda.

An Allied Artists Picture
Producer Walter Wanger
Screenplay Daniel Mainwaring, based on a story by Jack Finney
Photography Ellsworth Fredericks
Editor Robert S Eisen
Art Director Ted Haworth
Music Carmen Dragon
Running time 80 mins b/w

Cast
Kevin McCarthy (Dr Miles Bennell)
Dana Wynter (Becky Driscoll)
Larry Gates (Dr Danny Kauffman)
King Donovan (Jack)
Carolyn Jones (Theodora)
Jean Willes (Sally)
Ralph Dumke (Nick)

It Happened One Night

Frank Capra, USA, 1934

Screwball comedy

A cross-country journey from Miami to New York becomes a bench-mark in screen comedy.

The story

Absconding from Florida to New York on a long-distance bus, runaway heiress Ellie Andrews meets recently dismissed journalist Peter Warne. Affection replaces the initial antipathy between them as they outwit pursuing policemen, hitch-hike and pose as man and wife. A blanket draped between their beds, dubbed 'The Walls of Jericho', protects Elle's blushes. When Warne attempts to sell her story as a means of financing their marriage, his actions are misconstrued as those of yet another fortune-hunter. On the day of her wedding to another man, Ellie's father convinces her of Warne's sincerity and they elope, ensuring that the Walls of Jericho finally tumble.

Comment

Sweeping the board at the 1935 Oscar ceremony, *It Happened One Night* helped initiate the genre of screwball comedy and transformed Columbia from a poverty-row studio to a major Hollywood concern.

Myrna Loy and Robert Montgomery were among the first couples that Columbia had attempted to borrow for the leading roles but M-G-M boss Louis B Mayer refused to lend either of the stars. Miriam Hopkins, Margaret Sullavan and Constance Bennett are also known to have turned down the female lead and Paramount were equally unwilling to part with the services of Fredric March.

Director Capra's luck appeared to change when Mayer decided to punish Clark Gable for his recent salary and script demands and

considered a second-rate Columbia venture would soon bring him into line. Claudette Colbert was approached to be his co-star. Capra had directed her screen début in *For The Love of Mike* (1927) but sentimentality did not cloud her negotiating skills. She demanded $50 000 for four weeks' work that had to be completed in time for her Christmas vacation. Capra accepted the challenge and filming was completed in three weeks, six days and four hours.

The relaxed, improvisational approach to the material is reflected in the ease of the performances. Gable's good-natured, rugged masculinty shines through for really the first time on screen and is contrasted expertly with Colbert's aloof but not inaccessible beauty.

The clash of opposing personalities, the comic potential in the rich removed from the reassurance of their familiar trappings, the use of an extensive supporting cast and a feel for breakneck pacing would all become hallmarks of screwball comedy as it developed further through films like *Twentieth Century* (1934) and *Bringing Up Baby* (1938) (see p49).

A Columbia Picture
Producer Frank Capra
Screenplay Robert Riskin, based on the story
Night Bus by Samuel Hopkins Adams
Photography Joseph Walker
Editor Gene Havlick
Art Director Stephen Gooson
Music Louis Silvers
Running time 105 mins b/w

Cast
Claudette Colbert (Ellie Andrews)
Clark Gable (Peter Warne)
Roscoe Karns (Oscar Shapeley)
Henry Wadsworth (Drunk Boy)
Claire MacDowell (Mother)
Walter Connolly (Alexander Andrews)
Jameson Thomas (King Westley)

It's a Wonderful Life

Frank Capra, USA, 1946

Smalltown celebration

An angel called Clarence shows a man the true worth of his life.

The story

George Bailey's life of self-sacrifice and devotion to the family's building and loan company has left him embittered. When Uncle Billy lets the company's bankroll fall into the hands of unscrupulous banker Dr Potter one Christmas, he is faced with ruin and jail. Deep in despair, he contemplates suicide but an angel, Clarence, appears to show him how the town would have been had he never lived: called Pottersville, it is a vision of hell with his mother a lonely widow, his brother dead in a childhood accident and his wife a spinster librarian. Realizing the wonderful life and community he has created he is joyously reunited with his family and all the well-wishers who have rallied to make good his debts.

Comment

An irresistibly heart-warming paean to the common man and decency's right to triumph, *It's A Wonderful Life* may confirm some commentators' disdain for Capra's sentimentality and reactionary view of apple-pie America, but such carping is a small matter when discussing the near-perfect creation of a cinematic original that rivals the richness of Dickens's *A Christmas Carol*. Philip Von Doren Stern's short story 'The Greatest Gift' had been mailed to his friends as a Christmas card and received such a favourable response that it was subsequently published. R-K-O purchased the rights hoping to turn the story into a film for Cary Grant before Capra came to the property. Stewart, his first choice for the leading role, had also just returned from service and was keen to immerse himself in a

character who allowed him to explore the darker side of his all-American charm as Bailey resentfully sacrifices all his personal dreams and dearest wishes to make life better for those around him. Jean Arthur, Stewart's co-star in such previous Capra ventures as *You Can't Take It With You* (1938) and *Mr Smith Goes to Washington* (1939), had been the original choice to play his wife.

Making excellent use of a repertory company of supporting actors, emphasizing the emotional turmoil of Stewart's character through an effective deployment of close-ups and offering numerous set-pieces from Stewart and Reed's Charleston into a swimming pool to the joyous final moments, the film is a masterpiece of narrative exposition and emotion.

Nominated for five Oscars but unrewarded by the Academy, the film was also a commercial failure on its initial release, winding up some \$525 000 in the red. Time and audience affection have transformed it into one of the best-loved films of all time and a television Yuletide perennial.

A Liberty Films Production
Producer Frank Capra
Screenplay Frances Goodrich, Albert Hackett and Frank Capra, based on the short story 'The Greatest Gift' by Philip Von Doren Stern, with uncredited contributions by Michael Wilson, Clifford Odets and Jo Swerling
Photography Joseph Walker and Joseph Biroc
Editor William Hornbeck
Art Director Jack Okey
Music Dimitri Tiomkin
Running time 129 mins b/w

Cast

James Stewart (George Bailey)
Donna Reed (Mary Hatch)
Lionel Barrymore (Dr Potter)
Thomas Mitchel (Uncle Billy)
Henry Travers (Clarence)
Beulah Bondi (Mrs Bailey)

Jaws

Steven Spielberg, USA, 1975

High-seas horrors

Spielberg shows himself the master manipulator of audience fears with the hunt for a Great White Shark.

The story

As Amity Island becomes subject to shark attacks, the tourist-minded mayor evades the issue and tries to avoid adverse publicity. When a shark is captured the danger is assumed to have passed. However, expert Matt Hooper concludes that they should be looking for a Great White and, after a further attack, police chief Brody agrees with him. At a town meeting, old salt Quint offers to capture the shark for a fair price. Accompanied by Brody and Hooper he sets sail and they eventually spot the 28-foot beast. It pulls them out to sea and rounds on them, capsizing the boat and consuming Quint. With Hooper temporarily out of action, a desperate Brody fills the shark's mouth with an air tank and then blows it to smithereens.

Comment

A Hitchcock-like exploitation of man's primal fears, coupled with echoes of Steven Spielberg's own *Duel* (1971), Nixon's handling of Watergate and Ibsen's *An Enemy of the People*, *Jaws* was the film that established Spielberg as the man with the Midas touch, and was also the first of the mega-hits that would spawn a small industry of merchandizing and sequels.

A runaway bestseller, the project was offered to Spielberg after his feature début *The Sugarland Express* (1974). Describing his concept of the film as 'an experiment in terror' and 'a great episode of *Sea Hunt* mixed in with a little *Moby Dick*', he worked with author Howard Sackler, filmmaker John Milius and comedy-writer Carl Gottlieb on various drafts of the script before considering his casting options. Robert Shaw replaced Sterling Hayden as Quint, Spielberg held out for Roy Scheider over the studio's choice of Charlton Heston for the police chief, and chose Richard Dreyfuss (increasingly his cinematic alter ego) as ichthyologist Hopper after considering both Timothy Bottoms and Jeff Bridges. The biggest problem however was in making the mechanical shark, dubbed 'Bruce', convincing. Problems in this area resulted in the film's original schedule of 52 days stretching to 155 and the budget doubling. The results however were sensational and the film soon captured the title of the most financially successful ever made, won Oscars for Editing, Sound and the insistent throb of John Williams's Musical Score and earned extravagant praise like Pauline Kael's comment that 'there are parts of *Jaws* that suggest what Eisenstein might have done if he hadn't intellectualized himself out of reach'. Overlooked by the Academy, Spielberg has had nothing to do with the three sequels, all of decreasing merit.

A Universal Production
Producers Richard D Zanuck and David Brown
Screenplay Peter Benchley and Carl Gottlieb, based on the novel by Peter Benchley, with uncredited contributions by Howard Sackler and John Milius
Photography Bill Butler
Editor Verna Fields
Art Director Joseph Alves Jnr
Music John Williams
Running time 124 mins *colour*

Cast
Roy Scheider (Police Chief Martin Brody)
Robert Shaw (Captain Quint)
Richard Dreyfuss (Matt Hooper)
Lorraine Gary (Ellen Brody)
Murray Hamilton (Mayor Larry Vaughn)
Carl Gottlieb (Meadows)

The Jazz Singer

Alan Crosland, USA, 1927

The first talkie

Torn between family tradition and the call of the footlights, a cantor's son proves that the movies can talk.

The story

Young Jakie Rabinowitz runs away from home when his cantor father beats him for entertaining in a bar when he should have been attending synagogue. Changing his name to Jack Robin, he becomes a popular entertainer, forever guilt-ridden about his profession. Rising to success on Broadway, he is reunited with his mother but an unrelenting father declares his jazz music sacrilegious and rejects him once more. When his father falls seriously ill, he is torn between his big chance in the theatre or returning home. His mother is convinced that his talent belongs on a stage but he honours his dying father by singing the Kol Nidre at the synagogue. Later, a triumph in the show, he salutes his mother by singing 'Mammy' to her.

Comment

Although silent films were usually accompanied by at least a piano and often a house band playing specially composed music, the first synchronized sound system to come into general use was the recorded disc apparatus developed by the Vitaphone company for Warner Brothers in the mid-1920s. The John Barrymore swashbuckler *Don Juan*, also directed by Alan Crosland, which premièred in August 1926, was the first to benefit from the new technology (but as yet without synchronized speech). A number of test shorts designed to show off the movies' new toy were soon on show, but the initial feature with synchronized music and dialogue did not appear until October 1927 when Al Jolson's performance in *The Jazz Singer* created a box-office sensation and almost overnight ensured the new technology would be here to stay.

Jolson was the original inspiration for the basic story. George Jessel, successful in the role on Broadway, was initially cast in the film before being replaced by Jolson to whom audiences had responded more favourably in test shorts although such vaudevillians as Eddie Cantor and Harry Richman were also said to have been offered the part. It was therefore Jolson's stage catchphrase 'Wait a minute, wait a minute, you ain't heard nothin' yet' that was to be the first natural dialogue uttered on screen and his vibrant rendition of 'Mammy' which was to transcend the creakingly melodramatic material and remain irrevocably imprinted on the public imagination. The black-faced star's impact was to prove more substantial than that of the Vitaphone equipment which enabled him to burst into song in the first place – a year later it was gone, and Western Electric's sound-on-film system established as the new standard.

A Warner Brothers Production
Screenplay Al Cohn, based on the play by Samson Raphaelson
Photography Hal Mohr
Editor Harold McCord
Musical Director Louis (Lou) Silvers
Running time 89 mins b/w

Cast

Al Jolson (Jakie Rabinowitz/Jack Robin)
May McAvoy (Mary Dale)
Warner Oland (Cantor Rabinowitz)
Eugenie Besserer (Sara Rabinowitz)
Bobby Gordon (Jakie, aged 13)
Otto Lederer (Moisha Yudelson)
Myrna Loy (Chorus Girl)

' . . . in one word, Emotion'
The Nouvelle Vague

Allegedly coined by François Giroud, the term was given to the 'New Wave' of young French film directors who came to the fore in the late 1950s and 1960s. The nouvelle vague was a group of individual film enthusiasts whose critical writings in the journal *Cahiers Du Cinéma* championed an auteurist view of filmmaking in which the director is recognized as the sole auteur or author of a film, imposing his or her personal sensibility and artistic vision on every aspect of the production. The individuals involved such as François Truffaut, Claude Chabrol and Jean-Luc Godard proposed a cinema that discarded many of the fustian notions that they perceived to be responsible for the stultifying state of the French industry at the time. Eventually they put their ideas into practice behind a camera. Chabrol's *Bitter Reunion (Le Beau Serge)* (1958) is considered to be the first authentic expression of the 'New Wave', and over the next few years Truffaut directed *The 400 Blows (Les Quatre Cent Coups*, 1959), Godard made *Breathless (A Bout De Souffle*, 1959) (see p43) from Truffaut's idea and Alain Resnais created *Hiroshima, Mon Amour* (1959).

Revelling in the freedoms afforded by lightweight, hand-held cameras, they made extensive use of natural locations. Combining this with innovative story-lines, elliptical editing and unconventional use of sound, they created an alternative, more loosely structured cinema that placed less emphasis on smoothly rounded and resolved linear narratives. Thus the manner of presentation and the recognition of the artifice in cinematic storytelling became as important a part of the cinema experience as the emotions of the story itself and the philosophy was memorably vocalized by Sam Fuller in Godard's *Pierrot-Le-Fou* (1965) when he declares, 'The film is like a battleground, love,

hate, action, violence, death . . . in one word, Emotion.' Notable titles from the early flourishing of the nouvelle vague include Truffaut's *Jules et Jim (Jules and Jim)* (1961) (see p121), Resnais's *Last Year at Marienbad (L'Année Dernière A Marienbad)* (1961) and Godard's *It's My Life (Vivre Sa Vie)* (1962). The influence on all filmmaking of the past 30 years has been incalculable and can be glimpsed most readily in America though such films as *Bonnie and Clyde* (1967) (see p41) and *Easy Rider* (1969) (see p75). The pioneering individuals in the movement each chose radically different paths in their subsequent careers, Chabrol gaining renown for his ability to use a murder or act of violence as a mirror to observe bourgeois mores in films like *The Butcher (Le Boucher)* (1969) (see p42). Truffaut proved the most commercially successful of all the directors, revealing effortless charm and artistry in his approach to all genres, evoking the pain and pleasure of love through the series of films featuring his cinematic alter ego Antoine Doinel (played by Jean-Pierre Léaud) and delightfully capturing the pressures of the filmmaking process in the fictionalized *Day for Night (La Nuit Américaine)* (1973) (see p63).

Godard remained the most radical, politically and aesthetically, as he has striven, with variable success, to dismantle every individual element of the conventional dramatic and technical approach to filmmaking in a bid to revolutionize the medium and comment on the process of what is taking place. His most recent features include the cheekily entitled *Nouvelle Vague* (1990) starring Alain Delon. Clearly the term as a generic expression for the totality of these directors' work holds little value and perhaps as Chabrol once philosophically remarked, 'There is no new wave, only the sea.'

__Breathless__ (1959) Directed by Jean-Luc Godard (Jean-Paul Belmondo, Jean Seberg)

__Jules et Jim__ (1961) Directed by François Truffaut (Oskar Werner, Jeanne Moreau)

Aguirre, Wrath of God *(1972) Directed by Werner Herzog (Klaus Kinski)*

The Tin Drum *(1979) Directed by Volker Schlöndorff (David Bennent)*

Jean De Florette

Claude Berri, France, 1986

Deceit in rural France

A lavishly beautiful period drama which capitalizes on the stunning landscape of Provence.

The story

Provence, the 1920s. Ugolin returns to his native village with an elaborate scheme to grow carnations on his uncle César's farm, which he will inherit. They need the spring water from an adjoining property, but in the course of an argument, its owner, Pique-Bouffigue, is fatally injured by César. Ugolin and César hide the spring, but their plans are foiled when Cadoret, known as Jean De Florette, gives up his city job to inherit the farm. Ugolin pretends to befriend him, and convinces him the spring marked on his map is far distant. As summer drought takes it toll, Jean grows increasingly desperate, and is eventually killed by dynamite in an attempt to open a well and stave off financial ruin. As the stricken Cadoret family leave, his daughter Manon happens upon Ugolin and César unblocking the spring. The story is taken up in the sequel, *Manon des Sources.*

Comment

This beautifully filmed story about a French peasant society poised on the edge of inevitable historical dissolution struck a resonant chord not only in France, where it was a massive success, but also on the international market. Based on a novel by Marcel Pagnol (which had in turn grown out of a film written by Pagnol in the early 1950s), *Jean De Florette* is the first of a two-part account of the battle for inheritance, legal and illegal, of the vital, life-giving spring which irrigates the farmland.

It is a gripping story of greed, deceit and betrayal (conceived by Pagnol as a transposition of Greek myth to Provence), brilliantly acted by the leading players. Depardieu is especially compelling as Jean De Florette, the naive city-raised newcomer equipped for farming only by his books, and tragically outwitted by the venal but equally doomed peasants. Jean De Florette has one triumph over Ugolin and César, however, in that he has an heir to the property denied to both these childless men. Inheritance is one of the central strands which binds the peasant society together, and it sows the seeds of Jean's eventual vindication. The viewer must turn to the second film, *Manon des Sources* (1986), to see how that issue is resolved.

Much of the film's unexpectedly wide appeal, however, undoubtedly comes from the landscape of Provence itself, seductively shot by Bruno Nuttyen with a sensuous richness of colour and detail.

A Ren Productions/Films A2/RAI 2/DD Productions Production
Producer Pierre Grunstein
Screenplay Claude Berri and Gérard Brach, based on the novel by Marcel Pagnol
Photography Bruno Nuytten
Editors Arlette Langmann, Hervé de Luze and Noelle Boisson
Art Director Bernard Vezat
Music Jean Claude Petit
Running time 121 mins *colour*

Cast
Yves Montand (César Soubeyran)
Gérard Depardieu (Jean De Florette)
Daniel Auteuil (Ugolin Soubeyran)
Elisabeth Depardieu (Aimée Cadoret)
Ernestine Mazurowna (Manon Cadoret)
Marcel Champel (Pique-Bouffigue)

Le Jour Se Lève
(Daybreak)

Marcel Carné, France, 1939

French fatalism

The mood of pre-war France is captured in one man's inescapable destiny.

The story

The sounds of an argument emerge from a tenement block, a shot rings out and a man staggers and falls down dead. The police arrive but François, instead of surrendering, barricades himself into the flat and reflects on the circumstances that have led to this moment. A worker in a steel factory, he fell in love with flower-seller Françoise but grew jealous of her interest in dog-trainer Monsieur Valentin. When Valentin's partner Clara left him she came to François and they decided to live together. As more police arrive he recalls that it was Françoise who became the object of rivalry between him and Valentin and led to their argument. He uses the remaining bullet to kill himself as day breaks.

Comment

A key moment in that strand of 1930s' French cinema commonly termed 'poetic realism', *Le Jour Se Lève* marks a peak in the fruitful collaboration between director Marcel Carné and frequent screen-writer Jacques Prévert. Often considered in tandem with its companion piece *Quai Des Brumes (Port of Shadows)* (1938), the two Carné/Prévert classics evince a world-weariness that struck a deep chord with the French public and was very much a part of the national psyche as events tumbled towards the Fall of 1940.

The world suggested by the term 'poetic realism' is, in fact, anything but realist; *Le*

Jour Se Lève may take place amidst the grime of shadowy tenement blocks, but Carné's visuals are not so much an on-screen outpouring of social conscience as the outward expression of the protagonist's resignation to an inescapable destiny. The film's circular structure underlines the compelling mood of fatalism, beginning as a shot rings out and the murderer barricades himself in an attic, his only future to spend the night pondering his deeds before a second shot signals the breaking of dawn. Jean Gabin's performance as the doomed killer epitomizes his rough magnetism, allowing him to reprise the proletarian antihero type so evocatively paraded in Julien Duvivier's *Pépé Le Moko* (1936), while Prévert's dialogue – at times criticized for sentimentalizing the working-class – translates the banalities of the street into emotive shards of tough-guy lyricism. The overpowering melancholy of the final result is a tribute to the chemistry of the various creative participants, a blend whose delicately poised aura of sadness is completely absent in *The Long Night* (1947), the disastrous Anatole Litvak remake with Henry Fonda.

A Vog/Sigma Production
Screenplay Jacques Prévert and Jacques Viot
Photography Curt Courant, Philippe Agostini and Andre Bac
Editor Rene Le Henaff
Art Director Alexandre Trauner
Music Maurice Jaubert
Running time 85 mins b/w

Cast
Jean Gabin (François)
Arletty (Clara)
Jules Berry (Valentin)
Jacquelin Laurent (Françoise)
Bernard Blier (Gaston)
Jacques Baumer (Police Officer)

Jules et Jim

François Truffaut, France, 1961

Ménage-à-trois

Cinematic style and emotional resonance combine in a timeless ménage-à-trois.

The story

In Paris Jules and Jim become the best of friends until they are entranced by the mercurial Catherine. Eventually, Catherine marries Jules and they settle in Germany. World War I finds the friends on opposite sides of the conflagration, but afterwards Jim pays a visit to the seemingly contented family. Jules subsequently reveals that he is unable to retain the happiness or affection of Catherine and encourages Jim to sleep with her. Jim later returns to Paris and his girlfriend. Years later, Jules and Catherine settle in Paris. However, Jim realizes that their old gaiety cannot be recaptured and one day the ever-volatile Catherine drives them both to a watery grave in the Seine leaving Jules to grieve alone.

Comment

Jules et Jim remains for many viewers the most affectionately remembered film of the flowering of the French Nouvelle Vague. Based on a little-known autobiographical novel published in 1955 by Henri-Pierre Roche (at the age of 75), which immediately attracted the attention of the then film critic François Truffaut, this vital, mature and cinematically inventive chronicle of an ever-shifting *ménage à trois* across the decades from the Belle Époque to the depression-hit thirties is the most exquisite demonstration of the way in which its late director, out of all the post-*Cahiers du Cinéma* generation, carried the torch for the particularly Gallic lyricism which fired the earlier work of Jean Renoir and Jean Vigo.

Surprisingly, Truffaut's film retains its emotional resonance while riskily flaunting a plethora of cinematic devices – freeze frames, jump cuts, iris shots, stock footage etc – but the various effects provide an appropriate stylistic framework for the exuberance of the part-comic, part-tragic narrative. Although the complex relationship between Jeanne Moreau's volatile Catherine and her respective suitors, Jules and Jim, swerves unpredictably from one configuration to another, Moreau's entrancing central performance lends the swirling patterns of frustration and fulfilment both coherence and conviction. As all things to all men, her bewitching capriciousness still registers much more vividly than the best efforts of Margot Kidder in Paul Mazursky's spottily arresting American homage/remake *Willie & Phil* (1980). Truffaut himself returned to the work of Henri-Pierre Roche with *Anne and Muriel (Les Deux Anglaises Et Le Continent)* (1971), a less successful exploration of another triangular relationship.

A Les Films Du Carrosse/SEDIF Production
Producer François Truffaut
Screenplay François Truffaut and Jean Grualt, based on the novel by Henri-Pierre Roche
Photography Raoul Coutard
Editor Claudine Bouche
Music Georges Delerue
Running time 105 mins b/w

Cast
Jeanne Moreau (Catherine)
Oskar Werner (Jules)
Henri Serre (Jim)
Vanna Urbino (Gilberte)
Boris Bassiak (Albert)
Sabine Haudepin (Sabine)

Kind Hearts and Coronets

Robert Hamer, UK, 1949

Ealing comedy

British sangfroid carries off a black comedy of multiple homicide.

The story

On the eve of his execution, Louis Mazzini's memoirs reveal his unorthodox rise to the position of 10th Duke of Chalfont. Denied his birthright by the D'Ascoynes' disapproval of his mother's marriage, he exacts revenge by an ingenious pruning of the family tree that removes those who stand between him and the dukedom. Torn between the passionate Sibella and the more well-bred D'Ascoyne widow Edith, he marries the latter but is charged with murder on his accession to the title. Ironically it is for one he did not commit – Sibella's husband. Blackmailed into promising Edith's demise for Sibella's ability to produce an exonerating suicide note, he wins a reprieve, even though his incriminating memoirs remain within the prison.

Comment

Kind Hearts and Coronets remains perhaps the most remarkable offering to emerge from Ealing Films, but it is also one of the company's least typical productions. The Ealing phenomenon was largely the creation of studio head Michael Balcon, who must take credit for developing its pool of bright young cinematic talents and encouraging them to contribute to each other's work. With a gallery of variously distinctive character actors (among them Alec Guinness and Alistair Sim) from which to draw, this typically British form of celluloid group enterprise gave rise to an identifiable house style in the perennially popular run of Ealing comedies. Delighting in a sense of English quaintness, the world in films like Charles Crichton's *The Lavender Hill Mob* (1951) and Henry Cornelius's *Passport to Pimlico* (1948) is one peopled by eccentrics and driven by whimsical passions, yet in the incisive work by the director Alexander Mackendrick (*Whisky Galore*, 1948; *The Man In the White Suit*, 1951 etc) and in Hamer's elegant masterpiece *Kind Hearts and Coronets* we see the exceptions to such uniform cheeriness.

Hamer expressed his intention as, 'Firstly, that of making a film not noticeably similar to any previously made in the English language. Secondly, that of using this English language, which I love, in a more varied and interesting way. Thirdly, that of making a picture which paid no regard whatever to established, although not practised, moral conventions.' Remarkably, his story of dispossessed haberdasher Dennis Price who murders his way through the aristocratic d'Ascoyne family was a success on all three counts. Its Wildean verbal wit and poised visual humour achieved a rare piquancy and Guinness's performance as all eight upper-class victims offered an exercise in comic observation to savour.

An Ealing Studios Production
Producer Michael Balcon
Screenplay Robert Hamer and John Dighton, based on the novel *Israel Rank* by Roy Harniman
Photography Douglas Slocombe
Editor Peter Tanner
Art Director William Kellner
Music Wolfgang Amadeus Mozart
Running time 106 mins b/w

Cast

Dennis Price (Louis Mazzini)
Valerie Hobson (Edith)
Alec Guinness (Duke Ethelred/Banker/Reverend Henry/General Rufus/Admiral/Young D'Ascoyne/Young Henry/Lady Agatha)
Joan Greenwood (Sibella)
Audrey Fildes (Mamm)
Miles Malleson (Hangman)

King Kong

Ernest B Schoedsack and Merian C Cooper, USA, 1933

Monster sensation

A jungle sensation and an urban woman illuminate the beauty and the beast myth.

The story

Film producer and showman Carl Denham hires Ann Darrow as the star of his latest mysterious production to be shot on the remote tropical Skull Island. On the location, Ann is abducted by natives as a sacrifical offering for their god Kong. He proves to be a gargantuan ape who carries her off into the jungle. Many of Denham's crew are lost in the struggle to win her back but they manage to subdue the beast with the aid of a gas bomb and return to New York where they place him on public exhibition. However, he escapes and runs amok, seizing his beloved Ann from the window of a skyscraper. The pursuit of the beast ends at the top of the Empire State Building where a fleet of fighter planes gun him down.

Comment

Billed on its initial release as 'The Eighth Wonder of the World', *King Kong* continues to hold an impressive sway over the moviegoing imagination. For all its technical brilliance, the film's enduring fascination lies in the richness of the myth it has indelibly etched on the movie screen. The giant ape Kong is both sympathetic tragic figure and troubling psychological fantasy. Certainly he is savage nature brutally tamed by man's murderous technology but, as showman Denham finally remarks, 'It wasn't the airplanes, it was Beauty killed the Beast.' The famous image of Kong's huge fingers unpeeling heroine Fay Wray's clothing points to the statuesque primate as the outpouring of all our socially repressed sexual and violent urges, a release which of course must be stemmed when the ape is finally destroyed by the forces of the big city.

Hardly any of these notions would have been considered were not the on-screen execution of this tall tale so utterly credible. Recent advances in back-projection and matte work allowed effects maestro Willis O'Brien to integrate the actors and studio settings with the 18-inch stop motion model of the fierce ape, though full scale versions of Kong's face and hands were required for close-up sequences that still retain their power to disturb.

Ernest B Shoedsack hastily directed a dismal, comedic sequel *Son of Kong* (1933) and a virtual reprise in *Mighty Joe Young* (1949) which was not without its moments. Highly unofficial Japanese versions include *King Kong Vs. Godzilla* (1963) and *King Kong Escapes* (1968), while we have maverick producer Dino De Laurentiis to thank for the disappointing 1976 big-budget remake *King Kong* and a further rather desperate follow-up in *King Kong Lives* (1986).

An R-K-O Radio Pictures Production
Producers Ernest B Schoedsack and Merian C Cooper
Screenplay James Creelman and Ruth Rose, based on a story by Merian C Cooper and Edgar Wallace
Photography Edward Lindon, Vernon Walker and J O Taylor
Editor Ted Cheesman
Art Directors Carroll Clark, Alfred Herman, Mario Larrinaga and Byron L Crabbe
Music Max Steiner
Special effects Willis O'Brien
Running time 99 mins b/w

Cast

Fay Wray (Ann Darrow)
Robert Armstrong (Carl Denham)
Frank Reicher (Englehorn)
Bruce Cabot (Driscoll)
Sam Hardy (Weston)
Noble Johnson (Native Chief)

The Last Picture Show

Peter Bogdanovich, USA, 1971

Rites of passage

The end of an era in a dusty Texas town is evocatively captured.

The story

1951. Anarene, Texas. Sonny Crawford begins an unlikely affair with Ruth Popper, the wife of the football coach, whilst his friend Duane continues to pursue the aloof Jacy who has set her sights on acceptance by the rich Bobby Sheen. Sonny learns of Sam the Lion's past romance with Jacy's mother Lois and is saddened by the older man's death. Frustrated by Jacy's behaviour, Duane leaves town and enlists for Korea. Jacy then toys with Sonny who is badly injured by a jealous Duane on his return. An attempt by Duane and Jacy to elope is intercepted by her parents and Duane spends his last night in town with Sonny at the final performance of the cinema. When the retarded Billy is killed it is Ruth that Sonny turns to in his grief.

Comment

Film journalist turned filmmaker Peter Bogdanovich had already displayed his skill as a director with the taut and unusual thriller *Targets* (1967), and then firmly established himself as one of American cinema's most promising young talents with this beautifully-judged and evocative account of the frustrations, aspirations and unfulfilled longings of the populace, both young and old, in a small, dusty, declining Texas town of the 1950s that is captured in elegiac monochrome images by cameraman Robert Surtees. Striking in its painterly sense of composition and its mature grasp of characterization, the film is almost unique in contemporary American cinema for its ability to distil the essence of an era and illuminate the hollow lives of individuals within a well-defined community. This is accomplished with a potent combination of accuracy, sympathy and unflinching emotion that is more in the manner of a filmmaker like Renoir or Satyajit Ray than the more broadly populist or less class-conscious statements generally given voice in American cinema. Equally surprising was the commercial success of Bogdanovich's film which earned over $13 million at the American box-office and eight Academy Award nominations, winning richly deserved Supporting Performance Oscars for both veterans Cloris Leachman and Ben Johnson, who had been persuaded to accept his role by the intervention of Bogdanovich's friend, director John Ford.

Texasville (1990), a sequel set many years later, reunited Bogdanovich with the original cast in a patchwork story of middle-age malaise and disillusionment set against the backdrop of their small town's centennial festivities, but failed to repeat either the critical approbation or public acceptance accorded the original.

A BBS/Last Picture Show Production
Producer Stephen J Friedman
Screenplay Larry McMurty and Peter Bogdanovich, based on the novel by McMurty
Photography Robert Surtees
Editor Donn Cambern
Art Director Walter Scott Herndon
Music Various 1950s recordings
Running time 118 mins b/w

Cast
Timothy Bottoms (Sonny Crawford)
Jeff Bridges (Duane Jackson)
Cybill Shepherd (Jacy Farrow)
Ben Johnson (Sam the Lion)
Cloris Leachman (Ruth Popper)
Ellen Burstyn (Lois Farrow)

Last Tango in Paris
(Ultimo Tango A Parigi)

Bernardo Bertolucci, Italy/France, 1972

Identity crisis

An excoriating exploration of sensuality and grief marks Bertolucci's succès de scandale.

The story

Paris. Paul and Jeanne meet when viewing an empty flat and make love. Afterwards, he returns to the hotel where his wife has recently killed herself and Jeanne meets her fiancé, filmmaker Tom. The next day Jeanne returns to the flat, Paul is there and they decide to pursue their sexual obsession without revealing any of the details of their lives. An increasingly degrading relationship results in which Jeanne is torn between humiliation and love. After using butter to sodomize her, Paul breaks the rules – telling her of his life, begging her to marry him and dragging her to a tango contest. The spell has been broken and she shoots him dead, already preparing a convincing story about an unknown assailant.

Comment

A milestone in the frank treatment of sexuality on screen, Bertolucci's *Last Tango in Paris* was an act of liberation for the entire medium. Its highly favourable box-office reception and prosecution under the Italian obscenity laws made it something of a *succès de scandale*, but nevertheless it did offer conclusive proof that most audiences (and many censors) were prepared to accept the most intimate discussion and depiction of physical relations outside the context of mere pornography. A towering, self-revelatory central performance by Marlon Brando undoubtedly helped. Arriving with the baggage of his own star image he is at times brutish, at times tragic, as he confronts the emptiness of his marriage and his wife's recent suicide. His presence raises film acting to a new peak of soulful credibility and results in yet another Best Actor Oscar nomination (one of two accorded the film along with Bertolucci's Best Director).

Unfortunately, however, Schneider's efforts are no match for him and although Bertolucci's script ostensibly puts the focus on her choice between carefree physicality in sexual possession by Brando or conventional courtship and marriage as recorded by incorrigible filmmaker boyfriend Jean-Pierre Leaud, we learn less about the anxieties of a young woman trying to preserve her sense of self than we do of the older man's self-deluding search for communion in the darkest recesses of sensuality. Still, even with its flaws, *Last Tango* burns with an emotional truthfulness, its unforgettable scenes like Brando's tearful collapse in front of his wife's corpse or the troubling moments of mutual depravity in which the couple indulge, representing for each and every viewer the kind of contemporary epiphany only too rare in filmic art.

A PEA Cinematograficia/Les Artistes Associes Production
Producer Alberto Grimaldi
Screenplay Bernardo Bertolucci, Franco Arcalli and Agnes Varda
Photography Vittorio Storaro
Editor Franco Arcalli
Art Director Fredinando Scarfiotti
Music Gato Barbieri
Running time 129 mins *colour*

Cast
Marlon Brando (Paul)
Maria Schneider (Jeanne)
Jean-Pierre Leaud (Tom)
Darling Legitimus (Concierge)
Catherine Sola (TV Script Girl)
Mauro Marchetti (TV Cameraman)

Laura

Otto Preminger, USA, 1944

Film noir

The face in the misty glow becomes the focus of an influential murder mystery.

The story

When an unidentifiable corpse is discovered in Laura Hunt's flat, detective Mark McPherson investigates her death. Waspish columnist Waldo Lydecker recalls how Laura became his jealously guarded protégée before falling for playboy Shelby Carpenter. Carpenter subsequently admits his philandering ways and involvement with model Diane Redfern. When Laura unexpectedly returns from holiday, Redfern is revealed as the murder victim; Carpenter had been present but in hiding when she was shot by an unknown hand. Laura is arrested as a ruse to draw out the real murderer. Lydecker is identified as the culprit, having mistakenly shot Redfern instead of Laura, and is slain by the police when he makes a second attempt on Laura's life.

Comment

An influential production in the development of film noir, *Laura*'s disputed authorship and chequered production history are now almost inconsequential to the cohesive style, ambience and taut suspense that emerge in the finished film. Developed by Otto Preminger from the Vera Caspary novel, the film was destined to become a Fox B-picture before studio head Darryl Zanuck intervened to give it A-level production values. The relatively untested Preminger was not permitted to direct the film and Walter Lang and Lewis Milestone had been approached for the task before Rouben Mamoulian was signed. Jennifer Jones and Hedy Lamarr both rejected the role of the alluring Laura before Gene Tierney accepted and Zanuck had to be wooed and won over to the casting of Clifton Webb as the waspish Waldo Lydecker (a character inspired by noted Algonquin Round Table wit Alexander Woolcott).

Filming eventually proceeded, but then Zanuck, dissatisfied with the results, decided to dispense with Mamoulian. Preminger was appointed in his place, thus allowing him to direct the film he had always wanted to make and he replaced cameraman Lucien Ballard with his own choice of Joseph La Shelle. Mamoulian was later to assert that his conception of the film is still the one that became public property although Preminger claims to have scrapped everything and started over again. Whichever is true, *Laura* established many of the tenets of film noir in its atmospheric, heavily-lit camerawork, use of flashbacks, haunting theme song by David Raskin and Johnny Mercer, and ability to examine an elusive central figure through the testimony and shifting perspectives of a host of vividly etched secondary characters. Nominated for five Academy Awards, it won a solitary Oscar for Best Cinematography.

A Twentieth Century-Fox Production
Producer Otto Preminger
Screenplay Jay Dratler, Samuel Hoffenstein, Betty Reinhardt, Ring Lardner Junior and Jerome Cady, based on the novel by Vera Caspary
Photography Joseph La Shelle
Editor Louis Loeffler
Art Directors Lyle Wheeler and Leland Fuller
Music David Raskin
Running time 88 mins b/w

Cast

Gene Tierney (Laura Hunt)
Dana Andrews (Mark McPherson)
Clifton Webb (Waldo Lydecker)
Vincent Price (Shelby Carpenter)
Judith Anderson (Ann Treadwell)
Dorothy Adams (Besie Clary)

Lawrence of Arabia

David Lean, UK, 1962

Mercurial adventurer

Lean's lavish desert adventure subverts the conventions of the epic genre.

The story

After his death, the mercurial T E Lawrence is recalled by colleagues and friends. As a young lieutenant in Cairo, he ventures into the desert to visit Prince Feisal and meets Sherif Ali who becomes his strongest ally. He creates unity and restores morale among the fractious Arab tribes by leading a small force to conquer the Turkish port of Aqaba. Supported by the British, he becomes a hero to the Arab forces; however the brutality he experiences at the hands of Turkish captors makes him doubt his invincibility. Persuaded to continue, he conquers Damascus and establishes an Arab Council but watches in dismay as its unity quickly crumbles and the wily politicians Allenby and Feisal settle matters to their satisfaction.

Comment

The 1989 restoration and reissue of *Lawrence of Arabia*, a remarkable project requiring the original cast to redub footage trimmed after the first screenings, fostered a re-evaluation of David Lean's latterday critical reputation that had suffered in the wake of the intense disappointments voiced over the increasingly elephantine construction and vacuous romanticism most acutely apparent in *Doctor Zhivago* (1965) and *Ryan's Daughter* (1970). An intelligent and stirring epic, it demonstrates his expansive pictorialism tempered by a resonant psychological insight into the complex motivations of enigmatic English soldier and scholar T E Lawrence.

Lawrence's life had attracted a variety of previous film projects involving such figures as Robert Donat and Dirk Bogarde. Lean's $15 million venture had attempted to secure the services of Marlon Brando and dallied with the notion of casting Albert Finney before settling on Peter O'Toole whose previous cinema experience amounted to a mere handful of supporting roles. His performance of riveting intensity holds the film together and is superbly serviced by the detailed, unpatronizing screenplay of Robert Bolt.

Lean puts the desert landscape to rich use as both battlefield for predictably well-drilled military encounters and as the site of Lawrence's ongoing crisis of identity; whilst the film may offer the kind of spectacle we have come to expect from such lavish epics, *Lawrence* literally turns that genre inside-out, with its underlying impulse a challenging interior odyssey. Nominated for ten Academy Awards, it won seven including Best Picture and Best Director and earned some $17 million on its initial American release.

A Horizon Pictures Production
Producer Sam Spiegel
Screenplay Robert Bolt
Photography Freddie A Young
Editor Anne V Coates
Art Director John Stoll
Music Maurice Jarre
Running time 222 mins (1989 Director's Fine Cut 216 mins) colour

Cast
Peter O'Toole (Lawrence)
Alec Guinness (Prince Feisal)
Anthony Quinn (Auda Abu Tayi)
Jack Hawkins (General Allenby)
Omar Sharif (Sherif Ali)
Jose Ferrer (Turkish Bey)

The Leopard
(Il Gattopardo)

Luchino Visconti, Italy/France/USA, 1963

Aristocratic epic

The inexorable decline of an aristocratic order is richly conveyed.

The story

Sicily, the 1860s. Garibaldi is acting to unite the disparate provinces into an Italian state. Prince Don Fabrizio of Salina belongs to the old order of nobility but acknowledges that he must accept this changing world. During a balmy summer at the family's country retreat, his nephew Tancredi falls in love with Angelica, the daughter of the mayor Don Calogero, a prosperous merchant and a member of the rising middle-class. The union will cross class barriers and greatly assist the family coffers but at a grand ball to herald Angelica's arrival in society, the Prince is overcome with a bitter nostalgia for the past. The execution of four traitors further enforces his position as one among the last of a dying breed.

Comment

Distinctively combining nostalgia for the elegance of the past with a Marxian determinist's approach to the inevitability of social change, *Il Gattopardo* (*The Leopard*) remains perhaps the quintessential film by Milan-born aristocrat and avowed communist sympathizer Luchino Visconti. The publication in 1958 of the original novel by fellow nobleman Prince Guiseppe Tomasi di Lampedusa provided Visconti with the perfect material, enabling him to return to the key historical moment of the Risorgimento he had already visited in *Senso* (1954). An arrangement with Twentieth Century-Fox provided him with the finance to underwrite his epic. The original choice for the role of the Prince was Russian actor Nicolai Cherkassov with Laurence Olivier or Marlon Brando as possible contenders. When none of these men were available, Fox provided a short list of Spencer Tracy, Anthony Quinn or Burt Lancaster as the names they would consider acceptable for the part. Initially, against his better judgment, Visconti chose Lancaster but their partnership was a fruitful one resulting in a superlative performance, and they would work together again on *The Conversation Piece* (*Gruppo Di Famiglia In Un Inferno*) (1974).

The spectacular ball sequence, which took 36 days to shoot and takes up the last third of the film, contains some of the director's finest moments, capturing a mood marked more by elegiac resignation than any note of celebratory optimism. As Visconti's camera lingers over the authentic ballgowns, exquisite furnishings and finery, we are seduced by the richness and fluidity of his work but more than a little inclined to doubt the conviction or rigour of his leftist analysis. However, these contradictory impulses are precisely what makes the best of his films so fascinating.

A Titanus/SNPC/SGC Production for Twentieth Century Fox
Producer Goffredo Lombardo
Screenplay Luchino Visconti and others, based on the novel by Guiseppe Di Lampedusa
Photography Giuseppe Rotunno
Editor Mario Serandrei
Art Director Mario Garbuglia
Music Nino Rota
Running time 205 mins *colour*

Cast

Burt Lancaster (Don Fabrizio)
Alain Delon (Tancredi)
Claudia Cardinale (Angelica Sedara)
Paolo Stoppa (Don Calogero Sedara)
Rina Morelli (Maria Stella)
Romolo Valii (Father Pirrone)

The best years of our lives?
Post-war movie history

Many of the Hollywood filmmakers who had experienced wartime service returned to civilian life with a maturer edge to their talent. Thus, William Wyler reflected the problems of returning servicemen in *The Best Years of Our Lives* (1946) (see p32) and Frank Capra added darker resonances to his fanfare for the common man in *It's a Wonderful Life* (1946) (see p113).

The genres that flourished in American cinema after the war such as film noir and science-fiction seemed to reflect the starker mood of a country troubled by the nuclear age and virulently reflected the paranoia of the Cold War era, imaginatively so in a film like *Invasion of the Bodysnatchers* (1956) (see p111). The western as well, particularly in the collaborations between James Stewart and director Anthony Mann and in productions like *High Noon* (1952) (see p107) and *The Searchers* (1956) (see p189), chose to offer more psychologically complex explorations of the narrow shadings dividing good and evil. Ironically, the colourful escapism of the musical reached new heights of artistic expression in the productions of the Arthur Freed unit at M-G-M and such Gene Kelly works as *On The Town* (1949) (see p153) which took the musical on to natural locations, and the Oscar-winner *An American in Paris* (1951) (see p11) which broadened the appeal of ballet.

Many of the major figures in British cinema sustained the creative impetus that the war years had given to their careers and The Archers, formed by Michael Powell and Emeric Pressburger, continued to astound audiences with their seductive use of colour and very un-British desire to embrace cinema as a visual language and emotional force in films like *A Matter of Life and Death* (1946) (see p140), *Black Narcissus* (1947) (see p37) and *The Red Shoes* (1948) (see p180). David Lean displayed his mastery of editing and narrative with Dickens adaptations like *Great Expectations* (1946) (see p99), whilst Carol Reed impressed with *Odd Man Out* (1946) (see p152) and *The Third Man* (1949) (see p219) and Ealing comedies, like *Kind Hearts and Coronets* (1949) (see p122), found international favour.

In world cinema, Italian neorealism, with its documentary-like approach to the hardships of ordinary lives, flourished in films like *Rome – Open City* (1945) (see p183) and *Bicycle Thieves* (1948) (see p33) and influenced the greater realism in Hollywood filmmaking and the later kitchen-sink dramas of British cinema like *Room at the Top* (1959) (see p184) and *Saturday Night and Sunday Morning* (1960) (see p188). Japanese cinema also began to establish an international reputation with Festival successes and general audience approval of such works as Kurosawa's *Rashomon* (1951) (see p174) and *Seven Samurai* (1954) (see p190), Ozu's *Tokyo Story* (1953) (see p221) and Mizoguchi's *Ugetsu Monogatari* (1953) (see p229), whilst Ingmar Bergman's artistry was on view in *The Seventh Seal* (1957) (see p191) and *Wild Strawberries* (1957) (see p236).

The once indestructible power of the Hollywood studio system began to crumble in this era as it became illegal for the companies to run an integrated monopoly situation of both making films and operating the cinemas in which the films were shown. The advent of television was also seen as a massive threat to cinema's popularity but Hollywood struck back with 3-D, wide-screen spectacles in the shape of *The Robe* (1953), and more adult subject-matter in such films as *A Streetcar Named Desire* (1951) (see p208), *The Man With the Golden Arm* (1955) and *Anatomy of a Murder* (1959).

Citizen Kane *(1941) Directed by Orson Welles (Orson Welles)*

A Streetcar Named Desire *(1951) Directed by Elia Kazan. (Marlon Brando, Vivien Leigh)*

Ugetsu Monogatari *(1953) Directed by Kenji Mizoguchi (Sakae Ozawa, Masayuki Mori)*

The Seven Samurai *(1954) Directed by Akira Kurosawa*
(Toshiro Mifune, Ko Kimura, Takashi Shimura)

The Life and Death of Colonel Blimp

Michael Powell and Emeric Pressburger, UK, 1943

An examination of Englishness

Love, friendship and fair play are examined in a rich and ravishing English epic.

The story

1942. When Home Guard General Clive Wynne-Candy is angered by a surprise attack, he reflects on a lifetime of gentlemanly conduct. Awarded the VC in the Boer War, he subsequently went to Berlin, upheld British honour in a duel with German officer Theo Kretschmar-Schuldorff and acquiesced when Theo's love for English governess Edith Hunter proved more welcome than his own. In 1918, he married nurse Barbara Wynne and was later reunited with POW Theo who berated him for his sportsman-like approach to war. Barbara died in 1926 and in the 1930s the widowed Theo fled the Nazis. Recalled to duty, Clive asserts a belief in British traditions but the attack convinces him that more modern methods may have to be adopted against the Nazis.

Comment

Although it was the fifth film in the ongoing collaboration between English director Michael Powell and the Hungarian-born screen-writer Emeric Pressburger, *The Life and Death of Colonel Blimp* was significant as the first film to open with the distinctive target logo 'The Archers', announcing their unique writer/producer/directorship, and their return to the magical world of 1940s' Technicolor. The duo's previous monochrome propaganda efforts *The 49th Parallel* (1941) and *One Of Our Aircraft Is Missing* (1941) were little preparation for the uniquely eccentric, defiantly anti-realist investigation of Englishness that was hereby to follow, establishing The Archers as the great outsiders in the British film canon.

Loosely based on satiric cartoonist David Low's ageing military reactionary, Powell and Pressburger's approach to their Colonel Blimp, in the shape of Roger Livesey's General Wynne-Candy (a role intended for Laurence Olivier), is altogether more richly ambiguous, for while the film's central thesis affirms that the English notion of honour at all costs (as represented by old duffers like Blimp) must give way to the harsh realities of countering the Nazi threat, it is undercut by a good deal of nostalgic affection for the traditionalist's sense of fair play. With Deborah Kerr (in place of a pregnant Wendy Hiller) quite radiant as Wynne-Candy's thrice-lost love, an air of romantic pessimism runs through the complex flash-back structure, but it is in the General's lifelong friendship with the characteristic 'good' German, Theo Kretschmar-Schuldorff, that we find the perfect image of the Powell/Pressburger partnership and the main catalyst for wartime Prime Minister Winston Churchill's famous disdain which found expression in his attempts to prevent the film's production.

An Archers Production
Producers Michael Powell and Emeric Pressburger
Screenplay Michael Powell and Emeric Pressburger, based on the cartoon character by David Low
Photography Georges Perinal
Editor John Seabourne
Art Director Alfred Junge
Music Allan Gray
Running time 163 mins *colour*

Cast
Anton Walbrook (Theo Kretschmar-Schuldorff)
Deborah Kerr (Edith Hunter/Barbara Wynne/Angela Cannon)
Roger Livesey (General Clive Wynne-Candy)
Roland Culver (Colonel Betteridge)
Harry Welchman (Major Davies)
James McKechnie (Lieutenant 'Spud' Wilson)

Local Hero

Bill Forsyth, UK, 1983

Beguiling comedy

Magic and melancholy combine as a Highland community experience the glint of oil money.

The story

The proposed siting of an oil refinery at the village of Ferness, sends Texan MacIntyre to Scotland to clinch a deal for his boss Felix Happer. Met by Danny Oldsen, he is offered grudging hospitality by hotelier and village negotiator Gordon Urquhart who senses big money. Mac grows to appreciate the charm of the area whilst Danny falls for ocean-ographer Marina. Negotiations proceed amicably until it is discovered that Ferness beach actually belongs to the contented beachcomber Ben. Lured by talk of the *aurora borealis* in the skies, avid astronomer Happer flies in to conclude the deal but is also seduced by the area and decides to open a marine research unit. Mac returns to Huston retaining a nostalgia for Ferness.

Comment

Active as a filmmaker since entering the industry as a teenager, Bill Forsyth finally gained public recognition of his talents with the Edinburgh Film Festival première of *That Sinking Feeling* (1979) and the warmth of the international response to his comically-observed rites of passage tale *Gregory's Girl* (1980), which helped establish the viability of feature film-making within Scotland. Approached by Oscar-winning producer David Puttnam and shown *Whisky Galore* (1948) as a suggestion of the type of film they might make together, he then embroidered elements of a true story into a script ostensibly concerning the impact of oil and American money on a Scottish community but once again allowing him to reveal, in character and observation, his wry and melancholic view of the world and the imperfect people who inhabit it. Henry Winkler was considered for the part of MacIntyre before Peter Riegert was cast and although Forsyth wrote the role of Happer with Burt Lancaster in mind, Charlton Heston, Sterling Hayden and William Holden had been among the alternative possibilities should Lancaster decline the offer.

Breathtakingly shot in America and on an amalgam of Scottish locations by Chris Menges, the film is a lyrical work, conscious of the rugged beauty in its setting in the way that Powell and Pressburger were in their approach to Scotland in *The Edge of the World* (1937) and *I Know Where I'm Going* (1945), but tinged with an aura of sadness as it tackles such serious themes as isolation, love, friendship, money and their place in the hustle and bustle of the modern world. Seductive in the gentleness of its vision and Forsyth's ultimate (though sorely tested) faith in the goodness of mankind, it has proved the most successful film to date of this individualistic writer/director.

An Engima Production
Producer David Puttnam
Screenplay Bill Forsyth
Photography Chris Menges
Editor Mike Bradsell
Art Directors Adrienne Atkinson, Frank Walsh, Ian Watson and Richard James
Music Mark Knopfler
Running time 111 mins *colour*

Cast
Burt Lancaster (Felix Happer)
Peter Riegert (MacIntyre)
Denis Lawson (Gordon Urquhart)
Peter Capaldi (Danny Oldsen)
Fulton Mackay (Ben Knox)
Christopher Rozycki (Victor Pinochkin)

M

Fritz Lang, Germany, 1931

Serial killer

A highly symbolic child murderer stalks the streets of Weimar Germany.

The story

A German town lives in the grip of fear as an obsessive murderer stalks its children and is sought by both police and criminals alike. When pretty Elsie Beckmann becomes his latest victim, the criminals organize a network of beggars to inform them of any leads. Attracted to another potential victim, the whistling killer is recognized by a blind balloon-seller and marked with a chalk 'M' by a small boy. Fleeing in panic, he takes refuge in a cluttered attic but is discovered, wrapped in a carpet and taken to a makeshift trial. Before a kangaroo court, he disparages their right to judge him and claims that he has no control over the evil inside him. The crowd bays for his execution as the police break in and make an official arrest.

Comment

While the later crime thrillers of his American tenure, including *The Woman in the Window* (1944) and *The Big Heat* (1953), were to focus on dark cityscapes populated almost entirely by psychopathic felons and disaffected innocents, the finest expression of Fritz Lang's uniquely pessimistic vision could well be *M*. Based on the actual case history of a murderous paedophile in Düsseldorf and originally entitled 'Murderer Among Us', the film was written for the screen by Lang and his wife Thea Von Harbou and chillingly blends Expressionist and realist styles. The central character of a *petit bourgeois* who turns uncontrollable serial killer serves to emphasize the tension between weakening order and burgeoning chaos that was to mark the period in Germany under the Weimar Republic and that would create the conditions that led to the rise of Hitler.

M also marked the first time Lang had worked with sound but his mastery of the new medium is evident in the way he pushes the narrative along with both visual and aural information and in the innovative use of overlapping dialogue to draw parallels between both the police and the local underworld who are each attempting to apprehend the fiend in their midst. Moving towards a memorable climax, Lang has the trapped Beckert claiming that he's simply unable to help himself and pleading for clemency to the assembled gallery of ne'er-do-wells before the police finally arrive on the scene – typically the lines between innocence and guilt, law and disorder have become more blurred than ever.

Joseph Losey was to direct a substantially less effective and less resonant American remake of the film in 1951 with David Wayne taking the role of the murderer.

A Nero Film/A G Ver Star Film Production
Producer Seymour Nebenzal
Screenplay Fritz Lang and Thea Von Harbou based, on an article by Egon Jacobson
Photography Fritz Arno Wagner, Gustav Rathje and Karl Vash
Editor Paul Falkenberg
Art Directors Carl Vollbrecht and Emil Hasler
Music Excerpts from Grieg's Peer Gynt
Running time 118 mins b/w

Cast

Peter Lorre (The Murderer)
Otto Wernicke (Inspector Karl Lohmann)
Gustav Grundgens (Schraenker)
Theo Lingen (Baurenfaenger)
Theodor Loos (Commissioner Groeber)
Georg John (Peddler)

Mad Max

George Miller, Australia, 1979

Futuristic revenge opus

Gladiatorial conflict on the motorways of the future creates a cult hero.

The story

As the civilized order crumbles, motorways have become arenas for suicidal conflicts between bikers and law enforcers. When cop Max Rockatansky is responsible for the death of crazed biker The Nightrider, his lover Jessie insists that he quit the force. Meanwhile, psychopath biker The Toecutter and his gang collect the remains of The Nightrider and erupt into violence. Max and his partner Goose take gang-member Johnny the Boy into custody, but he is released on a technicality and vows revenge. When Goose is slain Max quits the force but a subsequent encounter with the gang leaves Jessie fatally injured and his son Sprog dead. Max rejoins the force and uses a super-charged Pursuit Special V8 car to track down and kill the bikers.

Comment

Charged with kinetic energy and brimming with death-defying stuntwork, *Mad Max* is both an imaginative, action-packed slice of post-apocalypse science fiction and an aggressive riposte to the then prevalent perception of Australia cinema as a world of period pieces, crinolines and lace. Director and co-writer George Miller was intent on using his futuristic setting to combine elements of the car action film and the horror genre in an examination of vehicular violence and the whole male cult of the car. A medical school graduate, Miller had lost three teenage friends in car accidents and witnessed many more less personal tragedies as a young doctor in the casualty department of a large hospital and this provided him with the raw material for a cathartic film that has the visceral impact of a car accident but with an equally potent emotional texture involving the aggrieved figure of cop-turned-vigilante Max.

Though released internationally as just another violent entertainment, the film soon found its supporters, although in America, with the Australian accents overdubbed for local consumption, it was merely lost in the shuffle. However, its success was such that a sequel was demanded and the high-octane more generously budgeted *Mad Max 2: The Road Warrior* (1981) surpassed the original in the flair and energy of its action sequences and was, in turn, followed by the more bloated and philosophical *Mad Max – Beyond Thunderdome* (1985). Mel Gibson starred in all three films, bringing the necessary physicality to the role but adding elements of vulnerability and the paranoia of the crazed and grief-stricken loner that rendered the character less of a conventionally clean-cut hero and more of a sympathetically complex cult figure.

A Kennedy-Miller Production
Producer Byron Kennedy
Screenplay James McCausland and George Miller
Photography David Eggby
Editors Tony Paterson and Cliff Hayes
Art Director Jon Dowding
Music Brian May
Running time 91 mins *colour*

Cast

Mel Gibson (Max Rockatansky)
Joanne Samuel (Jessie)
Hugh Keays-Byrne (The Toecutter)
Steve Bisley (Jim Goose)
Tim Burns (Johnny the Boy)
Roger Ward (Fifi Macaffee)

The Magnificent Ambersons

Orson Welles, USA, 1942

Family fortunes

Orson Welles's dynastic chronicle of love and decay equals the brilliance of Citizen Kane.

The story

Eugene Morgan is seen as the social inferior of the prominent Ambersons and loses the lovely Isabel to the wealthy Wilbur Minafer. Later a prosperous inventor and widower, he has hopes of rekindling a love for Isabel when Minafer dies. However, he is cruelly thwarted by her indolent son George who takes her to Europe. Morgan continues to enjoy good fortune but Isabel is struck with a heart attack and George finds the family coffers empty when old Major Amberson dies. Isabel dies and George is forced to close the once resplendent Amberson mansion. His aunt Fanny confronts him with his spiteful, worthless nature and he is almost killed in an accident but Morgan's intervention assures that he will be cared for in the future.

Comment

To follow the satisfying artistic triumph but disappointing box-office reception for *Citizen Kane* (1941) (see p55), Orson Welles originally had in mind a screen version of Charles Dickens's *The Pickwick Papers* to star W C Fields. When the star's schedule rendered the project unfeasible, Welles turned his attentions instead to the adaptation of Booth Tarkington's 1919 Pulitzer prize-winning novel *The Magnificent Ambersons*, the story of an aristocratic family's decline and fall. Eschewing the overt sentimentality of his source, Welles begins his chronicle as a jaunty picture of period foibles before darkening the tone to one of characteristically elegiac regret, a lament not so much for an era but for a whole set of values – although Welles's suavely omniscient narration retains some element of dispassionate distance on the dynasty's self-destruction.

Having edited his completed version to 148 and then 131 minutes, Welles ventured off to Brazil to start work on the abortive 'It's All True' project. Unfortunately, his absence coincided with a change of régime in the studio boardroom of R-K-O. Before long the new management – whose slogan 'Showmanship instead of genius: a new deal at R-K-O' was a clear declaration of intent – responded to an unfavourable preview by cutting it to 88 minutes, inserting a mawkish final scene not even directed by Welles, and opening the result on the lower half of a double-bill with the Lupe Velez vehicle *Mexican Spitfire Sees A Ghost*. The film returned a respectable enough $500 000 of the studio's $1 250 000 investment and even in its truncated form was nominated for four Academy Awards, including Best Picture. However, with his reflective masterpiece partially destroyed, Welles's turbulent relationship with the Hollywood system had only just begun.

A Mercury Theatre/R-K-O Production
Producer Orson Welles
Screenplay Orson Welles, based on the novel by Booth Tarkington
Photography Stanley Cortez
Editors Robert Wise, Jack Moss and Mark Robson
Art Director Mark-Lee Kirk
Music Bernard Herrmann
Running time 88 mins b/w

Cast
Joseph Cotten (Eugene Morgan)
Dolores Costello (Isabel Amberson Minafer)
Anne Baxter (Lucy Morgan)
Tim Holt (George Amberson Minafer)
Agnes Moorehead (Fanny Amberson)
Ray Collins (Jack Amberson)

The Maltese Falcon

John Huston, USA, 1941

Fool's gold

The quest for an elusive black bird defines the private-eye genre for the 1940s.

The story

When his partner Miles Archer and quarry Floyd Thursby are murdered, private detective Sam Spade protects the identity of his client Brigid O'Shaughnessy who shares an interest in a much-coveted black falcon statuette with criminals Joel Cairo and Casper Gutman. Later, Spade is visited by the mortally wounded Captain Jacobi who entrusts him with the safe-keeping of the elusive bird. He meets Gutman, Cairo, O'Shaughnessy and Gunsel Wilmer who had killed Thursby and Jacobi and will serve as a fall-guy if Spade is willing to negotiate a price for the falcon. The bird proves to be a fake and the criminals abscond leaving Spade to reluctantly hand O'Shaughnessy over to the authorities as Archer's killer.

Comment

Few today recall the first filming in 1931 of Dashiell Hammett's 1929 crime thriller *The Maltese Falcon* under the same title by Roy Del Ruth, or its 1936 incarnation as William Dieterle's *Satan Met A Lady* (1936) with Warren William as detective Ted Shane and Bette Davis as *femme fatale* Valerie, yet John Huston's scintillating directorial début with his 1941 version has long been established as a classic of Hollywood cinema.

Rewarded with his first venture behind the camera after many years service as a reliable screen-writer, Huston seized the chance to turn in a model of narrative concision that also bore out his maxim that 'The trick is in the casting'. Here Humphrey

Bogart inherited the leading role that George Raft had refused and created the archetypal trench-coated private dick, a sardonic yet romantic antihero. The experienced Mary Astor exuded alluring maliciousness, the pairing of Hungarian-born Peter Lorre and 62-year-old English stage actor Sydney Greenstreet created a delicious partnership in crime that was to run throughout the 1940s, and Huston's actor/father Walter made a brief good luck appearance as the luckless Jacobi.

The dark wit, constant deceit and rampant paranoia combined with the downbeat urban setting and brooding presentation to trace the first steps into the film noir genre that was to become increasingly baroque as the decade wore on. The subject matter – a motley crew of diverse types greedily pursuing a fabulous prize only to discover that the treasure is illusory – offered the first exploration of territory to which Huston would fruitfully return in the likes of *The Treasure of the Sierra Madre* (1947) and *The Man Who Would Be King* (1975) and which he affectionately spoofed in *Beat The Devil* (1953).

A Warner Brothers-First National Production
Executive Producer Hal B Wallis
Screenplay John Huston based, on the novel by Dashiell Hammett
Photography Arthur Edeson
Editor Thomas Richards
Art Director Robert Haas
Music Adolph Deutsch
Running time 100 mins b/w

Cast

Humphrey Bogart (Sam Spade)
Mary Astor (Brigid O'Shaughnessy)
Gladys George (Iva Archer)
Peter Lorre (Joel Cairo)
Barton MacLane (Lieutenant Dundy)
Lee Patrick (Effie Perine)
Sydney Greenstreet (Casper Gutman)

The Manchurian Candidate

John Frankenheimer, USA, 1962

Prescient political thriller

Political paranoia inspires a thriller of dazzling invention.

The story

Korea, 1952. An American patrol are captured and brainwashed. After their release, Captain Bennet Marco suffers nightmares, in which the supposedly heroic Raymond Shaw is an enemy cipher ready to kill on command. When another patrolman reveals similar nightmares, the army grows concerned. Meanwhile, Raymond's mother Eleanor triggers him to assassinate Senator Jordan and is prepared to have him kill again in a conspiracy to sweep her rabid, right-wing dupe of a husband Senator Iselin into the White House. Marco begins to crack Raymond's conditioning but he still follows orders to position himself at a Madison Square Gardens rally. However, at the crucial moment he shoots his mother and Iselin and then commits suicide.

Comment

Adapted from Richard Condon's 1959 novel, *The Manchurian Candidate* is one of the most cinematically audacious and imaginative political thrillers in the Hollywood canon, devised, according to producer/director John Frankenheimer, as a satire on 'the whole idea of fanaticism, the far Right and the far Left being exactly the same thing, and the idiocy of it'.

Lampooning the extremity of the anti-Communist figures who were flourishing in the shadow of red-baiter Senator Joseph McCarthy, it also presents a near-sacrilegious portrait of monstrous American motherhood in the figure of Angela Lansbury's power-wielding matriarch. Frankenheimer,

a graduate of live television, finds a feverish style to match the high-pitch melodrama of the events unfurling – allowing the domino theory of cause and effect to retain a chilling plausibility and yet heightening the reality through the use of specific lenses, television monitors and fast-paced editing. Casting throughout is exceptional, with Laurence Harvey's cold and aloof screen persona well deployed as the brainwashed Raymond, and Angela Lansbury, a mere three years his senior, excelling as the mother.

A critical and modest commercial success on its initial release, the film received only two Oscar nominations for Lansbury and editor Ferris Webster and was withdrawn from circulation after the assassination of John F Kennedy who had been instrumental in granting his blessing to the film's production. The subsequent slayings, conspiracies and treachery that have become almost commonplace in American politics have only served to lend greater credence to the plot and style of a film once dismissed in some quarters as fanciful, and its 1988 reissue saw universal confirmation of its classic status.

An M C Production
Producers George Axelrod and John Frankenheimer
Screenplay George Axelrod, based on the novel by Richard Condon
Photography Lionel Lindon
Editor Ferris Webster
Art Director Richard Sylbert
Music David Amram
Running time 126 mins b/w

Cast

Frank Sinatra (Bennet Marco)
Laurence Harvey (Raymond Shaw)
Janet Leigh (Eugenie Rose, 'Rosie')
Angela Lansbury (Eleanor Iselin)
Henry Silva (Chunjin)
James Gregory (Senator John Yerkes Iselin)

A kiss is just a kiss
Screen romance

Romance transcends all genres and has found expression in a variety of images from the solicitous behaviour exhibited by *King Kong* (1933) (see p123) towards Fay Wray, and Fred Astaire and Ginger Rogers gliding cheek to cheek through Art Deco Venice in *Top Hat* (1935) (see p222), to the noble self-sacrifice of Humphrey Bogart in allowing Ingrid Bergman to flee with husband Paul Henreid in *Casablanca* (1942) (see p51) and Gene Kelly's exuberant peregrinations through inclement weather in *Singin' In The Rain* (1952) (see p198).

The most potent and poignant romances have often been those that ended with the central couple apart as in *Gone With the Wind* (1939) (see p95) and *Brief Encounter* (1945) (see p45), or that culminated in tragedy like *Queen Christina* (1933) (see p171) or *Love Story* (1970). Liaisons of the happy-ever-after variety tend to come less readily to mind but, from the most classic period of Hollywood, would certainly include *The Philadelphia Story* (1940) (see p166), *Random Harvest* (1942) and *It's A Wonderful Life* (1946) (see p113).

A romance that blossoms from initial hostility has been one of the most well-worn paths in cinema history and the most renowned examples include news-hound Clark Gable and runaway heiress Claudette Colbert in *It Happened One Night* (1934) (see p112), Robert Donat handcuffed to Madeleine Carroll in *The 39 Steps* (1935), the unlikely union between prim spinster Katharine Hepburn and gin-sodden boatman Humphrey Bogart in *The African Queen* (1951) (see p4), and the mistaken identity that eventually brings Doris Day and Rock Hudson together in *Pillow Talk* (1959).

The battle-of-the-sexes has formed the basis of numerous comedy-romances, notably the series of vehicles teaming Spencer Tracy and Katharine Hepburn that began with *Woman of the Year* (1942). The directors who have been the most perceptive in their depiction of the romantic mood include Josef Von Sternberg in *The Blue Angel* (1930) (see p39), Ernst Lubitsch in *The Shop Around the Corner* (1940) (see p196), Marcel Carné in *Les Enfants Du Paradis* (1944) (see p77), Billy Wilder in *The Apartment* (1960) (see p17) (among numerous others including *Love in the Afternoon* (1957) and *Avanti!* (1972)), and Woody Allen in *Annie Hall* (1977) (see p16) and almost all of the films that have followed since.

For many, Cary Grant remains the ideal version of the romantic leading man with Greta Garbo the epitome of the enigmatic, alluring love goddess; however, a partial list of the most enduring romantic screen couples would have to include Janet Gaynor and Charles Farrell, Myrna Loy and William Powell, whose good-natured bantering and dry-martini wisecracks revolutionized the portrayal of married couples, Nelson Eddy and Jeanette MacDonald, Olivia De Havilland and Errol Flynn, Greer Garson and Walter Pidgeon and, more recently, Sophia Loren and Marcello Mastroianni and Elizabeth Taylor and Richard Burton.

The box-office fortunes of other genres may ebb and flow but romance is never out of fashion no matter how graphic the depiction or implausible the circumstances. *Fatal Attraction* (1987) (see p84) may have become a box-office sensation by depicting the stark consequences for a married man who strays from the path of fidelity but old-fashioned romance is still also very much to the cinemagoer's taste as has been proved by the recent welcome accorded such lightweight, warm-hearted examples of the genre as *When Harry Met Sally* (1989), *Pretty Woman* (1990) and *Ghost* (1990).

A Matter of Life and Death

Michael Powell and Emeric Pressburger, UK, 1946

Love conquers all

A commission to improve Anglo-American relations becomes an otherworldly romance of beauty and magic.

The story

Returning from a bombing mission, squadron-leader Peter Carter is forced to eject from his plane without a parachute. His last words are to American WAC June Carter. Miraculously, he survives and is washed ashore where he meets June and falls deeply in love. However, he has unwittingly cheated death and in the Other World a collector is dispatched to remedy this error. Peter refuses to join him and demands a hearing of his case. As Peter undergoes brain surgery, the recently deceased Dr Reeves fights his corner against Abraham Farlan, the first American killed in the Revolutionary War. The contentious issues between the two countries are debated but the sincerity of June's love wins the day and Peter is spared.

Comment

One peculiarity of Hollywood in the 1940s, illustrated in films like *Here Comes Mr Jordan* (1941) and *It's A Wonderful Life* (1946) (see p113), was its love of scenarios in which the earthly protagonists undergo a change in their situations that they can only ascribe to the real or imagined intervention of messengers from heaven. A sophisticated and stylish British variation on the theme came in The Archers' *A Matter of Life and Death* (released in America as *Stairway to Heaven*) which was selected as the first ever Royal Film Performance in 1946.

Commissioned to create a film that would improve Anglo-American relations, The Archers partnership had opted for a love story and were determined to make use of the human and technical resources gradually being made available to them with the cessation of wartime hostilities. David Niven was cast in the lead role after a number of other hopefuls, including Stewart Granger, had been considered, Kim Hunter replaced Powell's initial choice of Betty Field following the suggestion of Alfred Hitchcock, who had encountered her during screen tests for *Spellbound* (1945), and making use of Technicolor was once more a possibility. Shooting at Saunton Sands in North Devon and at Denham Studios, Powell handed the job of director of photography to Jack Cardiff for the first time and together they created lush colour visions of the Home Counties and an evocatively monochrome heavenly plane.

Powell would later claim the film as his favourite from among all The Archers' productions and ultimately it not only fulfils their brief of promoting greater understanding between the two nations concerned but is also an impassioned assertion of eternal love, a statement of faith in the individual and a visual *tour de force* as well.

An Archers Production
Producers Michael Powell and Emeric Pressburger
Screenplay Michael Powell and Emeric Pressburger
Photography Jack Cardiff
Editor Reggie Mills
Art Director Alfred Junge
Music Allan Gray
Running time 104 mins *colour* and *b/w*

Cast

David Niven (Sqdn Ldr Peter Carter)
Kim Hunter (June)
Marius Goring (Conductor 71)
Roger Livesey (Dr Reeves)
Raymond Massey (Abraham Farlan)
Richard Attenborough (English Pilot)

Mephisto

Istvan Szabo, Hungary, 1981

The price of fame

The rise of Fascism is mirrored in the moral quandaries of an ambitious actor.

The story

1920s Germany. Ambitious actor Hendrik Hofgen's advantageous marriage to Barbara Bruckner takes him to the State Theatre Company in Berlin where he placates all shades of the political spectrum and wins the role of Mephistopheles in an acclaimed production of *Faust* that brings him to the attention of a Nazi General. When the Nazis assume power in 1933, Barbara flees to Paris but Hofgen remains and wins increasing favour, however the price of his success is a divorce from Barbara, the end of his affair with Juliette and the betrayal of leftist former colleagues. He marries the actress Nicoletta and is hailed afresh for his *Hamlet* before humiliation at the hands of the General underlines the precariousness of his position.

Comment

'Our film is the story of an individual's brilliant capacity for self-adaptation. It is the story of a man who feels that the only thing he can achieve in life is to make others accept him,' declared writer/director Istvan Szabo on the release of *Mephisto*, his adaptation of Klaus Mann's 1936 *roman à clef*, allegedly based on the actor Gustav Grundgens. Winner of the 1981 Best Foreign Film Oscar, *Mephisto* provides a rare engagement with the sweep of history through the moral dilemmas of a fallible, less than heroic individual faced with acute and painful choices when every fibre of his body ironically seeks an untroubled life, security and a form of success that only endless compromise and betrayal can purchase. The central figure of an actor prepared to sacrifice his principles and loved ones for the hollow prize of a glittering career playing a character willing to sell his soul to the devil becomes an intertwined metaphor for the position of a German nation faced by incipient Fascism in the inter-War period. It is a credit to the conviction of Szabo's direction and the magnetism of Klaus Maria Brandauer's performance that our reactions to the character run the gamut from contempt to comprehension and yet retain a residue of sympathy throughout, and pose the uncomfortable question of how the viewer would have reacted in similar circumstances.

Brandauer and Szabo would subsequently be reunited on a further two films in what came to be described as a trilogy on the themes of charismatic men of destiny and the character flaws that cause their fall from grace or self-destruction. In *Colonel Redl* (1984) Brandauer is a careerist soldier in the Austro-Hungarian Empire and in *Hanussen* (1988) a wounded Austrian soldier who develops psychic powers.

A Mafilm/Manfred Durniok Production
Producer Manfred Durniok
Screenplay Peter Dobai and Istvan Szabo, based on the novel by Klaus Mann
Photography Lajos Koltai
Editor Zsuzsa Csakany
Art Director Jozsef Romvari
Music Zdenko Tamassy
Running time 144 mins *colour*

Cast
Klaus Maria Brandauer (Hendrik Hofgen)
Ildiko Bansagi (Nicoletta Von Niebuhr)
Krystyna Janda (Barbara Bruckner)
Rolf Hoppe (General)
Gyorgy Cserhalmi (Hans Miklas)
Peter Andorai (Otto Ulrichs)

Metropolis

Fritz Lang, Germany, 1926

Tomorrow's world

Fritz Lang's expansive futuristic vision establishes a model of science-fiction drama.

The story

In 21st-century Metropolis, the mass of drone-like workers survive in squalor while the ruling class enjoy life in the 'eternal gardens'. When Freder, son of the city's master Fredersen, falls in love with the worker Maria his eyes are opened to the grim conditions below. Meanwhile, his father commands scientist Rotwang to create a robotic decoy of Maria that will allow them to quell any insurgence. However, when the false Maria orders revolt the effects are catastrophic as the city grinds to a halt and the workers' quarters are flooded. The real Maria and Freder lead the children to safety and the robot is destroyed. Rotwang goes mad and on seeing the error of his ways Frederesen promises a more enlightened future.

Comment

The German economy may have been on shaky foundations during the 1920s, but that failed to prevent director Fritz Lang from mounting three of the largest film productions ever to have been attempted at that time. Thus the megalomaniac thriller *Dr Mabuse, Der Spieler* (*Dr Mabuse, the Gambler*) (1922) was followed by the Wagnerian legend of *Die Niebelungen* (1923) and then the utopian fantasy of *Metropolis*.

Taking almost 18 months to shoot, *Metropolis* would bankrupt the massive German Ufa studios before its much trumpeted release in January 1927. While Lang's political sympathies placed him on the left throughout his career, his then wife and co-scriptwriter Thea Von Harbou would in future become closely aligned with the Nazi party. Their joint scenario for *Metropolis* was simplistic enough to satisfy both of them, positing a future society where the technological luxury of a ruling class is maintained by an enslaved underclass who revolt and almost destroy the city before love wins the day. The climactic reconciliation ensures equally that right is reached and the moral underlined that 'the intermediary between the hand and the brain is the heart'.

The plotting and characters are dwarfed by the scale of the undertaking however, and Lang's impressive grasp of visual architectonics, all lavishly stylized sets and massive crowd scenes (involving a cast of 36 000), still ensures the power to mesmerize the viewer. With its mad scientist, evil female robot and expansive vision of futuristic technology, the film was to prove highly influential on later science fiction, while its respectful reception in the United States was at length to prove Lang's ticket to Hollywood.

A Ufa Production
Producer Erich Pommer
Screenplay Fritz Lang and Thea Von Harbou, based on her novel
Photography Karl Freund and Gunther Rittau
Art Directors Otto Hunte, Erich Kettelhut and Karl Vollbrecht
Running time originally 150 mins (most prints now run 120 mins; 1984 reissue: 83 mins) b/w

Cast
Alfred Abel (John Fredersen)
Gustav Frolich (Freder)
Brigitte Helm (Maria)
Rudolf Klein-Rogge (Rotwang)
Fritz Rasp (Slim)
Theodor Loos (Josaphat)

Napoleon

Abel Gance, France, 1927

Historical epic

From snowball fight to military conquest, the early life of Napoleon is rendered with cinematic sweep and innovation.

The story

At his military college, the young Napoleon shows his skills as a strategist during a snowball fight and seeks solace in the company of a pet eagle. Years later as an army lieutenant he tries to inveigle Corsica in the French Revolution and proves his worth in skirmishes with the British. During the Reign of Terror he is imprisoned for declining the command of Paris and meets Josephine. They fall in love and he is the toast of Paris for quelling a Royalist uprising. Appointed commander of the Army of the Alps he now envisages himself carrying the flag of the Revolution to new heights. Assigned a ragged, weary gathering of men, he inspires them with fresh purpose and leads them on a triumphant march into Italy.

Comment

Despite its length and scope, Abel Gance's *Napoleon* is only a sketch for a much more massive, ultimately unfulfilled project. The film was hailed on its opening in Paris as a vindication of the artistic spirit over the overt commercialism of pre-war filmmaking in France. Gance took a distinctly romantic view of great men throughout his films, and Napoleon was certainly no exception, but the film has been admired, then and now, as much for its extraordinary technical virtuosity as for its portrayal of the Emperor.

That portrayal is in any case a partial one, since the film only manages to take in his boyhood, youth and early military career; the remainder of the huge project to record his entire life was never committed to film,

thereby depriving Gance of the tragic ending which was so characteristic of his work. What he undoubtedly did succeed in doing, however, was to make full and unprecedented use of the possibilities offered by the camera, which swoops and twists through scene after scene in extraordinary fashion, and by film itself, including some visionary editing and cross-cutting techniques, and a version of the ending in which the closing scenes of Napoleon's entry into Italy are projected as a heroic triptych across three screens, rather than conventionally restricted, like the rest of the film, to one. Like most silent films, *Napoleon* does not exist in a definitive print. Even at the time of its original release, there were several different versions, while modern audiences have the choice of an edited American print generated by Francis Coppola or Kevin Brownlow's epic five-hour amalgamation of all extant footage. Neither can claim genuine authenticity, but Brownlow's tireless work is undeniably an impressive tribute to Gance's artistic vision.

A Westi/Societé General De Films/Les Films Historiques Production
Producer Abel Gance
Screenplay Abel Gance
Photography Jules Kruger, Jean-Paul Mundwiller and Leonce-Henry Burel
Editors Marguerite Beauge and Henriette Pinson
Art Directors Alexandre Benois, Pierre Schildknecht, Lochavoff, Jacouty, Meinhardt and Eugene Lourie
Music Arthur Honegger
Running time 270 mins b/w

Cast

Albert Dieudonne (Napoleon Bonaparte)
Gina Manes (Josephine De Beauharnais)
Edmond Van Daele (Maximilien Robespierre)
Alexandre Koubitzky (Danton)
Acho Chakatouny (Pozzo Di Borgo)
Antonin Artaud (Marat)

Nashville

Robert Altman, USA, 1975

American lives

Cynicism rather than celebration is the mood in Altman's bi-centennial fresco.

The story

Nashville, Tennessee. Presidential Candidate Hal Phillip Walker plans to launch his campaign with a rally involving the cream of country music stars. Veterans Haven Hamilton and Barbara Jean are among those asked to perform as the city fills with celebrities and drifters like young Kenny Fraiser, BBC reporter Opal and aspiring singer Albuquerque who has fled an unhappy marriage. Singer Tom Frank works his way though the female populace including Opal and gospel singer Linnea, wife of ardent Walker supporter Delbert Reese who eventually manages to secure Barbara Jean for the rally. However, at the concert Fraiser draws a gun and fires at the stage. In the ensuing confusion, Albuquerque seizes her chance and steps forward to sing.

Comment

The belated critical and commercial success accorded veteran director Robert Altman with the release of *M*A*S*H* (1970) allowed him access to funding for a succession of 1970s' projects that irreverently explored sacred American institutions and hallowed film genres. The results included the revisionist western *McCabe and Mrs Miller* (1971) and his far from stereotypical Raymond Chandler adaptation *The Long Goodbye* (1973). Noted for his distinctive style of multi-track sound, overlapping, seemingly spontaneous dialogue and persistent search for the antiheroic, his most expansive achievement came with *Nashville* which interweaves the lives of 24 characters into a kaleidoscopic depiction of the country music city, its denizens, and such fleeting celebrity guest stars as Elliott Gould, Julie Christie and The Misty Mountain Boys.

Hailed by Newsweek as an 'Epic of Opryland', the film manages to retain an intimacy amidst its sprawling richly-textured canvas as each cast member is allowed to suggest a complete life and illuminate some aspect of the general themes of isolation, the difficulties of communication and the hollowness to be found in pursuit of the American Dream. Altman's extraordinary cast includes many unknown or untested performers who went on to subsequent success. When Susan Anspach was forced to withdraw from the project, former singer Ronee Blakely was promoted to her role, whilst Lily Tomlin received her dramatic break in a role created from the experiences of actress Louise Fletcher and her deaf parents. Both performers received Best Supporting Actress Oscar nominations and Nashville was also nominated for Best Film and Best Director, winning the Oscar for Best Song 'I'm Easy', which was written and performed in the film by Keith Carradine.

An American Broadcasting Companies Production

Producer Robert Altman
Screenplay Joan Tewkesbury
Photography Paul Lohmann
Editors Sidney Levin and Dennis Hall
Art Director none credited
Music arranged by Richard Baskin
Running time 161 mins *colour*

Cast

Karen Black (Connie White)
Ronee Blakely (Barbara Jean)
Keith Carradine (Tom Frank)
Geraldine Chaplin (Opal)
Barbara Harris (Albuquerque)
Lily Tomlin (Linnea Reese)

A Night at the Opera

Sam Wood, USA, 1935

Marxist mayhem

'You can't-a-fool-a-me! There ain't no Sanity Claus!'

The story

Milan. Fast-talking entrepreneur Otis B Driftwood assures the wealthy Mrs Claypool that he will introduce her to American high society if she will invest in the New York Opera Company featuring Rosa Castaldi. They set sail with stowaways Riccardo Baroni, Castaldi's boyfriend, Tomasso, the dresser, and Fiorello, Baroni's agent. Accidentally hailed as heroic foreign dignitaries at New York City Hall, the team then head for their hotel. Meanwhile, Rosa spurns the advances of Rodolfo Lassparri and finds herself sacked along with Driftwood. However, they exact their revenge; disrupting the opening night of *Il Trovatore* and kidnapping Lassparri so that Ricardo and Rosa go on with the show and win tumultuous applause.

Comment

An anarchic force in screen comedy, the Marx Brothers found themselves temporarily without direction in the film industry when *Duck Soup* (1933) proved a box-office disappointment and ended their association with Paramount Pictures. However Irving Thalberg, the boy-wonder producer at M-G-M, was a fan and was also convinced that he knew the way to preserve the energy and manic inventiveness of their best work and yet place them in the kind of filmic context that would broaden their appeal. His solution was to include a romantic subplot and musical numbers within the structure of the script that did not detract from the central mayhem. He also allowed the Brothers, working for the first time without Zeppo, to go on the road in front of live audiences to test the comic sequences and material in *A Night at the Opera* before they set foot on a sound stage. Thus a potted version of the film, running at under an hour, played at four cities over a period of three weeks with writers Kaufman and Ryskind in the audience taking copious notes. The result was among the most polished and structured scenarios that the comedians had worked from.

A Night at the Opera proved to be one of their funniest and most successful comedies, earning some $3 million, and the exercise was repeated, with only marginally less pleasing results, on *A Day at the Races* (1937). Thalberg however died during the making of the latter film and other M-G-M executives were less concerned with the development of their careers. The broadening of appeal that Thalberg had begun soon came to mean the eradication of their more dangerous edges with children, lovers and big production numbers eventually overwhelming the larceny and lust that has once been their strongest assets.

An M-G-M Production
Producer Irving Thalberg
Screenplay George S Kaufman, Morrie Ryskind, Al Boasberg, Bert Kalmar and Harry Ruby, based on a story by James Kevin McGuinness
Photography Merritt B Gerstad
Editor William Levanway
Art Directors Cedric Gibbons and Ben Carre
Music: Herbert Stothart
Running time 90 mins b/w

Cast
Groucho Marx (Otis B Driftwood)
Chico Marx (Fiorello)
Harpo Marx (Tomasso)
Kitty Carlisle (Rosa Castaldi)
Allan Jones (Riccardo Baroni)
Margaret Dumont (Mrs Claypool)

The Night of the Hunter

Charles Laughton, USA, 1955

The poetry of fear

*Good and evil wage war
in a strikingly unique
psychopathological thriller.*

The story

West Virginia. Unemployed Ben Harper turns bank robber, stashing his takings and swearing his children John and Pearl to secrecy before he is apprehended. Prior to his execution, he is befriended by his cell-mate Harry Powell, a self-styled backwoods preacher who subsequently woos and marries his widow Willa. Frustrated at his inability to find the money, Powell terrorizes the children in search of information and ultimately kills Willa. The children escape downriver and find sanctuary in the home of the kindly Rachel Cooper. Powell doggedly tracks them down. However, he has met his match and Rachel holds him at bay until the police arrive. He is subsequently executed and the children find a new home with Rachel.

Comment

The Night of the Hunter is a curious anomaly in the history of Hollywood cinema, but an undeniably fascinating one. A religious allegory of the battle between good and evil cast in the form of a suspense thriller, it employed a self-consciously artistic approach in direction and editing which was largely inimical to the Hollywood way, and, as it turned out, to the film's own commercial success. One result of that failure was that actor Charles Laughton was robbed of any confidence that he may have possessed as a director and withdrew from plans to film Norman Mailer's *The Naked and The Dead*, never setting foot behind a camera again.

History, however, has allotted a more honoured place to his unique and highly personal vision in this flawed masterpiece than his contemporaries were prepared to do. The film betrays a certain lack of coherence in welding together its diverse concerns, but overcomes that weakness with a vividly atmospheric visual imagery and a highly inventive, dreamlike use of light and shadow. Its greatest strength, though, lies in the acting, particularly that of Robert Mitchum in arguably his greatest on-screen performance as the chillingly evil Harry Powell, remorselessly stalking the innocent children. He later recalled, 'Charles called me up and said "You play a diabolical crud". "Present!" I replied. Charles said, "I'm not supposed to know about such things. I am a professional non-crud." "Charles," I said, "I will take care of that department."'

The film retains much of its dark, fairy-tale power, redolent of the finest achievements in silent cinema than anything one would expect to find in the Hollywood canon.

1991 produced an American television remake with Richard Chamberlain attempting to fill Robert Mitchum's shoes.

A United Artists Production
Produer Paul Gregory
Screenplay James Agee, based on the novel by David Grubb
Photography Stanley Cortez
Editor Robert Golden
Art Director Hilyard Brown
Music Walter Schumann
Running time 93 mins b/w

Cast
Robert Mitchum (Preacher Harry Powell)
Shelley Winters (Willa Harper)
Lillian Gish (Rachel Cooper)
James Gleason (Birdie)
Evelyn Varden (Icey Spoon)
Peter Graves (Ben Harper)

Things that go bump in the night
The horror film

The 'horror film' tag can cover a multitude of gruesome variations from the relatively subtle suspense of a ghost story to the vile acts of miscreants created by scientists meddling in things best left alone. The classic monsters of the genre all made appearances during the silent era with Dracula appearing as *Nosferatu* (1922) (see p151), one of several imaginative German productions like *The Cabinet of Dr Caligari* (1919) (see p50) and *The Golem* (1920) which made inventive use of Expressionist ideas and chiaroscuro lighting effects. Lon Chaney Senior earned his reputation as 'The Man of a 1000 Faces' through a series of painful physical transformations into such figures as *The Phantom of the Opera* (1925) and the vampire in *London after Midnight* (1927) but the Golden Age of Hollywood monsters began with Bela Lugosi's repeat of his stage role as *Dracula* (1930), Fredric March's Oscar-winning performance as *Dr Jekyll and Mr Hyde* (1931) and the affecting poignancy of Boris Karloff's monster in *Frankenstein* (1931), directed by Englishman James Whale who returned with a deft mixture of black humour and the macabre in *Bride of Frankenstein* (1935) (see p44). With *The Wolf Man* (1941) Universal Studios now had a stable of monsters that were utilized in increasingly unworthy and implausible yarns. However, at R-K-O, home of *King Kong* (1933) (see p123), Val Lewton established a low-budget unit that made such films as *Cat People* (1942), *I Walked With a Zombie* (1943) and *The Seventh Victim* (1944) where the atmosphere of fear was the result of implicit, suggestive means and the skilful use of sometimes mundane settings.

The advent of 3-D brought a flurry of gimmicky horror films like *The House of Wax* (1953) and *The Creature from the Black Lagoon* (1954) but the genre was well overdue for revitalization by the time that British studio Hammer employed the likes of Peter Cushing and Christopher Lee to notable effect in *The Curse of Frankenstein* (1956), *Dracula* (1958) (see p72) and *The Mummy* (1959) which cumulatively created a distinctively gothic style that placed a new emphasis on the erotic appeal of horror. Roger Corman also made his contribution to the genre with a series of flamboyant Edgar Allan Poe adaptations, using the camerawork of Floyd Crosby, the thespian skills of Vincent Price and a Freudian interpretation of the author to illuminate the likes of *The Fall of the House of Usher* (1960) and *The Masque of The Red Death* (1964). Note should also be made of such Italian maestros as Mario Bava and Dario Argento whose orchestration of colour, music and *mise-en-scene* reached a pinnacle in *Suspiria* (1977) and *Inferno* (1980).

Mainstream horror films have gained an increasing commercial viability with the grand guignol excesses of *What Ever Happened To Baby Jane?* (1962) (see p233) initiating a cycle of films involving older female stars, and Alfred Hitchcock's *Psycho* (1960) (see p169) creating one of the cinema's most chilling figures in genial psychopath Norman Bates and inspiring a plethora of lesser productions involving indestructible maniacs at loose in *Halloween* (1978), *A Nightmare on Elm Street* (1984) and *Friday the 13th* (1980) and their innumerable sequels. *Night of the Living Dead* (1968) (see p150) and its sequels have used the zombie film to comment on modern America mores but the vast audience for *Rosemary's Baby* (1968) (see p185), *The Exorcist* (1973) (see p78), *The Omen* (1976), *The Evil Dead* (1982) and *Poltergeist* (1982) series, as well as countless low-budget video-destined imitations would suggest that audiences are more keen than ever to experience pure, unmitigated fear from the safety of a cinema seat.

Dracula *(1958) Directed by Terence Fisher (Christopher Lee)*

The Bride of Frankenstein *(1935) Directed by James Whale*
(Elsa Lanchester, Boris Karloff)

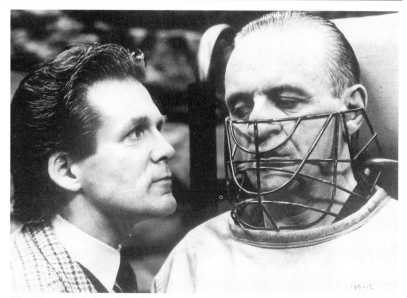

The Silence of the Lambs (1991) Directed by Jonathan Demme
(Anthony Heald, Anthony Hopkins)

Invasion of the Bodysnatchers (1956) Directed by Don Siegel (Kevin McCarthy, Dana Wynter)

Night of the Living Dead

George A Romero, USA, 1968

Zombie shocker

The dawn of the dead heralds fresh vigour in the horror genre.

The story

Visiting her father's grave, Barbara and Johnny are attacked by a zombie. Barbara flees to a nearby house containing the similarly scared Ben who barricades them in whilst combatting the increasing zombie hordes outside. Other stragglers are discovered cowering in the sanctuary of the basement. News bulletins inform them that zombies are overrunning the country and advise them to make for official emergency rescue stations. An abortive escape plan results in the deaths of young couple Tom and Judy. The zombies then attack the house, killing all save Ben who barricades himself into the basement. Armed vigilantes combat the zombies and, relieved to be rescued, Ben emerges from hiding only to be mistakenly shot dead.

Comment

Although restricted by its modest budget and functional acting, *Night of the Living Dead* still represented a chilling new direction in the development of the horror/science-fiction genre from imaginative 28-year-old director George A Romero who was injecting an explicitness into the on-screen gore whilst encouraging a more serious interpretation of the story as symbolic of its times in depicting traditional American values under siege from strange, rapacious forces. Devoid of the leavening black humour frequently employed in the genre, and nihilistic in its conclusions, the film eschews the traditional heroics of the horror field in which good ultimately triumphs over evil and the final reel offers heroic redemption or salvation. Romero's lack of financial resources and the resulting rather amateurish quality in the film also lends its story a greater edge of conviction in a manner reminiscent of the way Orson Welles used the reportage qualities of radio to scare an earlier generation of Americans with his broadcast of *War of the Worlds* in 1938.

The film proved to be the first of a series in which Romero utilized the commercial appetite for and dramatic possibilities of flesh-eating zombies to comment on ecological concerns (the original film explains that they are the result of radiation fall-out from a rocket) and criticize the less appealing facets of contemporary American life and consumerism. The sequels include the rather more professionally polished and nail-biting *Zombies – Dawn of the Dead* (1978) which offers a sharply satirical subtext, and the less imaginative *Day of the Dead* (1985). 1990 saw Romero collaborate on the script for an unnecessary colour remake of his original film.

An Image Ten Production
Producers Russell Streiner and Karl Hardman
Screenplay John A Russo
Photography George A Romero
Editor, Art Director, Music none credited
Running time 96 mins b/w

Cast
Judith O'Dea (Barbara)
Duane Jones (Ben)
Karl Hardman (Harry Cooper)
Keith Wayne (Tom)
Judith Riley (Judy)
Marilyn Eastman (Helen Cooper)

Nosferatu
(Nosferatu, Eine Symphonie Des Grauens)

F W Murnau, Germany, 1922

The vampire rises

The beauty and the horror of the vampire myth are captured in Murnau's production.

The story

Real-estate clerk Hutter leaves his bride Ellen in order to conduct business with the eccentric Garf Orlok. The journey instills an increasing sense of foreboding and he is unceremoniously dumped before a speedy coach comes to transport him to the castle. Dismissing his host's undue interest in the blood that oozes from his cut finger during their evening meal, Hutter eventually flees the castle when he discovers that Orlok is one of the undead. Attracted by an image of Hutter's bride, Orlok has his coffin shipped to Bremen and brings pestilence and plague in his wake. However, Ellen proves to be his temptress and his downfall as she delays his visit long enough for him to be destroyed by the rising sun's rays.

Comment

The subtitle 'A Symphony of Horror' does not seem misplaced for this first and most impressively realized of all the film versions of Bram Stoker's classic novel of Victorian sexual repression. At every stage in his career, Murnau was part of the German Expressionist movement, whose guiding lights unquestionably included the post-Victorian theories of Sigmund Freud, and his reading of the vampire myth is heavily weighted with that changing interpretation of its sexual significance. That is nowhere more apparent than in his decision to reverse the central relationship of the novel, turning the male character from strong destroyer of Dracula/Nosferatu into an ineffectual weakling, and foregrounding the female (Mina in the book, but Ellen in the film; the names were changed partly because no rights were paid for the use of the book, although some later prints confusingly reverted to Stoker's names). Ellen, whose own curiously emaciated appearance seems to prefigure her martyr's fate, then becomes both the victim of the vampire's desire, and the means of the vampire's destruction, inverting the book's symptomatic Victorian fear of female sexuality.

Inevitably, critics have explicated the Freudian references at great length, but for the contemporary viewer the main interest of the film may well be in the extraordinary visual qualities which Murnau brings to it, and the atmospheric, imaginatively Expressionist backdrops he invokes, many using real locations rather than the more customary studio sets. Dracula has been remade many times and in many ways, but Werner Herzog's *Nosferatu, The Vampire* (1979) specifically attempted, with very mixed results, to invoke the spirit, and often the letter, of this pioneering, and arguably still greatest, version.

A Prana Production
Screenplay Henrik Galeen, unofficially based on the novel *Dracula* by Bram Stoker
Photography Fritz Arno Wagner
Set Designer Albin Grau
Running time 75 mins b/w

Cast
Max Schreck (Graf Orlok, Nosferatu)
Alexander Granach (Knock, an Estate Agent)
Gustav Von Wangenheim (Hutter, His Employee)
Greta Schroeder (Ellen, His Wife)
G H Schnell (Harding, Shipowner)
Ruth Landshoff (Annie, His Wife)

Odd Man Out

Carol Reed, UK, 1946

British thriller

A wounded gunman on the run from the police signals a rare British masterpiece.

The story

Ireland, the early 1920s. Johnny McQueen, the leader of a proscribed political organization, has escaped from prison where he has been serving time for gunrunning. Needing money, he organizes the theft of a linen mill payroll. Shot and badly wounded, he is abandoned to survive on the streets as the police hunt him down. In a weakened state, his adventures take on a hallucinatory quality as he is painted by an artist and operated on by a failed medical student. His devoted girlfriend Kathleen manages to contact him and arrange for their flight to the docks. However, as the police move in, the couple realize the futility of further evasion and Kathleen shoots a gun to draw the fire which kills them both.

Comment

The indigenous British film industry blossomed in the immediate post-World War II years, and Carol Reed was among the handful of directors who put the new possibilities to best use. *Odd Man Out* is an imaginative, surrealistic and occasionally slightly overheated thriller that explores one of Reed's favourite themes of a lone protagonist caught in a situation over which he has no control and which he must struggle (often vainly) to overcome.

James Mason is excellent as the doomed romantic hero of the Irish rebellion (it is impossible to imagine a similar contemporary treatment of an IRA or INLA man) and is matched by a fine supporting cast, particularly Robert Newton as the artist who witnesses all the pain-induced sensitivity that he has always wanted to capture on canvas. Reed directs both the action sequences and the more suspenseful moments with immense style and, although the highly symbolic ending seems a little overdone, few would dispute Mason's latterday recollection: 'I think this was a great film, perhaps Carol Reed's best; certainly it was mine.'

The film remains one of the rare masterpieces of British cinema, and prefigures in many respects Reed's subsequent and even better known *The Third Man* (1949) (see p219), notably in its atmospheric monochrome photography by Robert Krasker, its underworld milieu, and its lone but dubious protagonist being hunted towards his tragic end. The director's approach echoes the style of wartime documentaries, allied to a developing taste for stark realism which was to dominate British filmmaking in the ensuing decades.

Odd Man Out was updated and remoulded to fit black Americans in the Civil Rights struggle as *The Lost Man* (1969) with Sidney Poitier in the Mason role but as such had a considerably lessened impact.

A Carol Reed/Two Cities Production
Producer Carol Reed
Screenplay F L Green and R C Sherriff, based on the novel by Green
Photography Robert Krasker
Editor Fergus McDonell
Art Director Ralph Brinten
Music William Alwyn
Running time 116 mins b/w

Cast
James Mason (Johnny McQueen)
Robert Newton (Lukey)
Robert Beatty (Dennis)
F J McCormick (Shell)
Fay Compton (Rosie)
Beryl Measor (Maudie)

On The Town

Gene Kelly and Stanley Donen, USA, 1949

Musical innovation

Three sailors on shore leave take the Hollywood musical on to the streets of New York, New York.

The story

Brooklyn, 6am. Sailors Gabey, Chip and Ozzie disembark for shore leave. When Gabey catches a glimpse of poster girl 'Miss Turnstiles' he sets off in pursuit of her. Chip meets cab-driver Brunhilde who joins the search, and at the Museum of Natural History Ozzie meets anthropology student Claire. They go their separate ways and meet later at the Empire State Building. Gabey discovers his girl, ballet dancer Ivy, but she is embarrassed by her job as a dancer at Coney Island and runs away. The gang follow her there in a stolen taxi with the police still on their trail. However, the dancers raise funds to pay for past damages, all are happily reconciled and later bid farewell at the navy yard as three other sailors leave for their day on the town.

Comment

Throwing aside the by now rather old-fashioned mould in which the Hollywood musical had been set during its classic decade of the 1930s, *On the Town* marks the beginning of the modern musical. Adapted from the long-running Broadway success, the film broke new ground in a number of areas, notably in shooting on the streets of New York rather than the omnipresent studio sets which had previously dominated the genre. Whilst prevented from shooting the entire film on location, Kelly and Donen made the most of their week in New York to create the opening number and finale. Equally significantly, the dance routines and big musical numbers were integrated into the action in a way which had not been considered necessary in the Fred Astaire musicals of the 1930s, far less those of a set-piece specialist like Busby Berkeley. Songs are never treated as an aside, but are used to advance the plot rather than stall it, or to establish relationships between characters, like Ann Miller's 'Prehistoric Man' routine in the Museum of Natural History which is tapped out for the benefit of Jules Munshin. The women whom Kelly and Sinatra meet are no shrinking violets either, but seem unusually outspoken and liberated for their day and every bit as dominant as the men.

The final factor which has established the film as a continuously vital one though, does not depend on its influence over subsequent generations of American musicals. Rather, it is the sheer exuberance and vitality of the cast, music and dancing; even without its ground-breaking role, *On the Town* would rate among the handful of great film musicals. Nominated in only a solitary Academy Award category it won Best Scoring of a Musical for Roger Edens and Lennie Hayton.

An M-G-M Production
Producer Arthur Freed
Screenplay Betty Comden and Adolph Green, based on their musical play from the Jerome Robbins/Leonard Bernstein ballet *Fancy Free*
Photography Harold Rossen
Editor Ralph E Winters
Art Directors Cedric Gibbons, Jack Marin Smith, Edwin B Willis and Jack D Moore
Music Leonard Bernstein and Roger Edens
Running time 98 mins colour

Cast
Gene Kelly (Gabey)
Frank Sinatra (Chip)
Betty Garrett (Brunhilde Esterhazy)
Ann Miller (Claire Huddesen)
Jules Munshin (Ozzie)
Vera-Ellen (Ivy Smith)

On the Waterfront

Elia Kazan, USA, 1954

Realist drama

The guilt-ridden redemption of a failed boxer gives Marlon Brando one of his finest roles.

The story

New York. Charley Malloy, a ruthless figure among the hoodlums who control the Longshoreman's Union, uses his brother Terry to lure an uncooperative docker to his death. The man's sister Edie and priest Father Barry are determined to bring his murderers to justice. Spying on his brother's behalf, Terry attends one of their public meetings and is attracted to Edie who asks for his help. When a potential witness is killed in an 'accident', Terry tells Edie of his guilt and ignores the pleading of his brother not to turn stool-pigeon. Charley is killed for failing to secure his silence and Terry testifies against the gang. The next day at the docks he is savagely beaten but survives to lead the dockers to work.

Comment

Despite some dissatisfaction with the ending, *On the Waterfront* has established a place as classic American realist drama, and boasts one of Marlon Brando's finest performances. Written by novelist Budd Schulberg from a series of newspaper reports on violence and corruption in the docks, the film was directed by Elia Kazan. Both men had been implicated in giving evidence to the House Un-American Activities Committee and some critics have seen Terry Malloy's rather sudden apotheosis from reviled 'stoolie' to lone hero as a self-justifying redemption for his creators as well. Interestingly enough, Schulberg chose a completely different, distinctly non-heroic ending for the novel he subsequently published.

The Christlike role of Malloy had once been earmarked for Frank Sinatra but has become one of the quintessential characters in defining the power, range and animal magnetism of Brando that had lit up the American screen annually since his cinema début in 1950. The famous 'I could have had class. I could have been a contender' speech that Terry delivers to his brother in the back of a cab has been much parodied over the years but is a genuinely moving moment and illustrative of the marvellous complexity that Brando could bring to a basically simple character. After nominations for *A Streetcar Named Desire* (1951) (see p208), *Viva Zapata!* (1952) and *Julius Caesar* (1953), *On the Waterfront* earned him his first Best Actor Oscar in the face of competition from Humphrey Bogart in *The Caine Mutiny*, Bing Crosby in *Country Girl*, James Mason in *A Star Is Born* (see p206) and Dan O'Herlihy in *The Adventures of Robinson Crusoe*. The film itself, the recipient of 12 nominations, won in eight categories including Best Picture, Best Director and Best Screenplay.

A Horizon Production
Producer Sam Spiegel
Screenplay Budd Schulberg, based on articles by journalist Malcolm Johnson
Photography Boris Kaufman
Editor Arthur E Milford
Art Director Richard Day
Music Leonard Bernstein
Running time 108 mins b/w

Cast

Marlon Brando (Terry Malloy)
Eva Marie Saint (Edie Doyle)
Karl Malden (Father Barry)
Lee J Cobb (Johnny Friendly)
Rod Steiger (Charles Malloy)
Pat Henning ('Kayo' Dugan)

One Flew Over the Cuckoo's Nest

Milos Forman, USA, 1975

Triumph of the will

A struggle for power in a mental asylum becomes a cinematic paean to the human spirit.

The story

When prisoner Randle P McMurphy fakes insanity to avoid a work detail he is transferred to a state mental institution. Bristling under the tyranny of head nurse Ratched, he tries to awaken his fellow inmates from their docility. He demands that they watch the World Series, initiates card games and even spirits them away for an unauthorized excursion. One evening he organizes a wild ward party. Next morning when Ratched discovers Billy Bibbit in bed with a girl, her threat to inform his mother leads to his suicide. McMurphy then attempts to strangle her but is subdued and later lobotomized. On his return to the ward, Chief Bromden gently smothers him and takes his chance to break out to freedom.

Comment

In 1963 Kirk Douglas made a shortlived Broadway appearance in Dale Wasserman's theatrical adaptation of Ken Kesey's celebrated anti-authoritarian novel. He then spent numerous, fruitless years attempting to secure the backing for a film version in which he would star. Eventually, he passed the film rights over to his son Michael, then best known for television's *Streets of San Francisco* and it was he who made the project a reality, raising the $3 million budget and securing an appropriate cast.

The most difficult role to fill was that of the harridan Nurse Ratched, once described as 'a misogynist's nightmare vision of the female as castrator'. Among those said to have refused the part are Anne Bancroft, Angela Lansbury, Ellen Burstyn and Geraldine Page. Louise Fletcher had only recently returned from a decade's retirement with a small role in her husband's production of *Thieves Like Us* (1974) when she caught the eye of director Milos Forman.

The first production since *It Happened One Night* (1934) (see p112) to capture all five of the top Oscars, *Cuckoo's Nest* is one of the most uncompromising and radical films to have emerged from contemporary Hollywood and postulates a marvellous triumph for the human spirit over the dehumanizing forces of repression and enforcement. It also retains enough of the implicitly allegorical dimension of the book to appeal to the immediate post-Vietnam disillusion of American youth with their political and social systems, and finds the perfect rebellious spirit in the committed performance of Nicholson. Ultimately, a rare recipient of critical acclaim and public acceptance, the film became one of the top ten grossers of all time with its take of $60 million.

A Fantasy Production
Producers Saul Zaentz and Michael Douglas
Screenplay Lawrence Hauben and Bo Goldman, based on the novel by Ken Kesey and the play by Dale Wasserman
Photography Haskell Wexler, William Fraker and Bill Butler
Editors Richard Chew, Lynzee Klingman, Sheldon Kahn
Art Director Edwin O'Donovan
Running time 133 mins *colour*

Cast
Jack Nicholson (Randle Patrick McMurphy)
Louise Fletcher (Nurse Mildred Ratched)
William Redfield (Harding)
Michael Berryman (Ellis)
Brad Dourif (Billy Bibbit)
Danny De Vito (Martini)

Orpheus
(Orphée)

Jean Cocteau, France, 1950

Death and regeneration

Jean Cocteau finds poetry in the cinema of the unreal.

The story

While entranced by the enigmatic Princess, Orpheus assists her when the poet Cegeste is killed by motorcyclists. At her house, he witnesses the man, back from the dead, pass through a mirror. Orpheus is haunted by the events and distraught when the Princess's chauffeur Heurtebise informs him that his wife Eurydice has also been killed. Passing through the mirror to the Underworld, he learns that Eurydice will be restored to life only if he never looks at her again. He breaks the promise when he glimpses her in the mirror of the Princess's Rolls Royce and is then killed by a mob. However, he is reunited with Eurydice as both the Princess and Heurtebise are led to face punishment for dabbling in the affairs of mortals.

Comment

The essential achievement of the cinematic strand of Jean Cocteau's diverse artistic endeavours is contained in what has become known as his 'Orpheus Trilogy', three disparate films made over a 30-year span, but linked by a remarkable continuity of vision. *Orphée* (*Orpheus*) stands between *Le Sang D'Un Poète* (*Blood of a Poet*) (1930) and *Le Testament D'Orphée* (*The Testament of Orpheus*) (1960), and is the most completely realized of all his films. Cocteau described the first film of this trilogy as a 'realistic documentary of unreal events', and that encapsulation is equally as effective for the method and matter of *Orpheus*.

Standing as an immense achievement of

European cinema, the film *Orpheus* illustrates Cocteau's philosophy that 'a poet must die several times in order to be born'. A wonderfully imaginative fusion of his obsession with Greek myth in general (and the story of Orpheus in the underworld in particular) with his own highly idiosyncratic ideas on the nature of the poet and the creative process, it depicts the adventures of Orpheus and his wife Eurydice on two different planes, one in contemporary domesticity, the other in a fantastic underworld. Cocteau formally demarcates the two realms through an inventive employment of such visual effects as reverse slow-motion, negative images, and a bath of mercury as the mirror through which they may pass over. The domestic existence of Orpheus however is shot quite realistically and the division serves as an emblem of the position of the artist, caught between mundane reality and the wonders of the imagination. Always challenging and often funny, *Orpheus* is Cocteau's masterpiece, and as close as he – and perhaps anyone else – came to his aim of realizing film as poetry.

A Andre Paulve/Films Du Palais-Royal Production
Screenplay Jean Cocteau
Photography Nicolas Hayer
Art Director Jean D'Eaubonne
Music Georges Auric
Running time 112 mins b/w

Cast

Jean Marais (Orphée)
Maria Casares (The Princess)
Marie Dea (Eurydice)
François Perier (Heurtebise)
Juliette Greco (Aglaonice)
Edoaurd Dermithe (Cegeste)

Paris, Texas

Wim Wenders, West Germany/France, 1984

Road movie

An attempt at family reconciliation marked a new departure in the director's fascination with road movies.

The story

Travis Anderson, missing presumed dead for four years, returns in a state of exhaustion to a small border town. Silent at first, he slowly begins to tell his brother Walt his story on the drive back to Los Angeles. Walt and Ann have adopted Travis's son Hunter, but when Travis decides to go and search for his wife Jane in Houston, Hunter insists on coming. Travis confronts Jane in a peepshow booth, but does not reveal his identity until their second encounter, which teases out the reason for their separation. Travis arranges the reunion of mother and son, and drives off.

Comment

While this austere but commerically very successful film extends some of the thematic strands evident in Wenders's earlier road movies like *Alice in the Cities* or *Kings of the Road*, it is unusual in his oeuvre in its focus on family relationships, albeit of an ultimately unresolved kind.

The film reflects the director's persistent fascination with the cultural clash between Europe and America. He has spoken of the crucial influence that, through books but mainly films and music, the post-war Americanization of European culture exerted on his own formative years in Germany.

That complex network is engaged here again, beginning with the very title. Paris, Texas, where Travis has bought a plot of land with the dream of settling his estranged family, is explicitly linked with the missing romantic ideal of Paris, France. Ironically, Travis attains neither; Paris, Texas proves to be as much a dream as its namesake.

The central core of the film lies in the relationships between Travis and his separated family. He makes his peace with his young son Hunter (at the cost of disrupting his brother's family life), and effects a reconciliation of sorts with his wife Jane (brilliantly played by Nastassja Kinski in her finest role to date), but the desired ultimate reunion proves impossible.

Ry Cooder's haunting soundtrack music and the wide-screen vistas of Texas which open the film remain powerfully in the memory, but the key scene, and one of the most brilliant in Wenders's films, is the painful confrontation between Travis and Jane through the peepshow mirror. In the end, though, the promise of resolution from endless wandering (the film is crowded with images of movement) is denied, and Travis is condemned to return to the road alone.

A Road Movies Filmproduktion/Argos Films Production
Producers Don Guest and Anatole Dauman
Screenplay Sam Shephard, adapted by L M 'Kit' Carson
Photography Robby Muller
Editor Peter Przygodda
Art Director Kate Altman
Music Ry Cooder
Running time 148 mins *colour*

Cast
Harry Dean Stanton (Travis Anderson)
Dean Stockwell (Walter R Anderson)
Aurore Clement (Anne Anderson
Hunter Carson (Hunter Anderson)
Nastassja Kinski (Jane)

The Passion of Joan of Arc
(La Passion de Jeanne D'Arc)

Carl Dreyer, France, 1928

The power of faith

Imaginative use of the close-up hauntingly expresses the martyrdom of Joan of Arc.

The story

Having inspired and led an army against the British forces, the teenage Joan has been captured by the Burgundians and stands trial in the Palace of Justice charged with witchcraft and heresy. She is denounced for wearing men's clothes and talking to St Michael but stands up to her captors claiming that her freedom will be secured by a great victory. She is ordered to renounce her visions but remains unrepentant despite gruelling torture, bleeding and fever. Promised the body and blood of Christ if she will sign a confession, she again resists. Further humiliated, she demands her punishment. Her head shaved, she is burnt at the stake. Her physical presence may be destroyed but her martyrdom and faith bring her eternal life.

Comment

Although not a commercial success on its initial release, Carl Dreyer's epic account of the trial of Joan of Arc has long been considered a great masterpiece of world cinema. Offered a contract to make a film on a French historical personage, the Danish director chose Joan of Arc who had been canonized in 1920. The film condenses her 18 months of interrogations into a single day, the last of her life, but takes as its real theme the battle for her soul, and the attainment of salvation through suffering.

Dreyer's relentless use of close-ups was considered revolutionary at the time, and is central to the realization of his need to involve the audience in the ordeal of the girl, as well as revealing the machinations of her persecutors, starkly framed without any softening make-up. This reliance on the close-up has perhaps been over emphasized in critical discussion of the film, to the detriment of its equally inventive use of other devices, notably the rapid cross-cutting as it moves into the climactic rythmn of the closing scenes. Having once considered the possibility of Lillian Gish for the role, Dreyer wrings a nakedly emotional performance from boulevard comedienne Renée Maria Falconetti in her only film appearance, and is said to have treated her remorselessly in the process. *La Passion de Jeanne D'Arc* took almost 18 months – and much expenditure on elaborate sets – to make, and was Dreyer's last silent film. As in all his work, his suffering heroine is defeated by a cruel and heartless world, but triumphs in what he saw as the ultimate realm of the soul. His shameless manipulations of chronology and historical fact are all aimed at drawing the viewer into this timeless struggle; generations of filmgoers have attested to his success.

A Société Generale De Films Production
Screenplay Carl Theodor Dreyer, based on the original records of the trial and the novels *Vie De Jeanne D'Arc* and *La Passion De Jeanne D'Arc* by Joseph Delteil
Photography Rudolph Mate
Art Directors Hermann Warm, Jean Victor-Hugo and Valentine Hugo
Music Victor Alix and Leo Pouget
Running Time 114 mins b/w

Cast

Renée Maria Falconetti (Joan of Arc)
Eugene Silvain (Bishop Pierre Cauchon)
Maurice Schutz (Nicholas Leyseleur)
Michel Simon (Jean Lemaitre)
Antonin Artaud (Massieu)
Louis Ravet (Jean Beaupère)

Pather Panchali
(Song of the Little Road)

Satyajit Ray, India, 1955

Indian landmark

A simple portrait of village life places Indian cinema on the international map.

The story

The 1920s. Mechanization is slowly changing the rural way of life. In one small village, Harihar lives with his wife Sarbajaya, children Apu and Durga and aged aunt. When Harihar decides that his Treasury pay is no longer enough to support his family, Apu is sent to a school for the poor and Harihar leaves home to earn money as a lay preacher. Apu and Durga amuse themselves by following the sweet-seller, listening to their aunt's ghost stories and catching sight of a train. Apu also learns of death with the passing of his aunt and Durga who catches a fever during a thunderstorm. Harihar returns when Durga is on her deathbed and subsequently takes Sarbajaya and Apu with him to Benares and a new life.

Comment

Satyajit Ray's début film opened up an entirely new subject-matter and set of aesthetic and formal possibilities in an Indian cinema previously dominated by escapist musical adventures and romances. For one thing, the film was in the Bengali tongue rather than the predominant Hindi one, and betrayed the influence of the Italian neorealists in its downbeat but lyrical mode. The novel had begun life as a serial in a Calcutta journal in 1928 and was considered a modern classic by the time Ray came to film it in the 1950s. Unable to secure much enthusiasm for his plans, he nevertheless began filming in October 1952 and resumed several months later in 1953. The completed footage was then edited and shown in vain to potential backers before a further year passed and filming resumed once more with backing from the Government of West Bengal and the promise that if completed it would be featured at an Indian exhibition planned for New York's Museum of Modern Art in April 1955.

From these most difficult of circumstances, Ray created a film that transforms everyday material into something almost literally magical. In the film's most famous scene, the boy Apu runs with his sister through a field of white kasha in order to catch a glimpse of a passing train, bound for the city. It is a supremely ordinary moment, but the characters' response invests it with a joy which both renders it marvellous, and implicitly reveals much about the wider context of their lives. The revelation of the social and political through the personal and intimately emotional is typical of the director's approach to his subsequent work, which includes the remaining two parts of the trilogy *Aparajito* (*The Unvanquished*) (1956) and *Apur Sansar* (*The World of Apu*) (1959).

A Government of West Bengal Production
Producer Satyajit Ray
Screenplay Satyajit Ray, based on the novel by Bhibutibhusan Banerjee
Photography Subrata Mitra
Editor Dulal Dutta
Art Director Bansi Chandragupta
Music Ravi Shankar
Running time 115 mins b/w

Cast
Kanu Banerjee (Harihar)
Karuna Banerjee (Sarbajaya)
Uma Das Gupta (Durga)
Subir Banerjee (Apu)
Chunibala Devi (The Aunt)

Paths of Glory

Stanley Kubrick, USA, 1957

The futility of conflict

Stanley Kubrick offers an eloquent indictment of the insanity engendered by military fanaticism.

The story

1916. A battle-weary regiment are ordered to advance on an impregnable German fortification. When this proves futile, the fanatical General Mireau orders the artillery to fire on their own men. The order is refused. As a scapegoat for his own incompetence, he organizes a trial on the charges of mutiny and cowardice. Colonel Dax is allowed to act as defence counsel but the event is a mere formality. Even when Dax learns of Mireau's orders to kill, his superior General Broulard will not act on the information. Three men are needlessly executed in the name of justice, but Broulard subsequently relents and announces that Mireau will face a court of inquiry.

Comment

Paths of Glory remains among the most powerful anti-war films ever committed to celluloid, and the harbinger of a re-evaluation of the depiction of war and the military in Hollywood over the en suing decades. Shooting on locations in Germany, some 25 miles west of Munich, director Stanley Kubrick pursues the logic of the script (which he co-wrote) with a relentless and unforgiving determination – savagely condemning the callousness of the French military, contrasting the grim scenes of trench life with the plush comfort of the chateau where the officers reside, and leavening his bitter view of man's inhumanity only in the film's closing moments when he focuses on the quiet dignity of Dax's commitment to his men.

Comparable in impact to Lewis Milestone's *All Quiet on the Western Front* (1930) (see p9), the film benefits from the director's insistence on compromising on authenticity only in the name of dramatic impact. Thus his trenches were dug six feet wide to allow the camera access for long tracking shots but an entire plot of ground was studiously transformed by 60 workmen into a muddy, debris-strewn battlefield to allow him to capture the slaughter experienced during the attack on The Anthill with a broad, unflinching sweep across acres of wholesale destruction.

Critically admired but a commercial failure, the film prefigured the more blackly comic anti-war sentiments of Kubrick's subsequent *Dr Strangelove (Or How I Learned to Stop Worrying and Love the Bomb)* (1964), and makes an interesting contrast with his more ambiguous reflections on the Vietnam War in *Full Metal Jacket* (1987), although the latter does share the theme of the dehumanizing effect of war on those drawn into its bloody compass.

A Harris-Kubrick production
Producer James B Harris
Screenplay Stanley Kubrick, Calder Willingham and Jim Thompson, based on the novel by Humphrey Cobb
Photography George Krause
Editor Eva Kroll
Art Director Ludwig Reiber
Music Gerald Fried
Running time 86 mins b/w

Cast
Kirk Douglas (Colonel Dax)
Ralph Meeker (Corporal Paris)
Adolphe Menjou (General Broulard)
George Macready (General Mireau)
Wayne Morris (Lieutenant Roget)
Richard Anderson (Major Saint-Auban)

Peeping Tom

Michael Powell, UK, 1959

Voyeuristic self-revelation

The portrait of a killer is a disturbing study of voyeurism and the craft of cinema.

The story

Mark Lewis works in a film studio, supplements his income taking 'girlie' photos for a local shop and films the faces of his female victims as he stabs them with his camera tripod. He becomes friendly with Helen Stephens, a downstairs neighbour, and lets her watch disturbing films of him as a child when his father used him to experiment in the psychology of fear. He subsequently murders model Vivian and films the police inquiry into her death. He is interrupted when watching the films by Stephens's blind mother who can sense that something is amiss. He finally arouses police suspicions and they follow him. At home, he discovers Helen watching the films of his murders and turns the camera on himself to record his suicide.

Comment

Successive generations of critical acclaim have rescued Michael Powell's disturbing and provocative shocker from the neglect into which his entire oeuvre had fallen. His account of the behaviour of a disturbed young man who takes his pleasure from murdering women with the sharpened leg of a camera tripod while filming them remains arguably the most genuinely shocking British film ever made.

Unlike films in the horror genre, though, there is no escape into the fantasy element for the captive viewer, who is forced not only to come to terms with Mark Lewis as a character whom we are invited to under-stand and even empathize with, but also to recognize his or her own complicity in the voyeuristic act of watching a film. Powell employs multiple films-within-films effects, including the films made by Mark, which he replays for his pleasure, and those made by his father (played by Powell) of experiments carried out on Mark as a child (played by Powell's son), which suggest the source of his perverse behaviour. That structure reflects Powell's obsession with the nature and form of film, a pre-occupation which runs through most of his major works, albeit in a less overt manner. His distinctive use of colour and lighting and the constantly shifting visual surface of the film make it the most stylistically radical of his works, and easily the most controversial. Vitriolically condemned by the critics on its release, the film is now recognized as an important contribution to contemporary cinema. If it has grown no more comfortable to watch, the passage of time and a changing social and psychological context have conspired to make it less of an oddity, and much more than the gratuitously nasty shocker it must have appeared to audiences in 1959.

An Anglo-Amalgamated/Astor Production
Producer Michael Powell
Screenplay Leo Marks
Photography Otto Heller
Editor Noreen Ackland
Art Director Arthur Lawrence
Music Brian Easdale
Running time 109 mins *colour*

Cast

Carl Boehm (Mark Lewis)
Anna Massey (Helen Stephens)
Maxine Audley (Mrs Stephens)
Moira Shearer (Vivian)
Esmond Knight (Arthur Baden)
Shirley Ann Field (Diane Ashley)

From the new wave to the movie brats
Movie history in the 1960s and 1970s

In films like *Breathless* (1959) (see p43) and *Jules and Jim* (1961) (see p121), the French 'nouvelle vague' awakened fresh notions about the technique and artificiality of filmmaking as well as asserting a director's right to use film as form of personal expression. The influence of such a philosophy can be seen in later American films like *Bonnie and Clyde* (1967) (see p41) and *Easy Rider* (1969) (see p75).

Italian cinema in this period consistently underlined its world-class status with a spectrum of productions from lucrative sword and sandal epics to the spaghetti westerns of Sergio Leone and the full artistic flowering of Federico Fellini in films like *La Dolce Vita* (1959) (see p70) and *8½* (1963) (see p76). Michelangelo Antonioni also displayed his measured approach to the search for self-fulfilment in works like *L'Avventura* (1960) (see p22) whilst the riches of Italian cinema were also to be found in the films of Pasolini and Bertolucci.

Ingmar Bergman continued to explore the darker side of the human condition with a rare sensitivity and rigour in films like *Persona* (1966) (see p165) and *Cries and Whispers* (1972) and the 1970s witnessed an unexpected flourishing of national cinema in both West Germany and Australia. The former brought to the fore such talents as Werner Herzog, director of *Aguirre, Wrath of God* (1972) (see p6), Volker Schlöndorff with *The Tin Drum* (1979) (see p220) and Wim Wenders, whose preoccupation with the influence of American popular culture on post-war Germany found expression in such films as *Kings of the Road* (1976) and eventually took him to America where he made *Paris, Texas* (1984) (see p157). The Australian renaissance focused attention on such figures as Gillian Armstrong, Fred Schepisi and Peter Weir who achieved success with *Picnic at Hanging Rock* (1975) (see p168), although *Mad Max* (1979) (see p135) destroyed the myth that Australian cinema consisted exclusively of a rose-hued nostalgia for the past.

Despite a changing world, Hollywood's greatest hits of the period often consisted of such old-fashioned and prehistoric entertainments as *The Sound of Music* (1965) (see p204), *Airport* (1969) and *Love Story* (1970) with studios placing their faith in increasingly gargantuan all-star productions like *How The West Was Won* (1962), *The Longest Day* (1962) or *It's A Mad, Mad, Mad, Mad World* (1963). Social changes and the demise of a restrictive censorship system brought such films as *Who's Afraid of Virginia Woolf?* (1966), *The Graduate* (1967) (see p96) and *Midnight Cowboy* (1969) whilst the phenomenal success of *Easy Rider* (1969) (see p75) opened up opportunities for an increasing cine-literate generation of filmmakers like Bob Rafelson with *Five Easy Pieces* (1970) (see p86), Peter Bogdanovich with *The Last Picture Show* (1971) (see p124), Francis Coppola with *The Godfather* (1972) (see p89) and Martin Scorsese with *Mean Streets* (1973). Indeed, by the early 1970s, the American cinema seemed to have achieved a balance of the commercial and the more artistic as the cycle of disaster films like *The Towering Inferno* (1974) and mainstream horror films productions such as *The Exorcist* (1973) (see p78) could happily co-exist alongside more adventurous works dealing with political and racial issues or questions of national identity such as *The Conversation* (1974) (see p59), *One Flew Over the Cuckoo's Nest* (1975) (see p155) and *All The President's Men* (1976) (see p10). With the falling age of the general cinemagoing audience and the box-office acclaim that greeted Steven Spielberg's work from *Jaws* (1975) (see p114) onwards that balance became less easy to sustain.

All The President's Men *(1976) Directed by Alan J Pakula (Dustin Hoffman, Robert Redford)*

Z *(1968) Directed by Constantin Costa-Gavras (Yves Montand in poster)*

Close Encounters of the Third Kind *(1977) Directed by Steven Spielberg*

The Exorcist *(1973) Directed by William Friedkin (Max Von Sydow)*

Persona

Ingmar Bergman, Sweden, 1966

Psychology and the cinema

The workings of a troubled mind bring a rare engagement with psychoanalaysis and the nature of cinema.

The story

Actress Elisabeth Vogler is hospitalized after losing the power of speech. There is no medical explanation for her condition but she remains in the care of nurse Alma who, by contrast, speaks incessantly. They move to a summer house by the sea and Elisabeth gains in strength while Alma confides her memories and desires. However, their relationship changes when Alma discovers a letter in which Elisabeth is less than complimentary about her. When Elisabeth's husband arrives, he is unable to distinguish between them and makes love to Alma. Alone once more, Alma voices Elisabeth's thoughts about the difficult childbirth that may have contributed to her breakdown. Alma leaves and Elisabeth is assumed to have resumed acting.

Comment

Ingmar Bergman's first film after a period of extreme ill health, *Persona* is an enigmatic and multi-layered masterpiece culled from the most basic of cinematic materials – a one-sided dialogue between a highly talkative nurse and her psychosomatically speechless patient. Most of the film is spent in unrelenting concentration on the relationship between these two women (who may well represent dual aspects of a single woman, a reading encouraged by a frequently repeated composite shot made up from half of each woman's face). The exceptions are a brutal pre-title sexual fantasy of a young boy, a psychiatrist who talks to both women early in the film, and the appearance of the patient's husband who seems unable to tell one woman from the other. The material from the pre-title sequence also returns in a surprising mid-film incursion. The film begins with a roll of film threading into a projector; at midpoint, and at a moment of physical crisis in the relationship, the film apparently burns away, introducing this extraneous material from the adolescent fantasy.

Few films have attempted to deal so directly and yet in such oblique fashion with psychoanalysis, both at the level of subject-matter and in the formal devices (there is, for example, almost no cross-cutting from one woman to the other, except in moments crucial to the evolving relationship). There are also few films so intent on breaking the relationship between viewers and subject-matter to remind them that the stark truth and reality they are experiencing are part of the illusion that cinema creates. Ultimately, *Persona* defies any easy solution or explanation of what the viewer has encountered on screen, and that ambiguity itself is unusual in a medium historically yoked to linear narrative and action.

A Svensk Filmindustri Production
Producer Ingmar Bergman
Screenplay Ingmar Bergman
Photography Sven Nykvist
Editor Ulla Ryghe
Art Director Bibi Lindstrom
Music Lars-Johan Werle
Running time 81 mins b/w

Cast

Liv Ullmann (Elisabeth Vogler)
Bibi Andersson (Nurse Alma)
Margarethe Krook (The Woman Doctor)
Gunnar Bjornstrand (Mr Vogler)
Jorgen Lindstrom (The Boy)

The Philadelphia Story

George Cukor, USA, 1940

Cocktail comedy

The sight of the privileged classes enjoying their privileges serves as the epitome of sophisticated screen comedy.

The story

Divorced from the still devoted C K Dexter Haven, spoiled socialite Tracy Lord is preparing to wed business tycoon George Kittredge. The devious Haven persuades a scandal magazine to suppress a planned exposé of Seth Lord's indiscretions in return for allowing reporter Macaulay Connor and photographer Liz Imbrie exclusive access to the high-society wedding of the year. An incensed Tracy reacts by lording it over the journalists. However, Connor's cynicism makes her acutely aware of her own deficiencies. An inebriated moonlight swim and a declaration of his love awaken her to the mistake that is about to be made. Her fiancé calls the wedding off but the marriage goes ahead with Tracy and Haven as bride and groom once more.

Comment

One of several stars labelled box-office poison in 1938, Katharine Hepburn contacted playwright Philip Barry about creating a suitable role for her return to Broadway. The result was *The Philadelphia Story* which opened in March 1939 and played for a triumphant 415 performances. Hepburn had purchased the film rights and, despite a number of offers, including one from Sam Goldwyn that comprised William Wyler as a director and Gary Cooper as her co-star, she chose M-G-M as the home for her project, with the possibility of Clark Gable and Spencer Tracy as the screen substitutes for stage colleagues Joseph Cotten and Van Heflin. She was happy to settle for her frequent partner Cary Grant and contract player James Stewart alongside George Cukor who had previously directed her in such films as *A Bill of Divorcement* (1932), *Little Women* (1933) and *Sylvia Scarlett* (1935).

The film boasts one of the most effective opening sequences in movie history, and does so without a single line of dialogue being spoken. Cary Grant is precipitately ejected from the front door of a splendid mansion; Katharine Hepburn appears in the door, breaks a golf club over her knee, then tosses the remainder after him and slams the door; Grant rings the bell, and when she answers, pushes her in the face. The entire film, widely regarded as the quintessential example of the screwball comedy, builds from that single scene as Cukor uses the witty script and rich supporting cast to play mischievously with the audience's expectations that these two Hollywood heroes will eventually get together again.

The Philadelphia Story smashed box-office records on its release and was nominated for six Academy Awards, winning the statues for James Stewart as Best Actor and Donald Stewart as the writer of the Best Screenplay.

A Metro-Goldwyn-Mayer Production
Producer Joseph L Mankiewicz
Screenplay Donald Ogden Stewart, based on the play by Philip Barry
Photography Joseph Ruttenberg
Editor Frank Sullivan
Art Directors Cedric Gibbons and Wade R Rubottom
Music Franz Waxman
Running time 112 mins b/w

Cast

Cary Grant (C K Dexter Haven)
Katharine Hepburn (Tracy Lord)
James Stewart (Macaulay Connor)
Ruth Hussey (Elizabeth Imbrie)
John Howard (George Kittredge)
Roland Young (Uncle Willie)

Pickpocket

Robert Bresson, France, 1959

Sin and redemption

The romantic undercurrents in Bresson's austerity emerge in the life of an obsessive thief.

The story

Lonely, impecunious student Michel begins a life of crime by stealing from a lady's handbag at a racecourse. Caught by the police, he is subsequently released. Upset by the death of his mother, he nevertheless acquires the necessary skills of the trade from a master thief and continues this obsession, despite the worries of friends Jacques and Jeanne. The arrest of two colleagues compels him to leave France. He returns quite some time later to discover Jeanne living alone with her child by Jacques. Assuming the role of breadwinner, he resumes his former trade and is caught in a police trap. Whilst serving his sentence, he is visited by Jeanne and the power of her love allows him a new purpose and peace of mind.

Comment

Pickpocket is a typically austere and rigorous piece of filmmaking from a director who eschews conventional film narrative and perspectives as a matter of course. Although it belongs to the period of the birth of the French Nouvelle Vague and was filmed on the streets of Paris at the same time as Jean-Luc Godard's *Breathless* (see p43), it takes a quite different approach to its subject-matter and style than any of the films associated with that movement. Michel is a young man who perversely defines his moral superiority through the act of stealing, not so much for gain – the door to his own unlocked room remains open throughout the film as a statement of his disregard for property – as for the act itself. Stealing has become obsessive, but has also become his way of interacting with the world and with other people, a symbol as much as an act. Bresson constantly signals this symbolic aspect of the thefts in his concentration on shot of near-disembodied hands, and in the way he momentarily but palpably suspends the stolen objects in the instant of their transferal from victim to thief, allowing the camera to linger meaningfully on them.

The film is unusual in Bresson's canon in that the protagonist is not simply allowed to outlive the end of the film, but is permitted a redemptive release from his obsession through the love he discovers for a woman. The film was inspired by Dostoevsky's *Crime and Punishment* but is in no sense a film of that book. Both narrative and dialogue are stripped to the barest essentials, which has the typically Bressonian effect of magnifying the smallest visual gestures, and weighing them down with significance. *Pickpocket* itself would serve as one of the inspirations for Paul Schrader's *American Gigolo* (1980)

An Agnes Delahaie Production
Screenplay Robert Bresson
Photography Leonce-Henry Burel and Henri Raichi
Editor Raymond Lamy
Art Director Pierre Charbonnier
Music Jean-Baptiste Lulli
Running time 80 mins b/w

Cast
Martin Lassalle (Michel)
Marika Green (Jeanne)
Pierre Leymarie (Jacques)
Jean Pelegri (Police Inspector)
Kassagi (Pickpocket)
Pierre Etaix (Accomplice)

Picnic at Hanging Rock

Peter Weir, Australia, 1975

Inexplicable mystery

A languid Victorian enigma proves a high point of the New Australian Cinema.

The story

St Valentine's Day 1900. A party of schoolgirls from an exclusive boarding school go on a picnic to the awe-inspiring Hanging Rock. During the heat of the afternoon, four girls decide to climb higher into the rock. Disturbed by the atmosphere around her, one of the girls turns back and informs the teachers of their actions. Miss McGraw sets off in search of the girls. None of the women reappear and a massive search gets underway to discover what might have befallen them. The aristocratic Michael Fitzhubert stumbles upon one of the girls in the rocks with her clothes torn. She has no recollection of what has happened and is unable to help in locating the others who are never heard of again.

Comment

The release of *Picnic at Hanging Rock* not only signalled the arrival of a major new talent in director Peter Weir, but also alerted international audiences to the remarkable upsurge then taking place in Australian filmmaking, drawing on distinctively Australian subjects and themes.

Following acclaim for his bizarre black comedy *The Cars That Ate Paris* (1974), Weir displayed his versatility and affinity with the mystical with this atmospheric, haunting account of the strange, unexplained disappearance of a schoolteacher and three of her pupils for which he had sought Deborah Kerr in the role now played by Rachel Roberts. The film captivated audiences with its eerie, sinister beauty and otherworldly atmosphere, augmented by gorgeous visuals and a hugely effective soundtrack. All these elements served to fill in the rather sparse storyline, given that the real fascination of the film lies not in what we see happen on the screen, but in what is not revealed to us about the mysterious disappearances. Like many of the other films emerging from what was quickly if unimaginatively dubbed the New Australian Cinema, *Picnic at Hanging Rock* looked back into Australia's hitherto unexplored (on film at least) past for a setting, and to the ambiguous relationship between the incoming modern residents of the continent and the mystical ways of its ancient indigenous populace. The attention to period detail, fresh and imaginative visual treatment, unconventional manipulation of the thriller genre, and unresolved air of mystery proved a potent combination, although Weir owes an enormous debt to the music of Gheorghe Zamphir – an evocative re-working on pan pipes of the second movement of Beethoven's fifth piano concerto.

Producers Jim McElroy and Hal McElroy
Screenplay Cliff Green, based on the novel by Joan Lindsay
Photography Russell Boyd
Editor Max Lemon
Art Director David Copping
Music Gheorghe Zamphir, Bruce Smeaton
Running time 110 mins *colour*

Cast
Rachel Roberts (Mrs Appleyard)
Dominic Guard (Michael Fitzhubert)
Helen Morse (Dianne De Poitiers)
Jacki Weaver (Minnie)
Vivean Gray (Miss Greta McGraw)
Kirsty Child (Dora Lumley)

Psycho

Alfred Hitchcock, USA, 1960

The cutting edge

Showering is never the same after a night at the Bates Motel.

The story

Fleeing with $40 000 of her boss's money, Marion Crane arrives at the Bates Motel where Norman rents her a room, much to the apparent displeasure of his mother. Later Norman discovers that Marion has been stabbed to death in the shower and disposes of the body. When a private detective arrives on Marion's trail, he too is hacked to death. Soon Sam Loomis and Marion's sister Lila arrive to investigate the disappearance. They explore the Bates mansion where Norman knocks Sam unconscious. Lila finds Mrs Bates's rotting cadaver and is about to be attacked by Norman dressed in his mother's clothes when Sam intervenes. Later under psychiatric care, Norman tries to convince the world that he wouldn't harm a fly.

Comment

A superbly orchestrated exercise in terror that has much to answer for in terms of the slasher genre it subsequently initiated, *Psycho* is one of Alfred Hitchcock's richest and most technically proficient late career works that shows the master of suspense at his peak in terms of narrative exposition, the use of the camera, music of Bernard Herrmann and sense of showmanship in the film's promotion – no-one was allowed into the cinema after the film had started.

Adapted from the Robert Bloch novel that had been inspired by the real-life activities of Wisconsin necrophiliac killer Ed Gein, the use of black and white and techniques employed within the film are a reflection of the speed and vigour Hitchcock had acquired working within television, and also of the

modest budget of $800 000 accorded the project by studio executives who were sceptical about its taste and commercial viability. The budget affected both the cast and crew possibilities and the length of the shooting schedule but Hitchcock was determined to enjoy his excursion into grand guignol, announcing to the press that he was considering either Helen Hayes or Judith Anderson for the role of mother and lavishing time and attention on the famous and much parodied shower sequence in which chocolate sauce served as blood. Cited by Hitchcock as an example of pure emotional cinema and dismissed by others as a cheap fairground ride, the film became Paramount's biggest grosser since *The Ten Commandments* (1956) and received Oscar nominations (but no awards) for Hitchcock, Janet Leigh, Cinematography and Art Direction.

Apparently restored to sanity, Norman reappeared in *Psycho II* (1983) and *Psycho III* (1986) (directed by Anthony Perkins), and the woefully unnecessary *Psycho IV* (1990) delved into Norman's childhood.

A Paramount Production
Producer Alfred Hitchcock
Screenplay Joseph Stefano, based on the novel by Robert Bloch
Photography John L Russell
Editor George Tomasini
Art Directors Joseph Hurley and Robert Clatworthy
Music Bernard Herrmann
Running time 109 mins b/w

Cast
Anthony Perkins (Norman Bates)
Janet Leigh (Marion Crane)
Vera Miles (Lila Crane)
John Gavin (Sam Loomis)
Martin Balsam (Milton Arbogast)
John McIntire (Sheriff Chambers)

The Public Enemy
(UK: Enemies of the Public)
William Wellman, USA, 1931

Gangster chronicle

James Cagney achieves stardom as the archetypal gangland hoodlum.

The story

Delinquent children Tom Powers and Matt Doyle become adult criminals under mentor Putty Nose. Their first major robbery results in two deaths and the suspicious disappearance of Putty. With prohibition, they grow rich on bootleg profiteering but Powers's family despise what he has become. The cocksure Powers flaunts himself with Kitty and blonde bombshell Gwen and mercilessly slays the two-timing Putty Nose when he reappears. When their boss is killed gang warfare breaks out; Doyle is shot dead and Powers is wounded when he kills rival gang leader Schemer Burns. He promises his family that he will go straight but is delivered from hospital by Schemer's gang wrapped from head to toe in bandages and shot through the head.

Comment

When first approached with the prospect of making *The Public Enemy*, Warner Brothers producer and future head of Twentieth Century-Fox Darryl Zanuck is alleged to have told director William Wellman, 'Look, Bill, the gangster picture's dead. We've had *Little Caesar* and *Doorway to Hell*. What do you think you can bring to this one that will possibly make it different?' Wellman replied, 'What I'll bring you is the toughest, the most violent, most realistic picture you ever did see.' 60 years on, the film may seem a little dated but it retains a raw, shocking power in the feral energy and amorality with which the gangster milieu is depicted and stands as the first gangster picture to tackle the social roots of crime as part of a genre film, linking environment and the stirrings of criminality in children.

The rise and fall of a prohibition-era gangster remains eminently watchable because of the explosive power and charisma of its star James Cagney playing a character said to be based on Chicago gangster Charles Dion 'Deanie' O'Bannion. A Broadway hoofer who had been a supporting actor in Hollywood for around a year, he was originally cast in the lesser role of Doyle, with Edward Woods cast as Powers. Recognizing his star potential, Wellman swapped actors after three days of shoting and Cagney snarled his way through the role in typically pugnacious style to establish the Hollywood archetype of the gangland hoodlum that would define and typecast him for the rest of his 30-year career. The moment when he approaches actress Mae Clarke with the words 'I wish you was a wishing well so I could tie a bucket to you and sink you!' and then plants a grapefruit on her unsuspecting physiognomy has taken on iconic status in film lore.

A Warner Brothers Production
Producer Darryl F Zanuck
Screenplay Kubec Glasmon, John Bright and Harvey Thew, based on the original story *Beer and Blood* by Bright
Photography Dev Jennings
Editor Ed McCormick
Art Director Max Parker
Music David Mendoza
Running time 84 mins b/w

Cast
James Cagney (Tom Powers)
Jean Harlow (Gwen Allen)
Edward Woods (Matt Doyle)
Joan Blondell (Mamie)
Beryl Mercer (Ma Powers)
Donald Cook (Mike Powers)

Queen Christina

Rouben Mamoulian, USA, 1933

Historical romance

*The legendary mystique of Garbo
achieves its most perfect incarnation.*

The story

17th-century Sweden. Weary of warfare, Queen Christina arranges a peace treaty. Out riding she encounters Spanish ambassador Don Antonio De La Prada and is so entranced that she disguises herself as a boy to discover his true nature. Her ruse is successful and she befriends him at a country inn. More attracted than ever, she reveals her disguise and they enjoy two days of blissfully happy communion. At court, she can only acknowledge him as an official representative but they continue to meet in secret. When her former lover Marcus discovers their affair, Christina sends Antonio away, promising to follow him to Spain. She abdicates, but Antonio is slain in a duel with Marcus. She takes his body and sets sail for a lonely exile.

Comment

Returning to Sweden during the extended renegotiation of her M-G-M contract, Greta Garbo's attention was drawn to the life of 17th-century monarch Christina by her friend Salka Viertel. Once more in Hollywood, Garbo insisted on *Queen Christina* as her next project and approved the casting of Laurence Olivier as her paramour. Initial encounters between the two performers were less than promising and Olivier was dismissed. Among the many considered as his replacement were Leslie Howard, Nils Asther and Franchot Tone. However, Garbo eventually selected her former lover John Gilbert, a silent-screen idol and co-star of *Flesh and The Devil* (1927) who was now struggling to maintain a career in the face of blatant sabotage by vindictive producer Louis B Mayer. Together, the two stars created a palpable romantic chemistry and the film remains perhaps the best example of the particular screen mystique that is forever synonymous with the name of Garbo. A highly romanticized version of historical events, the film nevertheless comprises some of the actress's finest moments. Hopelessly infatuated with her new lover she glides around the inn room, memorizing every moment for posterity in a scene that was shot to the sound of a metronome clicking to achieve the exact rythmn required by director Mamoulian. The most famous moment in all Garbo's career comes as she impassively sails into a loveless future, a climax requiring the camera to proceed from a long-shot to a final, extended close-up of the actress's unmoving face. Mamoulian recalled later telling the star, 'I want your face to be a blank sheet of paper. I want the writing to be done by every member of the audience.' Manifestly successful, the scene remains one of the most pure and moving expressions of a broken heart in cinema history.

An M-G-M Production
Producer Walter Wanger
Screenplay H M Harwood, Salka Viertel and S N Behrman, based on the story by Viertel and Margaret Levin
Photography William Daniels
Editor Blanche Sewell
Art Directors Alexander Toluboff and Edwin B Willis
Music Herbert Stothart
Running time 97 mins b/w

Cast
Greta Garbo (Queen Christina)
John Gilbert (Don Antonio De La Prada)
Ian Keith (Magnus)
Lewis Stone (Chancellor Oxenstierna)
Elizabeth Young (Ebba Sparre)
Sir C Aubrey Smith (Aage)

Raging Bull

Martin Scorsese, USA, 1980

A boxer's brutality

Scorsese explores the brutal ethos of masculinity with masterful skill.

The story

Driven by a ferocious desire for victory, Jake La Motta pulverizes his way through the list of opponents that stand between him and a shot at the middleweight championship. Mafia involvement in his career almost loses him his licence but he resumes fighting and wrests the title from Marcel Cerdan. The attainment of his goal results in a loss of discipline; he refuses to train, lets his weight balloon and displays an insane jealousy over his second wife Vickie's appeal to other men. Communicative only with his fists, he loses her, beats his loyal brother, and loses the title as well. As a nightclub owner he is jailed for serving underage girls but later settles for life as a cabaret act recalling the past error of his ways.

Comment

In US film magazine *Première*'s 1989 poll of critics and filmmakers, Martin Scorsese's *Raging Bull* topped the 'Film of the Decade' ranking with nearly double the votes garnered by its nearest rival, the acclaim almost unanimous for this most ferociously visceral and stylistically audacious work of its director's always challenging career.

The life of Jake La Motta also inspired Scorsese's frequent collaborator Robert De Niro to give one of his most dedicated and incisive performances – first training to gain the physique and technique of a prizefighter and then, whilst the production was closed down, gaining 56 pounds to portray the boxer in his declining years. The performance won him a Best Actor Oscar, one of the film's two victories along with Thelma Schoonmaker's editing, from a total of eight nominations.

During the film Scorsese balances the victim-hero's relentlessly punishing and self-punishing brutality inside and outside the ring against his developing sense of spiritual worth. Yet if, like almost all Scorsese's work, *Raging Bull* is on one level a reflective outpouring of typically Catholic body/soul anguish, on another level it is also a harsh portrayal of straitjacketing masculine values. As blood spurts from distorted faces in the shockingly stylized fight sequences, or terrifying family conflicts develop from La Motta's irrationally paranoid jealousy, we see the driving impulses of machismo in auto-destruct mode. Brilliantly shot in expressionist black-and-white by Michael Chapman, and displaying Scorsese's almost nonchalant formal virtuosity to staggering effect, the end result is a troubling explosion of unleashed physicality which no amount of pat schematizing can fully categorize.

A United Artists Production
Producers Irwin Winkler and Robert Chartoff
Screenplay Paul Schrader and Mardik Martin, based on the book by Jake La Motta (with Joseph Carter and Peter Savage)
Photography Michael Chapman
Editor Thelma Schoonmaker
Art Directors Alan Manser, Kirk Axtell and Sheldon Haber
Running time 129 mins b/w

Cast

Robert De Niro (Jake La Motta)
Cathy Moriarty (Vickie La Motta)
Joe Pesci (Joey)
Frank Vincent (Salvy)
Nicholas Colasanto (Tommy Como)
Theresa Saldana (Lenore)

Raiders of the Lost Ark

Steven Spielberg, USA, 1981

Cliff-hanging adventure

Gung-ho high adventure returns to the screen in the form of a whip-totin' archaeologist.

The story

1936. Escaping from a hazardous jaunt in South America, archaeologist Indiana Jones is then asked to assist in ensuring that the Ark of the Covenant doesn't fall into Nazi hands. In Nepal, he is reunited with his ex-girlfriend Marion before they take flight to Cairo where Marion is subsequently captured by Jones's arch-rival Belloq who is in league with the Nazis. When Jones discovers the Ark, the Nazis arrive, take the prize and leave him in a snake pit with Marion. They escape and pursue the Ark to a mysterious island but when the Ark's power is unleashed their German captors are reduced to ashes and the Ark reseals itself. Free at last, they dispatch the Ark to a vast warehouse and await further adventures.

Comment

Pretty much the master of American popular entertainment for the decade from *Jaws* (1975) (see p114) to his pursuit of artistic fulfillment in the likes of *The Color Purple* (1985), Steven Spielberg's love of Boy's Own-style high adventure found a perfect outlet in the creation of whip-totin', snake-hating adventurer Indiana Jones. The project originated in a conversation between Spielberg and George Lucas during a 1977 Hawaiian holiday. Flushed with the success of *Star Wars* (1977), Lucas asked Spielberg to name his dream project and received an answer somewhere along the lines of a James Bond adventure. Lucas told him the story of *Raiders* and the director was hooked. Lucas cited his inspiration for the

film as the cliffhanging weekly serials of the at-one-bound-he-was-free thrills and spills that he had enjoyed as a child. Spielberg felt that his approach was dictated more by his love of comic books like *The Green Lantern*, *Blackhawk* and *Sgt Rock*. Either way, the collaboration resulted in a breathtakingly paced scenario along the lines of cheap serials like *Flash Gordon*, but backed with all the technological resources and special-effects that could be bought on a budget of $22 million.

The first choice to play Indiana Jones was smalltime actor and commercials star Tom Selleck; however when he proved un-available Lucas's Han Solo, Harrison Ford, stepped into the part and made it his own. Soon any memories of Spielberg's misfire *1941* (1979) were obliterated by a film that found instant critical and public acceptance, won four Oscars and went on to feature in the top-five list of the all-time box-office champions. The character returned in the more flagrantly racist and less lighthearted *Indiana Jones and The Temple of Doom* (1984) and the exhilarating *Indiana Jones and the Last Crusade* (1989) featuring Sean Connery as Jones Senior.

A Lucasfilm Production
Producer Frank Marshall
Screenplay Lawrence Kasdan, based on a story by George Lucas and Philip Kaufman
Photography Douglas Slocombe
Editor Michael Kahn
Art Director Leslie Dilley
Music John Williams
Running time 115 mins colour

Cast
Harrison Ford (Indiana Jones)
Karen Allen (Marion Ravenswood)
Paul Freeman (Belloq)
Ronald Lacey (Toht)
John Rhys-Davies (Sallah)
Denholm Elliott (Brody)

Rashomon

Akira Kurosawa, Japan, 1951

Japanese breakthrough

*The search for objective truth
becomes a bravura exercise in
narrative construction.*

The story

Japan, eighth century. Caught in a storm,
a woodcutter tells his companions a story
which begins with his discovery of a corpse.
Accused of murdering the man Takehiro
and raping his wife Masago, the bandit
Tajomaru states that the incident was a fair
fight. Masago asserts that she was raped and
then she killed her husband when he
disowned her. Through a medium, the
husband claims to have committed hara-
kiri in response to the dishonour. The
woodcutter however vows that Takehiro
had been forced to fight and that Tajomaru
acted in self-defence. However even his
objective testimony may not be reliable.
The story depresses the priest but his faith is
restored when the woodcutter offers to care
for an abandoned child they discover.

Comment

Although production company Daiei were
rather reluctant to submit it, fearing
incomprehension if not ridicule, the stir
created by the prizewinning appearance of
Akira Kurosawa's *Rashomon* at the 1951
Venice Film Festival, where it received the
highest honour of the Golden Lion,
effectively opened up Japanese cinema to
appreciation and acclaim in the West. While
Japan's insularity during the later 1930s
and the wartime era had prevented the
export of much of her cinematic output, the
very exoticism of Kurosawa's work, often
underappreciated in his native land,
certainly contributed to *Rashomon*'s impact
across Europe and in America where it
received the Best Foreign Film Oscar.

However, the film's bravura camerawork,
strong performances and, above all,
innovative narrative construction, made
clear that here was rich artistic integrity
and not just the latest cinematic novelty
item.

Based on stories by Ryunosuke Akutagawa, who had committed suicide in the
1920s, the film's multi-layered, Chinese
puzzle structure is perhaps less of a
philosophic inquiry into the nature of truth
than some have affirmed. Kurosawa's own
reflection that it is about the sort of people
'who cannot survive without lies to make
them feel better than they are' is perhaps
more in keeping with the typically bitter
humanism voiced throughout a distinguished filmography. As with several of
Kurosawa's films, most notably the western-
ization of *Seven Samurai* (1954) (see p190) into
The Magnificent Seven (1960), *Rashomon* was
remade by director Martin Ritt as *Outrage*
(1964), with Paul Newman as an unlikely
Mexican bandit accused of the central rape,
Claire Bloom as the rape victim and
Laurence Harvey as the husband. The
result is not in the same league as the original.

A Daiei Production
Producer Jingo Minoura
Screenplay Akira Kurosawa and Shinobu
Hashimoto, based on the short story Yabu
No Naka and the novel *Rasho-Mon* by
Ryunosuke Akutagawa
Photography Kazuo Miyagawa
Art Director So Matsuyama
Music Fumio Hayasaka
Running time 88 mins b/w

Cast

Toshiro Mifune (Tajomaru)
Machiko Kyo (Masago)
Masayuki Mori (Takehiro)
Takashi Shimura (Firewood Dealer)
Minoru Chiaki (Priest)
Kichijiro Ueda (Commoner)

We don't need another hero
High adventure in the movies

From *The Thief of Bagdad* (1924) (see p218) to *Robin Hood: Prince of Thieves* (1991), the cinema's ability to appeal to the awe-struck child in all of us is undiminished by the passage of time or the unimpressionability of modern audiences.

The lithe grace and devil-may-care insouciance of silent-screen idol Douglas Fairbanks set a standard that few have been able to match and his son rightly dismissed the notion of following in his footsteps with the comment that they 'were so light that they left no trace for anyone to follow'. However, Fairbanks Junior proved no mean adventurer in films like *Gunga Din* (1939) and *The Corsican Brothers* (1941), whilst the sound era's most heroic and dashing hero came in the shape of Errol Flynn whose athleticism and mischievous twinkle enlivened such timeless classics of the genre as *The Charge of the Light Brigade* (1936), *The Adventures of Robin Hood* (1938) (see p3) and *The Sea Hawk* (1940).

During the studio-dominated years of American production, from the 1920s to the 1950s, many stars were called to arms and a few distinguished themselves with blade or gun or just the right amount of manly heroics to win a place in the roster of great screen swashbucklers. The Ronald Colman of *The Prisoner of Zenda* (1937), the Tyrone Power of *The Mark of Zorro* (1940) or the Stewart Granger of *Scaramouche* (1952) would all find their claims for inclusion undisputed.

In American film history however, the great heroic figures have fallen into three categories: the decent, gentlemanly men of the west like John Wayne and Gary Cooper; the cynical, jaded romantic loner swearing allegiance only to their own code of honour, like the Humphrey Bogart of *The Maltese Falcon* (1941) (see p137) and *Casablanca* (1942) (see p51);

or the smouldering rebels of Marlon Brando, Montgomery Clift in *From Here To Eternity* (1953) (see p87), James Dean in *Rebel Without A Cause* (1955) (see p179), Paul Newman or Steve McQueen.

Sean Connery's sexy, sardonic and indestructible secret agent 007 seemed to set the mood of 1960s and inspired a spate of inferior imitations from Matt Helm to Derek Flint, but the recent success of *Star Wars* (1977) (see p207), *Superman* (1978) and their respective sequels has sent producers scurrying to their favourite comic-books in search of characters to capture the public's imagination and hard-earned cash. The results have been variable from a camp *Flash Gordon* (1980) to the Jack Nicholson-dominated *Batman* (1989) (see p27), the technically proficient but emotionally uninvolving *Dick Tracy* (1990) and the pleasant but uninspiring *The Rocketeer* (1991).

The darker side of what an audience can experience through a figure acting out their fantasies has been thought-provokingly explored in the likes of *The Searchers* (1956) (see p189), *Death Wish* (1974) and *Taxi Driver* (1976) (see p217) and the vengeance-seeking mayhem inflicted by wronged law enforcer Mel Gibson in *Mad Max* (1979) (see p135) and its sequels certainly struck a chord. However, the contemporary figure who has come closest to embodying the old-fashioned virtues of the Douglas Fairbanks style of do-gooder with a more worldly cynicism and level-headed practicality is the whip-totin' archaeologist-adventurer Indiana Jones who was first seen in *Raiders of the Lost Ark* (1981) (see p173). The moment, suggested by actor Harrison Ford, when he pulls a gun to settle a dispute with a gleeful, knife-wielding opponent confirmed him as the ideal hero of our time.

What Ever Happened to Baby Jane? *(1962) Directed by Robert Aldrich (Joan Crawford)*

Rosemary's Baby *(1968) Directed by Roman Polanski (Mia Farrow)*

The Adventures of Robin Hood *(1938) Directed by Michael Curtiz (Basil Rathbone, Errol Flynn)*

Raiders of the Lost Ark *(1981) Directed by Steven Spielberg (Harrison Ford)*

Rear Window

Alfred Hitchcock, USA, 1954

Voyeuristic thriller

A tense thriller from the master of suspense implicates the audience in the act of voyeurism.

The story

Immobilized with a broken leg, photographer L B Jeffries amuses himself by spying on his neighbours. He takes a particular interest in the bickering couple of Lars Thorwald and his wife. When the wife disappears, Jeffries suspects foul play. The theory is dismissed by his police detective friend Doyle, but his girlfriend Lisa agrees to secretly enter Thorwald's apartment. She is discovered by Thorwald who subsequently breaks into Jeffries's apartment. Jeffries blinds him with flashbulb explosions but is hanging by his fingertips from a window ledge when saved by the timely intervention of Doyle. He falls three floors, breaking his other leg and requiring a further period of voyeuristic convalescence.

Comment

Alfred Hitchcock had previously collaborated with James Stewart on *Rope* (1948) in which the action was confined to one apartment and the director experimented with the narrative limitation of single ten-minute takes. The restrictions that applied in their second venture *Rear Window* were that the hero was confined to a wheelchair and that events would always be seen from his perspective, thus allowing the viewer to feel the claustrophobia of his predicament and share his voyeuristic impulses.

Made on one elaborate soundstage at Paramount, the film is also as much about the relationship between ace photographer Stewart and his fashion-model girlfriend Grace Kelly, as it is about the unmasking of murderer Raymond Burr. Throughout, Kelly is portrayed as the aggressive half of the partnership, exuding sexuality and challenging Stewart's manhood by her determination to drag him to the altar and her willingness to risk her life in pursuit of satisfying his curiosity. The scene where she produces a flimsy nightdress from her handbag with the promise that it is a preview of coming attractions is one of American cinema's sexiest moments from the 1950s, on a par with Marilyn Monroe's encounter with a sidewalk grating in *The Seven Year Itch* (1955). Yet, Hitchcock takes great delight in portraying her as both an object of desire and a threat; when Jeff lies asleep a menacing shadow falls across his features which is revealed as Lisa delivering a proprietorial peck.

It is the skilful mixture of sexual politics and tense thriller that maintained Hitchcock's reputation as the master of suspense whose films operate on a variety of levels, from pure entertainment to revealing psychological self-portraits.

A Patron Production for Paramount
Producer Alfred Hitchcock
Screenplay John Michael Hayes, based on the short story by Cornell Woolrich
Photography Robert Burks
Editor George Tomasini
Art Directors Hal Pereira and Joseph McMillan Johnson
Music Franz Waxman
Running time 112 mins *colour*

Cast

James Stewart (L B Jeffries)
Grace Kelly (Lisa Fremont)
Wendell Corey (Thomas J Doyle)
Thelma Ritter (Stella)
Raymond Burr (Lars Thorwald)
Judith Evelyn (Miss Lonelyhearts)

Rebel Without a Cause

Nicholas Ray, USA, 1955

Juvenile delinquents

One anguished actor serves as a symbol for misunderstood youth everywhere.

The story

Arrested as drunk and disorderly, moody adolescent Jim Stark starts life at a new high school. On the first day he meets Judy, is befriended by the orphaned Plato and finds himself bullied into a test of nerve against gang leader Buzz. They meet for a 'chicken run' race towards a cliff but when Buzz's sleeve is caught on the doorhandle he is unable to jump free and plummets to his death. Jim reports the matter to the police, despite his parents' advice to keep quiet. An attempt to find refuge with Judy and Plato is marred by the revenge-seeking gang's attack on Plato who kills one of them and takes refuge in the planetarium. The police surround the building. Jim persuades Plato to give himself up but as he agrees he is shot dead.

Comment

The mid-1950s' apotheosis of the 'teenager' was probably down to the creation of a new youth market as much as any of the social forces involved, for if the nation's youngsters were questioning their relationship to the status quo then their new found rebelliousness sought to solidify itself around rampant consumption of records, clothes, movies and suchlike to shape the new cultural identity that would mark the 'teenager' apart from the older generation. The 1955 release of both Elia Kazan's *East of Eden* and *Rebel Without A Cause* established a nervy young actor named James Dean as the voice of and icon for frustrated youth everywhere, a cult that continues to flourish as a style accessory more than three and a half decades after the ill-fated star's premature death in a car accident.

That the Dean phenomenon still has meaning today is in some part due to the effectiveness of *Rebel Without A Cause* in capturing the timeless pattern of conflict as restless adolescents seek their own values in a process of anxious self-determination, and the pained intimacy of Dean's performances still rings true even although the film remains in many respects a 'problem' picture in the old Warner Brothers style of the 1930s. However, the unrelenting focus on the central character codified a self-consciousness that was a definitive step forward from the docile construct of Andy Hardy or the screen's usual colourless young folks.

Although ultimately unrewarded by the American Academy, the film was nominated for three Oscars in the categories of Best Motion Picture Story, Best Supporting Actress for Natalie Wood, and Best Supporting Actor for Sal Mineo. Dean himself was to receive posthumous Best Actor nominations for *East of Eden* and *Giant* (1956).

A Warner Brothers Production
Producer David Weisbart
Screenplay Stewart Stern and Irving Schulman, based on a story by Nicholas Ray
Photography Ernest Haller
Editor William Zeigler
Art Director Malcolm Bart
Music Leonard Rosenman
Running time 111 mins colour

Cast
James Dean (Jim Stark)
Natalie Wood (Judy)
Jim Backus (Jim's Father)
Ann Doran (Jim's Mother)
Sal Mineo (Plato)
Dennis Hopper (Goon)

The Red Shoes

Michael Powell and Emeric Pressburger, UK, 1948

Pas de deux

The Archers achieve an artistic peak with an impassioned fusion of ballet and melodrama.

The story

Struck by the promise of ballerina Victoria Page, impresario Boris Lermontov welcomes her into his company at the same time as composer Julian Craster. Craster is subsequently asked to transform *The Red Shoes* into a ballet in which Page will dance the prima ballerina role. The performance is a success but Lermontov disapproves of the love that has grown between Page and Craster and becomes mercilessly critical of the latter's work. The lovers resign from the company and marry. Later, Lermontov begs Page to dance one performance of *The Red Shoes* and, against Craster's wishes, she agrees. However, powerless in the grip of the red shoes, she leaves the theatre and leaps in front of the Nice Express, dying in Craster's arms.

Comment

Revered by ballet *aficionados* as perhaps the greatest dance film ever made, *The Red Shoes* represents Michael Powell and Emeric Pressburger's commitment to a total cinema at its most impassioned and fully achieved. Deliriously fusing music, movement, colour, performance and camerawork, it is arguably the high-water mark of The Archers' peak period of creativity in the 1940s. Challenging the wisdom that ballet films are box-office poison, it was also a considerable commercial success in America and earned five Oscar nominations, including Best Picture, winning awards for Art Direction and Scoring.

Originally drafted by Pressburger some ten years earlier as a vehicle for actress Merle Oberon, the core of the narrative comes from Hans Christian Andersen's fairy-tale of the girl who is punished for succumbing to the lure of the red shoes. Returning to the material, The Archers team were able to cast titian red-haired Sadler's Wells ballerina Moira Shearer in the role of a dancer fatally driven on by the domineering influence of a Diaghilev-like impresario and her acting prowess was such that she embarked upon a secondary career that included an appearance in Powell's notorious *Peeping Tom* (1959) (see p161). Working with a brilliant production team which doubled the original budget in their quest for perfection, Powell and Pressburger elevated the look of the film to exquisite heights of theatricality without ever losing sight of the nightmare element of the material (the film has been criticized for the harshness of its climactic tragedy). The high romantic agony of a dedication to art that transcends even life itself has rarely been expressed on celluloid with such disturbingly zealous conviction.

An Archers Production
Producers Michael Powell and Emeric Pressburger
Screenplay Michael Powell, Emeric Pressburger and Keith Winter
Photography Jack Cardiff
Editor Reginald Mills
Art Directors Hein Heckroth and Arthur Lawson
Music Brian Easdale
Running time 133 mins *colour*

Cast
Anton Walbrook (Boris Lermontov)
Moira Shearer (Victoria Page)
Marius Goring (Julian Craster)
Leonide Massine (Grischa Ljubov)
Robert Helpmann (Ivan Boleslawsky)
Albert Brasserman (Sergei Ratov)

La Règle du Jeu
(The Rules of the Game)

Jean Renoir, France, 1939

A mirror to society

A country weekend reveals the moral decline of a decadent society

The story

During a weekend at the estate of the Marquis De La Chesnaye, his wife Christine learns of his infidelity with Genevieve and informs her suitor André that she is now prepared to leave with him. The gamekeeper is also aware of an unwelcome attraction between his wife Lisette and a poacher who has been engaged as a servant. Later, Christine changes her mind and opts for the company of childhood friend Octave but, deciding he is too old to please her, he sends André into the garden for their rendezvous. Mistaking Christine for Lisette, the poacher shoots André. The guests accept the Marquis's explanation that André had been mistaken for a poacher but assume that it was the Marquis who had disposed of a rival for his wife's love.

Comment

Greeted with much public approbation on its initial three-week run in Paris because it satirized the French ruling class in the run-up to war, heavily cut then banned altogether by the Vichy government, and then destroyed in an Allied bombing raid in 1942, *La Règle du Jeu* was not widely seen in the director's original version until some 20 years after its première. However, it survived such an inhospitable early reception to become regarded as Jean Renoir's supreme masterpiece and remains a regular feature of critics' all-time ten best lists. Rarely quoted in full, the film's emblematic line 'There's one thing that's terrible and that's that everyone has his reasons' is some indication of the richly ambiguous currents of drama, irony and social observation it brings to the basic material of an updated Beaumarchais boulevard comedy. Later Renoir would recollect, 'During the shooting of the film I was torn between my desire to make a comedy of it and the wish to tell a tragic story. The result of this ambivalence was the film as it is.'

With the camera fluidly marshalling the attention first towards one character then another, the eternal intrigue of the film lies in the tension between its mocking disapproval and the generosity of spirit it extends to these various dilettantes, depicting, with the director's characteristic humanity, the decadence of a social structure on the brink of its own destruction. Full of memorable set-pieces, from a fancy-dress party to a rabbit hunt and the final hypocrises surrounding the rationalization of André's death, it is also exquisitely acted, not least by Renoir himself, and is a rare creation that presents a different facet on every subsequent viewing.

A La Nouvelle Edition Française Production
Producer Claude Renoir
Screenplay Jean Renoir and Carl Koch
Photography Jean Bachelet, Jean-Paul Alphen and Alain Renoir
Editor Marguerite Renoir
Art Directors Eugene Lourie and Max Douy
Music Roger Desormières and Joseph Kosma, from Mozart, Monsigny and Saint-Saëns
Running time premièred at 115 mins b/w

Cast
Roland Toutain (André Jurieux)
Mila Parley (Genevieuve)
Paulette Dubost (Lisette)
Marcel Dalio (Robert, Marquis De La Chesnaye)
Nora Gregor (Christine De La Chesnaye)
Jean Renoir (Octave)
Roland Toutain (André Jurieux)
Mila Parely (Genevieve)
Paulette Dubost (Lisette)

Rio Bravo

Howard Hawks, USA, 1959

Western values

A state of siege in a border town tests the true grit of its law-enforcers.

The story

Sheriff John T Chance's arrest of the murderous Joe Burdette places the town of Rio Bravo under a siege mentality as his brother Nathan plots to free him. Initially Chance is supported only by his alcoholic deputy Dude and crippled jail-keeper Stumpy. Later he accepts young gunhand Colorado as a deputy and showgirl Feathers's quick thinking saves him from one attack. However, a further ambush results in Dude being taken hostage. Chance agrees to trade him for Joe at the Burdette warehouse. Working as an unorthodox team, and with the unfair advantage of dynamite, Chance and his men better the Burdette gang and Feathers is subsequently able to provoke the unemotional Chance into a declaration of love.

Comment

Recovering from the failure of his Egyptian adventure *Land of the Pharaohs* (1955), director Howard Hawks set about formulating a retort to the lone male mentality of *High Noon* (see p107) and produced perhaps the most cogent exposition of the themes that had interested him throughout his widely varied career.

Unlike the historical approach favoured by John Ford, Hawks's Texas town of Rio Bravo is no real moment in the development of the American frontier but an almost abstract background which the director can use to play off his favourite archetypal characters against each other. It is hardly suprising therefore that in its examination of the integrity of the male grouping it bears a strong resemblance to earlier Hawks action fare, most notably the Andean flying thriller *Only Angels Have Wings* (1939) and the Martinique-set wartime smuggling drama *To Have and Have Not* (1944). Here the relationships rather than plotting are emphasized with the central focus on the bond between sheriff John T Chance and his drunken buddy Dude, and the pair's interaction with plucky old jailer Stumpy, gunslinger Colorado and showgirl Feathers.

A leisurely and marvellously executed exercise in genre conventions, the film inspired Hawks to more or less repeat the same formula (to lesser effect, it must be said) in *El Dorado* (1967) and his final film *Rio Lobo* (1970), while John Carpenter virtually remade it in an urban setting as *Assault on Precinct 13* (1976), acknowledging his source by giving his own editor credit to a certain John T Chance.

Completely ignored by the Academy Awards, the film did make the box-office charts as the number eight attraction of 1959 in America.

An Armada Production
Producer Howard Hawks
Screenplay Jules Furthman and Leigh Brackett, based on a short story by B H McCampbell
Photography Russell Harlan
Editor Folmar Blangsted
Art Director Leo K Kuter
Music Dimtri Tiomkin
Running time 141 mins *colour*

Cast
John Wayne (John T Chance)
Dean Martin (Dude)
Ricky Nelson (Colorado Ryan)
Angie Dickinson (Feathers)
Walter Brennan (Stumpy)
Ward Bond (Pat Wheeler)

Rome – Open City
(Roma, Città Aperta)

Roberto Rossellini, Italy, 1945

Wartime realism

The streets of war-torn Rome provide the setting for the first flourish of neorealism.

The story

Rome. Mussolini's reign is over but the Allies have yet to reach the city where opposition rages fiercely. Communist resistance leader Manfredi avoids capture by the authorities and takes refuge with Francesco on the eve of his marriage to the widow Pina. Manfredi continues to evade the police but Francesco is arrested and Pina is shot. Francesco subsequently escapes and hides with Manfredi in the apartment of the latter's former mistress Marina. A lovers' quarrel results in Marina betraying Manfredi to the Gestapo. He is arrested when visiting the trusted priest Don Pietro and tortured to death. The priest is shot. Francesco, the one-legged Romolo and a young gang of saboteurs continue the struggle.

Comment

Critics continue to debate whether Luchino Visconti's 1942 James M Cain adaptation *Ossessione* or Roberto Rossellini's 1945 *Roma, Città Aperta* might be termed the first flowering of Italian neorealism, but while the earlier offering was consciously designed to cohere with a set of realist artistic principles, Rossellini's chronicle of life under the Nazi occupation was more concerned with preserving on screen real historical incidents – filmed in the real locales wherever possible, and utilizing a largely non-professional cast to gain a greater feeling of authenticity.

Shot within two months of the Allied liberation of Rome, the project had been in development since the previous year but the director's wealthy sponsor soon ran out of money and Rossellini was left to sell his clothes and even his furniture to scrape together the funds required to purchase leftover lengths of newsreel stock. The adverse conditions under which the film was evidently put together however lends its grainy images, rough performances and downbeat locations an immediacy that speaks emotively of a certain historical experience. Still moving today when its documentary-influenced techniques have become part of film language, the film's raw vigour aroused a considerable stir on its initial release. Analytically speaking, its melodramatic plotting, manipulative music and sentimentalized use of children hardly render it a model of objectivity along doctrinaire neorealist theoretical lines, but the humanism that suffuses so much of Rossellini's work here transcends such narrow representational nitpicking, while the piece's international success was to rejuvenate the home industry and offer much encouragement to the subsequent careers of his Italian peers, Visconti and Vittorio De Sica.

An Excelsia Production
Screenplay Roberto Rossellini, Federico Fellini and Sergio Amidei based on a story by Amidei and Alberto Consiglio
Photography Ubaldo Arata
Editor Eraldo Da Roma
Art Director R Megna
Music Renzo Rossellini
Running time 100 mins b/w

Cast
Anna Magnani (Pina)
Aldo Fabrizi (Don Pietro Pellegrini)
Marcello Pagliero (Manfredi)
Marai Michi (Marina)
Harry Feist (Major Bergmann)
Francesco Grandjacquet (Francesco)

Room at the Top

Jack Clayton, UK, 1959

Kitchen-sink drama

A young social climber pays a bitter price for his success in a landmark of British drama.

The story

Employed as a clerk in Warnley, the ambitious Joe Lampton is determined to advance himself and doggedly pursues Susan Brown, the daughter of a local business magnate. When he overcomes her father's opposition to win her affection, she is sent abroad. He embarks on an affair with Alice Aisgill, an older, married woman with whom he falls genuinely in love. However, when Susan returns, their relationship is resumed and when she announces her pregnancy he accepts a position in the family business in return for marrying her. He ruthlessly abandons Alice who kills herself in a car crash and it is a miserable Lampton who weds Susan – the price of achieving his dreams the forfeiture of happiness.

the careers of a number of innovative new talents – notably the loosely-aligned Free Cinema grouping including directors Karel Reisz with *Saturday Night and Sunday Morning* (1960) (see p188), and Lindsay Anderson with *This Sporting Life* (1963).

Looking at these later offerings contextualizes Jack Clayton's *Room At The Top* as a transitional work, its much-touted sexual frankness less significant perhaps than its grim Northern setting (it was shot on location in Bradford) and harsh assessment of the means necessary to surmount the ossification of the British class system.

Nominated for six Academy Awards, the film received Oscars for Neil Paterson's screenplay and for Simone Signoret as Best Actress and launched Laurence Harvey on to a brief period of international stardom. He reprised his characterization in *Man at the Top* (1965), directed by Ted Kotcheff, while Joe Lampton, as played by Kenneth Haigh, was further revived for a British television series, *Man at the Top*, which spawned a movie spin-off under the same title in 1973, the third year of its run.

Comment

Britain in the late 1950s saw a burgeoning resistance to the apparent changelessness of its society during the austere post-war period, a sense of youth revolt founded on a hostility to the Establishment and/or working-class consciousness and culturally defined by rock'n'roll and the so-called 'angry young men' of the theatre (John Osborne, Arnold Wesker) and of the literary (John Braine, Allan Sillitoe, Stan Barstow). In film terms, the screen adaptation of Osborne's *Look Back in Anger* (1959) and Braine's *Room at the Top* were to provide a new impetus for the British film industry, with the substantial international success of the latter film in particular a key component of the growing confidence that was to launch

A Remus Production
Producer John and James Woolf
Screenplay Neil Paterson, based on the novel by John Braine
Photography Freddie Francis
Editor Ralph Kemplen
Art Director Ralph Brinton
Music Mario Nascimbene
Running time 117 mins b/w

Cast

Simone Signoret (Alice Aisgill)
Laurence Harvey (Joe Lampton)
Heather Sears (Susan Brown)
Donald Wolfit (Mr Brown)
Ambrosine Philpott (Mrs Brown)
Donald Houston (Charles Soames)

Rosemary's Baby

Roman Polanski, USA, 1968

The Devil to pay

A witch's coven in the heart of Manhattan is given a chilling credibility.

The story

New York. When struggling actor Guy Woodhouse and his wife Rosemary move into a new apartment they are befriended by neighbours Roman and Minnie Castevet, Guy's professional prospects improve and he suggests they have a baby. After consuming one of Minnie's desserts, Rosemary falls ill and awakes next morning with a bizarre recollection of having been raped by a horned monster. After some months of a debilitating pregnancy she consults her friend Hutch who dies mysteriously, leaving a book on witchcraft suggesting that Castevet is a warlock. Unable to convince anyone of her plight, she gives birth. Told that the child has died, she struggles to the Castevets' apartment and witnesses the coven celebrating the birth of the anti-Christ.

Comment

The first contemporary horror film to gain massive public acceptance, *Rosemary's Baby* was faithfully adapted from the Ira Levin novel and produced by William Castle, a man more renowned for his showmanship and gimmicky low-budget shockers like *The Tingler* (1959) and *Homicidal* (1961). His masterstroke was to offer the direction to Roman Polanski who was able to bring a stranger's eye to the familiar locale of Manhattan and the daily rituals of American life. Jane Fonda was originally approached to play the role of Rosemary before the inspired notion of casting the waif-like Mia Farrow. Robert Redford also rejected the role of Guy prior to John Cassavetes's acceptance. The film succeeds because of its refusal to sensationalize the events, and its decision to achieve its horror through the measured accumulation of believable suspense rather than outright gore or cheap thrills. Such familiar and endearing faces as Ralph Bellamy and Ruth Gordon lend a veneer of charm to their characters that makes it more difficult for the audience to wholeheartedly accept their diabolical actions and places the viewer in the same sceptical but fearful position as Rosemary herself. Evoking menace in the most innocent of locales and banal routines, Polanski created more genuine horror than any effects-laden, gore-spattered extravaganza and the film grossed some $15 million, received two Oscar nominations and won veteran Gordon a Best Supporting Actress Oscar. Its impact can be seen in a whole slew of pictures dealing with the Anti-Christ, from *The Exorcist* (1973) (see p78) to *It's Alive* (1974), *To the Devil A Daughter* (1975) and *The Omen* (1976). A television film, *Look What's Happened to Rosemary's Baby* (1976), directed by editor Sam O'Steen and again featuring Ruth Gordon, proved an unremarkable continuation of the original events.

A Paramount Production
Producer William Castle
Screenplay Roman Polanski, based on the novel by Ira Levin
Photography William A Fraker
Editors Sam O'Steen and Robert Wyman
Art Director Joel Schiller
Music Krzysztof Komeda
Running time 136 mins colour

Cast

Mia Farrow (Rosemary Woodhouse)
John Cassavetes (Guy Woodhouse)
Ruth Gordon (Minnie Castevet)
Sidney Blackmer (Roman Castevet)
Maurice Evans (Hutch)
Ralph Bellamy (Dr Sapirstein)

Safety Last

Fred Newmeyer and Sam Taylor, USA, 1923

Hair-raising comedy

Dangling from a high-rise clock face, Harold Lloyd establishes himself as the king of daredevil comedy.

The story

Seeking to impress his girl and earn his fortune, a young man heads for the big city. He secures employment as a clerk in a department store but embroiders his achievements in letters home. When she comes to visit he manages to create the impression that he is the store manager. Overhearing his boss says that he would pay $1000 dollars for a good publicity stunt, he convinces him to hire a daredevil who will climb the side of the building. Arranging to perform the stunt with his pal and split the money, he is forced to climb the 12 storeys alone when the pal is arrested. Overcoming such hazards as pigeons, a tennis net, a mouse and the mobile hands of a clock face, he makes the climb, secures the money and wins his girl.

Comment

Recognized along with Charlie Chaplin and Buster Keaton as one of the most inventive and popular of the silent comedians, Harold Lloyd's reputation as a king of daredevil comedy rests on his penchant for hair-raising comic antics that frequently involved skyscraper buildings and danger to his own life. *Safety Last* deftly combines these thrills with a degree of psychologically poignant character-building as subtle as anything in Chaplin's films and provides perhaps his most famous moments as the bespectacled employee dangling from the hands of a clock

face high above the streets of downtown Los Angeles. A double was used for long-shots and some of the filming was completed from a height of only three or four storeys instead of the 12 in the film, but regardless of the debate over the degree of danger that Lloyd actually faced, there is no doubting that it is the star of the film who is risking his life in the name of entertainment.

The idea for the film came to Lloyd in 1922 when he witnessed a crowd mesmerized by young steelworker Bill Strothers ascending a tall building, cycling round the edge and shinning along a flagpole before standing on his head. He later recalled thinking, 'My, if it can possibly do that to an audience – if I capture that on screen – I think I've got something that's never been done before.' The result thrilled audiences, provoked a shortlived craze of human flies and established *Safety Last* as one of the top five moneymakers of 1923 with a staggering gross of $1 588 545, of which some $643 842 went to Lloyd. The version of the film now shown on television includes an episode from another Lloyd film, *Hot Water*, adding eight minutes to the running time.

A Hal Roach/Pathé Exchange Production
Producer Hal Roach
Screenplay Hal Roach, Tim Whelan and Sam Taylor
Photography Walter Lundin
Editor Fred L Guiol
Art Director Fred L Guiol
Running time 70 mins b/w

Cast
Harold Lloyd (The Boy)
Mildred Davis (The Girl)
Bill Strothers (The Pal)
Noah Young (The Law)
Westcott B Clarke (The Floorwalker)
Mickey Daniels (The Kid)

Not in front of the children
Censorship in the cinema

Reports of Hollywood hedonism in the 1920s were what ultimately prompted the formation of a self-regulatory film industry body in America led by former Postmaster General Will H Hays. His task was to win the industry respectability and fend off any threat of state or federal censorship. Eventually he established the Motion Picture Production Code, or Hays Code. The British Board of Film Censors had existed since 1912 but it was this Code which promulgated the rules under which Hollywood and much of mainstream film production operated over the next 30 years. This Code forbade any form of explicit depiction or discussion of sexual matters, profanity, extreme violence or immorality, and could arbitrate as to the proper length of a kiss or the behaviour of a married couple – who were generally relegated to separate beds and permitted intimate physical contact only if both feet were kept on the ground. Thus, in *It Happened One Night* (1934) (see p112) when the unwed Clark Gable and Claudette Colbert share a room for the night, due propriety is maintained by the erection of a partition between them dubbed 'The Walls of Jericho', and actress Hedy Lamarr achieved notoriety merely by appearing naked in *Extase* (1933).

The standards of permissible language began to slip in the late 1930s with a shocking 'not bloody likely' allowed in *Pygmalion* (1938) and Clark Gable accorded the privilege of uttering a single 'damn' in *Gone With the Wind* (1939) (see p95). Differing national sensibilities provoke different reactions and whilst the heavy bosoms of distressed damsels in popular British bodice-rippers like *The Wicked Lady* (1945) did not cause riots in their native land they were considered too revealing for American audiences. A 1952 Supreme Court ruling on the film *L'Amore* (1948) freed films from censorship on religious grounds and brought the medium under the protection of the First Amendment. When Otto Preminger challenged the Code by releasing the films *The Moon Is Blue* (1953) with its daring mention of the words 'virgin' and 'pregnant', and *The Man With the Golden Arm* (1955) about drug addiction, bereft of the Seal of Approval, its days were numbered.

In Britain, kitchen sink dramas like *Room at the Top* (1959) (see p185) and *Saturday Night and Sunday Morning* (1960) (see p188) brought a more mature and explicit presentation of sex and *Victim* (1961) (see p231) was courageous in its stance on homosexuality which was then completely illegal. Language grew more explicit in films like *Who's Afraid of Virginia Woolf?* (1966), violence ripened in the likes of *The Wild Bunch* (1969) (see p239) and *Death Wish* (1974), whilst nudity, graphic depictions of the sex act and every conceivable immorality were soon common place with *Last Tango in Paris* (1972) (see p125) and *In the Realm of the Senses* (1976) (see p109), landmarks in screen sexuality.

Whilst in theory filmmakers are permitted total liberty in what they choose to portray, censorship is still a potent force. Many countries, particularly the pre-glasnost Soviet Union, ban films on political grounds and only recently have many controversial Russian productions seen the light of day in the West. In a highly-censored Britain the supposedly subversive *The Wild One* (1953) was banned until the late 1960s. In the 1990s violence seems an acceptable part of the cinema vocabulary, but sex is still something from which the viewer apparently needs protection. Thus the erect male member may become the last taboo of cinema censorship, although why tumescence is considered more of a threat to a nation's well-being than the numerous examples of stomach-churning violence, destruction and misogyny that are allowed on our screens remains a mystery.

Saturday Night and Sunday Morning

Karel Reisz, UK, 1960

Social realism

British cinema gains maturity with a virile portrait of a working-class lad.

The story

With a grin on his face and money in his pocket, Midlands factory worker Arthur Seaton is determined to enjoy life. Saturday evening is spent in the pub and then he pays a visit on Brenda whilst her husband is away for the night. Jack's change to night-shift allows the arrangement to become more frequent. However, the relationship changes when Arthur starts dating Doreen who offers more resistance to his amorous advances. Brenda however is pregnant. He makes an unsuccessful attempt to arrange an abortion and is subsequently beaten up by two squaddies, one of whom is Jack's brother. Showing more signs of responsibility, he becomes engaged to Doreen, but as they search for a house he claims that his happy-go-lucky days are far from over.

Comment

Saturday Night and Sunday Morning is the best of the stream of social realist films which dominated British cinema in the late 1950s and early 1960s. Tagged 'kitchen sink dramas' because of their focus on the domestic details of everyday lives, a subject which had not previously been deemed as generally suitable for serious filmmakers, they characteristically drew on the work of the new generation of novelists and playwrights then chronicling the mores of the working class, including such writers as Stan Barstow, John Osborne and Alan Sillitoe, whose novel provided the basis of this film.

Stage actor Albert Finney, seen but briefly in the film version of *The Entertainer* (1960), made a powerful and highly convincing début in a leading role and much of the enduring appeal of the film is down to his muscular, attention-demanding performance. Diana Dors was offered the part of the older, married woman but was unwisely persuaded to pass the opportunity by, thus gifting Rachel Roberts with one of the best roles in her film career; one of the other great strengths of the film is that the women are depicted as strongly individualized characters in their own right, rather than simply pawns in the male game. Finney's character himself is neither angry young man, like Osborne's Jimmy Porter in *Look Back in Anger* (1959), nor avid social climber like Joe Lampton in *Room at The Top* (1959) (see p184). His philosophy is simple: enjoy life as best you can, and 'don't let the bastards grind you down'. That rather self-defeating limitation, along with director Karel Reisz's gritty, semi-documentary approach, ultimately gives the film a dour, almost despairing air, but it remains a landmark in British cinema, particularly in its frank treatment of sexuality.

A Woodfall Production
Producer Tony Richardson
Screenplay Alan Sillitoe, based on his novel
Photography Freddie Francis
Editor Seth Holt
Art Director Ted Marshall
Music Johnny Dankworth
Running time 89 mins b/w

Cast
Albert Finney (Arthur Seaton)
Shirley Anne Field (Doreen)
Rachel Roberts (Brenda)
Hylda Baker (Aunt Ada)
Norman Rossington (Bert)
Bryan Pringle (Jack)

The Searchers

John Ford, USA, 1956

Psychological western

An obsessive quest for revenge explores the moral ambiguity at the heart of the western hero.

The story

Following defeat in the Civil War, Ethan Edwards returns to his brother Aaron's ranch but is absent with the Texas Rangers when the adults are slain by Commanches who abduct his nieces Lucy and Debbie. His desire for revenge is obsessive and, accompanied by Martin Pawley and Brad Jorgensen, he sets off in pursuit. En route, he discovers Lucy's body and faces Brad's death. The quest takes five relentless years and, when discovered, Debbie is reluctant to be saved. Only Pawley's intervention prevents Edwards killing her for the savage he fears she has become. An attack is organized on the camp and Pawley goes ahead to rescue her. When the fighting concludes, she confronts Edwards who spares her life and takes her home.

Comment

John Ford reached the summit of his achievement in the western genre with this dark, complex tale of revenge and self-discovery. The great strength of *The Searchers* lies in the way it takes one of the most basic of all western plotlines and transforms it into a psychologically and imagistically rich reflection on the genre itself and the myths it reflects. John Wayne gives one of his greatest performances as the Indian-hating Edwards who is himself more than halfway to the savage state. As the search for Debbie progresses, so the complexities of his character, and the moral dilemmas which he poses, multiply. His own behaviour, including the adoption of Indian customs like scalping, is as savage as any atrocity perpetrated by the Indians and it becomes increasingly clear that Edwards himself is caught in a strange no-man's land which is both psychological and territorial, a point made clear in the symbolic closing of the door as he hesitates outside in the final frame. He is trapped between the two poles of the film's central divide, excluded by custom and character from the civilization which the settlements represent, but unable to acknowledge his much closer connections with the Indians (and by extension the wilderness) he so detests.

The dilemma of this ambiguous character takes on added resonance from being played by Wayne, the quintessential embodiment of the classical western hero. The enduring appeal of *The Searchers* lies in the fact that it is a superb adventure story but one which expands to contain a revelatory probing of the values inherent in the genre itself and whose influence can be detected in numerous contemporary filmmakers including Martin Scorsese (*Taxi Driver*, 1976 (see p217)) and George Lucas (*Star Wars*, 1977 (see p207)).

A C V Whitney Production
Producers Merian C Cooper and C V Whitney
Screenplay Frank S Nugent, based on the novel by Alan Le May
Photography Winton C Hoch
Editor Jack Murray
Art Directors Frank Hotaling and James Basevi
Music Max Steiner
Running time 119 mins *colour* VistaVision Technicolor
Cast
John Wayne (Ethan Edwards)
Jeffrey Hunter (Martin Pawley)
Vera Miles (Laurie Jorgensen)
Ward Bond (Capt Reverend Samuel Johnson Clayton)
Natalie Wood (Debbie Edwards)
John Qualen (Lars Jorgensen)

Seven Samurai
(Shichinin No Samurai)

Akira Kurosawa, Japan, 1954

Japanese epic

The defence of a feudal community produces a physical and emotional epic of rare intensity.

The story

In 16th-century Japan farmers find their livelihoods under threat from marauding bandits. One village buys protection in the shape of samurai warrior Kambei. He recruits a select group and begins to fortify the village in preparation for attack. Three bandits scouting ahead of the main party are killed but an attack on the bandits leaves one samurai dead. The main battle finally commences and Kambei leads the villagers to victory. Only three samurai survive. Kambei and Shichiroji leave the villagers to their fields but Katsushiro decides to make his life in the village beside the farmer's daughter whom he has grown to love.

Comment

Akira Kurosawa's reputation as arguably the leading director of large-scale action in the world was built on the back of this epic adventure story. It is the most popular of all Kurosawa's films in the West, and that may be in large part because it so closely (and consciously) parallels the familiar conventions of the western genre itself. The director has acknowledged the influence of the western (and especially the classic westerns of John Ford) on this film, a correspondence underlined by its subsequent metamorphosis into John Sturges's Hollywood western *The Magnificent Seven* (1960), although its influence is equally evident in many other films of the period. Although set in 16th-century Japan, the central battle between the civilized settlers and the savage raiders with the tarnished defenders in the middle has been fought out in countless western scenarios, and has recurred again in Kurosawa's own work. The choreography of the ultimate violent clashes is breathtaking, and prefigures the kind of highly complex battle sequences which Kurosawa would create on a vaster scale for *Kagemusha* (1980) and *Ran* (1985).

The film's high standing in world cinema is due in part to its excellence as a totally absorbing adventure story, but it is equally attributable to the depth and intensity of emotions which the director succeeds in building around the framework of that adventure. The ultimate confrontation is carefully postponed while an intricate skein of relationships between the villagers and the samurai, at base two inimical groups, is developed. The climax, set amid the pouring rain so characteristic of the director, and making innovative use of multiple cameras and the telephoto lens, is all the more effective as a consequence.

A Toho Production
Screenplay Shinobu Hashimoto, Hideo Oguni and Akira Kurosawa
Photography Asakazu Nakai
Art Director So Matsuyama
Music Fumio Hayasaka
Running time 200 mins b/w

Cast
Takashi Shimura (Kambei)
Toshiro Mifune (Kikuchiyo)
Yoshio Inaba (Gorobei)
Siji Miyaguchi (Kyuzo)
Minoru Chiaki (Heihachi)
Daisuke Kato (Shichiroji)

The Seventh Seal
(Det Sjunde Inseglet)

Ingmar Bergman , Sweden, 1957

Facing mortality

A medieval knight's encounters with Death herald the maturity of a world-class artist.

The story

Returning from the Crusades, knight Antonius Block encounters Death and secures a brief reprieve from his call by challenging him to a game of chess. The knight finds his native land ravaged by disease and in the grip of a strange cult of self-flagellation. The remnants of his faith in God is shattered by what he witnesses but he also encounters the happier side of religious experience in the joy of travelling players Jof, his wife Mia and their child. Joined by a blacksmith and others, Block makes for his family castle. When Jof sees him playing chess with Death he gathers his family and departs – wisely so, as Death soon comes to pay a visit to Block and request the company of all who sit at his table.

Comment

This enigmatic and highly allusive allegory about man's relationship with God and Death established Ingmar Bergman as a major artist in world cinema. Described by the director as a film about 'the fear of death', it reflects something of his own troubled attitude to religious belief and stemmed from a play entitled *Wood Painting* which he had devised at drama school, inspired by the stained glass windows and murals he had witnessed as a child at his father's church services. Filmed over the summer of 1956, the title taken from a Bible reading of Revelation 8:1–2, 7–8 given by Block's wife just before Death enters their castle, it remains a remarkable piece of work, both in terms of the audacity of the subject,

and in the starkly etched visual style of Gunnar Fischer's almost bleached monochrome photography which lends an element of the poetic and the documentary to a brutal evocation of medieval life and a succession of striking religious tableaux that convey a hell on earth from which the goodness, love, mercy and compassion of a Christian God seem to be singularly lacking. The famous shot of the Dance of Death beneath an ominous cloud was not however the result of meticulous preparation as Bergman recalled in his autobiography *The Magic Lantern*: 'Most of the actors had finished for the day. Assistants, electricians, a make-up man and two summer visitors, who never knew what it was all about, had to dress up in the costumes of those condemned to death. A camera with no sound was set up and the picture shot before the cloud dissolved.'

The austerity of Bergman's perspective on religion and death, further emphasized by the stylized dialogue and mournful music, would develop in such future work as *The Virgin Spring* (1959) and *Through A Glass Darkly* (1961).

A Svensk Filmindustri Production
Screenplay Ingmar Bergman, based on his play *Tramalning*
Photography Gunnar Fischer
Editor Lennart Wallen
Art Director P A Lundgren
Music Erik Nordgren
Running time 96 mins b/w

Cast

Max Von Sydow (Antonius Block)
Gunnar Bjornstrand (Jons)
Bengt Ekerot (Death)
Nils Poppe (Jof)
Bibi Andersson (Mia)
Ake Fridell (Plog)

sex, lies and videotape

Steven Soderbergh, USA, 1989

Modern love

This intimate, low-budget account of tangled emotional relationships caused a sensation when it became the first début film to win the Palme D'Or at Cannes.

The story

John, a successful lawyer, is married to Ann, but is having an affair with her sister Cynthia. Graham, an old college friend of John's, comes to visit, and takes a friendly interest in Ann. She helps him to find an apartment in the area. She confides that she feels sex is overvalued, and he admits to being impotent. She later finds the collection of videotapes he has made of women talking about their sexual experiences. He tapes an intrigued Cynthia, and when Ann discovers the affair between her sister and husband, he interviews her at her own insistence. Ann tells John she wants a divorce, and he vents his ire on Graham. Graham destroys his tapes and begins a tentative relationship with Ann. Ann and Cynthia are reconciled, while John's career begins to slip.

Comment

When a clearly shocked Steven Soderbergh marked his acceptance of the Palme D'Or at the Cannes Film Festival in 1989 with the laconic observation that it was 'all downhill from here', he may have subconsciously realized even then the burden of expectation which would rest on his film, and, even more pressingly, on his *next* film.

sex, lies & videotape is an unassuming four-hander made on a very modest budget with no stars, although it established James Spader and launched Andie McDowell and newcomer Laura San Giacomo. Peter Gallagher, who is excellent as the unsympathetic John, tended to be undeservedly passed over.

The film is concerned with the weaving and subsequent unravelling of the complex web of relationships between the four protagonists, all circling around the enigmatic, passive figure of Graham. Video, Soderbergh suggests, has begun to function as a substitute for experience in our society, and Graham's replacement of emotional and physical engagement with videotaping women talking about their experiences and feelings is emblematic of that malaise.

Soderbergh succeeds in making the slightly schematic subdivision of character types seem entirely natural on screen, and handles the resulting emotional tapestry with consummate skill. The film explores complex areas of sexual and emotional experience too often disregarded in film, where it is always easier to show the act than to describe the feelings behind it, but was not really able to sustain the commercial expectations engendered by both its misleadingly lurid title and that Cannes accolade.

An Outlaw Productions Picture
Producers Robert Newmyer and John Hardy
Screenplay Steven Soderbergh
Photography Walt Lloyd
Editor Steven Soderbergh
Art Director Joanne Schmidt
Music Cliff Martinez
Running time 100 mins *colour*
Cast
James Spader (Graham Dalton)
Andie MacDowell (Ann Millaney)
Peter Gallagher (John Millaney)
Laura San Giacomo (Cynthia Bishop)
Ron Vawter (Therapist)

Shadows

John Cassavetes, USA, 1958–9

Improvisational piece

Cinéma vérité techniques establish the validity of American independent cinema.

The story

Manhattan. Black singer Hugh, his light-skinned brother Ben and sister Lelia share an apartment. Hugh seems content to settle for second-rate nightclub engagements but Lelia has aspirations that bring her into contact with various artistic types. Ben spends his days in the company of white friends Tom and Dennis. Lelia falls in love with Tony who abandons her when he discovers she is a mulatto. Hugh throws him out of the flat and Lelia reacts to further attempts at communication by dating a young black boy. Despite arguments with his manager, Hugh continues to accept the work he is given. Ben and his friends are attacked, prompting Tom and Dennis to make something more of their lives and leaving Ben to his aimless existence.

Comment

Director John Cassavetes's début film is quite probably more important for its groundbreaking role in establishing the credibility of the American Independent cinema sector than for its own intrinsic merits. The film is not Cassavetes's best, but it did allow him to demonstrate the deeply personal and highly spontaneous cinema which he envisaged could be translated into significant films. Made on a very low budget as an offshoot from a method-acting workshop involving unemployed actors which Cassavetes was then running, it was partly financed by his acting role in the television series *Johnny Staccato*. Shot in rigorously striking cinéma-vérité manner (hand-held cinematography, grainy images etc), and set in a curious underworld redolent of the Beat counter-culture of the late 1950s, the film is given real atmosphere by Charles Mingus's jazz music score.

Minimally scripted with a very loose plot line, *Shadows* allowed Cassavetes to let his actors explore the various human relationships and the issues of personal and racial identity which arise in the film, while simultaneously permitting them to explore the processes of acting itself through the considerable improvisational latitude allowed to them. It is inevitably a little rambling and even incoherent at times, but remains both a significant landmark and a fascinating achievement. The director would go on to refine the techniques he pioneered here in the search for a dramatically rendered emotional truth in a more fully realized and technically polished fashion in films like *Faces* (1968), *Husbands* (1970) and *A Woman Under The Influence* (1974), but the germ of his art is already fully present in this painfully realistic experiment in personal expression.

A Cassavetes-McEndree-Cassel Production
Producer Maurice McEndree
Photography Erich Kollmar
Editors Len Appelson and Maurice McEndree
Music Charlie Mingus
Running time 87 mins b/w

Cast
Lelia Goldoni (Lelia)
Ben Carruthers (Ben)
Hugh Hurd (Hugh)
Anthony Ray (Tony)
Rupert Crosse (Rupe)
Tom Allen (Tom)

She's Gotta Have it

Spike Lee, USA, 1986

African-American renaissance

A Spike Lee Joint heralds a renaissance for black filmmaking.

The story

Not the stereotypical one-man woman, Nola Darling appreciates different qualities in the three men who currently share her life. Jamie Overstreet is sensitive and caring, narcissistic model Greer Childs promises social mobility, and the garrulous Mars Blackman both amuses and endears himself to her. When both Jamie and Greer refuse to be part of this complex equation, she invites all three men to a disastrous Thanksgiving dinner. Afterwards she refuses Greer's invitation to join him on a working trip to the Caribbean. Jamie demands that she choose between the men and is disturbed by the violence she can unleash in him. She informs Jamie that she loves him but subsequently decides that monogamy is not for her.

Comment

Embarked upon when another film project had to be abandoned, *She's Gotta Have It* is a prime illustration of Orson Welles's stated belief that the enemy of art is the absence of limitation. Forced to conceive a film that could be made on a modest budget with a small but dedicated crew of actors and technicians, graduate filmmaker Spike Lee transcended these limitations to make a sexy, provocative drama of refreshing wit and inventiveness that travelled the world, earned him the Camera D'Or for best first feature at the Cannes Film Festival and initiated his career as the leading commercial black filmmaker of his generation. Made over 12 days for the paltry sum of $175 000 (partly financed by personal credit card), the film has been compared to *Rashomon* (see p174) in its structure of revealing a multiplicity of perspectives on events in order to arrive at some definitive version of the truth. Thus, Nola, her friends, family and lovers all directly address the camera in a device that is financially prudent but artistically valid and well deployed when, for instance, a plethora of would-be Lotharios deliver a mixture of witty, crude and improbable 30-second chat-up lines straight to the audience. Dedicated to expressing a richness of black culture that he had not previously witnessed on screen, Lee not only proved himself a valuable spokesperson for the black community but also a talented filmmaker. His characters, both male and female, have a richness and complexity of attitude, his dialogue is racy, humorous and credible, and the romantic in him is glimpsed when the film unexpectedly and engagingly bursts into colour as Jamie unveils a surprise birthday present. It is almost incidental that renaissance man Lee also distinguishes himself as no mean actor in the role of the fast-talking, overgrown adolescent Mars.

A Forty Acres and a Mule Production
Producer Shelton J Lee
Screenplay Spike Lee
Photography Ernest Dickerson
Editor Spike Lee
Art Director Ron Paley
Music Bill Lee
Running time 85 mins b/w and colour

Cast

Tracy Camilla Johns (Nola Darling)
Tommy Redmond Hicks (Jamie Overstreet)
John Canada Terrell (Greer Childs)
Spike Lee (Mars Blackman)
Raye Dowell (Opal Gilstrap)
Joie Lee (Clorinda Bradford)

The Shootist

Don Siegel, USA, 1976

Western swansong

The death of a legendary gunfighter serves as an elegy for the halcyon days of the western.

The story

Carson City, Nevada, 22 January 1901. Notorious gunfighter John Bernard Books arrives to consult with Dr Hostetler who diagnoses terminal cancer. Boarding with widow Bond Rogers, he befriends her son Gillom and attempts to disillusion the youngster about the glamour of his violent trade. Deciding to provide himself with a dignified exit, Books settles his affairs and arranges a saloon showdown with three gunfighters who would prize his name on their list of victims. He kills the three men but is seriously wounded before the bartender administers a fatal bullet. Gillom intervenes to kill the bartender but afterwards discards his weapon in disgust, an act that Books approves with his dying glance.

Comment

John Wayne's final feature film, *The Shootist* manages to celebrate the legacy of a cinema legend and lament the passing of the western genre in one of the screen's most poignant star swansongs.

Don Siegel reminds viewers of his early experience as an editor with a skilful opening montage of sequences from previous Wayne films, including *Red River* (1948) and *Rio Bravo* (1959) (see p182), which establishes the history of his character, whilst the cast includes numerous actors with a special place in the Wayne iconography. John Carradine, the gambler in *Stagecoach* (1939)

(see p205), is seen as the Carson City undertaker, Lauren Bacall was Wayne's leading lady in *Blood Alley* (1955) and James Stewart co-starred with Wayne in *The Man Who Shot Liberty Valance* (1962).

Redolent of Sam Peckinpah's *Ride the High Country* (1962) (UK: *Guns in the Afternoon*), the film treats its central character as a relic of a bygone era, much like the western itself. Books's newspaper informs him of Queen Victoria's demise and other details, from horseless carriages to electricity and running water, confirm that the establishment of civilization has signalled the death knell for wild frontiers and colourful gunslingers.

Wayne's performance is one of his most understated and affecting, the character's struggle with cancer reflecting his own off-screen battles, and the film's strong statement against the glorification of violence affords a welcome antidote to the gun-happy attitude of his more recent films like *The Cowboys* (1972). From the warm affection in his scenes with Lauren Bacall and Ron Howard to the fitting vigour of his demise, this is Wayne's valedictory hour.

Producers Mike J Frankovich and William Self
Screenplay Miles Hood Swarthout and Scott Hale, based on the novel by Glendon Swarthout
Photography Bruce Surtees
Editor Douglas Stewart
Production Designer Robert Boyle
Music Elmer Bernstein
Running time 100 mins *colour*

Cast
John Wayne (John Bernard Books)
Lauren Bacall (Bond Rogers)
Ron Howard (Gillom Rogers)
James Stewart (Dr Hostetler)
Richard Boone (Mike Sweeney)
Hugh O'Brian (Pulford)

The Shop Around The Corner

Ernst Lubitsch, USA, 1940

Tender romance

An exquisite tale of romance illustrates the finesse of 'the Lubitsch touch'.

The story

Budapest. One Christmas Klara Novak secures employment at Matuschek's shop. Alfred Kralik resents her presence but is preoccupied with a romance that has blossomed only by correspondence. The night he is meant to meet his sweetheart, Matuschek asks everyone to work late. Kralik protests but is fired because his boss suspects him of having an affair with his wife. Kralik keeps the rendezvous and discovers that the haughty Klara is the girl behind box 237. When Matuschek is later prevented from committing suicide the real adulterer is fired and Kralik is reinstated as store manager. The season is one of the most profitable on record and Kralik is eventually able to inform Klara of his identity and win her heart.

Comment

Celebrated as a master of sophisticated drawing-room comedies and frothy romances, director Ernst Lubitsch graced all his work with what came to be known as 'the Lubitsch touch': a mixture of wit, urbanity and visual elegance. Whilst his gossamer-light artistry is evident in the sparkling chic of *Trouble in Paradise* (1932) or the fine judgment displayed in skirting the precipice of bad taste in *To Be Or Not To Be* (1942), the warmth and charm of his work is perhaps best illustrated by *The Shop Around the Corner*. 'As for human comedy,' he later recalled, 'I think I was never as good as in *The Shop Around The Corner*. Never did I make a picture in which the atmosphere and the characters were truer.' Whilst the Budapest setting seems the kind of European never-never land that only ever existed on Hollywood backlots, the delicacy of the bittersweet emotions expressed and the sympathy for the characters and their foibles is indisputable.

Lubitsch's strength is to create compelling and emotionally satisfying drama from the subtle observation of the tensions and misunderstandings in everyday life: the romantic longings of a shop assistant, the antagonism between strangers unaware of each other's true natures, the conflicts provoked by inter-office rivalry, the trampled pride of a cuckolded husband. In this, he is greatly assisted by the calibre of the cast and in particular the screen chemistry of James Stewart and Margaret Sullavan who made four romantic pictures together in the short span between 1936 and 1940. Robert Z Leonard subsequently remade the film as the musical *In the Good Old Summertime* (1949) with Judy Garland and Van Johnson as the lonely-hearts lovers, and the material saw service once more as the 1963 Broadway musical *She Loves Me*.

An M-G-M Production
Producer Ernst Lubitsch
Screenplay Samson Raphaelson, based on the play *Parfumerie* by Nikolaus Laszlo, with uncredited contributions by Ben Hecht
Photography William Daniels
Editor Gene Ruggerio
Art Directors Cedric Gibbons and Wade B Rubottom
Music Werner R Heymann
Running time 97 mins b/w

Cast
Margaret Sullavan (Klara Novak)
James Stewart (Alfred Kralik)
Frank Morgan (Hugo Matuschek)
Joseph Schildkraut (Ferencz Vadas)
Sara Haden (Flora)
Felix Bressart (Pirovitch)

The Silence of the Lambs

Jonathan Demme, USA, 1991

Hannibal the cannibal

*'I'm having an old friend
for dinner.'*

The story

Trainee FBI agent Clarice Starling is
assigned to help Jack Crawford capture a
serial-killer dubbed 'Buffalo Bill'. To gain
vital information she continually confronts
imprisoned killer Dr Hannibal 'The Cannibal' Lecter. Meanwhile, Senator's daughter
Catherine Martin is kidnapped and a rare
death's-head moth is discovered in the throat
of the killer's last victim. Using clues
provided by Lecter, Clarice deduces that
their killer is creating a suit from the skins of
his victims. Lecter now seizes his chance to
escape. The moth clue leads Crawford to
suspect Jame Gumb but Clarice is already at
his lair where she rescues Catherine and
shoots Gumb. At her graduation ceremony,
she receives an admiring farewell call from
Lecter in Haiti.

Comment

A hugely popular thriller, with an American
box-office gross in excess of $130 million,
Silence of the Lambs focused attention on the
peculiarly American phenomenon of the
serial-killer, won fresh admiration for the
directorial prowess of Jonathan Demme and
acting abilities of Jodie Foster and, in
Anthony Hopkins's chillingly cultured and
intelligent mentor/killer, created the
cinema's most bloodcurdling bogey man
since the advent of Anthony Perkins's
Norman Bates in *Psycho* (see p169) 30 years
earlier.

The character of Hannibal the Cannibal
had already been played by Brian Cox in
Manhunter (1986), adapted from the Thomas
Harris novel *Red Dragon*, but Hopkins made

it his own with a silky smooth charm to
conceal the ferocity of the beast, a laser-like
stare and a grating intonation brought to
such now celebrated lines as: 'A census taker
once tried to test me. I ate his liver with some
fava beans and a nice Chianti.' Director
Demme heightens the character's impact by
restricting his on-screen appearances and
building a mystique through other people
recounting the horrors of his exploits. The
film however is also significant for Demme's
striking use of colour and pacing as well as
the marvellous performance from Foster in a
role initially offered to Michelle Pfeiffer. A
well-rounded central protagonist, vulnerably
making her way in a man's world and
courageously tackling the psychological
force of Lecter's mind and the physical
threat of Buffalo Bill, the character struck a
progressive blow for women in contemporary
mainstream cinema. Indeed, the only
criticism of the film is the sterotypical
portrait of the deviant killer Buffalo Bill. At
the time of writing, Harris, Demme, Hopkins
and Foster have all expressed interest in the
creation of a sequel.

An Orion/Strong Heart/Demme Production
Producers Edward Saxon, Kenneth Utt and
Ron Bozman
Screenplay Ted Tally, based on the novel by
Thomas Harris
Photography Tak Fujimoto
Editor Craig McKay
Art Director Tim Galvin
Music Howard Shore
Running time 118 mins *colour*

Cast
Jodie Foster (Clarice Starling)
Anthony Hopkins (Dr Hannibal Lecter)
Scott Glenn (Jack Crawford)
Ted Levine (Jame Gumb)
Anthony Heald (Dr Frederick Chilton)
Lawrence A Bonney (FBI Instructor)

Singin' in the Rain

Stanley Donen, USA, 1952

Joyous musical

Love finds its most sublime expression on a rain-swept sidewalk in the Hollywood of 1927.

The story

1927. After a Hollywood première, swashbuckling star Don Lockwood takes refuge from his fans in the car of aspiring actress Kathy Selden and is smitten by her, even though she proves resistant to his charms. As sound sweeps the industry, his next picture is to be a talkie. The production is a disaster with leading lady Lina Lamont's caterwaul of a Brooklyn accent laughed off the screen. However, Lockwood's friend Cosmo Brown has relocated Kathy and whilst the three of them commiserate he hits on the idea of making the film into a musical with Kathy dubbing Lina's voice. The ploy works and a jealous Lina's desire to conceal the fact is exposed at a public screening where Lockwood declares his love for Kathy.

Comment

One of the undoubted contenders for the title of greatest Hollywood musical, *Singin' in the Rain* was developed by producer Arthur Freed whose body of work as a lyricist, including the title song, would form the basis of the film's soundtrack. First announced in 1949 to star Ann Miller, the project took shape when Betty Comden and Adolph Green were hired as writers. The creators of *The Barkleys of Broadway* (1949) and adapters of *On the Town* (1949) (see p153) for the Kelly–Donen partnership, it was their idea to set the film during the 1920s rush towards sound and utilize the notion of a John Gilbert-like star facing ruin in the new era, but treating the situation for comic rather than dramatic effect.

The result is one of the most colourful and joyous of film musicals in which each component, from Kelly's sidewalk pitter-patter in the rain puddles to Donald O'Connor's manically inventive 'Make 'Em Laugh' number as well as Jean Hagen's 'shimmering, glowing star in the cinema firmament', makes a telling contribution.

As in *On The Town*, the musical numbers are generally used to advance the plot although the point here is not naturalism but a celebration of the never-never world of musicals which is achieved through the lavish use of colour, stylized sets and film-industry backdrop. However, one of the strengths of its caricatures is their basis in accurate observation; Millard Mitchell's studio boss is based on Freed himself and perennially apoplectic director Douglas Fowley conjures up memories of Busby Berkeley. The film received only two Academy Award nominations, for Hagen and Best Musical Score, neither of which it won. Posterity however has placed its reputation beyond the mere arbitrary awarding of statuettes.

An M-G-M Production
Producer Arthur Freed
Screenplay Betty Comden and Adolph Green
Photography Harold Rosson
Editor Adrienne Fazan
Art Directors Cedric Gibbons and Randall Duell
Music Nacio Herb Brown
Running time 103 mins *colour*

Cast

Gene Kelly (Don Lockwood)
Donald O'Connor (Cosmo Brown)
Debbie Reynolds (Kathy Shelden)
Jean Hagen (Lina Lamont)
Millard Mitchell (R F Simpson)
Rita Moreno (Zelda Zanders).

'And the winner is'
The Oscar

The American Academy of Motion Picture Arts and Sciences was established by 36 leading figures in the film industry who met on 4 May 1927 and selected Douglas Fairbanks as their first President. One week later three hundred guests attended an industry banquet to discuss the Academy's aims and purposes. Louis B Mayer suggested that the Academy should sponsor a series of awards to celebrate outstanding achievement in motion pictures. Art director Cedric Gibbons sketched a statuette on a tablecloth that was later sculpted by George Stanley into the Academy Award – a gold-plated figure standing on a reel of film carrying a sword. It is $13\frac{1}{2}$ inches high and weighs $8\frac{1}{2}$ pounds.

The responsibility for nicknaming the award 'Oscar' has been claimed by many, including actress Bette Davis, but the likeliest explanation seems to be that Academy Librarian Margaret Herrick once declared it to resemble her uncle Oscar and, from 1931 onwards, the name stuck.

The first awards to honour achievement between 1 August 1927 and 1 August 1928 were announced on 18 February 1929. The presentations took place three months later at a Banquet at the Hollywood Roosevelt Hotel on 26 May. Contemporary accounts of the event detail two highlights from the evening: a portable sound projector was used to show 'talkie' footage of Adolph Zukor receiving the Best Picture Award for *Wings* (1927) from Douglas Fairbanks in New York, whilst Al Jolson was there in person to sing for the assembled crowd.

Fairbanks presented those first awards in four minutes and 22 seconds and the whole evening had the air of a private party. The ensuing 60 years have turned the event into a gaudy, interminable spectacle dubbed, with good reason, 'the real star wars'.

Over the years the process has been streamlined; since 1935 the awards have covered a calendar year and other categories have been added including Best Foreign-Language Film, the Jean Hersholt Humanitarian Award and the Irving G Thalberg Memorial Award in recognition of 'the most consistent high quality of production achievement by an individual producer during that year'.

The Oscar ceremony now has an estimated global audience of around one billion viewers and, apart from prestige, an award is deemed to add millions of dollars to a film's gross takings and to immeasurably advance a career, hence the lavish amounts now spent by the major studios on campaigns to support their favoured films and stars. The actual effect of winning however is debatable. Certainly film like *Chariots of Fire* (1981) (see p52) benefited from its Best Picture 'Cinderella' win at the 1982 ceremony, but four Oscars could do nothing to prevent *The Right Stuff* (1983) from being a box-office flop and certain careers could not be said to have advanced from an Oscar win. Louise Fletcher, Best Actress for *One Flew Over the Cuckoo's Nest* (1975) (see p155) and F Murray Abraham, Best Actor for *Amadeus* (1984), have both suffered from a sense of anti-climax in the afterglow of their victories.

Based in Beverly Hills, the Academy has an active, often elderly, membership of around 3500 and devotes itself to research and education. Membership is by invitation only and members in specialist areas vote for nominations in their own field with the entire membership then eligible to vote from these nominations for a final winner. Since 1989, the Academy President has been actor Karl Malden.

To be accurate, the correct form of presentation is currently 'And the Oscar goes to . . .'

Chariots of Fire *(1981) Directed by Hugh Hudson (Ian Charleson)*

Local Hero *(1983) Directed by Bill Forsythe (Jenny Seagrove, Peter Capaldi)*

Day for Night *(1973) Directed by François Truffaut*
(Jean-Pierre Léaud, Jacqueline Bisset, François Truffaut)

Cyrano De Bergerac *(1990) Directed by Jean-Paul Rappeneau*
(Gérard Depardieu)

Snow White and the Seven Dwarfs

Walt Disney, USA, 1937

Animated fairy-tale

With a hearty 'Heigh Ho!' Disney's animated art reaches new heights of achievement.

The story

Raised by a wicked Queen, the orphaned Snow White dreams of being freed by a handsome man and one day is visited by Prince Charming. However, when the Queen's mirror declares that Snow White is the fairest in the land she orders her death. Unable to comply with this command, a huntsman tells Snow White to hide in the forest where she comes across a small cottage belonging to the Seven Dwarfs. Disguised as an old crone, the Queen visits Snow White and tricks her into eating a poisoned apple. Chased by the dwarfs, the Queen falls from a mountain ledge and perishes, and Snow White is restored to life by a kiss from Prince Charming and lives happily ever after.

Comment

Already renowned as the creator of Mickey Mouse and the 'Silly Symphonies' series of cartoons, Walt Disney was keen to take animation beyond its short-form restrictions to explore character and the possibilities of the medium within a feature-length story-line. He announced his intention to make a long-form fairytale in 1934, estimating that it might require a budget of $500 000. By the time of its Christmas 1937 première at the Cathay Circle Theater in Hollywood, the film had cost some $1 500 000, pushed Disney to the brink of bankruptcy and forced his staff of animators to devise and refine numerous new techniques. The drawing boards used in the studio had to be changed to accommodate the larger, more detailed images needed, whilst the development of the multi-plane camera helped to give a greater illusion of depth, augmented by much refined attention to small but telling details like the movement of smoke or rain, and other similar 'special-effects' which had not been considered worthwhile in the shorter format, but greatly enhanced the overall quality of the animation. Equally unprecedented attention was paid to developing characterization, both in the 'realistic' human figures like Snow White, the Huntsman, or the Prince, and in the dwarfs, each of whom was given a distinctive speech or action which the audience could recognize.

A work of pioneering innovation and magical, musical entertainment, *Snow White* employed 570 artists, used 250 000 drawings and set the benchmark by which all future Disney animation would be judged. By the end of its first year on release, it had grossed $8 500 000 and earned Disney a special Oscar in the shape of Snow White and seven small dwarfs, which was presented by Shirley Temple.

A Walt Disney Production
Producer Walt Disney
Screenplay Ted Sears, Otto Englander, Earl Hurd, Dorothy Ann Blank, Richard Creedon, Dick Richard, Merill De Maris and Webb Smith, based on the fairy tale *Sneewitchen* by the Brothers Grimm
Art Directors Charles Phillippi, Hugh Hennesy, Terrell Stapp, McLaren Stewart, Harold Miles, Tom Codrick, Gustaf Tenggren, Kenneth Anderson, Kendall O'Connor and Hazel Sewell
Music Frank Churchill, Leigh Harline, Paul Smith and Larry Morey
Running time 83 mins *colour*

Cast

Adriana Casselotti (Snow White)
Harry Stockwell (Prince Charming)
Lucile La Verne (The Queen)
Moroni Olsen (Magic Mirror)
Billy Gilbert (Sneezy)
Pinto Colvig (Sleepy/Grumpy)

Some Like It Hot

Billy Wilder, USA, 1959

Jazz age farce

Cross-dressing in the Roaring Twenties begets a timeless comic delight.

The story

1929. Witnesses to the St Valentine's Day Massacre, musicians Joe and Jerry disguise themselves as 'Josephine' and 'Daphne' and head for Florida in an all-girl band. At Miami Beach, 'Daphne' catches the eye of oft-married millionaire Osgood Fielding III, whilst Joe becomes a wealthy playboy to woo love-hungry singer Sugar. When a gangland convention brings Spats Columbo to Florida, Joe and Jerry are in danger again. However, Spats and his gang are killed by rival mobsters. Joe's disguise is revealed to Sugar who loves him regardless, and when 'Daphne' confesses to Osgood that he is a man, he is met with the tolerant rebuke that 'nobody's perfect'.

Comment

One of the most consistently funny and enduring of all comedies, *Some Like It Hot* was once considered as a vehicle for the partnership of Bob Hope and Danny Kaye. Later, writer/director Billy Wilder tailored the role of 'Daphne' especially for Jack Lemmon after having seen the actor in *Operation Mad Ball* (1957). Tony Curtis was cast as fellow musician Joe and Mitzi Gaynor was to be Sugar Kane. However, commercial considerations almost forced the replacement of Lemmon by the then more potent box-office attraction of Frank Sinatra. When Marilyn Monroe signed on as Sugar, the pressure was eased and the chemistry of Lemmon and Curtis allowed to develop fully.

A production that became notorious for the delays caused by Monroe's poor time-keeping and inability to remember the simplest of lines, *Some Like It Hot* is the film that caused Curtis to remark that 'kissing Marilyn was like kissing Hitler'. However, what is seen on screen is pure magic, combining a razor-sharp script with inventive performances, an adroit sense of timing, a complex, uninhibited examination of sexual identity and an affectionate pastiche of the gangland era with George Raft parodying his famous *Scarface* (1932) role.

The number-three film at the American box-office in 1959, it was nominated for six Academy Awards including Best Director and Best Actor for Lemmon. Coming up against the year of *Ben-Hur* (see p31) and the innate conservatism of the Academy, it received only one statue for Best Costume Design. The film did however initiate a long and fruitful collaboration between Lemmon and Wilder that resulted in such films as *The Apartment* (1960) (see p17), *Irma La Douce* (1963) and *Avanti!* (1972).

An Ashton-Mirisch Company Production
Producer Billy Wilder
Screenplay Billy Wilder and I A L Diamond suggested by a story by R Thoeren and M Logan
Photography Charles Lang Jnr
Editor Arthur Schmidt
Art Director Ted Haworth
Music Adolph Deutsch
Running time 120 mins b/w

Cast
Marilyn Monroe (Sugar Kowalczyk)
Tony Curtis (Joe/Josephine)
Jack Lemmon (Jerry/Daphne)
George Raft (Spats Columbo)
Joe E Brown (Osgood Fielding III)
Pat O'Brien (Mulligan)
Joan Shawlee (Sweet Sue)

The Sound of Music

Robert Wise, USA, 1965

Family musical

An old-fashioned musical becomes one of the world's favourite things.

The story

Salzburg, 1938. Tomboyish convent girl Maria is sent to work as a temporary governess for the widower Captain Von Trapp and his seven children. Her sense of fun and openness bring a refreshing warmth to the household but she returns to the Nonnberg Abbey when she realizes her regard for Von Trapp is turning into love. However, the Mother Abbess encourages her to pursue the romance and she returns to Von Trapp who breaks off his engagement to the Baroness Schrader so that they may be wed. Their happiness is shortlived as the Nazis insist that the Captain report for naval duties. He refuses and uses the cover of a large music festival to escape with the family and cross over the mountains to the safety of Switzerland.

Comment

Based on the true story of the Von Trapp family's escape to neutral Switzerland in 1938, *The Sound of Music* was developed from Rodgers and Hammerstein's rather weak stage musical which had provided another success for Mary Martin on Broadway in 1959. The film version was apparently offered to both directors Billy Wilder and William Wyler before being entrusted to the care of Robert Wise, an Oscar-winner for his co-direction of *West Side Story* (1961). Star Julie Andrews signed on for the film fresh from her screen début in *Mary Poppins* (1964) which would bring her a Best Actress Oscar.

Artistically, it is easy to dismiss the film for its blatant manipulation of sentiment (Plummer was apparently wont to describe it as the Sound of Mucus) but to do so would be to ignore the considerable brilliance of both director and performers, the staggeringly beautiful use of the Swiss scenery, the tuneful songs and the creation of an old-fashioned entertainment that crossed all boundaries of age and nationality in its appeal. Dwight MacDonald in *Esquire* magazine offered a backhanded but apt compliment when he wrote, 'There is something interesting about any man-made product that approaches perfection of its kind, also about any exercise of supreme professional skill, and this was both: pure, unadulterated kitsch, not a false note, not a whiff of reality.'

The public cared not a jot for the critical disdain and eventually pushed the film towards a box-office gross in excess of $80 million, thus toppling *Gone With the Wind* (1939) as the most popular film of all time. The Academy nominated the film in nine categories and *The Sound of Music* was to win five Oscars including Best Picture and Best Director.

An Argyle Enterprises Production
Producer Robert Wise
Screenplay Ernest Lehman, based on the stage musical by Richard Rodgers and Oscar Hammerstein II from the book by Howard Lindsay and Russel Crouse
Photography Ted McCord
Editor William Reynolds
Art Director Boris Leven
Music Rodgers and Hammerstein
Running time 174 mins *colour*

Cast

Julie Andrews (Maria)
Christopher Plummer (Captain Von Trapp)
Eleanor Parker (The Baroness)
Richard Haydn (Max Detweiler)
Peggy Wood (Mother Abbess)
Charmian Carr (Liesl)

Stagecoach

John Ford, USA, 1939

Prototype western

A hazardous journey becomes a landmark in the development of the western.

The story

En route from Tonto, a stagecoach party are joined by The Ringo Kid, a fugitive from justice seeking the men who have killed his father and brother. Despite the loss of their cavalry escort, they journey on, with the inebriated Dr Boone and prostitute Dallas assisting when Mrs Mallory goes into labour. The Indians finally attack and the Kid distinguishes himself in the fearsome skirmish that ensues although gambler Hatfield is killed before the timely arrival of the cavalry. On their arrival in Lordsburg the banker Gatewood is arrested for embezzlement and Ringo settles his score with the Plummer boys before Sheriff Wilcox allows him to ride across the border with Dallas whose heart has been won by his chivalry.

Comment

Although long regarded as one of the key figures in the historical and artistic development of the western, director John Ford had not worked in the field for a dozen years before embarking on *Stagecoach*, one of a number of releases in 1939, including *Jesse James*, *Union Pacific* and *Destry Rides Again*, which heralded a lasting upturn in the genre's popularity and prestige. Having purchased Ernest Haycox's 'Stage to Lordsburg' story from the April 1937 issue of *Collier's* magazine, Ford had selected John Wayne as his leading man but encountered numerous setbacks because of doubts over Wayne's box-office value. David O Selznick had expressed an interest in providing the $230 000 budget but only if he would cast Gary Cooper and Marlene Dietrich.

Eventually backed by independent producer Walter Wanger, the film was made, and proved to be crucial in the development of the western from its role as simplistic action vehicle into something capable of carrying more serious themes within its adventure narrative. The quality and tension of the action drama itself marked it out as a major development in the genre, notably the furious chase sequence in which Ford utilized the broad sweep of Utah's statuesque Monument Valley for the first time. Beyond that action level, however, the film suggested a more complex ambition within the relationships which grew up between the various characters who were to be models for many westerns to come. The characterization has more depth and complexity than anything which preceded it, and touched on such issues as racism and social and moral values, which had previously found no place in the unquestioning mores of the genre. Neither the 1966 remake nor the 1986 television version can hold a candle to the original.

A Walter Wanger/United Artists Production
Producer John Ford
Screenplay Dudley Nichols, based on the story 'Stage to Lordsburg' by Ernest Haycox
Photography Bert Glennon
Supervising Editor Otho Lovering
Art Directors Alexander Toluboff and Wiard Ihnen
Music Richard Hageman, W Franke Harling, John Leipold, Leo Shuken and Louis Gruenberg adapted from folk tunes of the period
Running time 97 mins b/w

Cast
John Wayne (The Ringo Kid)
Claire Trevor (Dallas)
John Carradine (Hatfield)
Thomas Mitchell (Dr Josiah Boone)
Andy Devine (Buck)
Donald Meek (Samuel Peacock)

A Star is Born

George Cukor, USA, 1954

One-woman show

The pressures on the union between a rising star and a fading idol create a memorable melodrama.

The story

Saved from embarrassment at a Hollywood première, alcoholic movie star Norman Maine meets his benefactor Esther Blodgett and is struck by the promise of her vocal talent. Re-christened Vicki Lester, she is groomed for success and ultimately achieves stardom. They are wed, but whilst Esther finds her star in the ascendant, Norman's roisterous reputation and fading appeal signal the twilight of his career. Wallowing in self-pity and alcohol, he shames Esther in public and, after a further binge, is released into her custody. Aghast that she is prepared to abandon her career to care for him, he commits suicide. A grief-stricken widow, Esther retreats from the world but makes an emotional return as 'Mrs Norman Maine'.

Comment

The tragic see-saw relationship between a showbusiness couple has been a hardy perennial of film drama for almost 60 years beginning with *What Price Hollywood?* (1932), also directed by George Cukor, the film that directly inspired the first official version of *A Star Is Born* (1937), an early Technicolor effort starring Fredric March and Janet Gaynor. This lavish 1954 remake is, above all, a showcase for the remarkable musical and dramatic talents of Judy Garland who was returning to Hollywood for the first time since the termination of her M-G-M contract in 1950 and subsequent triumph as a live performer in New York. Garland had played the role of Esther in a 1942 radio production of the story and was keen to repeat the experience on screen for her cinema comeback. Cary Grant was the original choice for the role of Norman Maine but rejected the offer. The second choice was James Mason who gives one of his finest performances, capturing the enthusiasm rekindled by Esther, the bitterness, self-loathing and self-sacrifice, and providing a well-modulated counterpoint to Garland's compelling emotional *tour de force* that was described by *Time* magazine, with only slight exaggeration, as 'just about the finest one-woman show in modern cinema history'. Nominated for six Oscars, including Best Actor and Actress, the film went unrewarded, with Garland scandalously passed over in favour of Grace Kelly's performance in *Country Girl* (1954), which was remarkable only for her daring to appear deglamourized. The decision was described by Groucho Marx as the biggest robbery since Brinks. With the setting switched from Hollywood to the rock world, 1976 saw a further unnecessary recounting of the story with Barbra Streisand and Kris Kristofferson, which lacks any of the virtues of the earlier versions.

A Transcoma Enterprises Production
Producer Sidney Luft
Screenplay Moss Hart based on the Dorothy Parker, Alan Campbell and Robert Carson screenplay from a story by William A Wellman and Robert Carson inspired by the film *What Price Hollywood?*
Photography Sam Leavitt
Editor Folmar Blangsted
Art Director Malcolm Bert
Music Harold Arlen
Running time originally 182 mins *colour*

Cast

Judy Garland (Esther Blodgett/Vicki Lester)
James Mason (Norman Maine)
Jack Carson (Matt Libby)
Charles Bickford (Oliver Niles)
Tom Noonan (Danny McGuire)
Lucy Marlowe (Lola Lavery)

Star Wars

George Lucas, USA, 1977

Space age heroics

'A long, long time ago, in a galaxy far away. . .'

The story

Captured by Grand Moff Tarkin, Princess Leia implants a hologram in robot R2D2 who flees with C3PO. Purchasing them from junk dealers, Luke Skywalker discovers her message and seeks out Obi-Wan Kenobi who informs him that his father had been a Jedi knight and tries to instruct him in the Zen-like power of 'The Force'. When his relatives are slain by Tarkin's men, Luke recruits pilot Han Solo to take him and Obi-Wan to the Death Star. Whilst the others save Leia, Obi-Wan perishes in combat with Darth Vader passing 'The Force' on to Luke. Arriving on the rebel planet, Skywalker volunteers for a bomber raid on the Death Star and, with Solo's assistance, succeeds in destroying it. Vader however escapes to fight another day.

Comment

Star Wars opened the floodgates for the series of high-budget, effects-laden action adventure spectacles that littered the box-office charts in the decade after its explosive arrival. George Lucas and Steven Spielberg were to dominate the field and, although both came from film school backgrounds, it was the Hollywood B-movies and low-budget serials of their childhoods that provided the inspiration for their most popular works. A conflict between good and evil, personified on the one hand by the youthful hero Luke Skywalker and on the other by his nemesis Darth Vader and the Empire he represents, the film does however acknowledge some progress from the simple morality of the *Flash Gordon* era.

Skywalker's righteous crusade is also a battle with the dark forces within himself (a notion made even clearer in *Return of the Jedi* (1983) where Vader is revealed to be his father) and his compatriots, notably Han Solo, are not exactly unambiguously clean-cut either. However, the robots R2D2 and C3PO and a variety of odd, furry extra-terrestrials fulfil the apparently necessary light relief and cuteness quotients and foreshadow the later success of Spielberg's *E. T.* (1982) (see p74).

If there is more to the film than just spectacular action, the expert accomplishment of that action is undoubtedly at the root of its enormous appeal and gross in excess of $165 million. It swept the technical Oscar categories, winning awards for Visual Effects, Editing, Sound, Art Direction, Costume Design and Original Score. Lucas once talked of the film and its equally popular sequels, *The Empire Strikes Back* (1980) and *Return of the Jedi* as being the middle trio of a nine-part epic cycle but no further additions to the mythology of the Empire have yet appeared.

A Twentieth Century-Fox Production
Producer Gary Kurtz
Screenplay George Lucas
Photography Gilbert Taylor
Editors Paul Hirsch, Marcia Lucas and Richard Chew
Art Directors Norman Reynolds and Leslie Dilley.
Music: John Williams
Running time 121 mins *colour*

Cast
Mark Hamill (Luke Skywalker)
Harrison Ford (Han Solo)
Carrie Fisher (Princess Leia Organa)
Peter Cushing (Grand Moff Tarkin)
Alec Guinness (Ben Obi-Wan Kenobi)
Anthony Daniels (See Threepio (C3PO))

A Streetcar Named Desire

Elia Kazan, USA, 1951

Maestro of method acting

Tennessee Williams's hothouse drama brings Marlon Brando to the forefront of screen actors.

The story

New Orleans. Blanche Du Bois arrives to visit her sister Stella and her husband Stanley who demands their share from the sale of the family home. Blanche admits that the money has gone. Resentful of her airs and graces, he unearths the secrets of her scandalous past including the suicide of her husband and her reputation as a scarlet woman. He relishes telling his enchanted friend Mitch the truth about genteel, ladylike Blanche. When the pregnant Stella is taken to hospital, Stanley and Blanche are left alone in the claustrophobic apartment. He rapes her and precipitates her final plunge into madness. Stella takes their newborn child and moves out, leaving him alone, bellowing her name.

Comment

Directed by Elia Kazan, Tennessee Williams's play opened on Broadway in December 1947 with a cast headed by Jessica Tandy and the 23-year-old Marlon Brando who caused a sensation with his electrifying performance as the brutish Stanley Kowalski. When it came to the film version, Kazan was retained to direct with many of the cast repeating their stage roles, except Tandy who was replaced by Vivien Leigh, thus establishing a contrast of techniques and personalities with Brando that would work to the advantage of the already highly-charged dramatic proceedings.

Despite the screen version's removal of any references to the homosexuality of Blanche's first husband, and substantial toning down of her nymphomania, it did represent a move towards a more mature approach to sexuality than that previously permitted under the primly restrictive Production Code, and marked Brando's emergence as a fully-fledged star. Following a screen début in *The Men* (1950), his performance as Kowalski astounded with its stark realism and adoption of the Method style derived from Stanislavsky and propagated in America by Lee Strasberg. The emotional intensity and authenticity of his achievement and determination to explore the psyche of a character from the inside out influenced all subsequent generations of actors and stands in sharp contrast to Leigh's equally effective style of classical English acting.

The film was nominated for 12 Academy Awards, winning Oscars for Leigh, Hunter, Malden and Art Direction. Brando lost to Humphrey Bogart's performance in *The African Queen* (1951) (see p4). A 1984 television version of *A Streetcar Named Desire* starring Ann-Margret and Treat Williams was able to be far more faithful to the original text.

A Warner Brothers Production
Producer Charles K Feldman
Screenplay Tennessee Williams and Oscar Saul, based on Williams's play
Photography Harry Stradling
Editor David Weisbart
Art Director Richard Day
Music Alex North
Running time 125 mins b/w

Cast

Vivien Leigh (Blanche Du Bois)
Marlon Brando (Stanley Kowalski)
Kim Hunter (Stella Kowalski)
Karl Malden (Mitch)
Rudy Bond (Steve Hubbell)
Nick Dennis (Pablo Gonzales)

Stromboli
(Stromboli, terra di dio)
Roberto Rossellini, Italy, 1950

Volcanic passion

The scandalous off-screen relationship between star and director eclipsed the impact of the film itself.

The story

A Czechoslovakian refugee marries a soldier in order to escape from a displaced person's camp at the end of World War II. He brings her back to his tiny native island of Stromboli. She attempts to adjust to the hard life on the bleak but beautiful island, but the natives are distrustful of newcomers, and she is isolated from the community. She makes friends with Sponza, the lighthouse-keeper, but her husband reacts jealously, and locks her in their house. When she discovers she is pregnant, the thought of bearing a succession of his children in this place is too much, and she attempts to escape over the volcano at the heart of the island, with the help of the lighthouse-keeper. She succumbs to fumes at the top, and when she recovers, determines to go back and face life on the island.

Comment

Rossellini is often described as the father of Italian neorealism, but *Stromboli* is equally typical of the increasingly dominant spiritual and transcendent values in his work. As such, it is something of a bridge between his acclaimed trilogy of near-documentary films about the effects of the war (*Rome, Open City*, 1945 (*Roma, Città Aperta*) (see p183), *Paisan*, 1946 (*Paisà*), and *Germany, Year Zero*, 1947 (*Germania, Anno Zero*)), and later more overt searches for a spiritual meaning to life in later films like *Voyage to Italy* (1953) (*Viaggio in Italia*).

Rossellini had achieved great success with non-professional actors in *Rome, Open City*, but the experiment was not as successful here, possibly because they looked considerably less convincing when placed alongside Ingrid Bergman. The combination is an uneasy one, and reflects the general uneasiness of Hollywood meeting a very different tradition which pervades both the off- and on-screen reputation of the film. The passionate relationship which developed between Bergman and Rossellini (their daughter is actress Isabella Rossellini) led to the actress leaving her husband, and caused a scandal, including the boycotting of the film in certain places.

On screen, Bergman's professionalism and star quality is often incongruous amid the rather wooden, self-conscious performances from the largely amateur cast. She does not allow that to distract from her own performance, however, while the island itself is a spectacular as well as an apt background for the director's exploration of the instability and insecurity of human relationships.

A Be-Ro/RKO Production
Producer Roberto Rossellini
Screenplay Roberto Rossellini, Art Cohen, Renzo Cesana, Sergio Amedei and C P Callegari
Photography Otello Martelli
Editors Roland Gross and Jolanda Benvenuti
Music Renzo Rossellini
Running time 81 mins b/w

Cast
Ingrid Bergman (Karin Bjiorsen)
Mario Vitale (Antonio)
Renzo Cesana (The Priest)
Mario Sponza (The Lighthouse Keeper)

Sullivan's Travels

Preston Sturges, USA, 1941

A lesson in life

Fired with a social purpose, an earnest director learns that there is no shame in creating pure entertainment.

The story

A successful director of light entertainment, John L Sullivan, yearns to make a searing drama of human suffering. His attempt to experience ordinary life becomes a publicity stunt but, dressed as a tramp, he tries again and meets a girl. Later, she returns to Los Angeles but he is robbed by a tramp who is subsequently killed and assumed to be him. Suffering from amnesia, a fracas with a railroad guard brings a six-year sentence of hard labour. The misery of prison life is relieved only by the joy experienced at a Mickey Mouse cartoon. Sullivan then confesses to his own murder and the resulting publicity leads to his recognition and release. Intending to marry the girl he is also determined that his future work will bring the world laughter.

Comment

Although his comet-like career as one of Hollywood's most inventive comic minds lasted but a handful of years, Preston Sturges's credits as writer/director include some of the sharpest and funniest entertainments to emerge from wartime Hollywood, including such films as *The Lady Eve* (1941), *Hail, the Conquering Hero* (1944) and *The Miracle of Morgan's Creek* (1944). His glorious, freewheeling comedies energetically combine slapstick, social satire and a gallery of outrageous characters that provided gainful employment for an unofficial rep company of seasoned scene-stealers. One of his few films to present an overt message in-between the humour and coruscating plot-twists, *Sullivan's Travels* was written by Sturges specifically for Joel McCrea and , in the director's words, was 'The result of an urge, an urge to tell some of my fellow playwrights that they were getting a little too deep-dish and to leave the preaching to the preachers.'

Impressed by Veronica Lake's performance in *I Wanted Wings* (1941), Sturges was adamant in wanting her as his leading lady and wrestled that concession from a studio that had hoped to cast the likes of Claire Trevor, Lucille Ball or Ruby Keeler in the part. Their price was that Sturges complete the film on a budget of $600 000 within 45 days. He complied and created a wickedly accurate satire of Hollywood pretensions that is informed by an insider's knowledge. The title of Sullivan's proposed epic of human degradation is *Brother, Where Art Thou* and one can sense the relish of Sturges vindicating his own beliefs as Sullivan is gradually stripped of the notion that great art can only be created in the serious depiction of social realism. *Sullivan's Travels* in itself is eloquent rebuttal to that misguided school of thought.

A Paramount Production
Producer Paul Jones
Screenplay Preston Sturges
Photography John Seitz
Editor Stuart Gilmore
Art Directors Hans Dreier and Earl Hedrick
Music Leo Shuken and Charles Bradshaw
Running time 91 mins b/w

Cast
Joel McCrea (John L Sullivan)
Veronica Lake (The Girl)
Robert Warwick (Mr Lebran)
William Demarest (Mr Jones)
Franklin Pangborn (Mr Casalais)
Porter Hall (Mr Hadrian)

Sunrise

F W Murnau, USA, 1927

The vagaries of love

A consummate use of light and shadow infuse a hymn to love with a rare poetry.

The story

In the heat of his affair with a city woman, a young farmer agrees to kill his wife and move to the city. He plans to stage an accident in the boat they use but is unable to carry out the deed and distraught by what he had contemplated. Joyously reconciled with his wife, they spend a day in the city, witnessing a wedding and enjoying the attractions of an amusement park. However, on the way home by boat a storm erupts and the sail breaks. Pushing his wife to safety, the farmer takes his chances in the sea and is safely washed ashore. The wife however is still missing. When the city woman arrives she assumes he has carried out their plan but when word arrives that his wife has been found alive, the ecstatic farmer rushes to her side.

Comment

Subtitled a 'Song of Two Humans', *Sunrise* marked the transition from Germany to Hollywood of noted director F W Murnau and also represents one of the finest expressions of the artistic heights scaled by silent cinema in the very moment it was to be made obsolete by the advent of talking pictures.

A painterly and poetic melodrama that creates its narrative by the use of light and space, the film incorporates much of the visual language of the German Expressionist movement, thus enabling Murnau to render an American tale within a very European sensibility. Along with screen-writer Carl Mayer, he may have opted to change the original novel's tragic denouement into a more conventionally happy ending, but this does not detract from the intensity of the anguish and tenderness which have been expressed throughout the story in the direction and the power of the visual images.

Murnau abandons the static conventions of silent cinema in favour of almost constant motion, to the point where the action is moulded to fit the needs of a fluid camera, rather than the other way around. The film jumps between scenes of highly stylized, expressionistic sets and acting, and those of a more naturalistic mode, following a rhythm perceived in the material by the director. The use of lighting effects in creating the moods of ecstasy, reconciliation or furtiveness appropriate to these stylistic and thematic shifts is extraordinary even by contemporary standards.

Although a commercial flop, *Sunrise* was recognized at the first Oscar ceremony with awards for Artistic Quality of Production, Cinematography and Best Actress for Janet Gaynor shared with her performances in *Seventh Heaven* (1927) and *Street Angel* (1928).

A Fox Film Corporation Production
Producer William Fox
Screenplay Carl Mayer, based on the novel *The Journey to Tilsit* by Hermann Sudermann
Photography Charles Rosher and Karl Struss
Art Director Rochus Gliese
Running time 117 mins b/w

Cast
George O'Brien (The Man)
Janet Gaynor (The Wife)
Margaret Livingstone (The Woman from the City)
Bodil Rosing (The Maid)
J Farrell MacDonald (The Photographer)
Ralph Sipperly (The Barber)

Sunset Boulevard

Billy Wilder, USA, 1950

The inside story

'All right, Mr De Mille, I'm ready for my close-up.'

The story

Stumbling across silent-screen idol Norma Desmond and her manservant Max, scriptwriter Joe Gillis accepts her offer of work and board. Lavished with gifts, he tolerates her need to bask in past fame but flees an intimate New Year supper for two. He meets script-reader Betty Schaefer again and she encourages him to pursue his own work. However, he stays with Norma when he learns she has attempted suicide. Allowed to believe she is in demand again, Norma visits Cecil B De Mille and prepares for her comeback in *Salome*. Gillis sees more of Betty but a jealous Norma exposes him as a kept man and when he tries to leave, she shoots him dead. As she is led away, the presence of newsreel cameramen convince her she is back at work.

Comment

One of the blackest and most merciless insider portraits of Hollywood and the tragedies behind the phoney tinsel, the Wilder-Brackett script for *Sunset Boulevard* bristles with dark humour, highly quotable dialogue and a dazzling inventiveness that sets a film noir-ish tone by having the plot related by Gillis's corpse as it floats in Desmond's pool. It is almost barbarically cruel in its treatment of leading actress Gloria Swanson who contributes a chillingly convincing performance as a character similar in circumstances, if thankfully not in temperament, to her own.

Montgomery Clift had originally been scheduled to play the impecunious hack Gillis but passed on the role one week before shooting. Unable to persuade Fred MacMurray to take the part, Wilder and Brackett hired William Holden. A number of older actresses including Mary Pickford, Pola Negri and a deeply insulted Mae West had been approached to play Norma before Swanson was chosen. Her casting alongside Erich Von Stroheim as her former mentor, ex-husband and now devoted manservant is perfect; both their careers dimmed with the advent of talkies and it was von Stroheim's lavishly indulgent direction of *Queen Kelly* (1928) that almost bankrupted Swanson and brought an end to many of their individual and communal Hollywood aspirations. Clips from the film are used within *Sunset Boulevard* and Norma's old friends in the film are played by Buster Keaton, Anna Q Nilsson and H B Warner – all real-life relics of the silent era who had known better days.

Nominated for eleven Academy Awards, the film received Oscars only for Best Story and Screenplay, Art Direction and Musical Score. Holden's performance lost to José Ferrer's *Cyrano De Bergerac* and Swanson was passed over in favour of Judy Holliday in *Born Yesterday*.

A Paramount Production
Producer Charles Brackett
Screenplay Billy Wilder, Charles Brackett and D M Marshman Jnr
Photography John F Seitz
Editors Doane Harrison and Arthur Schmidt
Art Directors Hans Dreier and John Meehan
Music Franz Waxman
Running time 110 mins *b/w*

Cast
William Holden (Joe Gillis)
Gloria Swanson (Norma Desmond)
Erich Von Stroheim (Max Von Mayerling)
Nancy Olson (Betty Schaefer)
Fred Clark (Sheldrake)
Lloyd Gough (Morino)

Sweet Smell of Success

Alexander Mackendrick, USA, 1957

Absolute power

The underside of the glamorous New York media world provides a corrosive study of power and corruption.

The story

Unprincipled press agent Sidney Falco will stop at nothing to win the approval of powerful New York columnist J J Hunsecker. Entrusted to crush the romance between Hunsecker's beloved sister Susie and unworthy musician Steve Dallas, he devises a smear campaign that loses Dallas his job and has him framed on a drugs charge. He is rewarded with the assurance that he will write Hunsecker's column while J J is on holiday. Susie however retaliates and arranges for J J to catch her in a seemingly compromising situation with Falco. J J now has Falco arrested on the drugs charge but his patriarchal power crumbles as Susie leaves home to be with Dallas.

Comment

Sweet Smell of Success is another of those Hollywood films that broke the rules a little too much for its merits to be fully recognized at the time of its release, leaving it to a later critical re-evaluation to establish its rightful standing. While James Wong Howe's celebrated camerawork, shot on the night streets of New York in evocatively moody fashion, align it most closely with film noir, it falls neatly into no specific genre, either in manner or subject-matter.

Hecht-Hill-Lancaster had already been responsible for such successes as *Marty* (1955) and *Trapeze* (1956) before placing its weight behind this corrosive study of power and corruption and it is to their credit

that they spotted previously untapped facets of the talents of both Tony Curtis and Sandy MacKendrick.

Better known for his beefcake appeal, Curtis finally asserted his acting credentials here with a scrupulously well-observed portrait of the venal, ambitious press agent. MacKendrick's reputation as a purveyor of the best in Ealing comedy, from *Whisky Galore* (1948) to *The Man in the White Suit* (1951), had done little to prepare one for the sense of suspense and pyschological menace he brought to the seamy revelations of the underbelly of the glamorous New York media world. The brittle dialogue of the Clifford Odets – Ernest Lehman script, evocative jazz score of Elmer Bernstein and the stylish realization of the film have lost none of their appeal, while the issues it raises are arguably even more pertinent in today's unrelenting wash of media-glare than they were when it was made.

MacKendrick subsequently worked on the Lancaster production of *The Devil's Disciple* (1959) before being replaced by director Guy Hamilton and was reunited with Curtis on the comedy *Don't Make Waves* (1967).

A Hecht-Hill-Lancaster Production
Producer James Hill
Screenplay Clifford Odets and Ernest Lehman
Photography James Wong Howe
Editor Alan Crosland Jnr
Art Director Edward Carrere
Music Elmer Bernstein
Running time 96 mins *b/w*

Cast

Burt Lancaster (J J Hunsecker)
Tony Curtis (Sidney Falco)
Susan Harrison (Susan Hunsecker)
Marty Milner (Steve Dallas)
Sam Levene (Frank D'Angelo)
Barbara Nichols (Rita)

The present day
Contemporary movie history

With work ranging from *Close Encounters of the Third Kind* (1977) (see p58) and *Raiders of the Lost Ark* (1981) (see p173) to *Star Wars* (1977) (see p207) and *E.T.* (1982) (see p74), Steven Spielberg and George Lucas have been responsible for the majority of films that now make up the official top ten list of the biggest box-office hits. However, their dominance of Hollywood production in the 1970s and 1980s narrowed the horizons of the major studios and fostered an adolescent view of the world that was underlined by the average age of American cinemagoers now falling to the late teens or early twenties. Hence, the dispiriting succession of films whose aspirations rarely rose above the level of the groin or beyond double-figure IQs, the popularity of romps like *Porkys* (1981), and the acceptance of measuring achievement in box-office dollars rather than by any other criteria.

The financial difficulties involved in the making of *Apocalypse Now* (1979) (see p18) and, more notoriously, *Heaven's Gate* (1980) (see p102) provoked a reaction of conservatism among the Hollywood studios. Thus, Martin Scorsese found himself following the acclaim of *Taxi Driver* (1976) (see p217) and *Raging Bull* (1980) (see p172) with much safer, commercial projects like *The Color of Money* (1986) before returning to more challenging material in the 1990s.

However, if the major studios were cautious, the burgeoning American independent filmmaking scene provided a home for such talents as Jim Jarmusch, John Sayles and Spike Lee whose success with *She's Gotta Have It* (1986) (see p194) launched a continuing career in the mainstream and gave him a platform as the unofficial spokesman for a new generation of African-American filmmakers. The mainstream too grew to accept such figures as Woody Allen,

David Lynch with *Blue Velvet* (1986) (see p39) and Jonathan Demme with *The Silence of the Lambs* (1991) (see p197).

In world cinema, old masters graced their autumnal years with such works as *Kagemusha* (1980) by Kurosawa, *That Obscure Object of Desire* (1977) by Buñuel, and *Fanny and Alexander* (1982) (see p79) which marked Ingmar Bergman's life-affirming farewell to the movies. At the opposite end of the age spectrum, Pedro Almodovar made use of the post-Franco freedoms to revel in an iconoclastic view of human relationships and became an art-house darling with *Women on the Verge of a Nervous Breakdown* (1988). The dour wit of Aki Kaurismaki emerged from Finland, the sentimentality of Giuseppe Tornatore won friends for *Cinema Paradiso* (1989) (see p54), new Chinese cinema briefly grew in strength and stature and France nourished the stylish endeavours of Jean-Jacques Beineix and Luc Besson whose *The Big Blue* (1988) was the most popular film of the decade in its native land although eclipsed by *Jean De Florette* (1986) (see p119) and *Cyrano De Bergerac* (1990) (see p61) in international recognition. Despite numerous obstacles British cinema has also endured in such diverse productions as *Chariots of Fire* (1981) (see p52), *The Draughtsman's Contract* (1982) (see p73), *Local Hero* (1983) (see p133), *Distant Voices, Still Lives* (1988) (see p66) and in the films of Derek Jarman.

Success in any area is never guaranteed and the blockbuster mentality of contemporary Hollywood can equally well produce the goldmine of *Batman* (1989) (see p27), the surprise popularity of *Dances With Wolves* (1990) (see p62) or the absolute turkey of *Hudson Hawk* (1991). However, sheer unpredictability is what keeps the joy in cinemagoing alive.

Five Easy Pieces *(1970) Directed by Bob Rafelson (Jack Nicholson)*

The Last Picture Show *(1971) Directed by Peter Bogdanovich (Cybill Shepherd)*

Apocalypse Now *(1979) Directed by Francis Coppola (Martin Sheen)*

Raging Bull *(1980) Directed by Martin Scorsese (Robert De Niro)*

Taxi Driver

Martin Scorsese, USA, 1976

Urban hell

Scorsese and De Niro collaborate on a searing and disturbing exploration of urban alienation.

The story

New York. Vietnam veteran Travis Bickle is sickened by the perversion that surrounds him. Working nights as a taxi driver, he spends his days watching porno films or collecting his troubled thoughts in a diary. He charms election campaign worker Betsy into going on a date with him but is swiftly rejected. He purchases a collection of firearms and gives vent to his anger by shooting a supermarket robber. He then meets 12-year-old prostitute Iris and makes it his mission to rescue her from the streets. He achieves this by shooting her pimp Sport, one of his men and Iris's client. A lack of bullets prevents his own suicide but he is hailed in the press for his heroic actions and treats Betsy with disdain the next time they meet.

Comment

Inspired by the Harry Chapin song 'Taxi', this quintessential picture of contemporary urban life as hell on earth could perhaps only have stemmed from a collaboration between avowedly Roman Catholic filmmaker Martin Scorsese and the sternly Calvinist-influenced screenwriter Paul Schrader. Partially inspired by the discomforting ambiguity at the heart of the John Wayne character in *The Searchers* (1956) (see p189), the Taxi Driver character of Travis Bickle juxtaposes the attitudes of a moralizing western hero with the capacity for carnage found within the psychopathic slayers endemic to the contemporary vigilante and horror genres. Scorsese described the film as 'a continuation of *Mean Streets*. It's a film dealing with religious anxiety, guilt and one man's attitudes toward women – attitudes that were arrested at age 13.'

Burning with disgust at the moral decay around him, De Niro's mesmerizing performance delineates an almost existential sense of frustration fed by his feelings of sexual inadequacy and paranoid disdain for his fellow man, whilst Scorsese finds a visual style for his state of mind in a nocturnal New York that is a sleek, gleaming, nightmarish vision. Throughout, the religious connotations are to the forefront of the drama, from the candles in the prostitute's room to the interpretation of Bickle as a character who journeys through purgatory to find his own redemption in the catharsis of violence.

Rejected by most of the Hollywood studios, the film returned some $12 million dollars on an investment of $2 million and earned four Oscar nominations, but the dismaying enthusiasm with which some audiences greeted the protagonist's crazed quest evinces the degree to which the film resonates with a disturbing and provocative sense of ideological imprecision.

An Italo-Judeo Production
Producers Michael Phillips and Julia Phillips
Screenplay Paul Schrader
Photography Michael Chapman
Editors Marcia Lucas, Tom Rolf and Melvin Shapiro
Art Director Charles Rosen
Music Bernard Herrmann
Running time 112 mins *colour*

Cast

Robert De Niro (Travis Bickle)
Cybill Shepherd (Betsy)
Jodie Foster (Iris Steensman)
Peter Boyle (Wizard)
Harvey Keitel (Sport)
Albert Brooks (Tom)

The Thief of Bagdad

Raoul Walsh, USA, 1924

Arabian Nights fantasy

Fairbanks's spectacular magic carpet ride marks a peak in cinematic fantasy.

The story

At the Palace of the Caliph, rapscallion Ahmed's heart is captured by the fair Princess. When suitors pay court, 'Prince' Ahmed is chosen as her husband but his duplicity brings a flogging and banishment. The Princess then promises her hand to whomsoever returns with the rarest treasure. Ahmed meanwhile embarks on a magical journey that secures him True Manhood and Power Over Men. Meanwhile, the Mongol Prince plots to overthrow the Caliph and poisons the Princess. She is rescued but then a Chinese army captures the city. Using his new powers, Ahmed conjures up an army, retakes the city and restores the Caliph to power. He then whisks the Princess on to a Magic Carpet and they fly off into the star-studded sky.

Comment

Arguably the most dashing, athletic and Ariel-like of all screen swashbucklers, silent screen idol Douglas Fairbanks Senior was much more than an agile swordsman and, with the phenomenal box-office popularity of films like *The Mark of Zorro* (1920), *The Three Musketeers* (1921) and *Robin Hood* (1922), had begun to take charge of every element involved in the creation of his lavish spectacles. Continually seeking to dwarf his own previous achievements and those of lesser continental rivals, he wrote, performed and produced *The Thief of Bagdad* intending to create the cinema's

most lavish Arabian Nights fantasy. Almost 70 years later it still impresses with its sense of scale and an incident-strewn scenario involving the Valley of Monsters, the Crystal Realm, the Cavern of Fire, a Flying Horse and, of course, a Magic Carpet.

Art Director William Cameron Menzies created Bagdad, the Magic City of the East, on a six-and-a-half acre site at the Pickford-Fairbanks Studio; when the initial sets proved unbecoming to the scrutiny of the camera, the entire one-and-a-half acre courtyard of Bagdad was covered in cement, painted jet-black and polished, thus allowing the surrounding buildings to be reflected in the gleam and creating a heightened illusion of a magical city suspended from the clouds. Renowned for performing his own stunts, Fairbanks mounted the magic carpet, suspended by six wires from a 90-foot crane, to fly over Bagdad and is even seen to confront a dragon consisting of a cunningly disguised crocodile shot in double-exposure with Fairbanks. In terms of the creation of cinematic fantasy, the result remains unrivalled with an ingenuity and invention that contemporary advances in special-effects pyrotechnics have done little to diminish.

A Fairbanks-United Artists Production
Screenplay Lotta Woods and Elton Thomas (Douglas Fairbanks Senior)
Photography Arthur Edeson
Art Director William Cameron Menzies
Running time 155 mins b/w

Cast
Douglas Fairbanks (Ahmed, The Thief of Bagdad)
Snitz Edwards (Evil Associate)
Charles Belcher (Holy Man)
Julanne Johnston (The Princess)
Anna May Wong (The Mongol Slave)
Winter-Blossom (The Slave of the Lute)

The Third Man

Carol Reed, UK, 1949

Viennese thriller

A lofty encounter on an Austrian Ferris wheel is a high point in an unforgettable British thriller.

The story

Writer Holly Martins arrives in Vienna to discover that his friend Harry Lime has died in a car accident. Major Calloway informs him of Lime's criminal activities. Lime's girlfriend Anna suggests his death may not have been accidental and a porter recalls a mysterious 'third man' at the scene of the death. Martins determines to uncover the truth. Leaving Anna's apartment one evening, he spots a man obscured by the shadows – it is Lime. They meet and Lime offers his friendship and suave justifications for his acts. However, when Calloway threatens to deport Anna, Martins betrays Lime to secure her freedom. A chase through the sewers beneath the city ends with Martins killing Lime. After the funeral Anna walks by him without speaking.

Comment

Successful partners on *The Fallen Idol* (1948) and *Our Man in Havana* (1960), writer Graham Greene and director Carol Reed achieved the peak of their collaboration on this original Greene story that is redolent of the themes of corruption and betrayal that mark much of his best fiction.

The financial involvement of American mogul David O Selznick necessitated extensive rewriting of the script and ensured his virtual veto over casting. His original suggestions for Harry Lime amounted to either Orson Welles or Noel Coward with Holly Martins to be played by Cary Grant or James Stewart. The ultimate choice of Joseph Cotten to play Holly made the reunion with his Mercury mentor and old friend Welles a casting stroke of genius. For while Reed's marvellously atmospheric location work throughout the narrow streets and shadowy sewers of the bombed-out city lends the film much of its visual panache, and he also takes credit for implementing zither virtuoso Anton Karas's insistently effective scoring, the influence of Welles imposes its distinctive stamp over much of the action. Certainly the angular camerawork and Robert Krasker's stylized chiaroscuro cinematography evoke Welles's own directorial personality, but it is his mesmerizingly charismatic performance as disturbingly cynical individualist Harry Lime that sparks true screen electricity, for as writer of his own dialogue he created one of the cinema's most delicious rationalizations of villainy.

'In Italy for 30 years under the Borgias, they had warfare, terror, murder, bloodshed. They produced Michelangelo, Leonardo Da Vinci and the Renaissance,' he purrs from the aerial perspective of a fairground Ferris wheel. 'In Switzerland they had brotherly love, five hundred years of democracy and peace. And what did that produce? The cuckoo clock.'

A London Films Production
Producer Carol Reed
Screenplay Graham Greene
Photography Robert Krasker
Editor Oswald Hafenrichter
Art Directors Vincent Korda, Joseph Bato and John Hawksworth
Music Anton Karas
Running time 104 mins b/w

Cast

Joseph Cotten (Holly Martins)
Orson Welles (Harry Lime)
Alida Valli (Anna Schmidt)
Trevor Howard (Major Calloway)
Wilfred Hyde-White (Crabbit)
Bernard Lee (Sergeant Paine)

The Tin Drum
(Die Blechtrommel)

Volker Schlöndorff, France/West Germany, 1979

An allegory of German history

A remarkable performance from 12-year-old David Bennent proved the key to the success of this allusive German epic.

The story

Poland, the early 1900s. A peasant shelters a fugitive beneath her skirts, and later gives birth to Agnes. After World War I, Agnes marries Alfred, a grocer in Danzig, but also has an affair with her cousin Jan, who may be the father of Oskar. Oskar resolves to stop growing at three, and becomes resolutely attached to his toy tin drum. Fascists take over Danzig, and Agnes dies after being forced to eat eels by Alfred. Oskar shelters beneath his grandmother's skirts. Alfred remarries. Oskar leads Jan to the besieged Polish post office, where he is captured and executed by the Germans. Oskar befriends Roswitha and joins a circus which performs for the Nazis. After the liberation, he returns to Danzig, where he sees Alfred shot as a collaborator. Oskar resolves to start growing again.

Comment

Günter Grass's famous novel presented alarming challenges to the screen adapter, but this film version of part of it manages to retain much of the book's central allusiveness and symbolic intent, while still achieving a cinematically coherent (if rather abstruse) whole.

The single most significant factor in the film's success undoubtedly lies in the performance of 12-year-old David Bennent in the role of Oskar. The part called for a three-year-old boy with the knowing ways of an adult, and Bennent's own misfortune became the key to an on-screen triumph.

Schlöndorff had rejected the idea of using a dwarf to play Oskar, and settled instead on the son of actor Heinz Bennent, who suffered from a genuine case of arrested development which left him with a face rather more mature than the rest of his body. The boy produces a startling performance, without which the film may not have been possible.

Inevitably in a film which ranges widely in time and engages with the broad dramatic sweep of German history, the narrative proceeds through a series of tentatively linked episodes rather than in a smooth linear flow, but is given unity and continuity through the character and perspective of Oskar, who has resolved not to grow, a decision he reverses only after the liberation of Danzig (now the Polish city of Gdansk) from the Nazis.

The film is a visual *tour de force* and an immensely powerful attempt at filming a literally impossible book. Schlöndorff later gave up on the idea of a sequel which would follow the rest of the novel through Oskar's maturity when it became obvious that Bennent's physical development would not be adequate for the adult role.

A Franz Seitz Film/Bioskop-Film/GGB 14 KG/ Hallalujah Film/Artemis Film/Argos Film Co Production
Producer Franz Seitz
Screenplay Jean-Claude Carrière, Franz Seitz and Volker Schlöndorff, based on the novel by Günter Grass
Photography Igor Luther
Editor Suzanne Baron
Art Director Bernd Lepel
Music Maurice Jarre
Running time 142 mins *colour*

Cast
David Bennent (Oskar)
Mario Adorf (Alfred Matzerath)
Angela Winkler (Agnes Matzerath)
Daniel Olbrychski (Jan Bronski)
Katherina Thalbach (Maria Matzerath)
Mariella Oliveri (Roswitha Raguna)

Tokyo Story
(Tokyo Monogatari)

Yasujiro Ozu, Japan, 1953

Everyday life

Subtle characterization and meticulous attention to detail serve to create an understated masterpiece.

The story

Post-war Japan. Shukishi and Tomi Hirayama live in a small town. They decide to visit their children in Tokyo. The children, though, consider the parents to be a burden, and send them off to a holiday resort. Feeling out of place, the couple return to Tokyo after one night, but they do not go to the children this time. Tomi takes ill on the train home the next day, and they stop at Osaka, where another son lives. When they finally reach home, Tomi's condition is critical, and the family is summoned. She dies before they all arrive. After the funeral, only the widowed daughter-in-law Norika, herself lonely, lingers on to help Shukisho and his daughter Kyoko. He thanks her, and advises her to return to Tokyo and find a new husband.

Comment

If Akira Kurosawa is the figurehead of a Japanese cinema which is epic in its scope, Yusujiro Ozu stands at the opposite extreme. His films are intimate and understated, rich in nuance and imbued with a deep understanding of the mores of daily life in Japan. These qualities led to his comparatively late discovery in the West, since his films were rarely seen outside Japan before 1965. The Japanese believed that Ozu was their most quintessentially Japanese film-maker, and his work would not travel well when lifted out of its native context.

His films, and *Tokyo Story* in particular, give the lie to that belief. It first played in London in 1965, and was released in the USA (as *Their First Trip To Tokyo*) in 1972, and established Ozu's international standing. It is concerned with familial obligation, and in particular the nature of the relationship between ageing parents and their grown children, who now have families of their own. That relationship is seen as a disappointing one, although Ozu is content to present the behaviour of his characters in a largely non-judgmental fashion.

The couple who travel hopefully to visit their children in Tokyo are doomed to a series of disappointments, but the bond which should unite families is not entirely missing, but simply misplaced, since it is their widowed daughter-in-law who proves to have the feelings and obligations proper to their children.

The subtle characterization, distinguished acting and meticulous attention to structure and detail elevates a simple story into a genuine masterpiece of modern cinema.

An Ofuna Studio Production
Producer Takeshi Yamamoto
Screenplay Yasujiro Ozu and Kogo Noda
Photography Yushun Atsuta
Editor Yoshiyasu Hamamura
Art Directors Tatsuo Hamada and Itsuo Takahashi
Music Takanori Saito
Running time 135 mins b/w

Cast

Chishu Ryu (Shukishi Hirayama)
Chiyeko Higashiyama (Tomi Hirayama)
So Yamamura (Koichi Hirayama)
Kuniko Miyake (Fumiko)
Mitsuhiro Mori (Isamu)
Haruko Sugimura (Shige Kaneko)
Nobuo Nakamura (Zurazo Kaneko)
Setsuko Hara (Noriko)
Kyoko Kagawa (Kyoko)

Top Hat

Mark Sandrich, USA, 1935

Musical perfection

Dancing cheek to cheek through Art Deco Venice, Rogers and Astaire create movie magic.

The story

London. Practising in a hotel room one evening, American dancer Jerry Travers unwittingly awakens fellow resident Dale Tremont and is instantly smitten when she calls to complain. He pursues her relentlessly and romance blossoms until a note mistakenly convinces her that he is the husband of her friend Madge Hardwick. Dale flounces off to Venice with her dress designer Beddini. Travers and Madge follow but Dale slaps him when he proposes marriage and decides to wed Beddini. However, when Madge learns of the mistake, she smooths over the difficulties, and when it transpires that the Hardwicks' disguised butler had officiated at Dale's wedding to Beddini and she is therefore free to wed Jerry, bliss is unconfined.

Comment

Although RKO's frothy musical *Flying Down to Rio* (1933) was ostensibly a vehicle for box-office attraction Dolores Del Rio, it was the pairing of fifth-billed former Broadway hoofer Fred Astaire and ex-vaudevillian Ginger Rogers in their featured dance number 'The Carioca' which caught the attention of the moviegoing public to such an extent that a starring movie of their own together was only a matter of time. In the next two years, the studio swiftly adapted two established theatrical properties *The Gay Divorce* (1934) and *Roberta* (1935) for the new dance sensations, but it was in the first film created specifically for their talents, *Top Hat*, that the particular screen magic of the coupling was to achieve its most fully realized expression. Here the featherweight scenario of mistaken identity matters less than the way in which Irving Berlin's marvellous tunes and the choreography – for which Hermes Pan and Astaire take credit – allow the emotional thrust of the material to be expressed through the production numbers. While the title song, synonymous with the Astaire legend, allows Fred to strut his solo stuff most admirably, the witty love-hate duet 'Isn't This A Lovely Day?' and the later highly-charged 'Cheek to Cheek' routine charts the fortunes of two people whose superficial hostility inevitably gives way to the most touching affection.

Typifying sophisticated 1930s' cool as their bodies swirled with precise grace across the screen, here was a professional chemistry that would stand the test of time and be good for another six movies together. Nominated for four Academy Awards, *Top Hat* went unrewarded but found ample compensation in its public acceptance; second only to *Mutiny on the Bounty* in the year's top earners, it returned over $3 million on a studio investment of $620 000.

An R-K-O Production
Producer Pandro S Berman
Screenplay Dwight Taylor and Allan Scott, based on the musical *The Gay Divorce* adapted from the play *The Girl Who Dared* by Alexander Farago and Aladar Laszlo
Photography David Abel and Vernon L Walker
Editor William Hamilton
Art Director Van Nest Polglase
Songs Irving Berlin
Musical Director Max Steiner
Running Time 101 mins b/w

Cast
Fred Astaire (Jerry Travers)
Ginger Rogers (Dale Tremont)
Edward Everett Horton (Horace Hardwick)
Helen Broderick (Madge Hardwick)
Erik Rhodes (Alberto Beddini)
Eric Blore (Bates the Butler)

Touch of Evil

Orson Welles, USA, 1958

Borderline thriller

Despite being re-cut by the studio, this classic study of a twisted lawman ranks with Welles's finest achievements.

The story

Mexico. A mobster is blown up on the US side of a border town, but by a bomb planted in Mexico. Vargas, a Mexican policeman, offers to help the monstrous Quinlan with the investigation. His wife is warned off by the leader of a drug ring, Uncle Joe Grand. He persists, and is shocked when Quinlan plants evidence to incriminate a young suspect, Sanchez. A racist motive for Quinlan's behaviour begins to emerge. Quinlan and Grand plot to get at Vargas through his wife, and she is kidnapped and held in a seedy motel. Quinlan kills Grand, and leaves the body with Vargas's drugged wife. Vargas strikes back, and discovers a vital clue in Quinlan's cane, which he has left at the scene of the crime. A fortune-teller predicts Quinlan's life is used up. Vargas and Menzies try to trap him with an incriminating tape, leading to a shoot-out in which Menzies and Quinlan die. As his bloated body floats in the river, Vargas hears that Sanchez has confessed his guilt.

Comment

The opening sequence of *Touch of Evil*, an unbroken crane-shot of three minutes' duration culminating in the explosion which sets up the film's decadent plot, is one of the most famous single shots ever committed to film. It is typical of both the bravado and the excess of the director.

Everything in the film is larger than life, including the monstrous figure of Welles himself as the ruthless lawman Hank Quinlan. Welles was originally hired as an actor, and ended up directing only because of a misunderstanding on the part of Charlton Heston, who assumed he would act and direct. The studio capitulated, but later had the film re-cut, while Harry Keller added a few (uncredited) close-ups.

Quinlan is an unforgettable creation, as physically repugnant as he is morally ambiguous. His morals and methods disgust the straight-laced Vargas, but we are also allowed to know that he has only trapped men he really believes to be guilty, and that he does so because his own wife was murdered by a half-breed who went free for lack of evidence. Quinlan, though, is a figure out of time, a throwback to the frontier era, while Vargas represents the new face of modern law and order. As Quinlan stoops to kidnap and murder in order to press his case, Vargas is forced to fight back, and attempts to trap the detective into a confession, leading to a fatal shoot-out (again echoing the old frontier).

The squalid death of Quinlan echoes the decadence which pervades the film, arguably Welles's greatest achievement after *Citizen Kane*. Despite its stylistic excesses, it remains a remarkably powerful evocation of evil.

A Universal-International Picture
Producer Albert Zugsmith
Screenplay Orson Welles, based on the novel *Badge of Evil* by Whitt Masterson
Photography Russell Metty
Editors Virgil M Vogel and Aaron Stell.
Art Directors Alexander Golitzen and Robert Clatworthy
Music Henry Mancini
Running time 95 mins (other versions 105 and 115 mins) *b/w*

Cast

Charlton Heston (Ramon Miguel Vargas)
Janet Leigh (Susan Vargas)
Orson Welles (Hank Quinlan)
Joseph Calleia (Pete Menzies)
Akim Tamiroff (Uncle Joe Grand)
Joanna Moore (Marcia Linnekar)
Marlene Dietrich (Tanya)
Ray Collins (Adair)
Victor Millan (Manolo Sanchez)

The Tree of Wooden Clogs
(L'Albero Degli Zoccoli)

Ermanno Olmi, Italy, 1978

Peasant epic

A mosaic of 19th-century life salutes the relationship between the land and the peasantry.

The story

Lombardy, the late 19th century. Four peasant families share dwellings in a large farm house. Minek attends school, the eldest of the Widow Runk's children secures employment with the miller, Finard is forever at loggerheads with his sons and the Brenas' daughter Maddalena becomes involved with the shy Stefano. Despite the hardships, there is magic in the air when a sick cow recovers after drinking 'consecrated' water and, during a Spring Festival, Finard finds a gold coin and Batisti's wife gives birth. Stefano and Maddalena are married. When Batisti chops down a tree to make a new clog for Minek, he is punished by the master and the family are expelled from their home.

Comment

Although citing the poetic film ethnology of America's Robert Flaherty as a major influence, regional filmmaker Ermanno Olmi's lengthy study of rural Lombardy is something of a return to the Italian neorealist tradition in its concentration and insistence on the nobility of the everyday experience of its non-professional cast of Lombardian peasants. Eschewing the posturing spectacle and fabulist tragicomedy of contemporary offerings drawing on similar material, namely Bernardo Bertolucci's *Novocento* (*1900*) (1976) and the Taviani Brothers' *Padre Padrone* (1977), Olmi's unhurried chronicling of the lives of four farming families across the seasons on the surface at least appears closer to screenwriter and theorist Cesare Zavattini's original, uncompromising neorealist ideal. The relaxed unfolding of the main narrative events – birth and marriage, the slaughter of a pig, the discovery of a gold coin – almost render the film a humanist documentary, were it not for more obviously fictive moments, like the miracle of the cow, allowing Olmi's optimistic Catholicism to shine through when prayers bring about the sudden recovery of a stricken animal. Indeed, perhaps because Olmi's authorial imprint is so delicately manifested, it is all too easy not to realize that the viewer is being gently but firmly guided towards definite spiritual and ideological positions. A careful consideration of the section from which the title is derived, wherein a young peasant boy breaks his shoe on the way home from school resulting in his father cutting the landowner's tree to make him a new sandal and in turn precipitating the eviction of the entire family, reveals a Marxian overview of class exploitation all the more potent for the undemonstrative lucidity of its expression.

A RAI-Radiotelevisione Italiana/Italnoleggio Cinematografico/GPC Production
Producer Giulio Mandelli
Screenplay Ermanno Olmi
Photography Ermanno Olmi
Editor Ermanno Olmi
Art Director Enrico Tovaglieri
Music Johann Sebastian Bach
Running time 186 mins *colour*

Cast

Luigi Ornaghi (Batisti)
Francesca Moriggi (Batistina, His Wife)
Omar Brignoli (Minek)
Antonio Ferrari (Tuni)
Teresa Brescianini (Widow Runk)
Giuseppe Brignoli (Grandpa Anselmo)

Triumph of the Will
(Triumph Des Willens)

Leni Riefenstahl, Germany, 1934

Cinema as propaganda

Impressive cinematic technique is shackled in dubious harness to the glorification of Nazism.

The story

A documentary-like record of the 1934 Nazi Party Nuremberg rally.

Comment

From the very outset of achieving power in Germany, Hitler and Minister of Information Josef Goebbels recognized that the film medium could play a significant role in communicating Nazi doctrine and achievement to the widest possible audience. Soon newsreels, shorts and documentary features became the tools of direct Party propaganda. This is the context in which former actress and director Leni Riefenstahl was appointed 'film expert to the Nationalist Socialist Party' and commissioned by Hitler to create a film record of the 1934 Nuremberg rally that would be specifically stage-managed for the benefit of the more than 30 cameras and staff of 120 that would be placed at her disposal. In the most basic of terms the film is thus a documentary, but Riefenstahl's control of composition and montage is so complete that the basic material of actuality is at length transformed into the stuff of repellent Wagnerian myth. From the messianic overtones of the Fuhrer's initial aeroplane descent from the clouds, to the constant motion of the 18-minute parade section or the massive architectural vistas of the wreath-laying sequence, Riefenstahl's masterly editing creates impressive abstract patterns of images and sounds. Constantly cutting from panoramic long-shot (a vast array of Nazi flags) to extreme close-up (one flag in one man's hand) she both dislodges the viewer's sense of perspective and creates an aura of visual harmony implicitly rhyming with the political message being put forward. It can be argued that such extraordinary formal skill transcends the content on view, thus compelling us to judge it as absolute film, but by concentrating on the glories of Riefenstahl's form are we then tacitly approving her work as Nazi propagandist?

Olympische Spiele 1936 (Olympiad) (1938), her subsequent work, is another propagandistic documentary of impressive technique that celebrates the Berlin Olympic Games as a 'song of praise for the ideals of National Socialism' and was given a gala première on Hitler's 49th birthday. Although receiving a 'clean bill of ideological health' by Allied de-Nazification units after the War she was, unsurprisingly, never able to fully resume her filmmaking activities, but did build a further career under the name of Helen Jacobs as a photojournalist, covering the 1972 Olympic Games and building a portfolio of work on the East African tribe of Mesakin Nuba.

An NSDAP Production
Producers Walter Traut and Walter Groskopf
Photography Sepp Allgeier
Editor Leni Riefenstahl
Music Herbert Windt
Running time 120 mins b/w

Twelve Angry Men

Sidney Lumet, USA, 1957

Courtroom drama

An isolated but resolute individual fights for justice.

The story

The outcome of a trial seems a foregone conclusion until the jury retire and one man registers a vote of not-guilty. Uncertain in his mind, he feels that the accused deserves a thorough discussion. The rest of the jurors resent the inconvenience of his decision; one had hoped to visit a baseball game, others entertain not one shred of doubt about the youth's guilt in killing his father with a knife. However, he gradually undermines their confidence, showing that the murder weapon is widely available to anyone and that the evidence of key witnesses is suspect. Gradually they are won round by his arguments and even the most bigoted of his fellow jurors reluctantly concurs with him. Their verdict is now a unanimous not guilty.

Comment

The hothouse dramatics and claustrophobic setting of the courtroom drama have long endeared it to film and television makers and with *Twelve Angry Men*, producer/actor Henry Fonda and director Sidney Lumet created one of the most revered examples of the genre. Adapted by Reginald Rose from his 1954 television play, the film marked Lumet's cinema début and established his concerns with the workings of the judicial system and fondness for central characters whose actions are dictated by conscience regardless of the personal consequences. The film also reflected the speed and efficiency for which Lumet would become renowned, utilizing the comparative rarity of a two-week rehearsal period to let the actors become familiar with their characters and also deploying the camera in such a way that lends fluidity and dynamism to a situation – the stifling confines of a jury room – that is in itself static.

Fonda praised Lumet for his 'total communication with an actor. Actors working with Lumet feel they have given their best performance.' Over the ensuing 35 years the feeling has often been valid precisely because they have given their best performance and *Twelve Angry Men* does make exemplary use of the authority and integrity that had innately accrued to the Fonda screen persona as well as creating an ensemble of well-delineated secondary characters from the bullying patriarch of Lee J Cobb to the undisguised bigotry of Ed Begley and the ice-cool detachment of E G Marshall. Such was the unity of the the cast and their familiarity with the text that Fonda once remarked that it had been the closest he ever came in the cinema to achieving the creative satisfaction he more readily found in the theatre. The film received three Academy Award nominations, including Best Picture.

An Orion-Nova Production
Producers Henry Fonda and Reginald Rose
Screenplay Reginald Rose, based on his teleplay
Photography Boris Kaufman
Editor Carl Lerner
Art Director Robert Markell
Music Kenyon Hopkins
Running time 96 mins b/w

Cast
Henry Fonda (Juror No 8)
Lee J Cobb (Juror No 3)
Ed Begley (Juror No 10)
E G Marshall (Juror No 4)
Jack Warden (Juror No 7)
Martin Balsam (Juror No 1)

'Keep watching the skies'
The science-fiction film

Using the vast resources of the cinema to envisage the future or the denizens of far planets has been irresistible to filmmakers since Georges Méliès's *Voyage to the Moon* (1902). However the genre was approached only intermittently in the first few decades of this century, most notably in Fritz Lang's potent allegory *Metropolis* (1926) (see p142) with its vast sets depicting a dehumanized city of tomorrow, and *Things To Come* (1936), H G Wells's vision of the future as realized by William Cameron Menzies.

Despite the popularity of cliffhanging serial *Flash Gordon* (1936) and the impact of Orson Welles's notorious radio broadcast of *War of the Worlds* in 1938, the genre did not become a permanent fixture of cinemagoing until the post-war era when close encounters with alien beings, usually hostile, provided a dramatic expression for the Cold War paranoia about the threat of enemy attack. The many examples of this include *The Thing* (1951), *War of the Worlds* (1953), *Invaders from Mars* (1953) and, most effective of all, *Invasion of the Bodysnatchers* (1956) (see p111). *The Day The Earth Stood Still* (1951) struck a rare note for an alternative view in the shape of a peace-seeking alien, whilst the perils of scientific advances in nuclear power and its unknown side-effects were cautioned in the likes of *Them* (1954) in which giant ants rampage through the south-west of America, and *The Incredible Shrinking Man* (1958), which focused on an alarming reduction in size rather than expansion.

Real-life space travel and the first landing on the moon coincided with some of the genre's most imaginative efforts including the still impressive *Planet of the Apes* (1968) and its sequels and Stanley Kubrick's *2001: A Space Odyssey* (1968) (see p228), combining state-of-the-art special-effects, near-psychedelic visual sequences and also a puzzling conundrum of meanings to challenge the mind as well as arrest the eye. Douglas Trumbull, who worked on Kubrick's film, made his directional début with *Silent Running* (1971) and the 1970s also witnessed grim visions of the contemporary world slipping into future dysfunction in *Westworld* (1973) and *Soylent Green* (1973) as well as the highly diverting and resourceful *Dark Star* (1974) and *The Man Who Fell to Earth* (1976) with David Bowie as an alien visitor. However, the genre reached its commercial peak with the phenomenal popularity of George Lucas's space-age high-adventure *Star Wars* (1977) (see p207), and Steve Spielberg's *Close Encounters of the Third Kind* (1977) (see p58) which brought an almost religious faith to its position of alien beings both existing and exuding an intelligent benevolence that had developed or degenerated into an endearing cuteness by the time of *E.T.* (1982) (see p74). The most financially viable genre of the period, science-fiction films were now used to conceal other genres; thus horror was transported into outer space with *Alien* (1979), the western was transformed into the frontiers of space with *Battle Beyond the Stars* (1980) a loose remake of *The Magnificent Seven* (1960), and *Outland* (1981), a virtual reworking of *High Noon* (1952) (see p107). There were new versions of *Invasion of the Bodysnatchers* (1978), *Flash Gordon* (1980) and *The Thing* (1982) *Star Trek* made it to the big screen in 1979 and Jeff Bridges contributed an engaging, Oscar-nominated performance to *Starman* (1984). In the 1990s however, only the continuing adventures of the Starship Enterprise and the muddled dystopian fantasy *The Handmaid's Table* (1990) kept the genre alive and whether its fall from favour is momentary or permanent only time will tell.

2001: A Space Odyssey

Stanley Kubrick, UK, 1968

Psychedelic science fiction

*The mysteries of life and creation
are explored in the furthest reaches
of the galaxy.*

The story

Prehistoric apemen discover a mysterious black slab but as their fear subsides it inspires an evolution in their thinking. In the present day when an identical slab is discovered buried on the moon and emitting signals to Jupiter, a spaceship is sent to investigate. It is manned by Bowman and Poole, three colleagues in suspended animation and the infallible computer HAL who engineers a malfunction, kills the sleeping astronauts and maroons Poole deep in space. Bowman disconnects its memory banks and proceeds alone. Close to Jupiter, he witnesses a black slab in orbit and enters a New dimension where he finds an older version of himself. Reaching towards a black slab, he is transformed into the foetus of a new Man.

Comment

The deliberate Homeric connotations of the title offer some indication of the thematic ambition of Stanley Kubrick's *2001: A Space Odyssey*, which tackles nothing less than the history and future development of all mankind and is exemplified in the celebrated cut from pre-historic man's bone-tool flying through the air to the similar outline of a huge spacecraft floating in orbit. Humankind, runs the general interpretation of a film described by its director as a 'non-verbal experience', has transcended the human state through technology but must move beyond that technology before rebirth as astral superman. For all its would-be grand Nietzschean theorizing on 'humanity' however, *2001*, like much of Kubrick's later work, is ironically flawed by its simple lack of warmth for the human race. Asserting man's dehumanization by his technology, the film's visual stress is on the magnificently conceived and executed future hardware, or the bravura imprint of its own directorial styling (most obviously signalled by the eccentric virtuosity of its choice of classical music score), rather than its cast of characters. Still, the final irony remains that this most cerebral of superproductions was championed by contemporary connoisseurs of psychedelia as 'the ultimate trip', a line later used on the poster for the film's reissue.

Nominated for four Academy Awards, the film received one Oscar for Special Visual Effects but returned a healthy $24 million American gross on a reported budget of $11 million. It was followed in 1984 by a clever and accessible but inevitably disappointing sequel *2010*, directed by Peter Hyams, in which a joint Soviet-American mission is dispatched to discover just what did happen during the *Discovery*'s mission to Jupiter.

An M-G-M Production
Producer Stanley Kubrick
Screenplay Stanley Kubrick and Arthur C Clarke, based on Clarke's short story 'The Sentinel'
Photography Geoffrey Unsworth
Editor Ray Lovejoy
Art Director John Hoesli
Music Richard Strauss, Johann Strauss, Aram Khachaturian and Gyorgy Ligeti
Running time 141 mins *colour*

Cast
Keir Dullea (David Bowman)
Gary Lockwood (Frank Poole)
William Sylvester (Dr Heywood Floyd)
Daniel Richter (Moonwatcher)
Douglas Rain (Voice of Hal 9000)
Leonard Rossiter (Smyslov)

Ugetsu Monogatari

Kenji Mizoguchi, Japan, 1953

Romantic ghost story

This remarkable ghost story introduced a new concept of fantasy and the supernatural to Western audiences.

The story

16th-century Japan. Genjuro, a potter, and his brother-in-law Tobei discover they can make money from his pottery. They drive themselves frantically in the production of pottery to sell in the market. Genjuro's wife is killed by soldiers after he leaves for town, and he is taken in by a beautiful woman who is actually a ghost. She imprisons him in a charmed estate, protected from the war outside. Tobei pretends to be a samurai, and claims to have killed a famous warrior. His wife is raped by soldiers, and turns to prostitution. He finds her in a brothel. Genjuro escapes from the ghost through the agency of a priest. Both men return to their village and revert to their former way of life, now watched over by the ghost of Genjuro's wife.

Comment

Ugetsu Monogatari (known as *Ugetsu* in the US) is based on two 18th-century ghost stories by Akinari Veda and one by Guy De Maupassant. It established Kenji Mizoguchi as an important international director.

The most remarkable feature of the film to Western audiences is the way in which it combines elements of everyday realism with fantasy and the supernatural. The transitions from the mundane realities of peasant life to the shimmering fantasy world of the ghostly Lady Wakasa are seamless rather than disruptive, part of a larger whole rather than contrasted entities.

It reflected Mizoguchi's own shift from the radical political standpoint of his earlier films towards a much more emphatic interest in aestheticism and spirituality. The striking, almost painterly beauty of his images, the original and dramatic marriage of sound and image, and the eerie insubstantiality of the supernatural sequences are testament to this shift.

Genjuro the potter undergoes both an aesthetic and a spiritual conversion in the course of the film, as does his brother Tobei, in a different fashion. The potter begins by making coarse everyday pots for mass use, but under the guidance of Lady Wakasa is shown a different world of exquisitely created objects. On his return, this time under the guidance of his wife's ghost, he sets about creating pots which reflect both the utilitarian usefulness of his earlier works, and the new beauty which has been revealed to him. While some critics have found fault with the movement away from his more ideologically committed works, the film remains widely regarded as a master work.

A Daiei Studios Production
Producer Masaichi Nagata
Screenplay Matsutaro Kawaguchi, based on Yoshita Yoda's adaptaation of two stories by Akinari Ueda
Photography Kazuo Miyagawa
Editor Mitsuji Miyata
Art Director Kisaku Ito
Music Fumio Hayasaka and Ichiro Saito
Running time 96 mins b/w

Cast

Machiko Kyo (Lady Wakasa)
Masayuki Mori (Genjuro)
Kinuyo Tanaka (Miyagi, Genjuro's wife)
Sakae Ozawa (Tobei)
Mitsuki Mito (Ohama, Tobei's wife)
Sugisaku Aoyama (Old Priest)

Vertigo

Alfred Hitchcock, USA, 1958

Romantic obsession

Hitchcock's unconventional thriller reveals a perverse study of romantic obsession.

The story

Suffering from acrophobia, 'Scottie' Ferguson retires from the police. He is hired by old friend Gavin Elster to follow his apparently suicidal wife Madeleine. Scottie becomes infatuated with her but, when they visit an old mission, he is paralysed by fear when she ascends the bell tower and plunges to her death. Recovering from the shock, he encounters Judy Barton whom he transforms into an exact double of his deceased love. Judy however had been hired by Elster to impersonate his real wife whom he murdered and threw from the tower. When Scottie deduces this, he overcomes his fear to return with Judy to the tower. She admits her guilt and her love for him but is startled by the sudden appearance of a nun and plunges to her death.

Comment

Arguably Alfred Hitchcock's supreme masterpiece, where his technical gifts mesh most completely with the richness of his material, *Vertigo* is also one of the bleakest, most perverse offerings to come out of mainstream American cinema in the 1950s.

The director has rarely seemed more dismissive of cinema conventions than in *Vertigo* – revealing the twist in the story half way through, letting the murderous husband go free and choosing not to explain how Scottie survives a perilous rooftop chase. However, subverting the narrative drive of the thriller only deepens the film's emotional and psychological impact, with perhaps the key scene the one in which Scottie fervently remodels (clothes, hairstyle etc) the new

Judy in the image of his former love. The director has described Stewart's role here as a man who 'wants to go to bed with a woman who's dead, he's indulging in a form of necrophilia'; but it is also that the film-maker is turning the everyday insecurities of human relationships into a cynical game of manipulation. Given the master of suspense's own voyeuristic proclivities and distinctive sexual fantasies, it is highly indicative of the personal obsessions with which he loaded the film that he has his protagonist transform the female lead into the paradigm Hitchcockian glacial blonde – a purely visual object of gratification.

A true ensemble success, *Vertigo* benefits from Robert Burks' photography of San Francisco, the music of Bernard Herrmann and the two central performances, particularly the mannequin-like Novak in a role that had been vacated by a pregnant Vera Miles. The film was unofficially remade by Brian De Palma as *Obsession* (1975) with Cliff Robertson and Genevieve Bujold.

An Alfred J Hitchcock Production for Paramount
Producer Alfred Hitchcock
Screenplay Alec Coppel and Samuel Taylor, based on the novel *D'Entre Les Morts/From Among the Dead* by Pierre Boileau and Thomas Narcejac
Photography Robert Burks
Editor George Tomasini
Art Directors Hal Pereira and Henry Bumstead
Music Bernard Herrmann
Running time 128 mins *colour*

Cast

James Stewart (John 'Scottie' Ferguson)
Kim Novak (Madeleine Elster/Judy Barton)
Barbara Bel Geddes (Midge)
Tom Helmore (Gavin Elster)
Henry Jones (The Coroner)
Raymond Bailey (The Doctor)

Victim

Basil Dearden, UK, 1961

Crusading drama

An expert British thriller breaks new ground in its depiction of homosexuality.

The story

Inspector Harris is puzzled by the case of Jack Barrett, a seemingly trustworthy man who has stolen from his employers. He is also baffled by Barrett's futile attempts to contact distinguished Queen's Counsel Melville Farr. When Barret is finally apprehended, he commits suicide. Farr then realizes that Barrett was being blackmailed and had sacrificed himself rather than reveal details of their homosexual liaison. Chastened, he agrees to risk his reputation and cooperate in the apprehension of the blackmailers who have used the illegality of homosexuality to prey on vulnerable men. Although his wife Laura is shocked by the anguished revelations of his love for Barrett, she vows to remain supportive.

Comment

Basil Dearden is widely regarded as a classic journeyman director in British cinema. His long professional relationship with producer Michael Relph and the Ealing Studios is reminiscent of the old Hollywood contract system, and the films that he turned out are generally seen as skilful but rather safe. There were a number of notable exceptions to that rule, however, of which *Victim* is not only the best but also the most controversial. As in the earlier *Sapphire* (1959), which used the murder of a prostitute as a vehicle for the study of racial prejudice, or the subsequent *Life for Ruth* (1962), which dealt with religious prejudice, *Victim* uses a tense thriller framework to investigate the previously taboo subject of homosexuality.

Although clearly in the Ealing tradition of well-intentioned, socially-conscious drama, *Victim* broke new ground in its thoughtful and entirely non-sensationalist approach to homosexuality, and was a brave film in its day for placing a gay hero at the centre of the drama and implicitly demanding tolerance for men branded as criminals purely on the grounds of their sexuality. The film was said to have played some modest role in influencing a change in public attitudes and leading to a limited decriminalization of homosexuality in England in 1967.

The film was also to prove crucial in Dirk Bogarde's move away from breezy juvenile leads to more challenging character assignments. He later recalled, 'I did have grey temples and I was broaching my own age, playing a man about 45. I wasn't the bouncy, happy doctor with a little perm in the front lock of my hair and my caps in. The caps came out, the hair was never permed again and a different audience came . . .'

An Allied Film Makers Production
Producer Michael Relph
Screenplay Janet Green and John McCormick
Photography Otto Heller
Editor John Guthridge
Art Director Alex Vetchinsky
Music Philip Green
Running time 100 mins *b/w*

Cast
Dirk Bogarde (Melville Farr)
Sylvia Syms (Laura Farr)
Dennis Price (Calloway)
Anthony Nicholls (Lord Fullbrook)
Peter Copley (Paul Mandrake)
Norman Bird (Harold Doe)
Peter McEnery (Jack Barrett)

Way Out West

James W Horne, USA, 1937

Bowler-hatted buffoonery

Mr Laurel and Mr Hardy follow Horace Greeley's famous dictum.

The story

Mr Laurel and Mr Hardy are on their way to Brushwood Gulch where they will deliver the title deed of a gold mine to the daughter of their deceased partner. At the town saloon, Laurel lets slip their task to larcenous owner Mickey Finn. The girl they seek is Finn's scullery maid Mary Roberts but he passes off his wife Lola Maxwell as the grief-stricken maiden and secures the deed. Made aware of the deceit, they attempt to retrieve the document which Lola finally wins by tickling Laurel to the point of exhaustion. By night they try to steal it back but are caught by Finn. In the ensuing chase, they capture Finn and force him to return what is rightly theirs. The two friends and Mary leave town to run the mine together.

Comment

Concentrating on feature films since the early 1930s, the affectionate buffoonery of bowler-hatted innocents Laurel and Hardy reached a peak in such achievements as *Bonnie Scotland* (1935) and *Way Out West* (1937) in which their well-established characters were placed within suitably promising situations and allowed to wreak the maximum amount of comic mayhem.

Laurel's ability to mastermind elaborate visual jokes of escalating indignity and superbly-timed slapstick as well as his penchant for verbal malapropisms is well to the fore; trying to indulge in small talk Hardy suggests, 'We've been having a lot of weather lately', whilst Stan tactfully tells Mary that her father 'was so deceased he died'. The feature-length format also allowed

them to indulge in several musical numbers. *Way Out West* features a delightful soft-shoe shuffle to the Avalon Boys' 'At the Ball, That's All' and also the famous 'The Trail of the Lonesome Pine' which became a posthumous recording hit for the duo in 1975 when it reached number two in the British singles chart.

Going through a number of working titles, from 'You'd Be Surprised' to 'Tonight's The Night' and 'In the Money', the western setting was apparently the suggestion of Stan's then wife Ruth and was filmed between August and November 1936 during a time of personal and professional difficulties for the duo: Laurel was in dispute with Hal Roach over the renewal of his contract, and both men separated from their respective spouses during the course of production, yet the film itself is untroubled and effortless fun that exemplifies the qualities in the team that still appeal to audiences half a century later in the pleasure of their trademark routines, the lack of malice in their childlike clowning and the personal warmth between the two amigos.

A Stan Laurel Production
Producer Stan Laurel
Screenplay Charles Rogers, Felix Adler and James Parrott, based on a story by Jack Levne and Rogers
Photography Art Lloyd and Walter Lundin
Editor Bert Jordan
Art Director Arthur I Royce
Music Marvin Hatley
Running time 65 mins b/w

Cast
Stan Laurel
Oliver Hardy
James Finlayson (Mickey Finn)
Sharon Lynne (Lola Marcel)
Stanley Fields (Sheriff)
Rosina Lawrence (Mary Roberts)

What Ever Happened to Baby Jane?

Robert Aldrich, USA, 1962

Gothic horror

Hollywood grand guignol revives the careers of legendary rivals Bette Davis and Joan Crawford.

The story

Wheelchair-bound former film star Blanche Hudson lives at the mercy of her increasingly deranged sister Jane. Blanche's decision to sell their house provokes a relentlessly sadistic war of nerves, and housekeeper Elvira is murdered when she attempts to rescue her. Planning to revive her childhood vaudeville act, Jane hires pianist Edwin Flagg. When he discovers Blanche, Jane drags her sister to Malibu beach, planning to bury her alive. A distraught Blanche finally admits that she had masterminded the accident that left her crippled and allowed Jane to harbour the guilt. As the police arrive, Jane has descended into total madness, offering a grotesque parody of her 'Baby Jane' act.

Comment

Hollywood's innate chauvinism and the film industry's emphasis on youth have posed great difficulties for its female stars. It is reckoned that once a woman passes the age of 40 opportunities drop precipitously, and many careers testify to this fact. By the time of *Baby Jane*, Joan Crawford and Bette Davis had been in Hollywood for over 30 years and their recent film work had been sparse and undemanding.

Despite reputations second to none and a shoal of Oscar nominations, no-one was keen to finance their appearance in a macabre gothic drama that had been termed the *Sunset Boulevard* (see p212) of the 1960s. Robert Aldrich funded it independently and shot the film in 21 days, paying his two stars $50 000 each and promising profit participation. The result was considered a sensation, presenting a psychological rather than visceral sense of horror. Aldrich added to the suspense with his use of black-and-white photography and the music of Frank De Vol which includes the song 'I've Written A Letter to Daddy'.

The low-budget film grossed $4 million in America alone and received five Oscar nominations, including Davis's tenth and final one as Best Actress. Aldrich later reunited Davis and Crawford on *Hush, Hush Sweet Charlotte* (1964) but illness found the latter replaced by Olivia De Havilland during shooting. The horror genre subsequently became a refuge for ageing female stars including Tallulah Bankhead in *Fanatic* (1964) (US: *Die! Die! My Darling*), Barbara Stanwyck in *The Night Walker* (1965) and Joan Fontaine in *The Witches* (1966) (UK: *The Devil's Own*). *Baby Jane* was remade for American television in 1990 with Vanessa and Lynn Redgrave as Blanche and Jane Hudson.

An Aldrich Associates Production
Producer Robert Aldrich
Screenplay Lukas Heller, based on the novel by Henry Farrell
Photography Ernest Haller
Editor Michael Luciano
Art Director William Glasgow
Music Frank De Vol
Running time 132 mins b/w

Cast
Bette Davis (Jane Hudson)
Joan Crawford (Blanche Hudson)
Victor Buono (Edwin Flagg)
Anna Lee (Mrs Bates)
Maidie Norman (Elvira Stitt)
Marjorie Bennett (Mrs Della Flagg)

White Heat

Raoul Walsh, USA, 1949

Gangster savagery

A mother-fixated hoodlum's demise signals a glorious end to the golden age of screen gangsters.

The story

The discovery of a body in a mountain cabin leads FBI agent Phillip Evans to the Jarrett gang who are wanted for a train robbery and double murder. Tailing Jarrett's beloved mother leads the FBI to Cody who escapes their net and avoids a certain death penalty by confessing to another robbery and serving a minor sentence. In prison he is befriended by informant Hank Fallon. Meanwhile Jarrett's wife Verna has taken up with Big Ed Somers and when Jarrett receives news of his mother's death he goes berserk. Breaking out of jail with Fallon, he kills Somers. The gang proceed to a payroll heist at an oil refinery with Fallon alerting Evans to their plan. Trapped at the refinery, Jarrett ascends an oil tank and is blown sky high.

Comment

With his galvanic performances in films like *The Public Enemy* (1931) (see p170), *Angels With Dirty Faces* (1938) and Raoul Walsh's *The Roaring Twenties* (1939), James Cagney had established himself as the quintessential screen embodiment of the cocky, vicious Hollywood gangster. His Oscar-winning role as George M Cohan in *Yankee Doodle Dandy* (1942) (see p239) and lesser work for his own production company on films like *Johnny Come Lately* (1943) and *The Time of Your Life* (1948) throughout the 1940s had allowed him to reveal other facets of his talent and thus taken him far from the worlds of criminal mayhem. *White Heat*, casting him in a more psychologically complex variant

on his most famous roles, returned him to his old stomping ground with a vengeance.

Cody Jarrett, a criminal with a mother-fixation and a tendency to blinding migraine headaches which serve to emphasize the psychopathic elements of his character, was apparently based on Arthur 'Doc' Barker with Margaret Wycherly therefore in the role of the infamous 'Ma' Barker. The blistering savagery, unpredictability and childlike qualities of this animalistic man are expertly conveyed by Cagney in an emotional *tour de force*. His famous demise on top of an exploding oil tank with the defiant cry of 'Made it ma, top of the world' has entered Hollywood lore and Cagney once explained the authentic intensity of his performance by recalling, 'I knew what deranged people sounded like because once, as a youngster, I had visited Ward's Island where a pal's uncle was in the hospital for the insane. My God, what an education that was! The shrieks, the screams of those people under restraint. I remembered those cries, saw that they fitted, and I called on my memory to do as required.'

A Warner Brothers Production

Producer Louis F Edelman

Screenplay Ivan Goff and Ben Roberts, based on a story by Virginia Kellogg

Photography Sid Hickox

Editor Owen Marks

Art Director Edward Carerre

Music Max Steiner

Running time 114 mins b/w

Cast

James Cagney (Arthur Cody Jarrett)
Virginia Mayo (Verna Jarrett)
Edmond O'Brien (Hank Fallon/Vic Pardo)
Margaret Wycherly (Ma Jarrett)
Steve Cochran (Big Ed Somers)
John Archer (Phillip Evans)

The Wild Bunch

Sam Peckinpah, USA, 1969

Western carnage

Out of their time, with nowhere left to run, western outlaws face bloody annihilation.

The story

Starbuck, Texas, 1914. Outlaw gang The Wild Bunch arrive to rob the bank but find themselves ambushed by bounty hunters led by their former comrade Deke Thornton. Shooting their way out, they head for Mexico where bandit 'General' Mapache hires them to hijack an American army munitions train. Pike Bishop outwits Thornton's men to accomplish the task but when Mapache discovers that Angel has given rifles to the Mexican revolutionaries he imprisons him. When Pike and the others return to demand his release, Mapache slits Angel's throat and is gunned down by Pike, thus precipitating a bloody confrontation in which they are all killed. Old man Sykes returns with the revolutionaries and when Thornton appears he decides to join them.

Comment

The Wild Bunch is arguably the most relentlessly violent mainstream western ever made but, unlike some of the equally graphic adventure films which followed in its wake, its appalling violence is framed in a consciously and carefully constructed moral context which borders on the mythic. The plot revolves around the most elemental of movie strategies, an extended chase, which opens and closes with two horrific massacres involving the eponymous Bunch of ageing outlaws faced by a changing world but holding on to their well-defined code of loyalty and honour. As the outlaws are hunted down, Peckinpah sets up a highly skilful moral dichotomy, representing the outlaws as simultaneously vicious disturbers of the social order and something close to folk heroes, an ambiguity which is never quite resolved even by their willed and astonishingly bloody death in the Mexican Revolution.

The film rewrote the vocabulary of the graphic representation of violence on screen with its use of lingering close-ups and almost operatic slow-motion which was justified by Peckinpah: 'Well, killing a man isn't clean and quick and simple – it's bloody and awful. And maybe if enough people come to realize that shooting somebody isn't just fun and games, maybe we'll get somewhere.'

Technically it is a *tour de force* to rival anything committed to celluloid but the capacity to disturb is not simply a consequence of the violence, which has sadly become commonplace, but rather is rooted in the fusion of extreme visual violence with a genuinely dark vision of the human condition, all framed in the context of characters with whom the viewer becomes inextricably involved. The formula is familiar enough but has seldom been realized with this degree of intensity.

A Warner Brothers/Seven Arts Production
Producer Phil Feldman
Screenplay Walon Green and Sam Peckinpah, based on a story by Green and Roy N Sickner
Photography Lucien Ballard
Editor Louis Lombardo
Art Director Edward Carrere
Music Jerry Fielding
Running time 143 mins *colour*

Cast
William Holden (Pike Bishop)
Ernest Borgnine (Dutch)
Robert Ryan (Deke Thornton)
Edmond O'Brien (Sykes)
Warren Oates (Lyle Gorch)
Jaime Sanchez (Angel)

Wild Strawberries
(Smultronstället)

Ingmar Bergman, Sweden, 1957

Life-affirming drama

An old man is brought face to face with the experiences of his life in Bergman's stark but compassionate classic.

The story

Professor Borg and his daughter-in-law Marianne travel to a ceremony honouring the old man. They pass his childhood home, where he recalls the girl he loved in his youth. They pick up a hitcher, Sara, a teenage girl who reminds him of his own sweetheart (played by the same actress), and her two friends. Their car is involved in a near-collision, and they pick up the couple from the other car. They prove argumentative, and the daughter-in-law throws them out. The remaining party stop for an outdoor meal, and discuss the existence of God. They continue their journey, and stop to visit the Professor's 95-year-old mother. He has a dream in which he fails to prove his professional worth. He receives the honorary degree, and Marianne announces her intention to return to her husband and bear the child she is carrying.

Comment

Wild strawberries are an emblem of rebirth and the coming of spring in Sweden, and they signal the ultimately affirmative intention of a film which spends much time looking back on lost opportunities in the life of Professor Isak Borg, a cold and distant man who has always experienced great difficulty in responding to simple human warmth, but who comes to understand its value.

Borg is played in a great autumnal performance by Bergman's predecessor as Sweden's greatest film director, Victor Sjöström. The car journey which he undertakes with his daughter-in-law becomes a journey through his past as well as his present, and the film is structured around a series of dreams which he has as they visit the locations of his earlier life.

The most famous of these occurs at the beginning of the film, when a coffin falls from a funeral wagon (a dream Bergman confessed to having himself) and a hand reaches out to clutch at Borg. When he looks inside, it is his own corpse he is struggling against. A subsequent dream revisits the unrequited love of his youth, while another subjects him to a humiliating examination of both his private and professional life.

The dreams reveal Borg's fears and anxieties as the end of his life approaches, and he comes to realize the mistakes he has made through his inability to deal with those close to him. Despite its occasionally harrowing moments and tendency towards over-analytical dissection, it is a compassionate and ultimately affirmative portrait, and one of Bergman's greatest achievements.

A Svensk Filmindustri Production
Producer Allan Ekelund
Screenplay Ingmar Bergman
Photography Gunnar Fischer
Editor Oscar Rosander
Art Director Gittan Gustafsson
Music Erik Nordgren
Running time 90 mins b/w

Cast

Victor Sjöström (Professor Isak Borg)
Bibi Andersson (Sara)
Ingrid Thulin (Marianne)
Gunnar Björnstrand (Evald)
Jullan Kindahl (Agda)
Folke Sundquist (Anders)
Björn Bjelvenstam (Viktor)
Naima Wifstrand (Isak's mother)

The Wind

Victor Sjöström, USA, 1928

Elemental drama

An unrelenting wind gives physical expression to emotional turmoil.

The story

An innocent young girl from Virginia arrives in Texas to live with her cousin. However, his wife resents her presence and refinement and she is asked to leave to prevent marital strife. Homeless and unnerved by the intensity of the elements around her, she hastily marries cowhand Lige who can at least offer a roof over her head. Left alone during a violent windstorm, she is visited by Roddy Wirt who tries to rape her. She shoots him dead and attempts to bury the body outside, but the howling wind and shifting sand continually uncover parts of the corpse and she is driven to the brink of insanity. However, when Lige returns home he is able to calm her and they decide to build a proper future together.

Comment

One of the last great silent features showcasing one of the last major roles performed by Lillian Gish, *The Wind* was shot amidst the barren terrain and scorching heat of the Mojave desert in what Gish subsequently described as 'one of my worst experiences in filmmaking'. However, the discomfort experienced by the cast and crew is vividly conveyed on the screen as the elements of wind, sand, temperature and topography become virtual characters in the merciless probing of a naive girl's emotional and psychological torment. Heading for Texas with romantic notions of life on a sprawling and civilized ranch, the girl encounters a harsh reality in which she is left homeless, forced into an unwanted marriage, violated by a stranger and forced to commit muder as a matter of self-defence.

Parelleling the increasingly nightmarish circumstances in which she finds herself, the film proceeds from a form of realism into full-scale hallucination as the sand seems to encroach upon every fibre of her body, the unrelenting wind becomes an inescapable part of her life, and the appearance of a white stallion signals a mind driven to the extreme edges of sanity. Initially, the film, like the novel, was scheduled to take this course of events to its grimly logical conclusion with the girl now insane and wandering at random through the desert, but M-G-M concluded that this would be too damaging to its commercial prospects and insisted upon a happy resolution. The decision detracts little from the impact of the film which is a stark reflection on the unpredictable elements that mould human existence and a testimony to both Sjöström's feeling for landscape and psychology and to Gish's expressiveness in delineating character and emotion through purely physical means.

An M-G-M Production
Screenplay Frances Marion, based on the novel by Dorothy Scarborough
Photography John Arnold
Editor Conrad A Nervig
Art Director Cedric Gibbons
Running time 74 mins b/w

Cast
Lillian Gish (Letty)
Lars Hanson (Lige)
Montagu Love (Roddy Wirt)
Dorothy Cumming (Cora)
Edward Earle (Beverly)
William Orlamond (Sourdough)

The Wizard of Oz

Victor Fleming, USA, 1939

Magical musical fantasy

'Somewhere over the rainbow . . .'

The story

Knocked unconscious during a tornado, Dorothy awakens in Munchkin Land where the good witch Glinda gives her a pair of ruby slippers and refers her to the omnipotent Wizard. En route, she meets a scarecrow in search of a brain, a tin man seeking a heart and a cowardly lion in need of courage. The Wizard agrees to help them if they secure the broomstick of the Wicked Witch of the West. When Dorothy and her dog Toto are captured, her three companions try to save her and the witch is destroyed. The wizard proves to be a phoney but her friends have found the qualities they sought through their own endeavours. Dorothy is then told to click her slippers together and utter the words 'There's no place like home' and is returned to Kansas.

Comment

Although there had been silent adaptations of the Frank Baum books in 1910 and 1925, this lavish M-G-M musical version remains the best known and one of the most tuneful and magical of all the fairy tales committed to celluloid during the golden age of the Hollywood studios. Although the role of Dorothy Gale has become inseparable from the performance of Judy Garland, and this film provided her with a life-long theme song of 'Over the Rainbow', the studio's original choice for the part was either Shirley Temple or Deanna Durbin. Garland, although strictly speaking too old for the role at 17, was considered a poor alternative, but brought just the right qualities of unsullied innocence, wonder and vulnerability to the character and won a special Oscar for the Best Juvenile Performance of the Year.

Frank Morgan's Wizard was originally offered to W C Fields and much coveted also by Wallace Beery, whilst Margaret Hamilton's definitely malevolent performance as the Wicked Witch was a substitute for Edna May Oliver or Gale Sondergaard. Begun by Victor Fleming, but completed by an uncredited King Vidor who is said to have directed the 'Over the Rainbow' number, *The Wizard of Oz* has, unlike such contemporary productions as *The Blue Bird* (1940), endured as one of Hollywood's most beguiling fantasies. No one factor can explain a phenomenon that is the product of many elements: the vibrant use of colour, the delightful Munchkins, the memorable art direction, effects and musical score, and the unforgettable performances from all the cast. Its influence on other filmmakers can be observed in such diverse productions as *Zardoz* (1973) and *Wild at Heart* (1990). 1978 brought a misguided, all-black musical version entitled *The Wiz* with Diana Ross, and a belated and unremarkable Disney sequel *Return to Oz* appeared in 1985.

An M-G-M Production
Producer Mervyn Le Roy
Screenplay Noel Langley, Florence Ryerson and Edgar Allen Woolf, based on the novel by L Frank Baum
Photography Harold Rosson
Editor Blanche Sewell
Art Director Cedric Gibbons
Music Herbert Stothart
Running time 101 mins b/w and *colour*

Cast

Judy Garland (Dorothy Gale)
Ray Bolger (Hunk/The Scarecrow)
Bert Lahr (Zeke/The Cowardly Lion)
Jack Haley (Hickory/The Tin Woodsman)
Billie Burke (Glinda)
Margaret Hamilton (Miss Gulch/The Wicked Witch)
Frank Morgan (The Wizard)

Yankee Doodle Dandy

Michael Curtiz, USA, 1942

All-American musical

Cagney impersonates Cohan in the patriotic musical par excellence.

The story

Born into a showbusiness family on 4 July 1878, George Michael Cohan is soon established as a stage star. Later, he writes *Yankee Doodle Dandy* and becomes engaged to Mary before penning *George Washington Jnr*, which unites the family for the last time. The failure of a straight play and death of his family are followed by his creation of the patriotic song 'Over There', a palliative for his sense of disappointment at being rejected for service in World War I. After the war, he travels and makes a belated return to Broadway in *I'd Rather Be Right*. The greatest moment of his career comes when the President presents him with a Congressional medal.

Comment

Often cited in later years by star James Cagney as his personal favourite from the titles in his filmography, *Yankee Doodle Dandy* is a highly conventional show-business saga that is raised to classic status by the energy and terpsichorean skill of Cagney in the role which won him his sole Best Actor Academy Award.

Very much a Cagney family affair with his brother William serving as associate producer and sister Jeanne cast as his screen sister, the film was the last under the actor's long-term contract with Warner Brothers and it has been suggested that the studio did not stint in meeting his requests in the hopes that he could be persuaded to re-sign with them. With a reported $1 500 000 budget, of which $100 000 went to the ailing Cohan,

the Cagneys and director Curtiz created one of the most patriotic musicals of all time that perfectly suited the mood of wartime America and also served as a riposte to the allegations of Cagney's Communism. Recalled in flashback from a reverent audience with President Roosevelt, the story never misses an opportunity to wave the flag from Cohan's birth on 4 July to the climactic moments amid the crowds of soldiers marching off to serve President and country at the onset of World War II.

Director Michael Curtiz can claim credit for the sense of pace and nostalgia he brings to the proceedings but it is Cagney's show all the way with his vast experience brought to bear on the eccentric form of dancing that was Cohan's speciality. A huge success in its day, the New York première at the Hollywood Theatre charged $25 000 for the best seat in the house and made a staggering total of close to $6 million for the war effort. The film itself soon become the studio's all-time top grosser.

A Warner Brothers Production
Associate Producer William Cagney
Screenplay Robert Buckner and Edmund Joseph, based on an original story by Buckner with uncredited contributions from Philip and Joseph Epstein and Joseph North
Photography James Wong Howe
Editor George Amy
Art Director Carl Jules Weyl
Music and Lyrics George M Cohan
Running time 126 mins b/w

Cast
James Cagney (George M Cohan)
Joan Leslie (Mary)
Walter Huston (Jerry Cohan)
Richard Whorf (Sam Harris)
Irene Manning (Fay Templeton)
George Tobias (Dietz)

Z

Constantin Costa-Gavras, France/Algeria, 1968

Political thriller

The exposure of a right-wing conspiracy juxtaposes political comment with nail-biting suspense.

The story

A Mediterranean country. Despite threats to his life, charismatic opposition MP 'Z' delivers his speech to a peace rally. He is subsequently knocked down by a van and dies from his injuries. The authorities insist that he was the victim of an unfortunate accident but an autopsy reveals a blow to the head. The driver Yago claims that he was drunk, evidence corroborated by his passenger Vago, but the magistrate comes to believe in a calculated act of assassination. The two suspects finally admit to their membership of an extreme right-wing organization and it is established that 'Z' was murdered. However, the men receive modest sentences and the high-ranking officials implicated in the case are not even brought to trial.

Comment

Z is widely held to be an exemplary model of the political thriller, and established the exiled Greek director Constantin Costa-Gavras as the leading filmmaker in that genre. Its greatest strength lies in its simplicity, and in the universality of the message which it contains. Based upon an actual incident and shot in Algeria, the film does not explicitly state its locale but clearly invokes the military government of Greece. However, Costa-Gavras's concern with human rights goes beyond a specific applicability to the Colonels' régime and is readily translated to any totalitarian regime or ruler.

Beyond that political dimension, however,

the film succeeds because it is a gripping and suspenseful thriller with actors of international box-office standing who grab and hold the audience's attention and sympathy. Jean-Louis Trintignant, who received the Best Actor prize at Cannes for his performance, is particularly noteworthy as the investigating magistrate attempting to expose the plot in the face of vicious intimidation, and the film's enduring appeal lies in this eternal conflict between individual and state machine. In America the film was nominated for five Academy Awards, including the rarity of Best Film and Best Foreign Film, and won Oscars in the latter category and for Best Editing.

The topicality of many political thrillers tends to date them quickly but this has not been true in the case of Z where its unusual combination of serious political comment and highly entertaining commercial appeal have helped it retain a freshness and impact and also established the characteristics of a style that Costa Gavras would deploy with similarly damning impact in such subsequent thrillers as *État De Siège* (*State of Siege*) (1973) and *Missing* (1981).

A Reggane Film/ONCIC Production
Producer Jacques Perrin
Screenplay Costa-Gavras and Jorge Semprun, based on the novel by Vassili Vassilikos
Photography Raoul Coutard
Editor Françoise Bonnot
Art Director Jacques d'Ovidio
Music Mikis Theodrakis
Running time 125 mins colour

Cast

Yves Montand ('Z')
Jean-Louis Trintignant (The Magistrate)
Jacques Perrin (The Journalist)
François Perier (The Public Prosecutor)
Irene Papas (Helene)
Georges Geret (Nick)

The films that never were

Imagine, if you will, Robert Redford as a family man and lawyer terrorized by convicted rapist Robert De Niro in *Cape Fear* (1991) or Kevin Costner and Debra Winger as a bickering married couple in *The War of the Roses* (1989) or Burt Lancaster writhing in the surf with Joan Crawford in *From Here To Eternity* (1953) (see p87) or a comical caped crusader portrayed by Bill Murray in *Batman* (1989) (see p27). These are just some of the casting notions that came to mind but never came to pass. The history of filmmaking is littered with unrealized projects – cherished dreams that remained forever on the drawing-board, or inspired last-minute casting switches that have literally changed lives and altered careers; it was only Claudette Colbert's ruptured disc that forced her withdrawal from *All About Eve* (1950) (see p8) and thus allowed Bette Davis one of the screen's most spectacular comebacks, and the repeated miscalculation of George Raft in turning down both *High Sierra* (1941) and *The Maltese Falcon* (1941) (see p137) that was immeasurably to the benefit of Humphrey Bogart.

For many years the best known uncompleted film was Joseph Von Sternberg's version of Robert Graves's *I, Claudius* (1937) starring Charles Laughton and Merle Oberon which suffered innumerable setbacks in the making and was finally abandoned altogether when Oberon was in a near-fatal car crash. The existing footage from the ill-starred production can be seen in the 1965 documentary *The Epic That Never Was*. With the decline in the influence of the studio system and the burgeoning of sometimes rather precariously financed independent productions, the number of films never completed has grown considerably; examples include *Something's Got To Give* (1962), shelved after the death of star Marilyn Monroe, *The Bells of Hell Go Ting-A-Ling-A-Ling* (1966) starring Gregory Peck and Ian McKellen which shot for only two weeks in Switzerland before being permanently shut down, and *The Jackpot* (1975) starring Richard Burton and Charlotte Rampling. Sometimes, a cessation of filming is merely the prelude to the film's ultimate salvation. In 1976, Robert De Niro segued straight from his gruelling stint as the *Taxi Driver* (see p217) to play a struggling actor in the altogether lighter Neil Simon comedy *Bogart Slept Here*, directed by Mike Nichols. After two weeks of filming with Simon declaring that the actor 'doesn't play joy very well', filming was suspended, Herbert Ross took over direction and the role was rewritten for Richard Dreyfuss who won an Oscar as the star of *The Goodbye Girl* (1977). Shortly afterwards, Roy Scheider received a Best Actor Oscar nomination for Bob Fosse's musical *All That Jazz* (1979) in a role that had been vacated by Richard Dreyfuss.

From the known projects that were never made, one's curiosity is certainly aroused by Jean Renoir's 1930s' idea of a life of Bonaparte starring Charlie Chaplin and Greta Garbo, or Max Ophuls's 1949 *La Duchesse De Langeais* with Garbo and James Mason, or the version of Conrad's *Nostromo* that was on the brink of production at the time of David Lean's death in 1991. Perhaps the figure most responsible for unfinished works is Orson Welles who is renowned for having fragments of partially completed productions scattered around the globe, including a version of *Don Quixote* begun in the 1950s and seen at Cannes 30 years later, *The Deep* (1967) starring Jeanne Moreau and Laurence Harvey and *The Other Side of the Wind* (1970–5), an exposé of the movie world starring, among others, the late John Huston. At the time of writing, Peter Bogdanovich would seem intent on finally unravelling the legal tangle that would allow the film to be publicly shown.

Index

Note: Entries in **bold type** refer to article headings on the pages referred to in the book. The index does not include cast and crew memnbers, which may be found listed in the boxes at the end of each film entry.